VOLUME I OF
NORTHWEST PASSAGES

by Bruce Calhoun

A collection of Pacific Northwest
cruising stories. These articles appeared under this title
in past issues of SEA & Pacific Motor Boat.

With updating footnotes by
Capt. William Berssen, USCG (Ret),
Editor PACIFIC BOATING ALMANAC,
assisted by the author.

Published by
Western Marine Enterprises, Inc.
Box Q
Ventura, California
1978

Dedicated
to Robert E. Walters

who preceded me in writing about the
Pacific Northwest and whose kindly guidance
and inspiration as friend and chief editor
of SEA & Pacific Motor Boat have been invaluable
in producing this collection.

Books by Bruce Calhoun

NORTHWEST PASSAGES Volume I
NORTHWEST PASSAGES Volume II
CRUISING THE SAN JUAN ISLANDS
MAC AND THE PRINCESS
(The story of Princess Louisa Inlet)

First Printing, April 1969
Second Printing, September 1969
Third Printing, April 1971
Fourth Printing, September 1972
Reprint Edition, June 1978

©1978 Bruce Calhoun
ISBN 0-930030-06-0

About this book

Many times during the past several years, the people I have met in yachting circles have said to me, in essence, "...your Northwest Passages cruising stories have been so valuable, we keep a looseleaf scrapbook of them aboard the boat for reference and for the enjoyment of our guests. That way, they fully appreciate what they are seeing."

The frequency of such remarks was an important factor in the decision to collect and reissue the articles in book form.

Some of these stories originally appeared several years ago. Wherever possible, the older material has been updated to conform with any changes known to have taken place in the areas discussed. The material has not been arranged chronologically, according to its prior publication dates. Instead, I elected to group the articles more or less geographically, by general area, for easier reader reference.

In gathering and re-editing this material for book publication, it seemed such a collection of cruising stories about the Northwest should also include some of the fine articles written by other authors. These have also appeared in recent issues of SEA and Pacific Motor Boat. To all those authors and photographers who responded and so generously gave permission to reprint their material, we are most grateful.

It is the sincere hope of the author and his publisher that this volume will prove of value to the yachtsman of the Pacific Northwest, his family and his guests. May it serve to enhance their enjoyment of these most wonderful cruising waters in all the world.

Bruce Calhoun

1978 POSTSCRIPT

This book, originally published in 1969, proved even more popular than expected, going through four printings. When the final stock was exhausted, the publisher decided the text was out-dated and there would be no further demand for it, so it would not have another printing. Since that time, yachtsmen from Olympia to Skagway, Alaska, have kept asking for it. Inquiries also have come from all of the western states as well as a few from the east.

Copyright to the book was obtained from the last publisher by the author and it is being re-issued and published by Western Marine Enterprises, Inc.

The reader should remember that, although the book was published in 1969, many of the articles used had previously been published in SEA and Pacific Motor Boat Magazine as far back as 1961. Thus changes that have occurred in the interim years make some kind of up-dating desirable. Tremendous increases in costs of paper, printing, binding and labor would drive the cost of re-writing and re-setting new type far beyond economic feasibility. The author and publisher agreed that the best plan would be to use the original plates and negatives and use footnotes to up-date the text wherever possible. It was also decided to use a soft cover in a further attempt to keep costs down.

It's quite possible, in fact likely, that some changes that should have been made slipped by. Please forgive us. Most of these, however, should not affect the basic value and pleasure of the book. You asked for it — here it is — we hope you enjoy it!

B.C.

Contents

Part V — The Inland Empire and Other Stories

Part VI — Selected Stories by Other Authors

Charts and Maps

Charts and maps in NORTHWEST PASSAGES–I are not to be used for navigation.

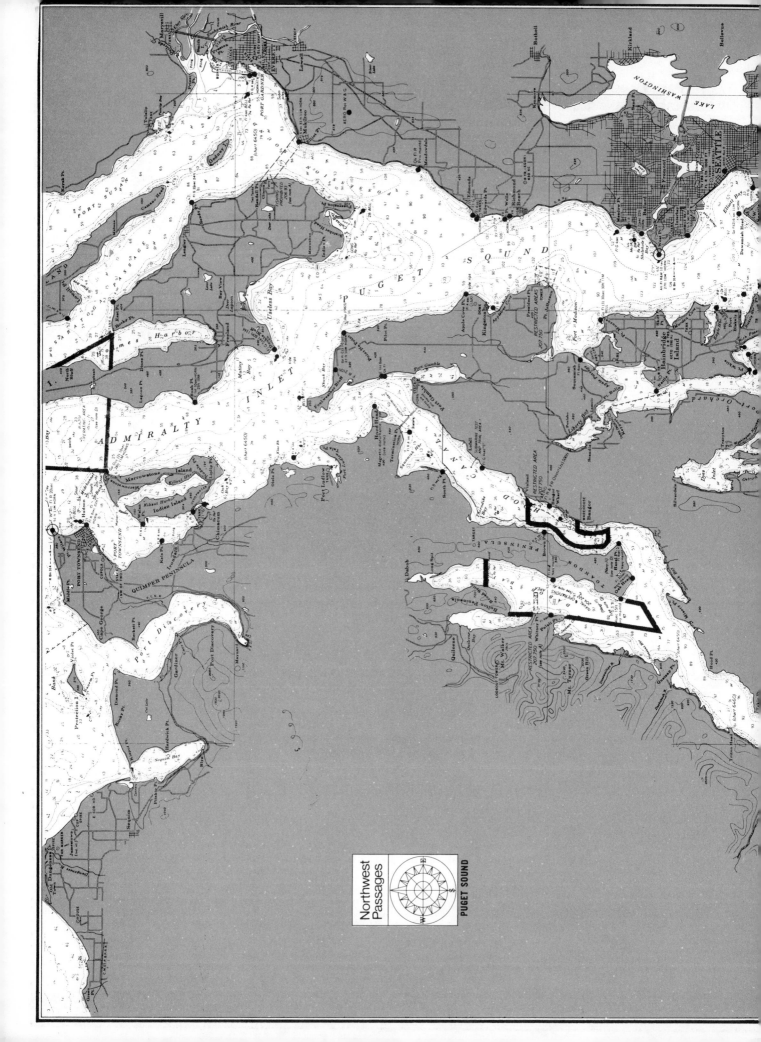

Northwest
Passages

PUGET SOUND

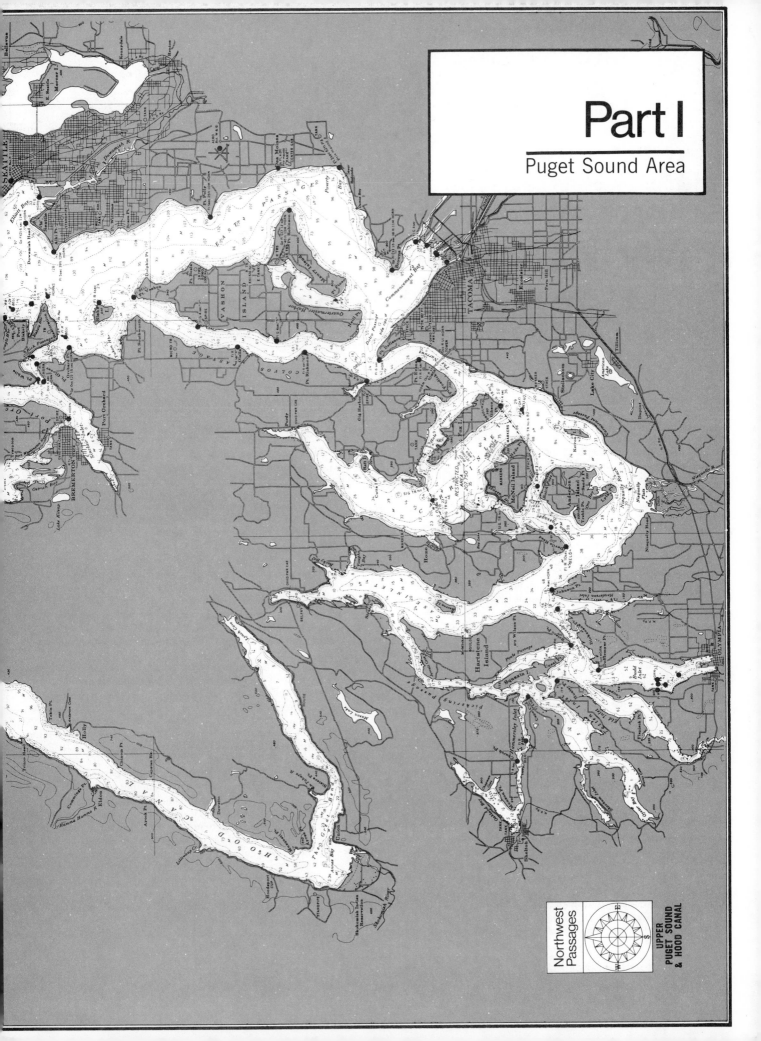

Part I

Puget Sound Area

Northwest Passages

UPPER PUGET SOUND & HOOD CANAL

Northwest Dividends for Small-Boat Yachtsmen

Morning came early. A receding tide called for tents and other camping gear to be stowed aboard the small cruisers at once so the day's run could be started before the boats became stranded on the gravelly beach.

Twin wakes merged to churn the silver spangled blue-green water into spreading Vs as two miniature ships sped out of the cove under the shadow of the purple-topped mountains, slowly turning a lighter green in the ascending sun's light.

Cruising in the Pacific Northwest, as elsewhere, is a way of life attracting more and more families every year. Formerly enjoyed only by the affluent in palatial yachts, the beauties and wonders of hidden coves, the intriguing surprises of narrow passages winding among forested islands and mountains rising sheer from the water's edge to snow-capped peaks or the broader expanse of waterways leading to all kinds of exploring adventure are now within the reach of almost anyone.

The difference is the small cruiser, either outboard or inboard/outdrive. The amazing development of this craft since the early 1950s with its trailerability, its speed, its easy maneuverability and its modest cost, means that literally hundreds of thousands of boaters scurry back and forth each summer to investigate the wide-spread inland waters of the Northwest—its rivers and its thousands of lakes.

Another contributing factor to the tremendous increase in small-boat cruising in the Northwest is the ever-growing number of marinas, resorts, state and provincial marine parks and camp grounds. Facilities range from the barest minimum of a landing beach and perhaps a few trails to well-kept floats, showers, laundromats, restaurants, stores, cabins, camp sites, fuel, water, ice and hull and motor repairs.

The Northwest states and British Columbia have recognized the growing need for public-owned marine facilities and are moving as rapidly as possible to acquire the property and, where desirable, to develop it for the yachtsman's use. Private marinas and resorts are also increasing in number and facilities offered.

Where does the small boat owner cruise in the Northwest? There is almost no limit to places to go and the answer depends on the amount of time available and the type of water or scenery desired. The area is so vast and the waterways so numerous that a person could spend a lifetime cruising and never cover it all.

Starting at the Oregon-Washington border the magnificent Columbia River offers many possibilities as it stretches northward to its source up in the interior of British Columbia. Broadening at times to beautiful lakes, some formed by huge dams, and joined by several navigable tributaries, this system of waterways is particularly well suited to the small cruiser. Also in eastern Washington, Idaho and western Montana are innumerable lakes of all sizes and shapes to intrigue the trailerboat owner with breath-taking scenery and excellent fishing.

Western Washington waters can be roughly divided into two segments. The first might include all of Puget Sound and Hood Canal as well as the inland passage running up behind Whidbey Island. Here the boater is in more or less civilized waters with shorelines generally somewhat populated although there are many stretches which must look very much the same today as they did to Peter Puget when he first saw them.

The second segment lying to the north is Washington Sound, a little used name for the waters between the Strait of Juan de Fuca and the Strait of Georgia including the storied San Juan Islands. Here is one of the cruising paradises of the world with 172 islands, numerous passages, bays and coves offering the small boat owner plenty of protection and his choice of civilized marinas or completely isolated coves.

Moving still farther north, the Gulf Islands of British Columbia are similar to the San Juans but different enough to write a new chapter in anyone's cruise log. Across the Strait of Georgia up the coast of British Columbia lies a vast series of waterways, all readily accessible to the small boat skipper either by cruising up from the south or by trailering to any of several convenient launching sites. This area might be arbitrarily cut off with the Desolation Sound-Discovery Passage waters to the northwest and would include Sechelt Inlet and the various reaches terminating in the famous Princess Louisa Inlet, generally considered a "must" for anyone cruising in the Northwest.

Do these skippers venture further? Indeed they do! They

explore the intricate networks of bays, inlets and reaches off Johnstone Strait and Queen Charlotte Strait. Then, moving northwestward along the British Columbia coast to Prince Rupert, tremendous inland waterways of southeastern Alaska await them with Juneau or even Skagway and Glacier Bay as a final destination.

These northern areas provide a real challenge for the outboarder, not so much because of weather and rough water, although in a few spots these factors are important, but because their remoteness and ruggedness call for careful advance planning for fuel and supply stops. It is amazing, as you round the bend of a channel or come around the point of an island, feeling as if yours were the only boat in a great silent world, to come upon a little cruiser or maybe two or three with their outboard motors purring smoothly as they speed on to new vistas and adventures.

Small boats in the Northwest have no lack of places to go, types of water or kinds of land surrounding the water. Taking a page from the books of their cousins in the larger cruisers, the small boat skippers have learned what is available to them and have adapted themselves and their boats to the greatest comfort and convenience possible in the enjoyment of this favored area.

Although small boat design and manufacture, along with motors, have improved tremendously in recent years, there are still problems which the owner must face. Skippers and their mates have devised many ingenious methods for achieving comfort in sleeping aboard or on the shore and ease of preparing meals, stowing gear of all kinds, carrying as much fuel and water as possible and even putting a small dinghy aboard.

One Seattle family has spent eight summers cruising in their outboard. Starting out with a 14 foot cruiser-fish-ing boat, the family was soon infected with that disease known as "two-footitis." Subsequent boats have each been two feet larger until they now cruise in a 20-foot fiber-glass cabin model with twin 50-hp motors. This sturdy little ship carries dad, mom, four youngsters from four to 12 years of age and—would you believe it—two medium size dogs.

Their ultimate goal is Alaska. Each year they explore waters a little further north, learning, through observation and their own inventiveness, new wrinkles to add to their comfort. They all sleep aboard the boat, although occasionally the sleeping bags will go ashore for a night on a sandy beach or under the pines.

Members of the Spokane Outboard Club, who cruise extensively in the lakes and rivers of eastern Washington and Idaho as well as interior British Columbia, sometimes trailering over west of Cascades for a taste of salt water, have become past masters in the use of foil in their cookery. One of the tastiest meals we've ever eaten was prepared over a beach fire on the shore of an Idaho lake. Except for the steaks, which were broiled on a folding grill, everything was cooked in foil, either wrapped in it or in pots fashioned of it. The salad was tossed in a foil bowl while the rolls were baked on a foil sheet with a foil reflector.

With the use of paper plates, cups and napkins there was very little dish washing necessary and no space in the boat was taken up with the storage of pots and pans. The only concession was a coffee pot.

Another interesting bit of cooking gear was seen on a Canadian outboard-powered cabin cruiser. It was an alcohol-primed one burner pressure kerosene stove, perhaps 14 inches square, with sea rails around the edges. The skipper had had a square pan constructed with two brackets on

A small outboard-powered cruiser nuzzles up to shore at the head of Von Donop Inlet on British Columbia's Cortes Island

each side which hung the pan from the rails. For frying, it was as large as any fancy electric fry pan, yet it could serve as a base for smaller pans and even be converted into a good dish pan.

Perhaps the ultimate in luxury and stowability is a Canadian-manufactured combination barbecue grill and rotisserie powered by flashlight batteries. It all folds up to about the size of an executive attaché case.

Cooking aboard the small boat is a subject of unlimited possibilities. Northwest skippers and/or their mates have become adept at changing from the relative luxury of the home kitchen to the limited facilities found afloat. Techniques vary from working in a tiny galley aboard to cooking alongside on a float or on the beach.

A boon to Northwest yachtsmen, especially those with small craft, is the wealth of food available in the sea. To tickle the palate of any crew it's hard to beat steamed little neck or butter clams with clam nectar, or small oysters pried from the rocks at low tide and placed on the barbecue grill until they open. Garnished with a piece of cheese and a dash of barbecue sauce, they are delicious.

The list of easily prepared dishes from clam, oyster, crab, shrimp, abalone and other denizens of the water and shore is nearly endless. Then there are the many varieties of lake, stream and salt water fish topped perhaps by that filet of King salmon caught that afternoon in the tide rips and done to a turn over the barbecue coals. It's a rarity when any explorer of Northwest waterways, whether his craft be large or small, ever goes to bed hungry.

An advantage enjoyed by the small boat owner in the Northwest is the availability of more nooks and coves. With his shallower draft, retractable propeller and simple maneuverability, he can more readily explore those places cluttered with kelp-covered rocks or driftwood logs than can the man with a large cruiser.

Because of the small cruiser, thousands and thousands more families in the Northwest are enjoying pleasures formerly reserved only for the wealthy. The sight of a misty bridal veil falls cascading down the side of a majestic, snow-capped mountain in Alaska, the rock-studded shores of a fir-clad island, the quiet whispering of the pines up-river from an Idaho lake, the new friendships made aboard other boats or among shore-side residents along the way, and the untold wonders of the Puget Sound-British Columbia inland waterways are just a few of the dividends paid annually to the owners of these craft.

2
Cruising Upper Puget Sound

Terminology can be confusing. It's called "Upper" Puget Sound, yet it's actually the southern part of the Sound. This paradox is something like the "head" of a bay, or the innermost part of a bay which, in many cases, we would tend to call the "foot."

Regardless of what it's called, that part of the Sound south of Tacoma is too much neglected by some cruising boat owners. True, the San Juan Islands and British Columbia Gulf Islands hold a charm and enticement that is hard to resist. This portion of our Northwest Nature's Wonderland holds forth an irresistible beckoning finger to both the neophyte who has heard about it and the old timer who's been there but wants to go back again and again to review familiar scenes and explore for new ones.

And well they should answer that call—all of them—for here are some of the most beautiful cruising waters on the face of the globe. There are those times, however, when northern distances are too great for that weekend when you must get out in the boat. Or the winter winds may discourage any long cruises, yet you know that motor ought to be warmed up and you do have a few days available.

These are the times to look to the south and rediscover some of its charm and beauty; the interesting and exciting cruising waters with which nature has endowed us — Upper Puget Sound.

Boat size and speed as well as your home port will determine your first objective but for the purposes of covering the entire area, let's begin with Gig Harbor and cruise the perimeter back to Tacoma and into Quartermaster Harbor.

Gig Harbor has everything the boatman wants or needs from gas and supplies or a complete repair job on motor or hull, to a shoreside cafe and bar with guest float. Approximately 25 miles from Seattle, the entrance is around 100 yards in width with the 10-foot channel offering some tricky currents at times.

By steering a center channel course midway between the western shore and the spit on the east, you'll have no trouble. Then hold to the eastern shore until well into the harbor when you can return to a mid-channel course.

You'll enjoy this story-book harbor on our inland sea which has long been a fishing port and is lately attracting more and more salty yachtsmen.

As we set a southwesterly course from Gig Harbor down through the Narrows, around Point Evans and Point Fosdick, we come into Hale Passage between the mainland and Fox Island. A right angle turn to the north brings us into Wollochet Bay, site of Tacoma Yacht Club's port away from home, and the settlement of Wollochet on the eastern point near the entrance. This two-mile-long finger-bay offers a well protected anchorage area with some nine feet of water in as far as the yacht club floats. Larger boats have 11 to 12 fathoms with a sticky bottom in mid-channel around 0.3 mile inside the entrance.

One thing we soon discover in cruising this part of the Sound is that we are in the midst of a more populated area than in northern waters. This may be somewhat restricting to the smaller boats which must depend on getting ashore more frequently for beach cooking or camping. Although there is considerable undeveloped waterfront, a good share of it is privately owned and skippers should use care in getting permission before setting up a beachhead for any purpose including clam or oyster collecting.

Continuing northwesterly through Hale Passage a fascinating area comes into view as we round Ketner's Point. You may want to do a little beachcombing (waterside, that is) and there's plenty of water, even 3½ fathoms behind Tanglewood Island. A fair anchorage can be found on either side of Tanglewood Island and the village of Sylvan is on Fox Island to the east of Tanglewood's southern point.

Under the bridge which connects Fox Island to the mainland and around the head of Fox Island we come into Carr Inlet. Rounding Green Point on a northerly heading soon brings us to the entrance of Horsehead Bay. You may want to do a little salmon trolling around Green Point before heading into the bay.

Although only a mile in length, Horsehead Bay is a delightful anchorage affording good protection in almost any weather condition. Many craft anchor just inside the spit but you'll find at least 2½ fathoms three-fourths of the way in toward the head.

An exploratory trip up Carr Inlet is a rewarding experience. Here are many enjoyable bays and little coves into which you'll want to poke your bow. The eastern shore features Raft Island, Lay Inlet and Rosedale. Purdy, near the north end, boasts an excellent sea food restaurant just below the bridge crossing Burley Lagoon.

On the west shore Huge Creek and Glen Cove will interest only the smaller boats. The former is a pretty little finger-bay while the latter is well protected but both are nearly dry at low tide.

Further south is Von Geldern Cove on which is situated the village of Home. Like several places many of us can recall on the Sound, local names vary from those given on

This small basin off Heron Bay on the east shore of Case Inlet offers the small boatman a peaceful hideaway for a lunch or a nap.

A sandy hook near the entrance is one of the features of Mayo Cove or Lakebay, as it is known locally. A county dock and floats at the head give ready access to the village of Lakebay.

the chart. The background of Von Geldern is obscured in the mists of history, or possibly his first name was Joe, for local residents call this Joe's Bay. A fair bit of the bay drains with the ebbing tide but there are still three feet at low water if you stay in the middle.

Mayo Cove, just to the south a bit, also changes name locally to Lakebay as it takes on the name of the village at its head. Here, too, the low tide leaves plenty of water, up to six feet, in the middle. Both of these bays have county docks and floats with some supplies available.

Penrose Point forms the south boundary of Mayo Cove and is the site of a 53-acre state park. This part of the cove is unprotected and does not offer a good anchorage except in the best of weather. If conditions are good, however, there is a nice sandy beach for swimming as well as picnic and camping facilities.

Rounding the point, we cross a wide bay and come around South Head, a long peninsula pointing northeast. Here there is a choice to be made. Pitt Passage, between the mainland and McNeil Island is a scenic bit of the area but not recommended at low tide as there are several rocks and shoals. If due caution is observed and the chart carefully checked, passage can be made, but unless the tide is in the nervous type should probably take a swing around McNeil Island, site of the federal penitentiary, and come back through Balch Passage into Filucy Bay. Landing on McNeil Island is not permitted.

Filucy Bay is a well protected harbor one and one-half miles long and is marked by an abandoned lighthouse tower* on McDermott Point, a spit at the south side of the entrance. A muddy bottom and six to eight fathoms of water afford a good anchorage with two to two and one-half fathoms at either end of the bay and in the small cove at Longbranch. This village offers some supplies, a county dock and floats. Marine service is found near the town dock and gas and diesel oil are available. This bay is a favorite rendezvous for many of the boats cruising these South Sound waters.

Leaving Filucy Bay, we head south in Drayton Passage, turn west around Devils Head, then northwestward into Case Inlet. Here is another broad expanse of water stretching to the north for some 14 nautical miles and with many more scenic coves, bays and islands awaiting your leisurely inspection and exploration. For sheer beauty and peaceful charm, smaller boats will want to look into Taylor Bay and Whitman Cove if the tide is high.

About half way up the inlet along the east shore is Heron Island, restricted to resident-members. The sign on the dock for the ferry connecting the island to mainland insists that "Guests Must Have Cards." Slightly further to the north is Heron Bay and village.

On up the east shore is an interesting shallow finger-bay called Dutcher Cove and two miles further is Vaughn Bay. Here is a good-sized harbor with a sand spit nearly closing off the entrance. Better hit this at something better than mean lower low-water which leaves only two feet in the entrance channel. Once inside there is plenty of water except close in to shore. The village of Vaughn is on the northern shore about one-half mile from the head. Some supplies are available and there is a launching ramp near by.

Around Windy Bluff and still further to the north is another scenic bay but without much protection and a bit on the tricky side at low water because of rocks and shoals. It's well worth poking your nose into Rocky Bay, however, if you are conscious of your boat's draft and the condition of the tide and you keep a good check on the chart.

Case Inlet narrows at its northern head to a very shallow bay with the villages of Victor on the east side and Allyn on the west. A launching ramp, gas, provisions and a restaurant will be found at Allyn.

Gig Harbor, looking from the inner bay out toward the entrance. Besides being steeped in history and home port to a sizable fishing fleet, it offers just about everything the cruising yachtsman could want.

*The tower is no longer there.

The placid waters of Horsehead Bay provide scenic beauty and a secure anchorage to those cruising the Upper Sound.

3

The Choice Offerings of Upper Puget Sound

Continuing to cruise in the southern waters of Puget Sound which are correctly known as "Upper Puget Sound", we wonder why more Northwest Yachtsmen don't take advantage of this delightful area.

Cruising down the west shore of Case Inlet, confusion persists as we approach what the chart lists as Reach Island. We aren't long in discovering, however, from both the local populace and various signs that everyone knows it as Treasure Island. Access is limited to property owner "members" only according to the sign on the little one way bridge which connects the island to the mainland.

Larger Stretch Island to the south is more hospitable. Here are acres and acres of grape vines and the St. Charles Winery formerly invited the boatman to stretch his legs a bit with a tour through its museum and winery with "tasting" included. The Winery has now been closed. Gas is available at the dock and there is a smooth beach launching area on the mainland near the village of Grapeview*

The narrow channel between the mainland and the two islands and under their connecting bridges provides picturesque scenery but isn't recommended at low tide because of shoals, rocks and shallow water.

A swing to the right next brings us into the entrance of Pickering Passage between Hartstene Island and the mainland. On the right is another of those charming little coves which lure the exploring skipper to poke his bow in for a view of the sylvan scene composed of cool water with green trees to the water's edge. McLane Cove is beautiful and restful but don't try it at low tide.

Another mile and a half on the left is the entrance to Jarrell's Cove. Actually it's so tiny and secluded that it could easily be missed, yet it is another of the state marine parks and can accommodate boats up to 70 or 80 feet. It has long been an anchorage and haven for small boats in spite of a previous name which appears on old charts as Bay of Despond. Fresh water is available as well as floats, picnicking and camping facilities and toilets. Official charts do not show water depths but at least two fathoms prevail at mean lower low water in most of the bay except the extreme points and the anchorage is well protected from any winds.

Continuing down Pickering Passage we are faced with

a decision to make as the waterway forks at the top of Squaxin Island with Peale Passage taking off to the left along the east side of the island. Since our cruise plan calls for a visit to Shelton, we choose to keep to the right, rounding Hungerford Point to turn into Hammersley Inlet.

This narrow approach to Shelton and Oakland Bay presents problems to a skipper but if he accepts the challenge and pays attention to available aids to navigation he will be well rewarded.

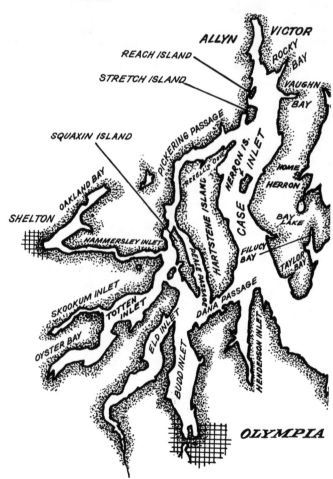

We're not sure whether fuel is available.

Jarrell's Cove is a popular State Marine Park in South Puget Sound Waters

Hammersley Inlet is about six miles long with an average width of 0.2 miles. The town of Shelton is at the far west end with Oakland Bay extending three and one half miles in a northeasterly direction. Shoals and current velocities up to five knots at the entrances are the hazards. Shoals are well charted, however, and experienced pilots advise favoring the north shore entering the inlet until past Cape Horn, then swinging to the south shore until Cannery Point is rounded. Midchannel the rest of the way is all clear except that Skookum Point might be favored a bit to avoid a four-foot shoal midway between Skookum and Church Points. Shelton offers moorage floats and docks, gas, oil, water, ice and other supplies, launching ramp and marine repairs.*

Leaving Hammersley Inlet we turn southwest into Totten Inlet, one of the three major fingers comprising the very southern extremities of the Sound. Although shorelines in this area are almost entirely privately owned and provide little or no opportunity for landing, these inlets do present an interesting and changing scene for the boatman whose philosophy of cruising includes leisurely enjoyment of passing scenery rather than the hurried pressure of speeding from starting point to destination.

About half way in Totten Inlet another smaller arm takes off to the west. This is Skookum Inlet which is navigable only at the higher tide levels. Oyster Bay, forming the head of Totten Inlet, is also taboo at low tide. These are the inlets and bays famous the world over for the small Olympia oyster as well as regular oysters and clams. Although these waters abound with favorite sea foods, woe unto the boatman who tries to harvest them for himself. The beds are all privately or commercially owned and maintained.

From a northerly heading to leave Totten Inlet we turn southeastward into Squaxin Passage around tiny Steamboat Island, a picturesque land-connected spot with both permanent and summer homes filling all available space. Hope Island is on our left as we cruise by Carlyon Beach where a small center furnishes outboard boat rentals, picnic sites, bait, tackle and small stores with gas in cans sometimes available.

On the southern end of Squaxin Island is a state marine park at Coon Cove which is receiving attention from several of the northwest cruising clubs.

Swinging to the southwest again we enter Eld Inlet, very similar to Totten scenically with the addition of many large log rafts stored in its inner reaches. Here again the skipper should avoid the inner third of the inlet at low tide although he will find the depths well charted.

Leaving Eld Inlet and rounding Cooper Point to turn south again into Budd Inlet we are startled by the impressive vista to the north and east. The dark green of the solemn firs on Squaxin and Hartstene Islands in the background forms a jagged horizon which supports a sky flecked with white cloud puffs. This fades to a lighter green along the shoreline reflecting in the clear blue of the broad expanse of water sparkling with dancing diamonds ahead of us. The deeper blue of cool shadows narrowing into Dana Passage on the right almost beckons us to explore but Olympia is our immediate goal so we turn to the south once again.

Budd Inlet is wider than its sisters and about half way in we pass the berthing area where a mothball fleet of merchant ships rusts in silence.† Keeping them to port, we approach the only serious hazard in the inlet—Olympia Shoal which bares at mean lower low water. It is well marked and charted. By following the channel indicated by lights and buoys until reaching Butler Cove, you can pick up the range and follow the dredged channel which is also well marked all the way in.

The western shore of Budd Inlet has several small boat anchorages with Butler Cove and Tykle Cove perhaps the most popular. Members of recognized yacht clubs will find a hearty welcome and good moorage awaiting them at Olympia YC's quarters at the very head of the inlet.

From here the capital city of Washington with its extensive commercial center offers everything the yachtsman could need from supplies of all kinds to a variety of amusements. Olympia visitors should include a shore trip to the capitol building to enjoy the floral display and a panoramic view from the Capitol Dome of the waterways they have been enjoying or expect to enjoy. All types of marine services and needs are readily found in Olympia with several complete marinas, launching ramps and marine supplies and services.

15

*Marine repairs are not available, but there is a tidal grid for do-it-yourselfers.
†The mothball fleet is now just a memory.

4
Autumn Doesn't End the Boating Season

Autumn, in many parts of the country, ends the boating season. Boats are hauled out, winterized and put to bed in canvas wraps for the icy months. It's different in the Pacific Northwest, where boating can be enjoyed the year around in protected waters such as the Snohomish River Delta where the blustery winds and storms of fall and winter can't reach them.

Skipper John knocked the ashes out of his pipe. Standing on the flying bridge of his *Pooka Too*, he watched as the crew carried the last cartons of food aboard. As he refilled and lighted the pipe, the pungent smoke brought memories of the dying summer and its cruising pleasures. He glanced at the clear sky and bright sun, smelled the woodsmoke in the crisp air and listened to the throaty "thrum-thrum-thrum" of the idling engines.

Lines were cast off and *Pooka Too* backed out to join a fleet of a dozen boats milling around the basin like a flock of ducks awaiting their mother. "Head for Priest Point," ordered Pilot/Cruisemaster Dave Gregory. "Take it slow until we're through the gap." Leaving Everett's 14th Street Boat Basin in single file, the boats ran north to Preston Point inside the long sand bar protecting the waterfront.

This was the annual October Snohomish River Cruise of the Edmonds Yacht Club. Fleet Captain John Moran's 36-foot *Pooka Too* was the pilot boat. The rest of the fleet, inboard, inboard/outdrive and outboard cruisers fell into formation behind, following the leader carefully in order to avoid the shoal areas in the many-fingered sloughs of the Snohomish where it empties into Puget Sound.

After two days of cold, blustery winds and rains, everyone was delighted to have such a beautiful day for this trip of exploration. These protected waters are generally considered ideal by Puget Sound yachtsmen for a one-day or a weekend cruise when fall or winter winds are blowing the spindrift off the tops of waves in outside waters. The dark river runs slowly, providing a perfect mirror for reflecting the dazzling autumn colors of alders and vine maples.

Heading for the mouth of Ebey Slough, Dave related the history of the breakwater. It is made up of navy barges of World War II vintage which wouldn't tow properly, were condemned, and now protect the large log booming area. He also pointed out the beautiful homes on Priest Point with

climbing roses festooned on fences and bare flower beds awaiting the renascence of spring.

Bridge tenders had been alerted of the fleet's expected arrival time so there was no delay passing Marysville. The swampy look, with cattails and scrub alders on both sides of the tortuous channel, soon turned to firm ground with farms and pasture lands presenting a picture of rural peacefulness. Long straight furrows marked the empty fields with

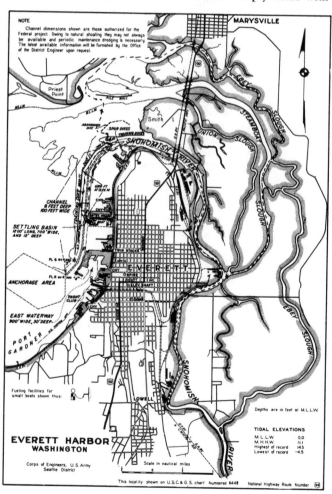

When the winds are blowing "outside," the quiet waters of the Snohomish with rioting fall colors along the shores offer an intriguing invitation

occasional corn-shuck tepees standing guard. A black V of Canadian geese etched the blue sky.

Coming to a watery crossroads where two of the river's fingers joined and crossed, Dave called for a course up Steamboat Slough. Here autumn had been particularly lavish with colors, splashing the maple leaves with a variety of reds and yellows against the background of the evergreens. Cattails, looking like burned out cigars, peeked out of little bayous and swayed gently to the wakes of the boats. A father was teaching his young son some of the secrets of fishing along the river's shore.

Dave pulled out the chart of the Delta area to show the many miles of pleasurable cruising in the maze of waterways which join, cross and recross each other in their run to the sea. He told how the best cruising is in the fall and winter, as in spring the river runs faster and is likely to be cluttered with deadheads and debris. Yacht clubs and local citizens are pulling hard for a portion of this area to be set aside as a marine recreation reserve.

He also suggested that shallow draft boats cause less concern about grounding and noted that some of the bridges are unattended so a 2-hour advance notice is required for opening.

The Snohomish runs slowly in the fall and life along its banks seems to become more leisurely. A cow raised her head from grazing to contemplate the passing boats invading her privacy. A little further along a woman sat comfortably in a rocking chair as she fished from her front porch overhanging the river. It almost seemed as though the boats stood still while the river flowed slowly past them. Then, suddenly, the waterway emerged from its sylvan setting to cross Union Slough and join the main stream of the river in Everett's backyard. Both Dave and skipper John were ever alert to water depths, staying well to the outside of curves and bends where the current digs a deeper channel. Occasionally the banks would be lined with pilings provide a booming area for logs awaiting their trip to the sawmills.

Crossing under the Hewitt Avenue bridge, the fleet continued up-river as far as Lowell. Dave explained that sometimes the cruise went further up-river to the city of Snohomish. But this was a one-day trip and a beach party

had been planned on the sandspit, so the parade of boats did a column left about. As the wider Snohomish wound northward along Everett's eastern limits Dave called attention to various points of interest—sawmills, shipyards and marinas.

The river continued to broaden as it passed under highway and railroad bridges to flow into the Sound. A turn to port took the parade of boats behind the sandspit and to a small dock and float maintained by the city of Everett. Rafting that many boats on both sides of the little float seemed impossible but they all made it. Soon whole families were lugging the makings of a potluck picnic to the open air kitchen with its windbreak on the outer side of the jetty. Driftwood was gathered and fires started while children played in the golden sand on one of the finest beaches in the Puget Sound area and adults went on hikes of exploration along little paths through the tall sand grass or sat on white drift logs to watch the breakers roll in over the shallow sand and crash on the beach.

A few of the more ambitious set out for the mile distant hulk of the *Equator*, a proud bit of maritime history which, with other old hulks and abandoned barges, has helped build up the sand jetty. Launched in 1882 at San Francisco, the schooner *Equator* served as a South Seas trader. In 1889 famed author Robert Louis Stevenson chartered her for a six-month Pacific cruise which provided inspiration for "The Wrecker" which he co-authored with his brother-in-law Lloyd Osbourne. Two other Stevenson stories, "Feast or Famine" and "Ebb Tide" are said to have been the results of his cruise of the *Equator*.

Everett Kiwanians long harbored a dream of refloating the tired old boat but their last efforts in 1966 were unsuccessful. Early in 1967 an organization called Equator, Inc., acquired title to the hull and planned to make another attempt to move the 82-foot craft which ended her active career in 1956 as a tug. They hope to restore the ship to her sailing days' appearance.

By the time the explorers returned from their hikes, the cooks had a delightful meal ready which everyone enjoyed as the sun retreated behind the Olympics. Crews returned to the boats for the homeward journey well satisfied with a pleasant fall outing.

5

Master Whidbey Proved the Deception

Northwest Passages invited Lois Jean Perkins to write our story of Whidbey Island. Mrs. Perkins is eminently qualified to tell the story of her favorite island as she was born in the old Alexander home at Coupeville and has always had a keen interest in the island's early history. Her great-grandfather, Captain Robert Fay, was a world sailor who retired on Whidbey and became a government Indian agent. Her grandfather, Abram Alexander, was the first white boy born on Puget Sound. She says that her family has always kept historical items and documents and that she cut her baby teeth on a very old copy of Bowditch. She and her husband, Cecil, a yachtsman in his own right, returned to Whidbey Island some years ago to make their home near Coupeville.

The first pale shafts of sunlight slanted across the deck in the sharp freshness of dawn. The riffled waters of the bay beat rhythmically along the sides of the cruiser's hull. The aroma of simmering coffee and sizzling bacon arose from the galley and another day of a Northwest Passages cruise began.

Within an hour after breakfast we were under way and headed for Whidbey Island. As we crossed Rosario Strait my thoughts wandered back in time to the spring of 1792 when Master Joseph Whidbey and his exploring party sailed a ship's boat from the *H.M.S. Discovery* over this same course. It was Master Whidbey who proved that the narrow passage we call Deception was not really a small bay, as charted by the Spaniards, but was a channel completely dividing the mainland from its supposed Peninsula. That lovely, long, wooded finger of land was indeed a large and beautiful island. In honor of this discovery the area was later re-charted as Whidbey's Island. General usage through the years has shortened the name to its present form.

Whidbey, largest of the 172 islands in Washington State coastal waters, has an area of some 235 square miles, is 38 miles long as the crow flies, and varies in width from one to ten miles. Yet no point on the island is more than five miles from salt water. Along her wooded shores are many delightful bays and sandy beaches with excellent clams, fish and crab to help replenish the larder.

As you approach Deception Pass, off the starboard bow lies one of Whidbey's most interesting and unusual beaches. This beach is actually a narrow strip of sand separating the open salt water from a beautiful fresh-water lake called Cranberry Lake. On this shore, according to record, was held Whidbey Island's very first picnic. The time was early spring in the year 1853. The schooner *Exact*, carrying a group of pioneer settlers bound for Penn Cove, was forced to lay over to await the turn of the tide before entering Deception Pass and the Captain decided to drop the hook in the calm waters off the Cranberry sand spit. Because the day was clear and warm and the passengers eager to stretch their legs on land, the good-natured captain ordered a boat over the side and all went ashore for a picnic.

At that time Cranberry Lake was a salt-water lagoon with the tides running in and out across the sand bar to mingle with the fresh waters from the lagoon's underground springs. Through the years, however, the sands gradually built up along the spit until finally Cranberry became a fresh water lake. The area is now a part of Deception Pass State Park. Modern bathing and picnic facilities have been installed and the lake is kept stocked for anglers. Cranberry is still a favorite picnic spot and each year hundreds of swimmers enjoy the moderate temperatures of the fresh-water lake while, only a few feet away, the cold surf breaks along the outer reaches of the sand fill.

Before entering Deception Pass yachtsmen should check charts and tide tables. In this narrow channel, swirling tides really boil through, sometimes reaching as high as 11½ knots at maximum flood. In the days of sailing ships the Pass was considered quite a challenge, but it was left to the daring Captain Thomas Coupe to really meet that challenge with a flourish. Captain Coupe was known as a man who carried all possible sail at all times, regardless of weather or tides. In the spring of 1851, true to form, he sailed his full rigged barque, the *Success*, through Deception Pass at flood — the only man known ever to attempt such a feat.

Many a yarn has been spun about smuggling operations through the Pass in the 1800's when unscrupulous skippers defied the Federal Government to run Chinese laborers to Whidbey's shores, keeping their human cargo locked in the hold to avoid detection. One tale is told of a skipper who saw the Federal boats closing in and decided to destroy the evidence. Quickly opening the hatch, the skipper called the Chinese on deck one by one, cracked them on the head with a belaying pin and dropped them over the side into the

Looking across Admiralty Inlet from Teronda Lodge on Whidbey's west shore . . . in the distance, the snow-capped Olympics

Cloud-spattered skies and wide vistas form an extravagant backdrop for Whidbey Island silhouettes

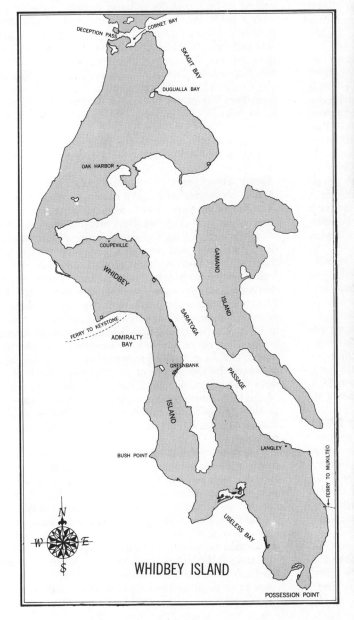

WHIDBEY ISLAND

DECEPTION PASS
CORNET BAY
SKAGIT BAY
DUGUALLA BAY
OAK HARBOR
COUPEVILLE
WHIDBEY
GAMANO ISLAND
SARATOGA
FERRY TO KEYSTONE
ADMIRALTY BAY
GREENBANK
PASSAGE
ISLAND
LANGLEY
FERRY TO MUKILTEO
BUSH POINT
USELESS BAY
POSSESSION POINT

Cornet Bay Marina boat basin
Langley Marina and wooded shoreline

swift-running current. When the Federal men pulled along side to make their arrest the evidence had completed disappeared.

Opium was another illicit and golden cargo here in early days which sometimes had to be disposed of quickly. On one such occasion a smuggler hastily beached his craft and hid the cans of opium in the woods near an isolated farm house. Before he could return for his precious cargo it was found by the farmer. Thinking the thick, brownish-red material to be paint, the farmer promptly painted the weather side of his barn with about $3,500 worth of opium. After learning the truth, the embittered farmer is said to have sworn never to paint his barn again.

Just inside Deception Pass lies jewel-like Cornet Bay. Here, in one of the loveiest settings imaginable, yachtsmen will find a modern marina catering to every need. Both open and covered moorage is available. Groceries, marine supplies and hardware are on hand. Salmon fishing is only minutes from moorage and the Deception Pass gateway to open water just around the corner. Also you'll find a delightful change of pace in the excellent fare served in the relaxed atmosphere of the marina's Galley Restaurant overlooking the boat basin. Don't miss it.

Then, if you are in a mood to stretch your sea legs a bit, a pleasant walk down the road in a northerly direction from the marina will lead you through a shaded lane to a dead-end at water's edge where you may still find some evidence of a long-ago dock. This is a memorable spot to old timers for here, long before the building of the Deception Pass bridge, travelers of the horse-and-buggy era came to board a ferry to the mainland. A small rickety dock jutted out into the water there at roadsend and from a post beside the dock hung a large, rusty, circular saw. To call the ferry, which had no schedule, one simply struck the saw several times with a mallet provided for this purpose, and then sat back to wait. In due time a flutter of white flag could be detected on the far shore, signifying that Mr. Blount had heard your call.

In a little while a tiny ferry would take shape in midstream and eventually struggle up to the dock. This ferry was a small open-ended scow lashed to a noisy little launch. Mr. Blount would call out when he was ready to load. Slowly and carefully the horses had to be led aboard the scow and firmly held throughout the crossing. Carriage passengers always dismounted and walked onto the scow for it was considered too dangerous to remain in the carriage. Once on the other side of the channel, a pleasant hour was always a certainty. Mrs. Blount waited eagerly to greet her husband's passengers, most of whom were old friends with news to share.

Cruising on down the eastern shore of Whidbey Island you pass the entrance to Dugualla Bay. This was a spot revered by the Indians long before the coming of the white man. From this bay a narrow finger of sea water reaches far into the low fields, actually seeming to be a small river. This channel, with brush and trees growing close, offered shelter to Indian canoes as well as water birds and other wild creatures. Named by the Indians, Dugualla means sanctuary from the anger of both men and Nature Gods.

From Dugualla, past Crescent Harbor and on in to Oak Harbor the Navy has claimed a large portion of the area for their operations. On this northern end of Whidbey the Navy maintains both land- and sea-plane bases as well as large housing units for personnel. The Seaplane Base is adjacent to the city of Oak Harbor and for a number of years Navy security made it necessary to restrict the waters of the harbor. Now, however, restrictions have been lifted and a channel is open at all times.

At present Oak Harbor has no facilities for visiting yachtsmen, but according to drawing board plans, an installation should be in operation in a few years. Oak Harbor stages an old fashioned Fourth-of-July celebration each year with a day-long program planned to include something for everyone. Parades, games, food and fun galore fill the daylight hours. With darkness comes a fireworks display on the city beach.*

Southwesterly from Oak Harbor lies Penn Cove and nestled along its eastern shore is the little town of Coupeville, county seat of Island County. Many a deep-sea captain chose to retire here where sailing ships found good anchorage and protection from storms in one of the best of natural harbors surrounded by lush forests and shining mountains. These forests also produced golden cargo for the taking. The trees proved to be unusually tall and straight, providing spars of such a premium quality they were soon in demand by the British and French navies. From this area were loaded the first spars ever to clear from Puget Sound bound for Europe, thus opening Washington Territory to European trade. Captain James Henry Swift of Coupeville carried that first shipment to Falmouth, England on his barque Anadir, clearing from Port Townsend December 1, 1855. Whidbey and Camano Islands also supplied the piles for building the San Francisco docks.

Coupeville has installed a float for the convenience of visiting boats, with water and gasoline available from the attendant. Stairs up the bank lead to the refurbished Front Street of this charming and picturesque little town. Here you will find a friendly, relaxed atmosphere amid well preserved old store buildings from a by-gone era, many still showing their original false fronts.

Each year, during the second week in August, Coupeville fills Front Street with various displays for its Arts and Crafts Festival. The Festival lasts through the three day weekend and includes such extras as a salmon barbeque, a fishing derby and antique collections. Be sure to visit the Alexander Blockhouse just a few yards from the head of the dock. This memento of pioneer days was built on its present site in 1855 to serve as a protection from hostile Indians in case of war — a war that never reached these shores. Beside the blockhouse, resting in their own special rack, you will find several authentic Indian canoes of varying sizes. Each of these canoes was shaped by hand from a single cedar log. In front of the blockhouse, inside a glass case, is the oldest memento in these parts of the bringing of Christianity to Whidbey's shores. The story of this old cross is there too for your pleasure.

Serene beauty awaits you all the way as you cruise on through Saratoga Passage between Whidbey and Camano Islands. Approaching Greenbank and Holmes Harbor, you pass the narrowest point on Whidbey Island. Across this narrow neck barely a mile of land lies between Saratoga Passage and Admiralty Inlet on the west shore. From here, and sweeping on up to Greenbank's high ground, stretches the largest loganberry farm in the world.

Langley is the next port of call. In this pleasant harbor the Langley Marina has made every effort to extend a welcome to all boats and to supply their every cruising need. Re-

*The Oak Harbor Marina, now completed, offers complete facilities.

pair service on all makes of motors is available. An extra float has been installed to meet increasing traffic and five new mooring buoys have been set in the harbor. Langley Yacht Club makes its headquarters at the marina and center-of-town shopping is only two blocks away. Langley Marina proudly claims to be the only marina on Puget Sound offering yachtsmen *free* ice!*

Nearing the southern end of Whidbey you will pass the Columbia Beach Ferry Dock, where travelers embark for Mukilteo and the mainland. Only a few cruising minutes beyond the Ferry Dock the brooding heights of Possession Point come into view, jutting into Puget Sound like a proud and defiant sentinel guarding the southernmost reach of Master Whidbey's Island. Beyond Possession Point you enter the more open waters of Admiralty Inlet, the link between the lower Sound and the Strait of Juan de Fuca.

Midway down the western shore of Whidbey, near the present site of the Keystone Ferry Landing, was once enacted an exciting bit of drama which might have had a far-reaching effect on the future of Washington Territory but for the quick thinking of a watchful mother. It all happened in the year 1856, during the Indian War then threatening the destruction of pioneer white settlements on Puget Sound. At that time the wife and four daughters of Isaac Stevens, first governor of the Territory, were visiting the Crockett

family on Whidbey Island. The island was considered to be safer than the mainland because local Indians were in sympathy with the whites. One especially warm day found Mrs. Stevens and the girls bathing in the cool waters of the cove adjacent to the Crockett farm. Suddenly a huge Indian war canoe filled with braves in full war dress swung around the point of Admiralty Head and made straight for the bathers on the beach. Instantly the alert Mrs. Stevens realized what a bargaining lever the Governor's family could mean to the embattled Indians. With a scream of warning to the older girls, Mrs. Stevens grabbed the baby in her arms and they ran at top speed to the safety of the near-by Crockett Blockhouse Compound. Had the Indian raid been successful it might also have meant loss of life to many Whidbey Island residents. Northern Indians, often quick to retreat at the failure of a tactic, were also often carried away with success to the point of wholesale destruction once launched into a raid. Islanders learned later that kidnapping the family of "Hyas Tyee" Stevens had indeed been the intention of the Hydah raiding party.

The ghost of Master Whidbey seems to hover near the shores of his Island discovery, inviting you to see yet another bay or hear another tale. But to the west across the Inlet the smokestacks of Port Townsend are clearly visible and the skipper has changed course to follow the lowering sun.

Deception Pass, first thought to be a small bay, was later proved to be a deep and turbulent passage between two major islands

21

Barney Heim, manager of Langley Marina, says that offer of free ice still holds good!

6

Cornet Bay Area

Another conveniently located facility for cruising Northwest yachtsmen is the Cornet Bay Marina just inside Deception Pass.

Although actually opened in the summer of 1963, few skippers realized it was there until the following year when they took full advantage of it. Lying beyond the State Park Dock it is between the northeast end of Ben Ure Island and the Navy Dock. Red and black numbered pilings clearly mark the ten-foot entrance channel to the well dredged basin.

The floats accommodate 115 boats — 65 permanent and 50 transient moorages with electrical power and water easily accessible. A Chevron gas dock provides complete sales and service with a full line of Chevron marine products.

Ashore the skipper and his crew will find clean restroom facilities, good inexpensive food, complete grocery store, marine hardware, ice, bait, tackle and a nine-ton hoist. Shower and laundry facilities are to be installed in the near future.

Since cruisers started plying the waters of the San Juan Islands, the inside passage and Deception Pass have been the favored route and Cornet Bay has provided a convenient place to await favorable conditions in the pass where, at times, the current velocity can be dangerous for small boats, particularly the slower ones. The Cornet Bay Marine Company, recognizing the strategic location of the bay and a need for better facilities for yachtsmen, has dredged and built the present harbor.

It all actually started when a group of boatmen who were Whidbey Island residents sought a place to moor their boats. Officers and directors of the company are local businessmen. The general manager of the marine is Oliver Deckwa.*

One of the outstanding features of this installation is the feeling of welcome and cordiality which is evident the minute the courteous and helpful dock boys take your lines upon arrival and everything in their power is done to make all visitors feel at home. This is the primary aim of the marina.

Cornet Bay Marina offers 65 permanent and 50 transient moorages; additional moorages are planned.

*Rena Deckwa, general manager of the Cornet Bay Marina, says they now have open and covered moorings with accommodations for about 80 boats, 65 permanent and 20 transient. Showers and laundry facilities are available.

Like other marinas in the vicinity, the Cornet Bay Marina has become popular with eastern Washington, Seattle and out-of-state boat owners as a place to leave their boats for the summer while they drive or fly between there and their homes or places of business. The easy access to island cruising waters eliminates the long runs from further down Puget Sound and allows many more hours of boating pleasure.

Winter activities have also become a part of the life at the marina. Northwest yachtsmen particularly, and some others, have discovered that winter fishing in the area is excellent while hunters use their boats for transportation to various islands or favorite remote spots for deer and bird hunting. Still others have found the enjoyment to be found in winter cruising with the mild climate and usually less winds than in summer. Here, again, Cornet Bay provides an ideal rendezvous spot, layover moorage or temporary berth for the boat.

Ready road access is found by taking the Mount Vernon to Oak Harbor highway and turning left at the first road after crossing the Deception Pass bridge. The marina is only a half-mile down this road.

Future plans call for the development of additional moorage space by further dredging along already acquired shore property. This part of the bay is well protected no matter how strong or what the direction of the wind.

For many years there has been confusion among yachtsmen as to the correct name for this bay. Older charts show it as Coronet while later ones list it Cornet. Bob Blain straightened the whole thing out for us by saying that the original name, Coronet, was given by Capt. Vancouver. Through the years this was somehow shortened to Cornet and local residents are most insistent that today the correct name is Cornet.

Three fine state-maintained launching ramps as well as picnic grounds and other resort facilities are adjacent to the marina with plenty of car and trailer space available. A new and larger launching ramp is scheduled to be built just north of the marina in the near future.*

As boating continues to grow in the Northwest so do the services and facilities for yachtsmen. The Cornet Bay Marina should be added to the ever-growing list of fine installations dotting the waterways of our fabulous Northwest cruising waters.

*The state ramp has been completed.

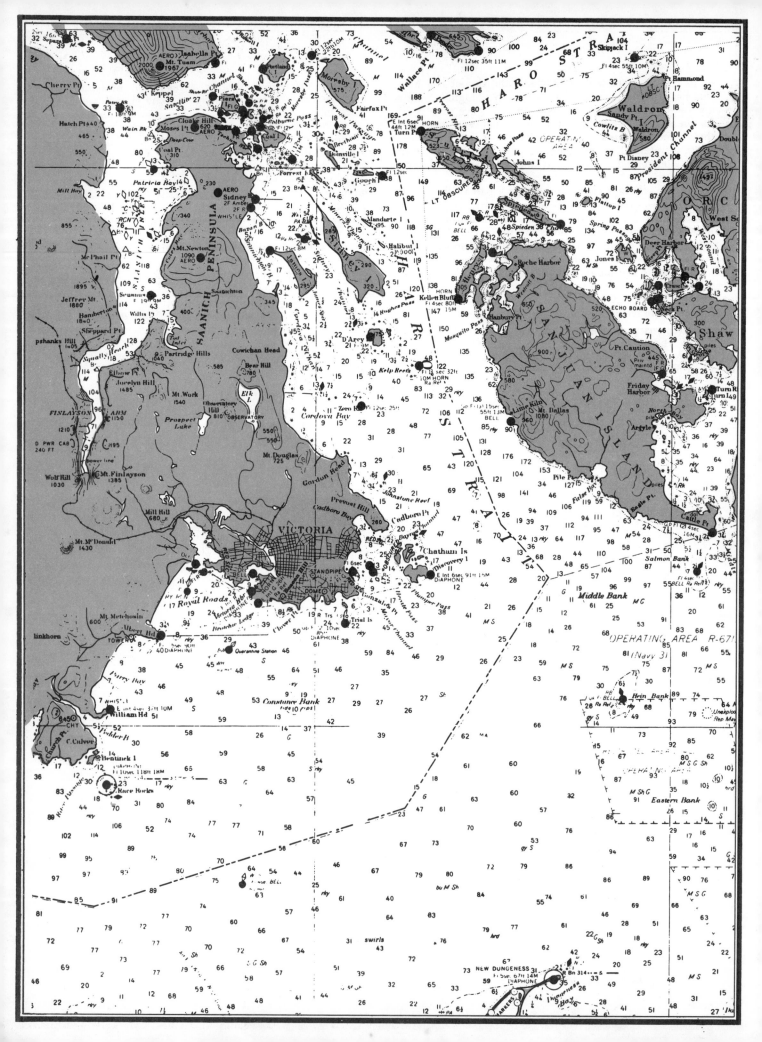

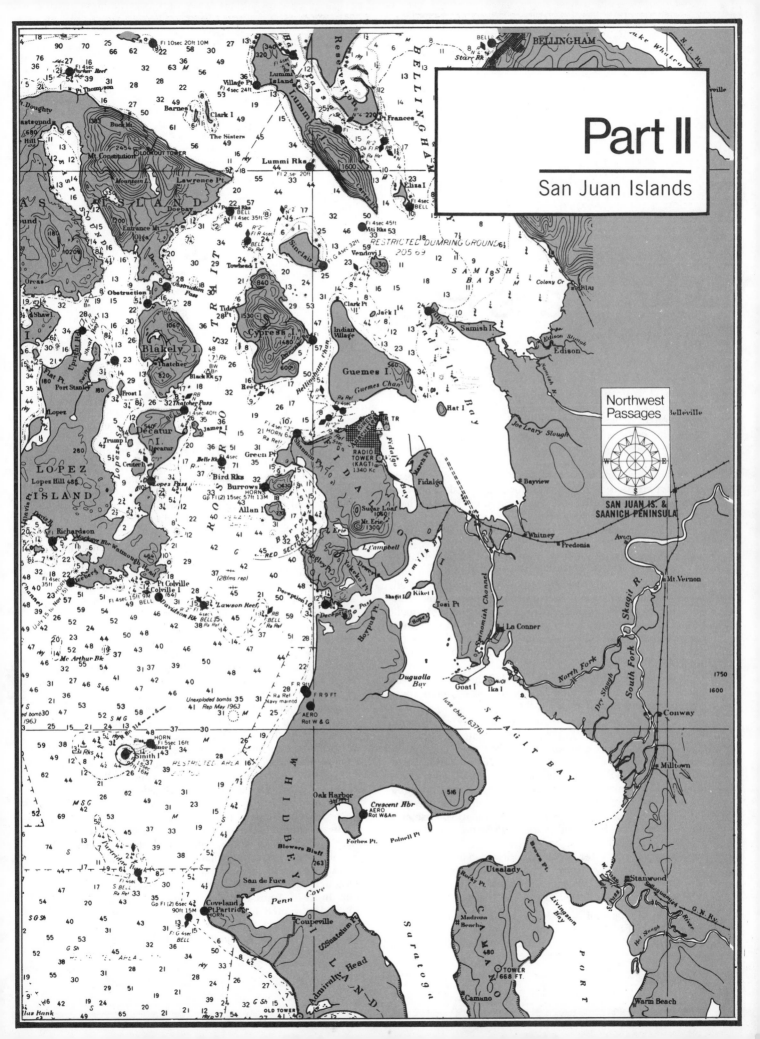

Part II

San Juan Islands

Northwest
Passages

SAN JUAN IS. &
SAANICH PENINSULA

7
San Juans East

Take one part of July sunshine, add to it generous portions of azure blue water and fresh air with the tang of salt. Sprinkle with forested isles and rocky islets against a backdrop of green hills rising to snow-capped peaks that meet the endless blue of the sky. Garnish with seagulls swirling gracefully above and in the center place yourself in the boat of your choice.

Recipe for contentment — outline for adventure — inspiration for creativity — prescription for living — take your own choice of a title as befits your mood but know that you have the makings of pure enjoyment.

Nature provides these ingredients in varying proportions at selected locations around the world but nowhere is she so generous with all of them as in the San Juan Islands.

Northwest skippers, families, crews and guests have been partaking of these pleasures for years. With the more recent advent of the planing hull and faster boats these same boaters have taken to ranging farther for additional enjoyment and exploration, many merely passing through this fascinating archipelago on their way. And, of course, there is the annual new group of boaters ready to sample the San Juans the first time.

Capt. Francisco Eliza has been called the "Father of the San Juans," and quite properly so, for he explored them thoroughly and named many of them.

How many islands are there? The number of different answers is in direct ratio to the number of times the question is asked of different people. At low tide with large rocks and reefs exposed, counts vary between 760 and 786. When the tide rises to its full height there are still somewhere around 457 peaks of this sunken mountain range visible above the water. Actual islands with names number between 170 and 175 depending on which chart or map you use and how you treat double islands with single names. Most often seen are the numbers 172 and 174.

To have some order in our consideration of this famed area, we arbitrarily divide it into nine parts. In this our first story, we are concerned with those islands which might be called the Eastern San Juans.

Seldom thought of as an island or considered one of the San Juans is Fidalgo Island but a check of the charts will show that it is actually surrounded by water. Eliza named

it for Salvador Fidalgo who aided him in his exploration of these islands.

Two well known waterways are adjacent to Fidalgo Island, Deception Pass and Swinomish Channel, more often called Swinomish Slough.

Having been through Deception Pass many times we decided to start our tour of these eastern islands in a counter-clockwise direction. We had armed ourselves with a large-scale chart of the area and had no trouble locating the channel from Skagit Bay, past Goat Island to the main channel. It is well marked with lighted buoys, red nun and black can buoys, lights and pilings.

Swinomish Channel itself provides an interesting trip, much like cruising on a river, with the historic old Indian town of La Conner along the way and sandy banks fading into fertile fields on each side. There are rocks and danger spots but they are well marked and the curves which are apt to shoal have regular range markers.

The channel into Padilla Bay is likewise well marked and it is good practice to pay attention to the markings as the water is shallow and sometimes it's quite a stretch to the next high tide for a grounded boat. This route is used by those who wish to by-pass Deception Pass or take a shorter run across Rosario Strait.

Since names and their sources are always interesting, there is a long one we should consider, for Eliza used various parts of it in this area. He was sailing under orders of the Mexican Viceroy and held him in great respect. This gentleman bore the following somewhat cumbersome name: Senor Don Juan Vicente de Guemes Pachecho y Padillo Orcasitees y Aguayo Conde de Revilla Gigedo.

In our immediate area Padilla Bay and Guemes Island come from this name. There is some question about Orcas, some maintaining that it was derived from the Orcasitees part of this name while others hold that it is from the Spanish word *orcas*, for whale.

As we leave Padilla Bay, Anacortes is on our left. Originally settled around 1860, it was known as Ship Harbor. In 1876 Amos Bowman bought the site and platted a town. He wanted to give it the maiden name of his wife, Anna Curtis, but purposely changed it to Anacortes to sound Spanish in keeping with Fidalgo and the other Spanish names nearby.

Here the yachtsman can supply all his needs. The several fine marinas including Skyline, Robinson's, and Gateway offer everything from permanent or temporary moorage to hull or engine repairs and even a swimming pool. Anacortes, known as the Gateway to the San Juans, is the jumping off place for many boaters who keep their craft here or launch them, after trailering from other points.*

Our heading was on little Huckleberry Island just off the east side of Guemes with Hat Island to our right. The sun at its zenith and our built-in automatic appetite meters both told us it was near noon. The water was so calm the twin V's of our bow wave and regular wake rolled lazily and unimpeded on either side of us for hundreds of yards.

Saddlebag Island, so called because of its shape, with its little sister, Dot, suddenly became the perfect place to stop for lunch, a bit of leg stretching ashore and to catch a few crabs for dinner.

We anchored in the north bay with a wary eye on the depth finder. After lunch the whole crew explored the scenic path across the island for a look at the south bay and Dot Island. Returning to the boat we lifted our crab trap to find an even dozen of the clawing creatures. After untangling them and sorting them out we kept the seven legal ones and tossed the others back to grow up for a future catch.

It was here we discovered a new way to crab. Two men and a boy were wading in the shallow water to the northeast of the island and were raking up crabs from the long seaweed with large rakes that resembled a hay rake with wooden tines about six inches long. It not only looked like fun but was obviously rewarding as well.

Leaving Saddlebag we swung over for a look at little Boat Harbor, behind a spit on Guemes Island, and made a mental note that we'd stop there for lunch next time. This small bay is the only harbor of any kind on the otherwise straight shoreline of this triangular shaped island.

Running between Guemes and Jack Islands we swung around the north end of Vendovi Island with Viti Rocks to the left. This island, which is privately owned and thus offers nothing to the yachtsman, was named by Capt. Charles Wilkes for a native of the Fiji Islands he had captured and brought with him. Viti Rocks he named for one of the Fiji Islands, presumably the home of the native, Vendovi.

A swing around Carter point, the southern or southeastern tip of Lummi Island brought us between Lummi and Eliza Island. This island, named for the explorer himself, (be sure to pronounce it *El-eeza*) is one of the most beautiful in this group. With its contrasting sandy and rocky shores it is a popular summer spot for Bellingham residents. Be careful though, coming from the south it can make you look twice at your chart as its two parts, connected by a low sand beach, make it appear as two islands. Its eastern shore and the north and south ends are lined with rocks but the two bays on the western side, while not offering much protection, are sloping sand and gravel.

Bellingham Bay and the town of Bellingham lie to the north and northeast. They were probably named for Sir William Bellingham who checked over Vancouver's supplies and accounts as he was leaving England. The bay, charted

1. Village Point silhouetted against Lummi Island's 1740-ft. mountain.

2. Eliza Island has sandy beaches on the western side. The eastern shoreline is rugged and rocky.

3. Little Chuckanut Island protects the entrance to Chuckanut Bay.

4. Both summer and year-round homes line the beach of Lummi Point on Lummi Island. The northern side of the point offers good protection from southeasterlies.

5. Hope Island is the center of a salmon fishing area where many big ones have been caught.

1.

2.

4.

5.

Today Anacortes has the following fine marinas: Cap Sante Boat Haven, Gateway Kove, Anchor Cove, Wyman's (formerly Robinson's) and Skyline Marina in Flounder Bay.

by Joseph Whidbey under Vancouver, is quite shallow and with a southeast wind can become fairly rough.

Just south of Bellingham is beautiful Chuckanut Bay guarded by Chuckanut Island and Rock. Chuckanut is an old Indian name meaning "unknown." The bay is protected by two arms and, with the small island in the opening and its picturesque trees and rocks, presents one of the most scenic spots in the area.

Cruising up Hale Passage between Lummi Island and the long arm which is the Lummi Indian Reservation, we stopped at Lummi Point , a long sandy spit, for a pleasant visit at the home of the Art Nordtvedts, Dick Hudsons and Jack Thomas's, all of United Boatbuilders in Bellingham. The point offers a fairly protected anchorage on either side, depending on which way the wind is blowing.

Long and narrow Lummi Island is mountainous on its southern end, rising to 1740 feet while the northern half is flatter with many nice sand or pebble beaches on both sides. A store at the ferry landing serves the 225 year-round residents and across the island Hawley's Marina offers marine service for the yachtsman.* Good crabbing and clamming in Hale Passage is another attractive feature for the cruising boatman.*

Saddlebag Island means good crabbing. Skippers and guests from Dave Thompson's The Misty Four and Ed Cushing's Cagy enjoy a dockside feast of the tasty crustaceans.

Swinging around Pt. Migley, the northern tip of Lummi Island, we coasted the east shore line down past Village Point and into Legoe Bay for a closer look at the large fleet of reef netters with their tall lookout towers. Heading on Boulder Reef Buoy, north of Sinclair Island, we encountered the strong tide rips of an incoming tide. Sinclair is a lower island than some of its neighbors and has poor anchorages so it is of small interest to the cruising boatman. Wilkes, in keeping with his practice of honoring distinguished officers of the U.S. Navy, named it after Arthur Sinclair Sr., Commander of the *Argus* in the war of 1812.

We swung around the top of little Towhead Island, wooded and rocky, and cruised down the east side of Cypress Island. Narvaez originally called it San Vicente, another of the Mexican Viceroy's names, but Vancouver, thinking the junipers were cypress trees, gave it the name of Cypress. He and his crew also enjoyed wild strawberries while anchored in the bay on the west side and so named Strawberry Island and Strawberry Bay, both scenic with not too much protection for anchoring but excellent fishing.

The Cone Islands, a group of small islets and rocks east of Cypress Island, are rocky, wooded and steep and offer some interesting exploring and photographic possiblities. The skipper of a large boat would be wise to use his large scale chart and depthsounder carefully or resort to the dinghy.

Cypress is well forested and quite high with steep rock walls. The eastern side has several interesting coves and

bays. Eagle Harbor with a dock which was part of a defunct real estate development, provides anchorage but is shallow. Deepwater Bay itself doesn't offer too much protection from the southeast although Secret Harbor at its southwest extremity makes a good anchorage. There's also an interesting little cove behind the bight at the northern end.

Cruising down Bellingham Channel and acrosss Guemes Channel we circled Burrows and Allan Islands in Burrows Bay. Both of these were named by Wilkes — the former for Lt. William Burrows and the latter for Capt. William Henry Allen of the U.S. Navy. As so often happens when biography is transferred to geography the spelling is changed so charts now show it as Allan Island. A reasonably protected anchorage as well as good fishing can be found between Burrows Island and its little satellite, Young Island, but a wary eye must be kept on the charted rocks.

Careful piloting is also needed to enter Reservation Bay just off Northwest Pass on the way to Deception Pass but a look into this interesting cove is worth the effort.

Deception Pass, well known to old time Northwest skippers, is always both beautiful and awesome. The deep, narrow gorge with 500 foot high rocky banks on both sides and an island in the middle is topped off with a high bridge where tourists stand and watch the whirlpools and boils of a fast torrent that attains a speed up to nine knots at times. A look at the chart shows how much water on either side of the pass must pour through this narrow hourglass in each direction as the tide ebbs and flows at approximately six hour intervals. The wise navigator, particularly of a slower boat, checks his current tables carefully to figure on running the pass somewhere near slack water.

Planning a cruise through any of the passes where it is necessary to take a tidal current into consideration always brings to mind the advice of experienced skippers. They say if you can't hit the slack exactly, and intend to run a pass either before or after slack, be sure to run against the current. If you find it's too strong you can always turn around and go back. If you're running with it, however, and get into trouble it sometimes isn't easy or always possible to turn back.

Just inside the pass is Cornet Bay, an excellent place to wait for good current conditions or to spend a night. The state marine park has both moorage and anchorages available and the Cornet Bay Marina, just beyond, offers complete facilities for the yachtsman.

Around the corner from Deception Pass lies Hope Island, with surrounding waters famous for record catches of the fighting salmon.

Too frequently we tend to think of the San Juan Islands only in terms of Orcas, Lopez, Shaw, San Juan and adjacent islands but the "magic of the islands" applies just as fully to those east of Rosario Strait. When you've spent time cruising through the enchanting blue waters which surround green-timbered islands, beach-combed along a sandy beach, searched for agates on a pebbly one, or explored along a craggy rock shore, gathered your share of clams, oysters or crabs, poked your bow into scores of friendly coves and finally dropped anchor in a quiet harbor to partake of a meal from the sea and watch the western sky fade from brilliant gold to a symphony of oranges and purples and at last to the gray of dusk, you will attest to the proclaimed "magic." You'll agree the San Juans, including the eastern group, live up to their billing and are truly spell-casters, not to be by-passed lightly.

*Hawley's Marina is now Village Point Marina on Legoe Bay Drive.

8
The Northern Perimeter Islands

The Northwest had just been returned from the laundro-mat after a night of washing. An early morning sun dispersed the last vestiges of rain clouds. The islands seemed to preen themselves from their high timbered hills and green valleys down to their craggy rock cliffs and sheltered sandy beaches in the sparkling mirror at their feet. The freshly washed air made us breathe more deeply in anticipation of a beautiful cruising day.

Rounding Lawrence Point, Orcas Island's easternmost extremity, called for a slow bell and a bit of fancy maneuvering to stay clear of all the fishermen and their crisscrossed lines. The pace wasn't boring, however, for we enjoyed watching two lucky anglers win their battle with the wily salmon and boat fish that must have weighed in the neighborhood of 25 pounds each.

Stifling an urge to stop and join them, we continued on for another day of rediscovering this San Juan archipelago — this magnificent paradise of islands — which so many skippers in fast boats by-pass these days in their hurried quest of cruising waters farther north.

Our first objective was a run up betweeen Barnes and Clark Islands with their smaller satellites, the Sisters. Like so many islands of these inland seas, they have been known be several names. In 1791 Capt. Francisco Eliza named the group Islos de Aguayo, part of the long name of his sponsor, the Mexican Viceroy. Later, in 1841, Capt. Charles Wilkes gave them their present names in honor of U.S. Naval heroes.

The Sisters, off the southeastern end of Clark Island are large rocks and provide innumerable convenient crannies which the sea gulls utilize as apartment homes. The many picturesque rocks, large and small, offer interesting photographic possiblities.

Both Clark and Barnes Islands are wooded. Barnes presents the rockier shoreline while Clark has several sand and gravel beaches. The channel between the islands has plenty of depth but the wise skipper will pay close heed to the charted rocks, particularly those extending north from Barnes Island.*

Leaving this group, we headed northwesterly, not quite sure whether we were technically in the northern reaches of Rosario Strait or the very southern part of the Strait of Georgia. The chart isn't very clear on the subject.

This brings up an interesting point. We in the Northwest tend to think of Puget Sound as extending from Olympia on the south to the Canadian border on the north. Actually it runs north only as far as the Strait of Juan de Fuca. The area between the southern end of Vancouver Island and the mainland on the east, and between the Strait of Juan de Fuca and the Strait of Georgia, the area containing the San Juan Islands, is officially Washington Sound although most charts fail to note it and few of us ever hear it called that.

Cruising among the islands, one is captivated by their charm and beauty. There's always some new wonder — a hidden cove or a picturesque bay, a sandy beach or a rugged rock cliff just around the next point. A calm serenity encompasses the entire setting and no matter how often you visit, you never quite feel you have discovered all that is there. And you haven't, for each return trip will produce something new, a different vista, an exciting reach or a half-familiar scene repainted in exotic colors on an entirely different canvas.

Matia Island is such a place, really intriguing in more ways than one. You hear it called "Matey" by some, "May-shia" by others, but an honest look at the record proves it should be "Mah-teé-ah".

Eliza called it Isla de Mata. Wiles charted it as the Edmonds Group. The U.S. Coast Survey of 1854 listed it as Matia and certainly a name of Spanish origin requires a broad, soft "a" so "Mah-teé-ah" it is.

It has also been said that Eliza's First Pilot Juan Pantoja called it Mal Abrigado or Bad Anchorage and that Matia, meaning no protection, from a safe anchorage viewpoint, was shortened from that name but the better authorities credit Eliza with naming it.

The group has been described as an exclamation mark with little Puffin Island on the east end forming the dot. Puffin was so named for the tufted puffins nesting there, although it was once charted as "Matia East." It is also a favorite rendezvous for seals.

All of Matia was set aside as a lighthouse reservation from 1875 until 1937 although a lighthouse was never established. The government kept 145 acres as a migratory bird refuge and in 1958 the State Parks & Recreation Commission applied for permission to use the balance of it for recreational purposes. Today the two coves on the northwestern

*Clark Island is now a state marine park.

end have been made a marine park.

For beauty and tranquility the bays of Matia are hard to beat although they are small and require attention to chart and depthsounder on moderate-sized cruisers. Larger craft will probably not be too anxious to try these.

Matia is an island for explorers and exploration is always more exciting when you have a background of history.

The first known settler of any permanence was probably Skookum Tom, an Indian wanted for murder in British Columbia and suspected of murdering a white man on Orcas Island and another on Waldron Island. He was there prior to 1883 and from then until 1889 several attempts were made to settle on the island with a couple of squatters named Evans and Lovering apparently the only successful ones.

In 1892 Captain Elvin H. Smith, a strong quiet, six-foot civil War veteran from Wisconsin and a lawyer friend from Fairhaven (Bellingham) bought the squatters out. Smith lived there for two years and, by then, thoroughly in love with the island, he paid the lawyer $1150 for his share.

Smith became the Hermit of Matia Island and built his home, consisting of several small compact buildings, below the bluff on the east end of the island. He cleared five acres, raised much of his food in his garden and fished by placing a net across the entrance of the bay at the east end. With the sheep, chickens and ducks he kept and plenty of wild rabbits, he and his dog and cat made out very well.

Since he had no dock for a mail-boat stop, the skipper would whistle if he had mail and Smith would row out for it. On Saturdays he usually rowed the 2½ miles to Point Thompson on Orcas, then walked two miles to Eastsound for whatever supplies he needed and to keep up with news of the rest of the world.

When outboard motors were first developed he had an early 2½-horsepower model. It wasn't much faster than rowing but considerably easier.

Returning from Orcas in February of 1921 with a friend, Civil War veteran Capt. George Carrier, they ran into a

At anchor in a peaceful bay on the western end of Matia Island

storm and were never heard of again. Wreckage of the boat with the motor was found later by Indians near Blaine.

Today as you explore the island, hiking along the path through the woods which connects the harbors, you can still see the remains of the old orchard, the clearing and the ruins of the hermit's cabin. As you mentally reconstruct the scene or enjoy the several scenic sandy beaches of Matia Island, you can understand why Capt. Smith loved his island paradise retreat.

It's only a short run from Matia to the famed Sucia Islands. Here we find another paradise only with different characteristics. Sucia is perhaps the most exotic of the San Juans having a definite South Seas flavor which becomes more obvious as you explore along Chinaman's Rock in Shallow Bay, dig fossils at the head of Fossil Bay and observe the charcoal-black cormorants with their long necks or an occasional rare sea parrot.

Youngsters head for shore at Sucia Island's Shallow Bay

Even its name has a romantic ring until you discover its meaning. Eliza called it Isla Sucia. In Spanish Sucia means dirty and he applied the term in sea-going language because of the dirty or rocky shore.

Capt. Wilkes named it the Percival Group in honor of Capt. John Percival, distinguished U.S. naval officer. But in 1847 British Capt. Henry Kellett restored the name Sucia for which we can all be thankful.

We can also thank the far-sightedness of leaders of the Puget Sound Interclub Association and the generosity of hundreds of yachtsmen and yacht club members who bought Sucia just as it was about to be sold to private interests and turned it over to the state. It is now a state marine park and can be enjoyed by yachtsmen for all time to come.

Like Matia, Sucia has a history of being held for a government use which never materialized. In 1896 after a group of settlers had requested it to be opened for homesteading, the 490-acre island was held as a military reservation for coastal defenses.

There was also a period of commercialization when in 1902 a company was formed to quarry sandstone. Many early-day streets in Seattle and other Puget Sound communities were paved with sandstone blocks from Sucia.

Sucia's many charms, her five bays — each with entirely different characteristics — her sylvan trails, her rocks and caves with a hint of smugglers and rum-runners of the past, her beauty, her romance and all the rest are too well known by yachtsmen to need further detailing. It's sufficient to say that once you've been there, once you've watched a sunset from Shallow Bay or seen its reflection on Mt. Baker from Echo Bay, and enjoyed all that is there simply for the taking, you'll come back again and again.

While Sucia is well known to most yachtsmen, fewer of them have bothered to look in on Patos, northernmost of the San Juans. If you are guilty of such an oversight it should be corrected.

Called Isla de Patos, island of the ducks, by Galliano and Valdez in 1792, Wilkes changed it to Gourd Island and Kellett restored Patos. Alden Point, as well as Alden Bank to the east, were named in honor of Lt. Cmdr. James Alden of the steamer *Active* with the Wilkes expedition. He also took part in Indian wars on Puget Sound in 1855-56. Active Cove of Patos and Active Pass were named for his ship.

The entire island is a government-owned lighthouse reserve. Originally built in 1893, this important lighthouse was rebuilt in 1908. A radio beacon was established in 1937 and new living quarters constructed in 1958.*

With only one small sheltered anchorage in Active Cove just south of the light, it's easy to understand why Patos hasn't achieved the popularity of some of the other islands. Yet she has attributes which shouldn't be ignored.

For those interested in sea life the island is a natural laboratory. At low tide little pools in the sandstone are miniature aquariums containing a host of undersea life not generally easy to see but here spread out for the visitor to study and wonder at. Still further investigation of the large variety of sea creatures is easy in the shallow water off shore from a small boat.

Nature has been generous with her artistic talents with the waves and breakers of a sometimes angry sea sculpturing interesting shapes and patterns from the sandstone. At low tide the visitor can examine this fascinating gallery where overhanging ledges protect walls containing bits of fossilized coal and wood and the floor is covered with a maze of interesting designs.

The southern shore has several sand and gravel beaches between its rough rocks while the northern shore is almost all low level with flat solid rocks and plenty of driftwood.

In spite of its remoteness and the heavy tide rips and whirlpools in front of the lighthouse, several hundred visitors call on the men and their families stationed there each year.† Active Cove, where both customs and Coast Guard craft have lain in wait in days past for reported smugglers, offers fairly good protection but care should be used on entering. Minnie's Beach at the east end was named for a lighthouse keeper's wife who sunned herself there.

If the wind and sea aren't kicking up from Georgia Strait, Patos is well worth a visit.

Leaving Patos we headed our bow southwesterly for a look at Waldron Island and its children, Skipjack and Bare Islands. Pantoja is credited with passing near Waldron and calling it Lemos but Wilkes named it Waldron in 1841. There is some question as to whether the name was for Captain's Clerk Thomas W. Waldron of the expedition's brig *Porpoise* or for R. R. Waldron, purser on another vessel of the expedition, the *Vincennes*.

Wilkes charted the two smaller islands as Skipjack Islands, probably for several species of fish by that name. The U.S. Coast Survey of 1853, noting the difference in covering of the islands, called the larger one "Wooded" and the smaller "Bare" Island. Capt. Richards in 1858 restored the original name for the larger one and changed the smaller one to Penguin Island and still later the U.S. Coast and Geodetic Survey used Skipjack, but rejected Penguin for Bare, the way the charts read today.

Waldron Island can perhaps be called the last frontier of the San Juan group. Entirely owned by its inhabitants, it has no public beaches and no protected bays, and is of little interest to the yachtsman. The dock in Cowlitz Bay is difficult to get to because of Mouatt Reef and is exposed to both southwest and southeast winds and strong currents. Even the mail boat occasionally has to resort to using a small cove on the other side of the island.

With this natural isolation from the rest of the world the island has retained nearly all of its pioneer charm. Its population, numbering in the thirties, still lives rather primitively but they like it that way. Several authors and artists live there with fishing and farming as occupations for others.

Although Waldron Island is different, still it contributes its share to the overall mood of the San Juans. Wherever you cruise among them, wherever you drop anchor or snug down for the night, whatever you choose from the long list of possible daily activities, you end up realizing that you have been "taken over" by the islands.

The forested, rocky north end of Barnes Island silhouetted against Orcas Island's Mount Constitution

*There is no longer a radio beacon on Patos Island.
†The island is uninhabited. Patos Island Lighthouse was fully automated on July 2, 1974.

9
Orcas and Its Satellite Islands

There are many descriptive names applied to the San Juan Islands and each year, as more people discover and rediscover them, more are added. Each reflects a mood or feeling induced in an individual by the magic that seems to pervade these emerald gems so beautifully set by the Master Artisan in the blue-green stained glass of this inland sea.

Isles of Delight, Treasure Islands of the Northwest, The Charmed Land, Sunshine Belt, Theme for Writers, Inspiration for Artists, Subject for Word Pictures, Paradise Isles, Magic Islands — these are just a sampling. Those who have been there will agree that these appellations are most fitting or they will have some others of their own.

In our effort to cover this delightful archipelago, we have divided it into arbitrary sections. Having already cruised the eastern islands and those around the northern perimeter, we now consider Orcas and some of its satellites.

With its 57 square miles, Orcas is the largest of the group, shaped something like a pair of well-filled saddlebags. There is some question as to the source of its name. Capt. Francisco Eliza, who first explored and named many of the islands, about 1791, called it Isla de Orcas, either from "Orcasitees," part of the long name of the Viceroy of Mexico, or from "Orca," the Spanish word for blackfish or killer whale which are frequently seen in these waters.

In 1841 Capt. Charles Wilkes, in his effort to honor U.S. naval heroes, called it Hull's Island after Commodore Isaac Hull who commanded the U.S. Frigate *Constitution* and captured the English vessel *Guerriere*. He also named Mt. Constitution and called East Sound "Old Ironsides Inlet" after the frigate's pet name. West Sound he called "Guerriere Bay" after the captured ship.

Mt. Constitution is the only one of these names which remains today. Capt. Kellett called it Orcas on his chart of 1847 and Capt. Richards used East Sound, West Sound and Deer Harbor on the British admiralty chart #2689 in 1858-60.

Leaving the float at Olga in Buck Bay near the entrance to East Sound after a visit to the store, we swung to the left for a cautious look into the shallow inner bay. Olga was named after the wife of John Ohlert who built and operated the first store, hotel, Post Office and dance hall there in 1870.

Planning to cruise around Orcas counterclockwise, we chose Obstruction Pass to get into Rosario Strait. It's always a toss-up between this and Peavine Pass, running parallel about a mile apart and separated by Obstruction Island. These passes in the San Juans need cause no concern for the skipper. True, maximum flow of the tidal currents can run up to five knots but they are not to be compared with some of the passes in Canadian waters.

Entering the dog leg of Obstruction Pass we again made the same mental note made many times before to some day stop and explore the cozy little cove with its sandy beach on Obstruction Island. Before making the turn to starboard we swung up past Obstruction Pass Resort with its cottages marshaled in parade formation on the shore and its hospitable gas dock.*

The day was warm with only a breath of breeze rippling the water as we emerged from the pass, rounded Deer Point and coasted the southeast shore of Orcas, staying in as close as we dared. Doe Bay Resort and Sea Acres Lodge along with many nice homes dominate this shore looking out over Peapod Rocks. Wilkes originally named these large barren rocks because of their shape. They are a favorite haven for large numbers of sea gulls and during the nesting season literally thousands of these graceful birds on the rocks, in the water and in the air present an intriguing picture.

Our course turned 90° to the port at Lawrence Point, named for the naval hero James Lawrence of "Don't Give Up The Ship" fame. The northeastern shore of Orcas with its steep banks rising eventually to 1890-foot Mt. Pickett and 2450-foot Mt. Constitution offers little of interest to the yachtsman.

Approaching North Beach we cruised between Pt. Thompson and Parker Reef lighted buoy. George Parker, for whom Wilkes named this reef, was a petty officer with the expedition. Our next objective was a stop at Bartel's Resort on North Beach where Power Squadron friends had reported the warm hospitality and friendliness of proprietors Dave and Roxie Church.† Here we were happy to find, in addition to an excellent resort with tennis courts and heated pool, a complete gas dock and store with groceries, ice, fishing gear and marine accessories. This is a welcome facility in this

32

*Obstruction Pass Resort, Doe Bay Resort and Sea Acres Lodge are no longer operating.
†Though Dave and Roxie Church still live on the island, they no longer operate Bartel's Resort.

Lookout spots on the way up Mt. Constitution offer varying vistas of the island-dotted waters of Washington Sound

Jones Island State Marine Park offers pleasant anchorage, mooring buoys, floats, campgrounds, wooded trails and inviting beaches

Grindstone Harbor on the south shore of Orcas Island has been a popular spot for over a hundred years

area because of its convenience to nearby Sucia. From the outside or on the chart the approach may look inhospitable but as you get closer a channel can be seen through the kelp marked by colored buoys.

Leaving Bartel's, we headed for Pt. Doughty which Wilkes named for another of his petty officers, John Doughty. This is still the charted name for this point but it is sometimes known by the more picturesque "Bill of Orcas" and another popular name is Cole's Point.

Entering President Channel between Orcas and Waldron Islands, which Wilkes named in honor of the frigate *President*, we encountered heavy tide rips. Every Northwest cruising skipper has experienced this uncomfortable type of water caused either by the surging of two meeting bodies of water at a tidal change or by tidal currents as they meet from different directions. Sea waves in an open body of water have a certain honesty about them as they run in a more or less regular and predictable pattern. Tide rips, however, are uncontrolled fiends with no sense of direction. The waves come from nowhere, go nowhere, yet in their mad scramble they assume varied shapes and sizes as they seem to attack a ship from all sides, lifting, dropping or turning it with the most erratic fervor. All the helmsman can do is maintain as straight a course as he can and hope he gets out of them as soon as possible.

Just inside Pt. Doughty we passed a fleet of small boats filled with boys from the YMCA Camp Orkila on their way to an overnight camp-out on Sucia Island.

Around the next point, which we gave a wide berth because of several rocks, lies West Beach, one of the finest beaches in the islands, and West Beach Resort, another excellent facility for yachtsmen with gas dock, store, diver's air station, etc.

Coasting down the northwest shore of Orcas with the Turtleback Range rising to 1500 feet behind, we recalled the story of the mysterious anchor. On a grassy slope near Turtleback's top lies the replica of an old sailing vessel type anchor laid out in rocks each six to eight inches in diameter. Old timers say it has been there as long as the memory of the first white settlers can recall.

The most popular theory is that remains of a wrecked sailing vessel found long ago off Steep Point were from an early exploring ship and that her survivors left the anchor as a memorial to the ship. Further support of this theory is that the rocks are not of a type native to this area and their uniform size and shape indicate they could have been part of the ballast of the wrecked ship.

Our course was now set directly for the bay indenting the north shore of Jones Island. This is a favorite rendezvous for many Northwest skippers. It is a state marine park with permanent mooring buoys, floats, dock, well, pump and camp grounds. Island trails offer an opportunity for leg stretching and some good photographic possibilities. The island was named by Wilkes for Master Commandant Jacob Jones who in the U.S. Sloop-of-War *Wasp* captured the British Brig *Frolic* on October 18, 1812.

In spite of many romantic tales that the Wasp Islands were so named because of pirates who hid there and attacked boats using Wasp Passage, Wilkes gave the name in 1841. He also called Upright Channel between Shaw and Lopez Islands "Frolic Strait" but Capt. Richards rejected this in his 1858-60 chart while retaining the Wasp Islands and giving them their separate names.

The afternoon was a pleasant one at Jones Island. One can nearly always find a friend or turn acquaintances into friends in this beautiful cove. With the sun over the yard-arm and the mainbrace properly spliced we continued to boat hop until a striking ship's clock reminded us it was time to be off. We had shore side dinner reservations.

It was only a short run down Spring Passage with a hard-a-port turn up North Pass to Deer Harbor. Time didn't permit our taking advantage of the Keppers' invitation to explore their little Fawn Island but circling it at least gave us an idea of what it was like.

The floats at Deer Harbor were nearly full but we managed to find mooring space. When time permits we like to walk the short distance to the Deer Harbor Inn. Besides being a pleasant hike, it whets the appetite for even more helpings of that famous family style chicken dinner. Originally known as Norton's and started early in the century, this was the first resort on Orcas Island. For years many cruising families have not considered a San Juan cruise complete without a call at this port for a chicken dinner. If time doesn't permit or you don't feel like walking, a telephone call from the store will bring a car to take you to the Inn. The store is well stocked and the marina has a gas dock as well as moorage.

We were all up early next morning and, after a good breakfast, we headed out toward Pole Pass. This is the narrowest pass in the area and was so called because the Indians string nets on long poles to knock down the ducks as they came through the pass.

West Sound has been a favorite since early days when the Lummi Indians camped around its shores. Today many beautiful homes are snuggled into the cedars, firs and hemlocks which seem to preen themselves in the sparkling mirror at their feet.

Bartel's Resort on the north shore of Orcas offers facilities for yachtsmen. Fuel, groceries, ice and fishing supplies are available as well as a complete resort with cottages, heated pool and tennis courts.

The bay hasn't always been the scene of peace and beauty, however, as some of the nearby names attest. Massacre Bay, Skull Island and Victim Island are reminiscent of days past when marauding Haida Indians came out of the north in their big war canoes to raid the peace-loving Lummi's. Both Haida Point and Indian Point as well as Massacre Bay were sites of more than one bloody battle.

Behind Picnic Island in White Beach Bay is the West

Sound Marina, with gas dock, moorage and repairs. The Orcas Island YC is around the bay to the left as is the West Sound store. A circle tour of West Sound is worth anyone's time even if no stops are planned. We always enjoy skirting the shoreline, poking the bow into the many little coves and exploring in behind the small islands. The bay behind Double Island is a particularly scenic spot.

Coming out of West Sound and around the corner to the east is Orcas. This is where the ferry lands and a fuel dock, liquor store, and complete grocery and meat market make it a popular provisioning stop for yachts of all sizes. If you're looking for some top grade steaks for the barbecue or hibachi or good meat of any kind, "Buss" Sheehan is the man to see behind the meat counter at the Orcas store.*

Heading eastward through Harney Channel there are three coves of interest. The first is behind the little island, or sometimes peninsula, just around the corner from Orcas. I've never been able to find a name for it but have always been intrigued by the lovely sandy beach in that bight.

Grindstone Harbor actually isn't too much of a harbor although it is a sheltered anchorage and a beautiful spot. The two large rocks at its entrance are charted, marked with kelp and usually with navigational markers. Two fathoms of water in the inner bay and nice beaches have made this a favorite spot since the mid-1800's when Paul Hubbs ran a store here until it burned in the 1860's.

Another smaller but deeper cove, nameless on the chart, lies between Foster Point and Shag Rock. A pair of sandy beaches at the head make this an enticing spot for an afternoon stop but there is no protection from southeast winds.†

Six-mile-long East Sound nearly cuts Orcas into two islands with the village of Eastsound at its head. As we cruised from Shag Rock around Diamond Point to Twin Rocks the youngsters decided that one lower and two higher peaks of Entrance Mountain on the opposite side above Olga looked like the head and double humps of a huge camel crouched down waiting to be loaded.

Although Eastsound is the largest village center on the island with an excellent store, post office, school, churches and a fascinating historical museum, there is no easy access for the boater. There is a Standard Oil fuel dock but no floats which makes fueling a difficult operation, particularly for smaller boats. Well known resorts are on both Fishing Bay and Ship Bay at the head of East Sound.‡

Halfway down (or up) the east shore is Rosario. This is the famous resort which Mr. and Mrs. Gil Geiser have developed from the former Moran estate. With its marina, fuel dock, guest moorages, store, lodge, boatel, heated pools, showers, laundromat, recreation program, excellent meals and other fine facilities, it has become one of the top yachtsman's resorts in the islands. No matter how we enjoy

the peace and solitude of a remote anchorage, there still comes a time on most cruises when the First Mate appreciates a day or more ashore where she can clean up, get some laundry done and eat someone else's cooking. The small fry also like a chance to relieve their cabin fever and enjoy the many shore-side activities.

Another means of recreation has been added in recent years by some of these resorts catering to yachtsmen. It's the chance to do some land exploring aboard a Honda motor scooter.§

This is an especially appealing activity at Rosario where skipper and crew can go for a joy ride to the top of Mt. Constitution. Although it had been many years since the skipper had been aboard a motor-driven two-wheel vehicle and the First Mate had never tried it, we rented a couple of these mechanical bucking broncos. After a few words of instruction from the dock staff and a couple of short trial spins around the grounds we put-putted up the hill, each with a youngster behind us, toward the seven-mile distant mountain.

The ride was exhilarating as we wound through the deep forest, past beautiful Cascade Lake and headed for the summit. The day was so bright and warm there was no need for the sweaters and jackets we'd brought along. The shafts of sunlight filtered through the cool shade of the evergreens as the pine and cedar scented air combined to insist on full appreciation for the wonders of nature.

At the top we climbed the stairs in the stone observation tower, drank in the awesome beauty of the 360° vista of green islands and blue water backed up with sparkling white-capped mountains in the distance.

The view of mile-long Mountain Lake from the tower called for a short side excursion to inspect it more closely on our return trip. Thy sylvan beauty of this lovely jewel nestled among the mountains is an unforgetable picture, worthy of treatment by artist or poet.

We returned to Rosario just in time to shower and clean up for the fabulous sea food buffet in the dining room of the lodge. The day's activity had added yet another new and never-to-be-forgotten experience which we highly recommend as a part of any cruising itinerary. Another worthwhile Honda trip is one we tried later when Rosario's Jim Dahl loaned us his more powerful vehicle for a spin to Eastsound and a most interesting afternoon at the historical museum with its fine collection of Indian and early pioneer artifacts and exhibits.

The more time one spends in these magical islands, the more one can find to do and the more fascinating places to visit. It isn't recorded that Mark Twain ever visited the San Juans but paraphrasing his graphic description of some other islands, it could certainly apply to the San Juans, "the loveliest fleet of islands that lies anchored in any inland sea."

---

*A few changes at the ferry landing—the barber shop and ice house are gone as is "Bus" Sheehan behind the meat counter. It's still a good store!
†Though still nameless on the chart, this is Guthrie Cove.
‡The resorts are gone leaving only the Outlook Inn.
§Hondas have given way to rental cars as the best way of exploring the island.

10

Historic Rosario

Even the most ardent yachtsman and certainly First Mates, guests and small fry enjoy time ashore occasionally. While we all revel in meals of fish, clams, crabs, oysters, shrimp—seafoods found so abundantly in our Northwest waters—still a good steak, roast, chop or bit of chicken, cooked by someone else, can offer a welcome change.

It's also necessary at times to replenish ship's stores, supplies of ice, water, fuel, etc., and it's always pleasant to have a convenient rendezvous point to meet with friends from other boats. Shoreside games and entertainment add variety to a cruise, too.

For reasons such as these a new type of marine resort has been born in recent years which caters to the cruising skipper and his family. Besides offering a pleasant interlude during a cruise, it can also serve as a convenient place to leave the boat and the family if the skipper finds it necessary to get back to his office for a few days. Scheduled air service is available at the East Sound Airport.

Rosario on East Sound, the long stretch of water that nearly cuts Orcas Island in half, isn't exactly new but it is new in the last few years as a major marine facility for yachtsmen.

The name "Rosario" is found in several places in the San Juan archipelago and apparently was first introduced by the Spanish explorer Francisco Eliza in the late 1700s. As a great organizer and map maker, he charted the islands and has been called the "Father of the San Juans." It was to the Gulf of Georgia that he gave the name "Gran Canal de Nuestra Senora del Rosario la Marinera."

In order to fully appreciate Rosario, enjoy its elegant charm and partake of its atmosphere, one must delve into history a bit. Robert Moran was a native of New York who followed Horace Greeley's advice and came west with plenty of hope and ambition but with less than a dollar in his pocket. Things worked out for him as he became an important shipbuilder, mayor of Seattle at the time of the great fire and a great philanthropist in the islands. The battleship USS Nebraska was built in his yards.

At about the turn of the century doctors gave him only a year to live. Coming to the San Juans, he fell in love with Orcas Island, bought Cascade Lake, the Cascade Lumber Company and adjoining property and ultimately owned some 6,000 acres. In 1905 he started the construction of his home on Cascade Bay to be the focal point of his beautiful estate. Regaining his health, he lived another 40 years of a full and active life.

The mansion of solid concrete with walls a foot thick, contains 54 rooms. All of the windows that open are of 7/8-inch thick porthole plate glass. Guests are sure to notice the rare wood paneling, the solid mahogany doors with special hinges, the original works of art and the luxurious Oriental rugs—everything still there for present day enjoyment. It took three years to install the tile and teakwood parquet floors.

The original living room with its massive fireplace and beautiful view of East Sound now serves as the main dining room. *Still very much as it was in days past is the music room, acoustically perfect and graced with stained glass windows. The giant Kimball pipe organ with its 1,972 pipes, the antique Steinway grand piano and the electric player piano are still in good condition and frequently used. Modern electronics come into the scene with a Wurlitzer electric organ, radio and television. The room is also fully equipped with a complete theatre projection booth.

There are 18 single sleeping rooms, two-bedroom suites and bedroom-sitting room suites all with fine furnishings and a beautiful view on the upper floor while the lower floor contains an indoor swimming pool, a game room and a cabaret theatre. The estate also had its own museum, a power plant and extensive gardens which people came from all over the world to see.

In 1921 Mr. Moran deeded most of the land to the state for what is now Moran State Park and kept only 1320 acres for his own use. In 1937-38 the estate was purchased by Mr. Donald Rheems and in 1958 it was sold to the Falcon Corporation of Waco, Texas, which subdivided some of the property, built seven houses and installed a new water system.

Gilbert Geiser, the present owner, bought Rosario

*The main dining room has been moved elsewhere.

in 1960 and in June of that year opened it as a resort. Since then he has been improving and building it until today the visitor will find, in addition to the old world charm of the main lodge, a modern boatel, gay and colorful in decor, with rooms and suites all having a shower and overlooking the outdoor, heated fresh-water swimming pool, the lagoon and the new boat moorages. The houses have been converted to housekeeping cottages. Rosario was a pioneer in installing modern panel electric heating.

Boaters are welcomed by dock boys to help tie up and will find a marina, complete gas dock, water, ice, grocery store, snack bar, showers and laundromat. The main dining room is open for three full meals each day with certain nights set aside for a smorgasbord or a seafood buffet. The chefs have built such a reputation for fine food and the dinners have been so popular that reservations have become a "must" if one wants to be sure to eat.

Two cocktail lounges, a cabaret theatre presenting live plays, and dinner dancing round out the possibilities for indoor entertainment. Talented college students and teachers spend their vacations at Rosario doubling as dock boys, life guards, play supervisors, musicians, strolling minstrels and cabaret actors and entertainers. Wherever you are in the main lodge you'll find live entertainment of some kind.*

In addition to cabaret type entertainment the theatre offers a series of plays under the direction of professionals which were well received last summer.

The Rosario concept of outdoor activities doesn't end with merely providing the facilities. A well organized and supervised program includes badminton, volleyball, shuffleboard, (popular with both children and adults) archery range and instruction, special games, hikes and wiener roasts, and a completely equipped playground area for the small fry. A swimming meet and pool show is staged once a week with young guest swimmers competing and displaying their talents.

The adult has the choice of relaxing or being as active as he desires. Activities can be as mild as a leisurely bit of beachcombing for agates or driftwood or as robust as a hike through the beautiful countryside, a trip up to Mt. Constitution on a Honda, or a round of golf on the nearby 9-hole course. Horseback riding is also available on the island and a stable of horses at Rosario is in future plans.

The yacht harbor and moorage at Rosario have been recently improved.

Gil Geiser, the genial host of Rosario, is constantly around to see that the needs of guests are satisfied and also works hard all year to build and improve the resort for the next season.

The summer vacation cruising season is all too short but northwest boatmen do not limit their cruising to summer months. More and more these island resorts are being used for off-season trips, hunting or winter fishing headquarters or just a relaxing spot to get away from it all for a special mood weekend, Thanksgiving, Christmas or New Year's holiday.

Gil tips us off that winter blackmouth fishing in Rosario's Cascade Bay is unsurpassed anywhere, practically un-publicized in sportsmen's circles, yet most guaranteeable and, if you wish, he'll even notify you when the run comes in.

Most of these marine type resorts, Rosario included,

This beautiful mansion, built by millionaire shipbuilder Robert Moran, is now the main lodge of Rosario.

now offer winter holiday special packages with traditional meals, suitable activities and entertainment and low off-season rates. One winter quite a fleet from one of the Seattle yacht clubs cruised north for the New Year's weekend.

The evolution of Rosario from millionaire's luxurious estate to marine resort has been a fortunate one for the yachtsman. It has become so popular, however, that if one desires accommodations, it's necessary to write, call or radiotelephone ahead for reservations or get there early in the afternoon, or there won't be an empty berth available.

In coming up the East Sound, the big white mansion is easily visible on the right. The entrance to the boat harbor can be confusing. Turn into Cascade Bay, head for the gas dock sign to the right of the rock breakwater and then swing to the left around the end of the breakwater. A dock boy will direct you to a berth.

Rosario is a most welcome addition to the ever-growing roster of popular marine resorts in the Northwest.

*Rosario had a few changes—only one cocktail lounge remains, no theatre, no actors, musicians or cabaret, but still excellent food and accommodations.

‖
Winter Fishing's Great in the San Juans

The man at the helm called down to his wife in the galley as he watched the black clouds moving into the northwest, taking the rain with them, "Things are going to improve fast, now, and we'll get our fish."

Two hours of slow trolling had produced only two bites and one landing. As the sky lightened, the two men in the cockpit of the small cruiser shed rain gear, flexed cold fingers and prepared for the promised battle with wily blackmouth by re-baiting.

"With the rain gone and a change of tide due, conditions are perfect," said the skipper. And he was right! Within the next two hours everyone on the boat, including the first mate, had limited with an even dozen beautiful blackmouth salmon from 13 to 28 pounds.

Fishing in the San Juan Islands is a great summer-time sport. And it's a great winter-time sport, too. More and more Northwest sportsmen are finding this out every year with their ranks increasingly augmented by ardent fishermen who fly up from the southwestern states for a taste of this exciting game.

Unlike most areas where salmon are fished, there is salmon fishing in the San Juans twelve months of the year. In fact, the winter period is exceptionally good, for that is when the blackmouth congregate in these waters. These are immature king salmon running up to about 35 pounds. They are primarily interested in finding food. When they find it they stay around, for the long inlets, shallow water and many bays serve as spawning grounds for the herring, candlefish and other kinds of feed they like.

The blackmouth is an extremely sporty fish, very good to eat and exceptionally good when smoked. They are generally best caught by trolling very deep with a heavy weight. Favored bait is dodger and herring or Pink Lady with strip rig. Some are caught on herring with spoon and some on flies.

Jack Young, one of Orcas Island's leading professional guides and charter boat skippers, doesn't mind passing out a few hints now and then. "Salmon are not converged at all points here, as would be the case around river mouths, for example," he says. "They are constantly moving, either following their migratory path or just searching for food so you have to go out and find them where they are.*

"Trolling is the ideal way of fishing for them. After you locate them by trolling, then, if you wish, you can switch to other methods such as mooching or spinning. The real secret, however, is found in that statement made by the late Henry Cayou, who is believed to have caught more salmon in his lifetime than any other human being. He said, 'You have to think like a fish to catch one.'"

Blackmouth fishing begins in the San Juans in November with fish running from 4 to 10 pounds. Best months are December and January with weights running from 20 to 25 pounds, occasionally up to 35. February is also good with the run usually lasting into mid-March and some years through April.

Orcas Island's East Sound is generally conceded to be the best area in the Northwest for blackmouth with the opening of the bay favored in early season and the fish moving further down East Sound and getting larger as the season progresses. Other good areas are Obstruction Pass, Harney Channel, West Sound, Pole Pass and Deer Harbor.

With the tremendous increase in popularity of winter blackmouth fishing, San Juan Island resorts which formerly had a three-month, or, at best, four-month season, are now busy the year around. Gil Geiser of Orcas Island's Rosario reports that many boats are moored in the harbor all during the winter fishing season and during the top months charter and rental boats must be reserved well in advance. Jim Dahl, Geiser's right hand man, goes fishing every day right outside the boat harbor until he has caught 60 fish and is generally successful in reaching his goal in less than a month. During the height of the season it is not unusual for a boat to limit in two hours. Recently two of a party of four went out in the morning, had their limit by noon, returned the boat for the other couple who went out in the afternoon and returned with the limit (three each) before dark.†

And the salmon fishing doesn't all end with the blackmouth. In May a fabulous run of Springs comes into East Sound, feeding on herring fry. They cruise along the east shore of the bay, following the bends of the shore line in shallow water. Sportsmen not only fish from boats in the usual manner, but from the shore. Springs running from

38

*Jack is no longer alive.
†Jim Dahl is busy now as Superintendent of Properties but he still keeps a watchful eye on the waterfront.

Mr. and Mrs. Jim Dahl caught a day's limit within two hours, just 1000 feet outside the Rosario Boat Harbor.

8 to 20 pounds are even caught from the sterns of boats moored in the Rosario boat harbor. It all becomes a regular field day with the fishermen going nearly crazy and crowds gathering to watch and cheer them when they land one.

Rosario, which has been becoming more and more popular as an off-season convention center, has met the challenge of this winter fishing with an increase in rental boats, rental gear and fishing tackle for sale. A special smoke house has been built for those who wish to take their salmon home smoked. Planes are met at the Eastsound airport on request, rental cars are available and it is now possible to buy an airline ticket from anyplace in the country direct to Eastsound.

Are you guaranteed a fish? Well, not quite. There are peaks and lows and the salmon is not a fish that is easily caught. It is one fish that takes a certain amount of technical know-how, skill and patience to catch but — it's a lot of fun!

12
San Juans West

Although Capt. George Vancouver didn't spend much time in the San Juan Islands, the magic and beauty of these emerald isles in an inland sea caught his fancy. His description of the entire area applies equally to this group.

He wrote, "Nothing can be more striking than the beauty of these waters without a shoal or a rock or any danger whatever for the whole length of this internal navigation, the finest in the world. Nothing can exceed the beauty of these waters and their safety. I venture nothing in saying that there is no country in the world that possesses waters equal to these."

Fundamentally, of course, he was right. Perhaps if he had spent some time enjoying the islands more intimately, he would have found a few rocks and shoals but Northwest yachtsmen acquainted with these waters basically agree with this overall concept.

To continue our rediscovery of this galaxy of islands, we now consider those in the western portion of the archipelago. Whether you've come from Deception Pass across the southern end of Lopez Island or north up Admiralty Inlet, you enter San Juan Channel through Cattle Pass. This pass, as well as Cattle Point, was so named when a ship was wrecked there and its cargo of cattle swam ashore to the point.

Our crossing of the strait had been remarkably smooth although these waters can kick up some uncomfortable seas at times. When they do it's best to stay clear of the islands on the east of the channel entrance to avoid the seas piled up by southwesterly winds between Whale Rocks and Iceberg Point.

After running midway between little Goose Island on the port and Deadman Island on the starboard, the wheel was swung slightly to the port to round what has recently come to be known as Cape San Juan with Harbor Rock off its northern point. A shoal area around the rock is well marked with kelp and no attempt should be made to go between the rock and the point.

We cut speed and continued a slow turn around Harbor Rock heading for Fish Creek on the southeastern tip of San Juan Island. This narrow little cove, about three-tenths of a mile long with one-and-a-half to two fathoms

of water, is an excellent haven from the winds "outside."

Like any of the other entrances to the islands, this one, too, seems immediately to "take you in." That magic feeling of peace and calmness settles over you as the usual tensions drop off and your blood pressure returns to a more normal state.

If you're interested in a shore-side hike, Fish Creek is a good point to start the two-mile trek to American Camp where U.S. forces under Capt. George Pickett were stationed during the famed "Pig War." The story of this "War," with a pig the only casualty, which played such an important part in the early history of both the island and the entire San Juan group, is too well known and documented elsewhere to cover here. The remains of the American and British camps, however, are always of interest to visitors.

San Juan Island has been likened to the general outline of North America. From Fish Creek we headed northwestward in Griffen Bay toward North Bay which would compare with the Gulf of Mexico. The chart shows this shore line dotted with rocks and shoals so we stayed fairly well off as we logged Low Point, Jensen Bay, Mulno Cove and Dinner Island.

While the shore line was beautiful with many lovely homes, the bays and coves, some with inviting beaches and driftwood, either didn't seem to offer sufficient protection for a good anchorage or appeared too private to merit closer exploration.

Heading next due east we rounded Pear Point with its rock and reef well marked with kelp then turned north toward Turn Island.

Our tendency, and probably that of many others, has always been to skirt the outside of Turn Island. Next time in this area, swing around behind it for as nice a bit of scenic beauty as you'll find in the islands. Take it slow, pay attention to that large scale chart (#6379) and let the kelp guide you. There's actually plenty of water if you're careful to keep in mid-channel all the way. You'll find it a worthwhile excursion and you might even decide to drop the hook for an afternoon or the night.

Incidentally, there is now a state marine park on Turn Island with picnicking and camping facilities as well as oysters and clams nearby.

Mooring buoys off Guss Island in Garrison Bay provide a comfortable anchorage whether you come for an afternoon of sunbathing, swimming and exploring or for a comfortable overnight stop in a beautiful setting

Friday Harbor, both the bay and the town, are well known to yachtsmen. Brown Island, which we recently noticed is called Friday Island in a real estate development folder, can be passed on either side; but attention should be paid to shoals extending off its eastern, southern and western shores.

The town, in addition to being a Port of Entry, is the county seat and offers complete service and supplies for the yachtsman with a port yacht moorage to the right of the main docks. The University of Washington Marine Laboratories around the bay from town are open to visitors between 2:00 and 4:00 p.m. on Wednesdays and Saturdays during the summer months. This is an interesting and educational side trip you'll enjoy.

Also of interest to boaters is the annual San Juan Rendezvous Celebration at Friday Harbor early in August. Featuring a huge free salmon barbecue, this affair is said to equal the famous July lamb barbecue of Saturna Island.*

Several stories are told about the naming of Friday Harbor. The most authentic seems to be that a Kanaka sheep herder grazed his flocks along the grassy slopes of the bay. He was called Joe Friday and the smoke from his shoreside shack was used by early boatmen to steer by. The bay became popularly known as Friday's Harbor.

Another popular story is that an officer of a survey boat entering the bay in the late 1850's called out to someone on shore asking, "What bay is this?" The man on shore, thinking he asked, "What day is this?" answered "Friday" and the survey officer marked his chart — Friday Bay.

Leaving Friday Harbor, our course swung us around Point Caution northwesterly again up San Juan Channel, past Rocky Bay, O'Neil Island and around Limestone Point into Spieden Channel. The northeastern and north shores of San Juan Island offer very little in the way of protected anchorages, although, as any place in the islands, the scenery is magnificent. Protection can be found behind Davison Head but don't go in too far as it shallows rapidly toward the head of the bay.

Rounding Davison Head we see little Barren Island with its tropical growth of cactus, then Posey Island and Pearl Island lying across the opening to Roche Harbor. Common entrance is around the west end of Pearl Island although many skippers enter by the east channel past the Reuben Tarte's beautiful home on the point.

You have hardly more than entered the bay before the unusual charm of the place is noticeable. The famous Hotel de Haro, the McMillin home (now the dining room), the old Roche Harbor Lime Co. loading pier and the little white chapel on the hill dominate the shoreline while the modern floats with hundreds of yachts extend out into the quiet waters. You are immediately aware of the enchantment of this one-time company town, restored and transformed into a modern resort, with all the facilities a yachtsman can ask for, by the hard working Tarte family.

Each year more and more yachtsmen discover the remarkable resort, not only in the summer months, but year-round when hunting and fishing seasons are at their peaks. With its air strip and taxi service to Friday Harbor, Roche Harbor has become one of the main centers in the islands. While the true cruising enthusiast likes his harbors out-of-the-way, quiet and untouched by civilization, there still comes that time when the small fry get cabin fever, the first mate tires of her own cooking and the skipper needs a shower, clean clothes and perhaps a replenishment of ice and ship's stores.

At these times installations such as Roche Harbor offer a welcome variety in the cruising schedule. Swimming pools, horseback rides, shoreside games, showers, laundromat, store and excellent meals, as well as the many familiar faces one finds, all add to the log of memories that we live on until the next cruise season starts.

Due west of the Roche Harbor floats, on the east shore of Henry Island, is a quiet little un-named cove which has become a favorite anchorage for many as has Nelson Bay just south of it.

Leaving Roche Harbor we entered Mosquito Pass, that beautiful narrow waterway between Henry and San Juan Islands. There are some shoals to watch for but most are marked with kelp and a mid-channel course will keep you out of trouble except at the south end where it is best to favor the east side a bit.

Once again the throttle was cut so that the ever-widening V of our wake was hardly noticeable. This gave us full opportunity to drink in the beauty of one of nature's finest pictures as we almost drifted along on a one or two knot ebbing current in the warm afternoon sunlight. Tiny Pole Island, grassy banks, little sandy beaches, tall evergreens reflecting in the water, even the rocks and reefs

41

appeared to be artistically grouped as though just waiting for the painter to transfer them to his canvas. We all agreed with Vancouver that these waters were truly incomparable.

We had to kick the rpm's up a little to make the left turn into Westcott and Garrison Bays. Past Horseshoe Bay and rounding the point into Garrison Bay we were impressed, almost to the point of envy, with the rustic

anchor buoys and the bay was alive with swimmers and sun bathers enjoying a perfect afternoon.

Mitchell Bay, south of Mosquito Pass, is another lovely spot although extremely shallow. The shoreline is mostly low level with some beaches and several houses. A moorage and gas dock are on the right as you enter the bay.‡

About two miles farther south, just beyond Low Island,

Stuart Island's Reid Harbor with its fine marine park facilities is a popular spot with northwest yachtsmen. Floats and dock at left lead to the camp and picnic sites and a trail to Prevost Harbor.

solitude of the cottages and cabins along the shore. What perfect places to "get away from it all" for a weekend, a vacation or forever!

Considering the ebbing tide and the fact that these bays are both comparatively shallow, we made fast to one of the anchor buoys off the point of Guss Island to continue our exploration in the outboard dinghy. A circle of Garrison Bay brought us to the English Camp of the Pig War where we went ashore for a closer inspection of the blockhouse, the old forge and what is left of a barracks building and commissary storehouse.* It was fascinating to hear Jim Crook and his sister Mrs. Anderson tell of the history of the place. Their father had homesteaded there after the British troops left and they have looked after it until now when it becomes a state historical park. We also took the short hike up the hill to the cemetery where eight British soldiers who passed away while in service are buried.

We continued our dinghy cruise into Westcott Bay which extends northeastward almost to the back door of Roche Harbor. Although quite shallow, this is also an excellent haven if the skipper checks the depths and watches the dense growth of eel grass which warns of the shoal areas. The Webb Camp School is ideally located on the east shore.†

Our return to the anchorage was followed by a swim which the kids insisted on after testing the water. By this time several other boats had taken over the rest of the

is Smallpox Bay where it is said the Indians jumped into the salt water in an effort to rid themselves of a smallpox epidemic. It is small, shallow and unprotected from the southwest. The rest of the west and south shore of San Juan Island is rugged and unprotected, of no particular interest to the yachtsman.

Open Bay on the south end of Henry Island, as its name implies, is too open to be much used.

North of San Juan Island is Spieden Island with its little satellite, Sentinel Island. These two islands, the smaller seeming to copy its big brother, are interesting for the peculiar growth pattern with the southern side completely bald of trees while the northern half is thickly forested. Viewed from either end they give the appearance of a head which has been clipped from front to back on one side only. Experts advance various theories about the distribution of vegetation by prevailing winds. In passing the western end of Spieden, we always enjoy the sudden change from hillsides of brown grass to the dark green of forested depths reflected into the cool water.

Most Northwest yachtsmen are acquainted with and most frequently use Spieden Channel to the south of the island. But for an interesting change and a scenic trip, try New Channel to the north next time. This takes you past the colorful Cactus Islands group ending with Gull Reef to the west. While most pictorial and enjoyable, you'll be more comfortable by paying close attention to that large-

*The blockhouse, commissary and barracks have been restored and become the San Juan Island National Historical Park.
†The Webb Camp School is no longer there.
‡This is the new Snug Harbor Marina Resort.

The British Garrison block house on Garrison Bay, built over 100 year ago during the "Pig War," is still in a good state of preservation. It is now a part of a state historical park.

Roche Harbor is famed for its beautiful flowers. Mrs. Reuben Tarte, shown here in one of her gardens, is responsible for them and has won many awards at local fairs and flower shows.

scale chart or at least keeping a close watch for the kelp marking the many rocks and shoals. Flattop Island and Gull Rock lie directly east.

To the northeast is Johns Island with Ripple Island off its southeast end. Some of the most picturesque cruising waters in the world are found in this area as you head for Johns Pass separating Johns Island from Stuart Island with as pretty a curving waterway as you'll find anywhere. We've heard of skippers who feel some trepidation about negotiating this pass; but with two hundred yards width at its narrowest point, from four to nine fathoms of depth in mid-channel, all rocks and obstructions well marked with kelp and a maximum current flow of three to five knots, there should be no cause for passing up this delightful passage if you are alert and use caution.

Stuart Island Airway Park, a waterfront and resort development on the eastern portion of the island, is adding another welcome facility for yachtsmen fronting on Johns Pass. Accessible only by water or air it is one of the last island hideaways left in the country. There are moorage facilities, boat and seaplane docks, air strip and other facilities available for the pleasure of the yachtsman.*

The two wonderful landlocked harbors of Stuart Island are well known to most boaters of this region. Reid Harbor to the south affords good anchorage on a soft bottom in depths of three to five fathoms with no dangers. There is a bit of foul ground on either side of the entrance but a mid-channel course will clear these without difficulty. A state park, moorage buoys, floats, camp ground and recreational area on shore make this an ideal spot. A sylvan trail leads across the narrow neck to like facilities on Prevost Harbor on the north. The shallow beach at the head of Reid Harbor is a good spot to get a bucket of clams at low tide.

Prevost Harbor is protected by Satellite Island. The passage to the west is recommended as the eastern passage is very shoal and rocky. The little village of Prevost, on the western shore of the bay, has a post office and there is about a one-mile trail leading from there to the Turn Point lighthouse. Good fishing is found from the entrance to the bay westward to Turn Point.†

We like Prevost for its sylvan beauty and quietness. After visiting the lighthouse, we chose an anchor buoy in the little cove of Satellite Island across the bay from the state dock. From here the small fry set out for a dinghy exploration. They came back loaded with marine biological specimens picked off the rocks and the sandy beaches at low tide.

As the day draws to a close with the sun painting the western sky in a variety of golds, reds, oranges and purples, one feels a certain sense of accomplishment. You started from some cozy cove or harbor, successfully made your passage through some of the world's most beautiful waters and have again come to another haven for the night.

With the anchor down, a good meal stowed away, and the dusk setting slowly over the water, you sense that feeling of quiet peace which is a part of this way of life. The stresses of civilization are remote. If you think of the world at all, you wonder how man can be at war with man in a creation so wonderful.

As the night darkens and your anchor light keeps watch above with only the lonesome wail of a loon heard across the bay, you might even think that if all men could only cruise the San Juans, there would be no strife. The wonder of God's creation would drive it from their minds.

One doesn't really need to own a boat to enjoy all this. There are many craft of all sizes available for charter. Or if you prefer sailing, Capt. Chris Wilkins runs six-day cruises from Orcas through the islands aboard his 60-foot ketch *Orcas Belle* or the 40-foot ketch *Idle Hour* can be chartered for weekly cruises from Capt. McBrayer of Eastsound.‡

Whatever your choice, power or sail, a few days or weeks spent cruising the San Juans will provide pleasant memories that will last a lifetime.

*The project was never developed.
†Prevost has no post office now.
‡Though these charters no longer run, others are available.

13
Roche Harbor

Daylight increased rapidly after the first pale tinges of pink had heralded the return of the sun in the eastern sky. J. S. rolled over in his big bed, rubbed his eyes and reached for his glasses. Although a quick glance out the window showed a filmy curtain of haze across the bay nearly hiding Pearl Island, he noted with satisfaction that the blue sky above was cloudless.

"Going to be a good day after all," he mumbled to himself as he sat on the edge of the bed and stretched.

J. S. knew he had to be up and about, for there was much to be done. He was accustomed to doing things in a big way, experiencing important events and meeting with famous people but this was July 13, 1906 and could well be the most memorable day he had yet lived in his 51 years. This was the day Theodore Roosevelt, President of the United States, would visit him at Roche Harbor.

John Stafford McMillin, owner of the biggest lime producing company west of the Mississippi, host to the President! His mind savored the thought as his eyes swept the harbor. There was the huge pier to the left, running well out into the bay, where his own ships and vessels from all over the world loaded his lime. There was the long dock running out to a cluster of sheds and boathouses to which his own yacht was moored practically in front of the house. To the right was another dock and floats and beyond lay the big flat barge which must be brought in and decorated. He could barely make out through the mist the log booms floating peacefully in front of the barrel factory on the point.

This was his own island empire and he was proud of it.

But this was not the time for idle dreaming. As he dressed he mentally checked off some of the things that must be attended to first. He must double check on room 10 in the company Hotel De Haro to make certain everything was perfect so Teddy could sleep well. He must make sure the barge was brought into the dock, cleaned up and decorated for the noon picnic trip to Point Mc-Cracken. He must see that the salmon and other food for the barbecue was ready and give the necessary orders for preparation of the evening meal in the De Haro

Banquet Court. Two other barges must be readied—one for the band, the other for the guests—for the dance that night in the middle of the harbor. Oh, yes, he must make certain that Mr. Young, the plant superintendent, had made all necessary arrangements for the tour of the kilns, the hatchery, Jap Town, and the rest of his company town. Yes, it was going to be a big day!

That was Roche Harbor in 1906. Roche Harbor now is probably known to nearly every yachtsman who cruises Northwest waters for it is one of the popular spots offering so many facilities for his pleasure and enjoyment—usually considered a "must" on any San Juan cruising itinerary. Part of the fascination of this place lies in its history. Throughout recent years visiting yachtsmen have heard many tales of the place and its past, some of them true or originally based on truth but, like most stories passed by word of mouth, embellished or changed with each telling.

It was with the purpose of searching out the true historical background that we spent some time digging out facts. Mr. Reuben Tarte, the late owner of Roche Harbor and president of the Roche Harbor Lime & Cement Co., generously permitted us the privilege of going through the archives and pictures, patiently answered our hundreds of questions and told us numerous anecdotes so we could devote this chapter of Northwest Passages to some of the intriguing history that adds so much to the charm of Roche Harbor as we know it today.

To start at the beginning, we must turn back the calendar to 1859 and the "Pig War" on San Juan Island. Among the pictures in the McMillin effects is one of a company of Marines stationed at the British Garrison. On the back of the picture is written, "Two brothers of these marines named Scurr bought Roche Harbor and started to mine lime. John S. McMillin bought from them"

McMillin's father, John King McMillin, homesteaded near Sugar Grove, Indiana, in 1830. John S., born in 1855, married Louella Hiett and the parents presented each of them with a wedding gift of $25,000. They came west to Tacoma in 1876 and John set up a law practice. In 1884 he bought the Roche Harbor property, incorporated the Roche Harbor Lime & Cement Co. in 1886 and began development of a business which, in 1929, had a net worth of $1,100,000. Much of the lime for cement and plaster used in rebuilding San Francisco after the earthquake came from here.

Roche Harbor, named after Lt. Richard Roche, who was a member of the boundary survey staff under Capt. J. C. Prevost, was first occupied as a Hudson's Bay Post.

In developing his island empire, McMillin attempted to make it as self-sufficient as possible. In addition to the quarries and the kilns, he established a barrel factory on the point where the Tarte's beautiful residence now stands. This was one of the first to make veneer barrels and was burned down by an anarchist sometime in the teens. During the rum-running days of the 20's a Coast Guard barracks occupied this site.

The McMillin company owned and operated three large sailing ships, *Star of Chile*, *Archer* and *Irving*, as well as smaller ships, tugs, work boats and barges. The *Star of Chile* was later sold to a movie company, the *Archer* burned and the final history of the *Irving* is not known. The ruins of the old tug *Roche Harbor*, used to get the sailing ships in and out of the bay and to tow barges to Seattle, can still be seen beached just beyond the swimming pool, and the Tartes hope some day to restore it.*

Another part of McMillin's complete community was his Bellevue Poultry Farm located at the head of Westcott Bay. This operation not only provided eggs and meat but also produced many prize-winning chickens and turkeys.

With an operation of this size many people came to Roche Harbor for both business and social purposes. To care for them McMillin built the 22-room Hotel De Haro using the old Hudson's Bay Post as the nucleus. Rewired and with modern plumbing, it is still in use today and in places the logs of the original Post building can be seen. Most of the rooms still contain the old furnishings which make antique collectors drool. Where replacements were necessary, the Tartes have used pieces in keeping with the original decor.

Roche Harbor today

Roche Harbor today with its modern moorages for 150 pleasure craft still has ties with the past with the chapel, old houses, hotel, lime kilns and a portion of the old pier.

One of the stories heard occasionally is that smuggled Chinese "slave" labor was used to work the quarries but, according to Mr. Tarte, this has no basis in fact. Workers were of varied nationalities although there was a large Japanese group and the remains of their "Jap Town" are still in evidence today west of the kilns.

The entire community had a population of up to 600 in its hey-day with a row of houses for the bachelor workers and 18 to 20 larger houses for families. Eight of these and the school house have been reconditioned and modernized to serve as resort cottages.

The little church building first served as a Methodist Church and was later used as a school. When the Tartes took over it was in poor condition but Mrs. Tarte undertook to restore it and today Catholic Mass is held each Sunday during the summer months with Father Healy, a professor of biology at Seattle University who spends his summers at the U. of W. Oceanographic Laboratories at Friday Harbor, conducting the services.

The altars came from an old church in Kirkland, the pews from one in White Center. Appropriately, since many of those attending are boating people, it is known

In its hey-day as a company town, Roche Harbor can be seen in this old picture taken before McMillin added the more ornate front to his home as we know it today. Hotel DeHaro is behind the stump at the right; in the distance is the barrel factory on the point.

John S. McMillin, industrialist and king of all he surveys, checks some item of business.

Early-day Roche Harbor

*The ruins of the tug are no longer there.

One of the company barges decorated with fir trees for a picnic or an evening dance on the bay.

This old picture shows a picnic on McCracken Point of Henry Island. Salmon are resurrected from the barbecue pits while John McMillin and his guests watch from the barge.

as our Lady of Good Voyage Chapel and Mr. Tarte had the statue of Our Lady of Good Voyage made in Italy at a cost of $600.

John McMillin, like many of the big industrialists of his time, was an autocrat who ran Roche Harbor as a dukedom. His employees worked long hard hours and, as the old song goes, probably "owed their souls to the company store."

He was just as strict with his family and modern psychiatry would no doubt attribute the serious problems which besieged some members of his family to his dictatorial attitudes.

His first son, John, died at birth. Next oldest was Fred who is said to have been his father's favorite. He was general manager of the company and died at the age of 42 in 1922. Paul, the younger son, took over management of the company when his father died in 1936 and it was from him that the Tartes purchased the company and property in 1956. He died in 1961. Mrs. McMillin

died in 1946 and, as far as is known, the only daughter, Dorothy, is still living in an institution.

The story is told that Fred and some of his buddies would take the family yacht *Calcite* on the pretext of going to Victoria to play golf. In reality they'd cruise around the corner to one of the many convenient bays for a drinking party. When father found out about it, he promptly built a golf course on the island and told the boys they had no further reason to go to Victoria.

Many visiting yachtsmen have hiked around to Afterglow Beach and have seen the ruins of Afterglow Manor there. This was the house built for Fred. It burned in 1946 from an electrical short circuit but the foundations and the long covered walkway from the house to the beach with its little summer tea house or bandstand can still be seen today. The ruins behind were the garage and servants quarters. The Spanish-type tile from the roof can be seen piled up along the roadway.*

Many visitors ask about the huge steel tanks which can still be seen in the ruins of the basement. Paul told Mr. Tarte that his mother liked to wash her hair in rainwater rather than hard well-water of the island which is so full of minerals. The tanks were installed to hold the rainwater which was caught by a massive system so that Mrs. McMillin would always have plenty for her shampoo.

Another spot which draws visitors is the old cemetery with many of the graves having the old fashioned fences around them. Lacking care for so many years, it is in poor condition but there are plans to clean it up and restore it in the future.

Don't be surprised if sometime you see fresh flowers on the grave with the little fawn statue. It seems that the son of a man who worked at the lime plant got into a fight with an Indian boy on one of the docks and was drowned. The mother, now a widow, works in Seattle but makes regular pilgrimages to Roche Harbor to place flowers on her son's grave.

John McMillin worked his employees hard but he worked hard himself. Still, he liked the good life and Roche Harbor had its share of social affairs. The two "Banquet Courts" which are to the left of the hotel were frequently used while many picnics and barbecues were held on Henry Island's McCracken Point, on Pearl Island and at Afterglow Beach. There are several pictures of a barbecue party on the beach which served a crowd of 1100. Sometimes the big barges were gaily decorated with fir trees and Japanese lanterns, one for a band, another for guests to dance on out in the bay.

Roche Harbor today is a beautiful place and one can't help but enjoy the atmosphere of its ties with a colorful past. Looking at the past, we are reminded of the transience of life. John McMillin realized this and made his plans accordingly. In building a memorial for his family, he enshrined the dreams and aspirations of his generation, his religious beliefs, his associations and his accomplishments.

Around a family table of native limestone, he visualized his family seated congenially after death for all eternity. The back of each chair is inscribed with the name of a member of the family and the seats serve as crypts for their ashes.

With a deep sense of love and respect for the Masonic Order, he utilized its teachings and symbolism for the overall design. Masons will easily recognize and understand the meanings behind the Brazen Pillars, the Flight

The ruins are no longer there.

of Winding Stairs to reach the Middle Chamber, the sets of three, five and seven steps and the Broken Column.

A leaflet describing the mausoleum and its Masonic symbolism is available for those who are interested.

John S. McMillin was the First Grand Consul of the Sigma Chi fraternity, a confidant of Presidents of the United States, a respected advisor to both the state and national Republican Party and at one time just missed by a small minority being a U.S. senator.

The yachtsman mooring at Roche Harbor will still find it a "company town" in many respects but with members of the Tarte family and their staff devoted to a different concept. Some of the original 4000 acres have been sub-divided so that today's Roche Harbor can be a resort for retired people as well as yachtsmen.

Among its facilities are moorages for 150 boats, complete gas dock, showers, laundry, store, hotel, sporting clothes store, cottages, restaurant and cocktail lounge, heated fresh water swimming pool, horseshoe pits, children's recreation area, riding horses, a competent engine mechanic on duty seven days a week, an airfield with 4000-foot runway and a dance hall where teenagers, properly supervised, hold forth every Friday night during the summer.*

The Roche Harbor Yacht Club is one of the oldest in the state and lists John S. McMillin as a past commodore as well as many prominent Seattle yachtsmen as members. It has quarters on top of one of the old piers, and was rejuvenated in its present form by the Tartes.

The flower gardens are a principal attraction to many. These were started by Paul McMillin who hired an English gardener to care for them. Today Mrs. Tarte supervises their care and many prizes and blue ribbons from county fairs attest to their quality.

In addition to its many summer time facilities, Roche Harbor is fast becoming a year-round resort. With accommodations for up to 150 people, it is attracting many conventions while sportsmen have discovered that fishing and hunting are excellent during the winter months.

Winter King salmon running from 16 to 25 lbs. are easily taken from December through May in Mosquito Pass, off Davidson Head or in Speiden Channel. Deer, pheasants, ducks and geese abound during the fall and early winter hunting seasons and rabbit hunting and netting is a year round sport. Hunters come by boat, by car (via ferry) and more frequently every year, by plane. Some yachtsmen have established traditional Thanksgiving or New Years weekend cruises.

There is an atmosphere or a mood about Roche Harbor that cannot be described—it must be experienced. As you stroll the grounds, inspecting the old cemetery, the mausoleum, the ruins of Jap Town, the quarries and kilns, the workers' houses, the company store, the big dock, and can envision the glory of what was once Afterglow Manor with its beautiful beach, or some of the grandeur of a dinner in the banquet court, the stately elegance of the hotel and enjoy a meal in the dining room which was once McMillin's home, the past becomes more alive.

Finally, when you come to the end of a full day, watch the impressive ceremonies for the lowering of the various burgees, pennants and Canadian and American flags to the music of national anthems, and hear the clear tones of the bugle sounding taps out across the blue water as the setting sun spreads its golden afterglow across the western sky, you'll have memories of Roche Harbor that will not soon fade.

A barbecued suckling pig dinner in the De Haro Banquet Court. Inscription over the fireplace, "Friendship's fires are always burning," can still be seen.

47

*In addition to the slip accommodations, there are moorings for 50 boats. The teen age dances are no more, nor does the Roche Harbor Yacht Club have its clubhouse there.

14
San Juans Hub

One of the many bonuses of San Juan Island cruising is the easy availability of a placid harbor, easily reached, when you decide it's time to snug down for the night. You don't have to start a search or make a long run. The islands abound with innumerable cozy little coves where you can drop anchor and safely pass a peaceful quiet night.

With the intention of exploring around Shaw Island, often called "The Hub" of the San Juans because it is the geographical center of the county, we had spent the night in the little cove behind the ferry slip at Shaw. We had been given permission to lay at the gas dock float for the night if we left early enough so the mail boat could get in the next morning. There is also good anchorage in this little cove.

As we pulled away from the float and around the ferry slip to head west, the magic of the islands once again descended upon us. The decks sparkled with millions of vari-colored gems deposited by the dew of the night while the refracted light of the early morning sun turned the island-studded glassy water into a magnificent painting splashed with all the radiant blues, greens, yellows, grays and purples blended from a master palette. Crisp fir and cedar scented air made deep breathing a conscious process later accentuated by the man-made addition of coffee and bacon aromas. And thus began another day of cruising these paradise isles.

As one spends more time exploring this delightful archipelago, it becomes more apparent that each island, large or small, has an entirely different character from its neighbors. Each is an individual in its own right.

So it is with Shaw. In some respects it might be called the last frontier of the civilized islands of the group. There are no resorts on Shaw and, as far as its residents are concerned, they don't want any. They came close, however. In the 1940's Harold Salvesen, well known Northwest skipper and yachtsman, had a dream of a unique resort on Blind Bay. The old *Admiral Rogers* was to be rehabilitated and beached alongside a dock to serve as a swanky beach hotel. Plans didn't materialize and the idea was abandoned.

Until a few years ago Shaw was inhabited almost entirely by old time residents who made a living in farming, fishing, cattle and chicken raising, fruit growing and truck gardening. It was a tightly knit community of folks who liked their island the way it was and wanted to keep it that way. A few summer homes were hidden in the trees here and there along the shore.

Today Shaw still maintains a certain aloofness and older-generation mood although there are now more summer residents and retired people who, recognizing the charms, have become addicted to this way of life.

Crossing the mouth of Blind Bay, we recalled the many times we have dropped anchor there. With little Blind Island in the entrance, this is a well protected anchorage. One must use caution, however, for rocks and reefs dot the entrance and there are shoal areas inside at low tide. With careful attention to the chart and tide tables the skipper should have no trouble. Best entrance is southeast of Blind Island, midway between it and the charted rock. Large scale chart #6379 is recommended not only for added assurance and safety but increased enjoyment in cruising the waters it covers.

Broken Point with its low connecting arm offers some protection on either side with the west side preferred by many who want a good stop-over spot for lunch.

As we continued westward and entered Wasp Passage Bell Island lay on our right. Although small, it is beautifully wooded and its rocky shores are fairly low. A tiny harbor just big enough for a small boat with a nice house overlooking it seemed to be the epitome of private-island living.

Although we've been through this much travelled passage many times, we throttled down to almost a drift in order to pay close attention to the shores on both sides of us. Larger Crane Island on our starboard with its higher, rocky shore is well wooded with an occasional neat cottage peeking out from among the trees. To the port the shoreline of Shaw is indented with several small bays and coves which appeared too private to be intruded upon.

At this point we determined to take time out for something we've always wanted to do—explore the Wasp Islands more thoroughly. The thought often occurs that too frequently, particularly in these days of faster boats, people are in such a hurry to get to some predetermined harbor that they by-pass some of the most picturesque spots, thus cheating themselves out of some of the best features of pleasure cruising.

We certainly have no fault to find with the large resort-type harbors of the better known bays and anchorages and we enjoy spending a share of our cruising time at such places. We also contend that this doesn't constitute all the pleasure and enjoyment which is so readily available in these waters to the cruising yachtsman.

There's a thrill of discovery and a challenge to a skipper's ability to pilot his craft off the beaten courses, into narrow inlets, picturesque coves and on the other side of some emerald isle. It provides a present pleasure with excellent opportunities for photography, swimming, clamming, crabbing or peaceful private sunbathing as well as a good topic of conversation when boating friends gather around a blazing fireplace on a blustery winter night to exchange cruising experiences.

We turned northwestward between the fairly high rocky shores of Cliff Island on the left and Crane Island on the right. Still cruising along on a slow bell, we wove in and out and between the dozen or so islands, islets and large rocks making up this group which Capt. Wilkes named for the U. S. Sloop-of-War *Wasp*.

This name brought to mind the many stories of early day pirates who were said to have hidden here to strike at boats going through Wasp Passage and the smugglers who knew the islands, passages, rocks and reefs so well they were able to evade the government revenue cutters or customs boats. First wool, then opium, diamonds, Chinese, and finally whiskey and rum were the principal items bringing a much higher price in the United States than in Canada.

Most famous of the smugglers was Lawrence Kelly, a skillful sailor with a fast sloop who knew every channel and reef. He operated for 20 years until he was finally caught in 1909.

Victor McConnell another famous smuggler who knew the waters well and had a fast boat specialized in

Chinese with a standard fee of $50 a head. He was last heard of running a filling station in Seattle and has been immortalized by having the largest island in the Wasp group named after him. Most of the other islands seem to have been named by Capt. George Henry Richards on his British Admiralty Chart #2689 of 1858-59.

We found the Wasps to be a most pleasant little family of islands, very scenic and sparsely populated with nice people in nice homes or gulls and other water fowl on the more barren isles and rocks. Exploring them was a rewarding two hours during which we made good use of the large scale chart (6379) to keep off the many reefs and shoals.

Shaw's Neck Point took our attention next. Besides a goodly collection of well weathered driftwood it seemed as if this were a natural depository for all kinds of treasures drifted in from the seven seas of the world.

Coasting along the western shore of Shaw Island in San Juan Channel we poked our bow into at least half a dozen little coves, some of them in behind protective rocks and islets. Apparently the waterfront dwellers see numbers of boats going up or down the center channel but have few of them coming in close. As we cruised by several doors opened and we were greeted with a hail or a friendly hand wave.

Parks Bay, in behind Pt. George, has long been a favorite anchorage for yachts cruising the San Juans in spite of the fact that its shores are all privately owned and well posted against any landing. If your crew includes a dog that needs shore-side exercising, this bay isn't for you.

Hicks Bay and Hoffman Cove on the south end of the island offer only fair anchorages with no protection from the south. A scattering of some rocks and reefs along this shore again makes that large scale chart a comfort to have aboard.

Swinging the helm to port on a northeasterly heading up Upright Channel we turned in for a closer look at Squaw Bay. This would make a nice anchorage if it had water. It is almost landlocked but is too shallow for boats of any draft. On the outer portion of the bay are

Little Blind Island protects the entrance to Shaw Island's Blind Bay

Shaw Island Cove, with ferry slip, floats, store and gas dock

the floats of Mr. Robert Ellis who is occasionally host for the steamboaters of the northwest at his beautiful estate. His trim, steam pinnace *Oceanid* can usually be seen berthed here when not out cruising.*

Around the next point is perhaps Shaw's most famous feature. Shown on the chart as Indian Cove and nestled in behind Canoe Island lies one of the finest sand beaches in the islands. It is known to islanders as well as many yachtsmen as South Beach and is included in a 60 acre county park which was bought from the U.S. Government by residents of the island. It is a favorite spot for outboarders who enjoy the excellent camping facilities and is a wonderful place to spend an afternoon on the beach, swimming, picnicking or sunbathing.

Canoe Island is a shady wooded isle. There is a shoal about the middle of the passage between it and the shore of Shaw, which can be avoided by staying fairly close to Canoe Island. Around another point to the northwest is Picnic Cove, a small, fairly shallow bay but deep enough if you don't get too close to shore and with enough protection to make a good anchorage. †

The balance of Shaw's coastline, around its northeast point, is rocky and quite steep. Approaching the store and ferry slip in Harney Channel is Hudson Bay, quite open and with no protection from the northwest but still a nice place to drop the hook in good weather.

Shaw Island, named by Wilkes in honor of John D. Shaw, a U.S. Navy officer who served prominently in the war against Algiers in 1815, is the smallest of the large islands in the San Juan group. Its character, its bays and beaches make it an integral part of this yachtsman's paradise which has attracted boatmen from far and wide and enthralled them with its magic.

An old legend telling of the creation of these islands describes the peaceful spirits who guarded them and removed the cause of pressure, strife and noise when they lowered them gently into the sea so that the ocean greets the mountain streams with friendly favor. These same kind spirits are supposed to have tended the forests, hills and lakes as they grew a playground for the coming builders of a new empire. They are said to still guard this Paradise closely so that the ambitious workers will not rush in and thoughtlessly squander the lovely resources which were planned for their Sabbath.

Those who have cruised the San Juans and know them like to believe in such a legend and hope these kind spirits will always be on guard so that these Treasure Islands of the Northwest will continue to provide a charmed Sabbath for generations of future workers in our new empire.

50

*No longer.
†Canoe Island is now privately owned and during the summer is a camp of the Institute Francais.

15
San Juans South Central

It was after one of those regrettable but necessary interruptions of cruising for a return to town for business. A clear morning sky with a brilliant August sun made a day perfect for driving or any other summer activity but our only thought was to get back aboard the boat and head across those cool blue waters to continue our re-discovery of the San Juan Islands.

The boat had been temporarily berthed at Skyline, one of the fine marine facilities in this "Gateway to the San Juans."

As we left the Flounder Bay, just the essence of a breeze stirred the water into little ripples which reflected the sun in millions of dancing diamonds. Already the pressures of civilization had slipped from our shoulders and we took long deep breaths of the clear air in anticipation of once again embracing the magic of the islands.

We couldn't help but remember Sophie Walsh's description in her "History and Romance of the San Juans." She wrote, "Nature put barriers about them like the rind of a melon and set them in the midst of a beautiful sea. They are, in fact, a natural gateway between two seas — The Canadian Strait of Georgia and Puget Sound on the American side."

There was no need for any navigation so the bow was headed on the buoy of Cypress Island's Reef Point for the run up Rosario Strait, past Strawberry Island and across to Blakely Island and Peavine Pass.

Blakely got its name in 1841 from Wilkes in honor of Johnston Blakely, a naval hero of the war of 1812. A man of iron nerve and bold activity, he commanded the sloop of war *Wasp* in many daring exploits until ship and crew disappeared without a trace in another of history's unsolved sea mysteries. Wilkes also named Obstruction Island, that little traffic divider that separates Obstruction and Peavine Passes.

These passes in the San Juans are always a joy to northwest yachtsmen. Although, at times, moderate currents and tide rips can run, they are not of sufficient force to cause trouble yet they add just a dash of spice to pep up the enjoyment of a tranquil cruise. Then there's always that vista of beauty opening up as you reach the other end.

One isn't really quite out of Peavine Pass before the lovely bay opens up on the south which is the site of Blakely Marina. Here is another of those excellent facilities, designed for the yachtsman where he can find fuel, ice, groceries, marine supplies, fishing gear, boat hoist, outboard service, rest rooms, showers, laundry and a warm welcome. A cozy inner harbor offers protected moorage and nearby is Blakely House Restaurant with its Peavine Room and delicious meals, the Boatel and an unusual gift shop.*

Blakely is often called "flying island." Purchased in 1954 by Floyd Johnson, he has developed it into a retreat for aviation and yachting enthusiasts. A lighted landing strip, 2400 feet long, has clear approaches over water at both ends. Property has been platted so that whether one has a plane or a boat, he lives only a short distance from his craft on an island which has been dedicated to the preservation of its primitive and natural beauty, its unbroken wilderness with a pioneer's moss covered cabin and a crumbling 19th century one room log school house.

While somewhere between 150 and 200 families live on Blakely, they are far outnumbered by some 2300 tame and protected deer. The island's two lakes are well stocked with fish; Spencer Lake with large and small mouth bass and Horseshoe Lake with trout. Both lakes are excellent for swimming.

Leaving Blakely Marina, we turned south along its rugged steep banked western shore. Just below Bold Bluff is a delightful little bay which appeared to be a good anchorage with nice beaches, but a large "No Trespassing" sign discouraged further exploration.

We ran inside little Willow Island, scenic, fairly high with steep sides and sparsely wooded, to turn east through Thatcher Pass, with Blakely on the north and Decatur Island on the south.

Decatur is an island with much of interest to the yachtsman. It was named by Wilkes for Stephan Decatur who first came to fame for cutting out the *Philadelphia* in the Tripolitan War in 1804. Admiral Nelson of the British Navy called it the most daring act of the age. He achieved many other successes before he died in a duel and a ship

*The restaurant, gift shop and boatel closed in 1972.

Blakely Marina, on the north end of Blakely Island just off Peavine Pass, is one of the fine facilities in the San Juans

named for him was instrumental in saving the infant village of Seattle from an Indian attack.

Leaving Thatcher Pass our course rounded Fauntleroy Point and turned south for a look at that beautiful area between Decatur and James Islands. Here Decatur Head extends to the northeast connected by a narrow spit which forms a graceful sandy beach in a pleasant bay. Although unprotected from the northeast, this is still a popular spot with large numbers of skippers and the little cove indenting the east side of James Island with a lovely beach is equally inviting. A cruise around James Island at trolling speed with lines in the water could be a rewarding experience.

James Island was named by Wilkes, probably in honor of Reuben James, an American sailor who saved Decatur's life by interposing his own body before the saber of a Turk.*

There are several rocks and shoals in this area which call for close attention to the chart and to their markings of kelp but which shouldn't keep one away. It's an ideal place for a bit of afternoon loafing even if you don't choose to spend the night.

Heading next for Lopez Pass, we were careful to stay far enough off Decatur's shore to avoid the row of rocks protecting the beach. This pass, between Decatur and the southeast toe of Lopez Island is the southernmost of the four passes from Rosario Strait to the central group of the islands. About 400 yards wide, it has depths from 12 to 14 fathoms and care should be used in laying a course once inside.

Ram Island and other islets and rocks lie inside the pass. Choose either a course in the narrow channel between the rock on the northern end of Ram Island and another unnamed rock to the north, or run between Ram Island and the toe of Lopez being careful to avoid the sunken rock about 400 yards off the southern end of Ram Island.

Lopez Sound has several intriguing bays and coves of interest to the boater. To the south are Hunter Bay and Mud Bay. The former provides excellent anchorage with depths of two fathoms or more and some fine clam beds are exposed at low tide. Mud Bay is shallow and not recommended for anything except dinghy exploration.

Center Island lies to the north after coming through Lopez Pass and is connected by a sandy shelf to Decatur Island. This is covered by an average depth of about two fathoms at low tide.

Still further to the north is little Trump Island of about 30 acres. To the northeast is a little cove frequently used by boaters although it is unprotected from southerly winds. Continuing to the north and around the peninsula is a charming cove, nameless on the chart but known to some as Kan Kut Harbor. It is a favored anchorage about 500 yards long by 200 yards wide with a good beach at the head.

Clams are reported along the east shore of Kan Kut and for those needing a bit of leg stretching or exercise following a too-big meal, there is a trail starting at the old dock site which runs a mile or so south to the old settlement of Decatur.

Our course continued north heading close to Frost Island, named by Wilkes in honor of John Frost, a boatswain on the *Porpoise* of the expedition. We rounded tiny Flower Island for a look into Swifts Bay, too unprotected and shallow to be of much interest to the yachtsman. Shoal Bay, between Humphrey Head and Upright Head of Lopez Island is fairly well protected except from the north and northeast.

Lopez Island, with 54 square miles, is the third largest of the San Juan Group, twelve miles long by four miles wide. History isn't too specific about the source of its name with some writers claiming it came from Lt. Lopez Gonzales De Haro, one of the early Spanish explorers who mapped the archipelago, and others saying it was the name of the lookout on watch when Capt. Eliza's ships first espied the group. Actually it could be possible it was one and the same man in both cases.

Wilkes changed the name to Chauncey's Island in 1841. Now Chauncey was probably a fine man and deserving of such an honor but we can all be thankful to Capt. Kellett for restoring the more musical Spanish name in 1847.

Lopez is one of the more fascinating islands of the group although there is no town, as such, on the island. The only sign of civilization at the ferry landing on Upright Head is Upright House, an excellent restaurant.†

*James Island is now a state marine park.
†Upright House is closed.

52

The main community center is called Lopez and is located on the west side on Fisherman's Bay. Here is a post office, store, church, inn and service station.

Lopez was one of the last strongholds for the old "central" operated "number please" telephone system complete with hand-cranked instruments but even that has gone modern now.

First white man to live on the island was James Nelson who settled on the north end. He, like so many of the early-comers, was too active to be tied down in more conventional circles and contributed a great deal to settling the surrounding wilderness.

Arthur Barlow, better know as Billy, was the second settler on Lopez Island. He came with a British naval surveying crew and when he first saw the beautiful bay near the south end of the island which still bears his name, he exclaimed, "Here is my future home."

Some time later, in 1854, when the surveying was finished and the ship had returned to Esquimault on Vancouver Island, he and three companions crowded into an Indian canoe they had bought and headed across the Strait of Juan de Fuca toward New Dungeness. Modern yachtsmen, who know what this strait can be like and who have been taught some of the basic elements of safety at sea, gasp when they hear that these men made that trip with only three inches of freeboard in their canoe.

Two years later Barlow returned to "his" bay on Lopez and raised a family of nine children which included that former well known Puget Sound and Island pilot, Capt. Sam Barlow.

The first storekeeper on Lopez was H. E. Hutchenson who arrived at Fisherman's Bay in the early fifties just as a large delegation of Alaskan Indians was giving the local red men a bad time. Being equipped with a goodly supply of firearms and realizing the intentions of the raiders, he joined the fray on the side of the home team and soon put the enemy to rout.

Hailing him as their deliverer, the Indians offered him anything they had if he'd stay. He evidently liked the idea for he opened a store at the point known as Lopez Landing and ran it for many years.

Lopez today, as it has throughout its civilized history, depends mainly farming and fishing. Well suited for agriculture with good soil and a more level terrain than the other large islands, it has fostered some profitable farms and orchards.

While fishing isn't as good as it was earlier in the century still many Lopez residents make their living at it. Most of the early day activity centered at Richardson on one of the many rock cluttered little bays at the south end of the island. The village was named for George Richardson who settled there in 1871. This was also the first port of call in the islands when steamer service was inaugurated from Seattle via Port Townsend to Bellingham.

In addition to the regular residents, the Henderson Camps for boys and girls and several fine resorts, Lopez is also fast becoming a favorite summer haven for Boeing Aircraft personnel.*

Leaving Upright Head, we always enjoy the cruise down Upright Channel past Canoe Island on the starboard and picturesque Flat Point on the port. Our destination was Fisherman's Bay on the west side of Lopez. This is one of the favorite coves in the San Juans but the entrance is easily missed. Best course after rounding Flat Point is to keep fairly well in towards shore but not too close as there are some rocks along the shoreline. Just about the time you decide you'll have to turn to starboard, the narrow entrance will open up. It's best to stay close to the spit on the right coming through the entrance, then head around the spit on the left, giving it plenty of room. The little cove inside the first spit offers good protected anchorage or you can anchor in the bay proper. A southwest wind can sweep across the low narrow neck of land but the bay isn't large enough to permit a sea to build up.

Inside the bay, on the east shore is Pantley's Resort, with float, gas dock, restaurant and cocktail lounge, cabins and laundromat. The resort is operated by Roberto and Lois Ann Pantley, who have remodeled and enlarged the former Ebb Tide Inn.†

There is an enlarged eating area and a new bar known as the Pagan Hut Room featuring exotic refreshments, entertainment and dancing. The restaurant menu includes both American and Chinese food. The decorations are authentically Hawaiian.

Mr. Pantley is of Greek extraction and has spent much time in the Hawaiian Islands. In addition to being an excellent chef he is also an accomplished entertainer, a master organizer and a builder.

Fisherman's Bay has always been a popular haven for boaters cruising the San Juan Islands.

After a satisfying meal at the resort we returned to the boat to enjoy the fading beauty of another fabulous San Juan sunset. As the reds and oranges were replaced with the deeper purples we couldn't help but agree with the poets who said that the San Juan Islands came into being after the Creator had practiced on the rest of the world to add a last touch to a grand and glorious picture.

As we wrap up this cruise of rediscovery of these gems of the inland sea, we can't resist repeating what has been

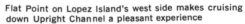
Flat Point on Lopez Island's west side makes cruising down Upright Channel a pleasant experience

*Jack and Jan Helsell's Camp Nor'Wester has replaced the Henderson Camps.
†Pantley's is now Islander Lopez owned and operated by Bill and Florence Burke, offering resort and marina facilities.

said before about the magic of the islands. These incredibly beautiful cruising waters of the Northwest, extending all the way from the southern tip of Puget Sound, through British Columbia and on up to Alaska are the finest in the world. In these days of fast boats the urge is to roam ever farther and farther but the skipper who has never cruised the San Juans and speeds through them on his way to more distant waters, is missing some of the finest cruising in the world.

We must agree that any cruising is good, some better, some poorer, but until you've let the San Juans "take you over," you really haven't lived.

So, for ourselves, and for the people of the islands, we borrow from the Chinook language of the Indians and early settlers to say, "Klahowya Tillicum," or "Good Bye, come again, friends."

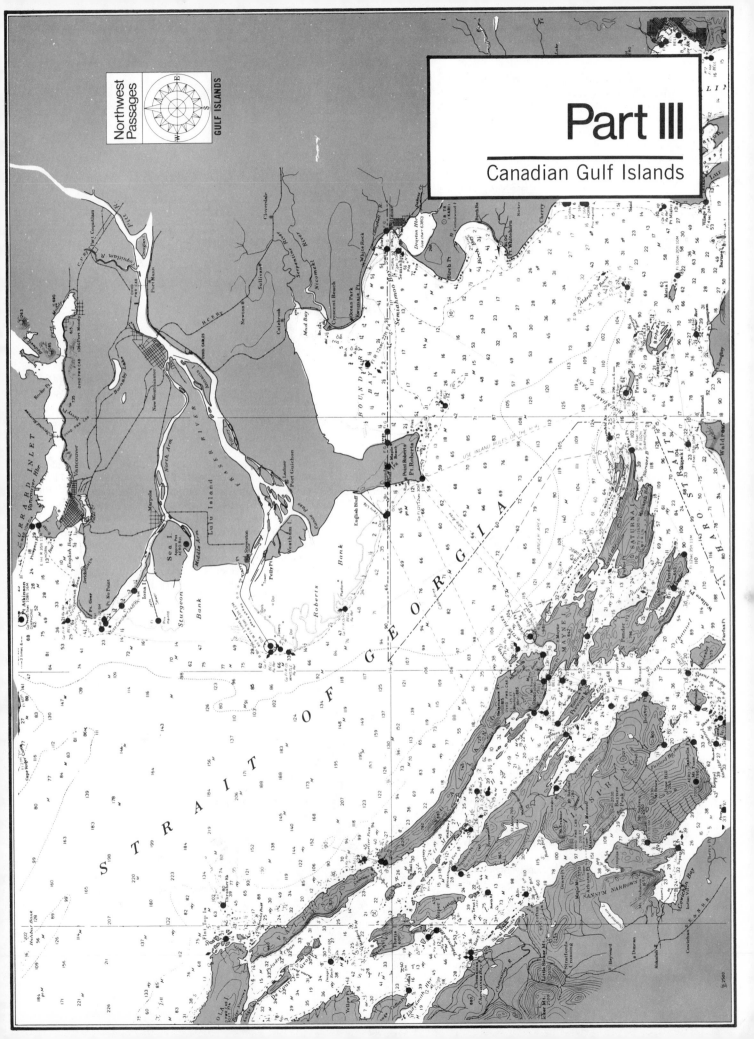

Part III

Canadian Gulf Islands

16
Canadian Gulf Islands

What a perfect cruising area! Sparkling blue-green waterways separating large, forested islands; lush, pastoral islands; tiny, lighthouse-capped islands; rugged, rocky islands, all scattered so as to form a sheltered group in a corner of the Gulf of Georgia which seems to have been specially designed for the yachtsman.

British Columbia's Gulf Islands are occasionally referred to as the Canadian San Juans, possibly because they are practically an extension of the American San Juan Islands across the International Border. This is not correct, however, and they should be accorded the dignity of calling them by their right name.

These beautiful gems are set in their inland sea along the southeast coast of Vancouver Island for nearly 50 miles from Nanaimo to the International Boundary. All too frequently their charms are by-passed by the yachtsman as he hurries through, bound for waters farther north.

We do not mean to detract from the more northern waters, but have always felt the San Juan Islands and the Gulf Islands should be fully explored, savored and enjoyed before setting a course for the more distant areas.

One of the major attributes of the Gulf Islands is the climate. Like the San Juans, they lie in that peculiar "banana belt" which runs northward from the Olympic Peninsula to bathe the area with warmer air and considerably less rain than the rest of the Northwest.

Nature must have had the yachtsman in mind when she created this cruising paradise, for it is loaded with attractions. Besides an easy atmosphere of relaxation, there are literally hundreds of secluded bays, coves and harbors for an overnight anchorage or longer stays while island-hopping. In some spots a beige sandy beach or a sand-stone shelf, worn smooth by the ever changing tide, invites swimming, picnicing or camping ashore. Clams, oysters and crabs are bountiful and, for the fisherman, these are favorite waters for the Spring, Blueback, or Coho salmon. Resorts, marinas and towns are conveniently located for re-stocking, re-fueling, laundry, showers, that occasional meal ashore or other needs.

In addition to these physical characteristics, the charm of the Gulf Islands is enhanced by a rich heritage of the past, full of legends and lore dating back to early Spanish and English explorers whose names are memorialized in many of the islands, rocks, reefs, points, bays and passages. Knowing the source of these names makes for a keener interest in cruising but, rather than scatter them through our narrative, we have listed them together at the end for ready reference.

In the previous section we presented an intimate study of the San Juan Islands for the yachtsman. The next several chapters will consider the Canadian Gulf Islands. There is no easy way to divide them into convenient groups so we will arbitrarily cruise through them, stick our bow into as many bays and coves as possible and invite you to enjoy it all with us.

Since crossing an International Boundary carries with it certain legal requirements, a skipper naturally charts his course for the nearest Port of Entry. Bedwell Harbour, between North and South Pender Islands, offers probably the

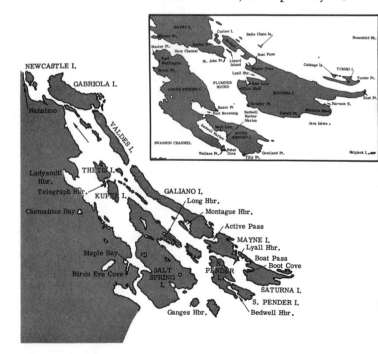

most convenient point for most yachtsmen to go through the necessary formalities of entering Canada. Besides, it's a most charming harbor with plenty of attractions and less than five miles from Prevost Harbor, 10 miles from Roche Harbor and 11 miles from Jones Island.

In early days the Pender Islands were one large island before the canal was dug in 1903 to separate them. It then rated two names: Sayas and San Eusbio, and Bedwell Harbour was then known as Harbor of San Antonio.

The Gold Rush of 1858 brought the boundary dispute to a head as well as several British Hydrographic Survey ships to the scene. Captain Daniel Pender of the Royal Navy arrived in these waters in November, 1857 as Master of H.M. Surveying Vessel *Plumper*. Second Master was Captain Henry George Richards who later commanded *H.M.S. Hecate*. These two men were responsible for many of the names found in our cruising charts today.

Pender, who died in England in 1891, was never to know that less than half a century after his work in these waters the island which Richards had named for him would become the home of one of his family.

It was in 1911 that William Ustick Pender of Cornwall, England, was literally washed ashore on South Pender. On Christmas Eve, during a howling gale, he was accompanying Herbert Page of Saturna Island in the latter's small boat from Victoria when they grounded. Later Pender bought some property on the island which he held until 1946.

The Customs and Immigration station in Bedwell Harbour is next to the Bedwell Harbour Marina on South Pender Island. Here Mr. and Mrs. Stan Lettner operate complete facilities for the yachtsman the year round. A separate fuel float provides all the essentials including premium gas, a special outboard fuel mixer pump and 80-88 octane gas for planes.*

A store offers groceries, fresh meats and a variety of items including charts, fishing gear, bait and ice. Outboard rental boats and motors, engine repairs, cottages, telephone, showers and laundromat are also available. A restaurant with licensed premises and a 25 by 60-foot heated saltwater pool, covered for winter and Sauna baths make this one of the yachtsman's favorite facilities, not only during the cruising season, but in winter months as well when, Stan reports, the fishing is excellent. A golf course is located on North Pender Island.

The place is located in a spot which was popular with the Indians as a potlatch area for hundreds of years as evidenced by the tremendous number of clam and oyster shells in the hills. An interesting Indian stone kitchen can be seen in front of the dining hall and a bench mark established in 1905 shows where *H.M.S. Egeria* started a hydrographic survey of the Gulf Islands.

Although hundreds of boats of Canadian and American registry visit Bedwell Harbour during the year, one never knows which boating friends he might meet there. Our visit was highlighted by seeing the *Danginn* of Monrovia come in to anchor. Owned by a Mr. Ludwig of Texas and New York, she is reportedly the largest privately owned yacht in the world. Built in Japan in 1960 and outfitted in Hong Kong, she carries a crew of 28 and her 257' length and 16' draft literally house a floating palace.

After a night at the Marina we were ready to start exploring. It was only a short hop out to Peter Cove just inside Wallace Point on the southeastern tip of North Pender. The morning was clear and bright under a pale blue sky as we slowly made our way past the large rocks guarding the entrance of this peaceful little cove to drop the anchor in a comfortable 20 feet of water.

The shore of the bay is rock-bound with two lovely beaches divided by a gigantic boulder. According to the large scale Canadian chart #3474 there are two to four feet of water at low tide almost up to the shore. Entry can be made on either side of the rocks in the middle but

The little bay in back of Skull Islet has a nice beach and is a popular spot for boaters to picnic, camp, or just spend a relaxing afternoon. Beaumont Marine Park is in the background.

*The Lettner's no longer own the resort.

careful attention should be paid to an uncharted rock as you head for the northerly of the two beaches.

A shore side hike took us along the ridge toward Wallace Point where we sat watching the hurrying boats on their way to or from Customs. We couldn't help but wonder if, being in such a hurry, these folks perhaps didn't miss many secluded little beauty spots such as this.

Sitting in the shade at our lookout point, we watched several cruisers partaking of the good fishing off Wallace Point and along the south shore of South Pender. We also recalled stories of American prohibition days when Peter Cove was a favorite rendezvous of rum runners as they transferred their liquor cargo from Canadian boats to fast American boats for the run across the border. A double murder of father and son is said to have taken place here with the two murderers later apprehended. It was hard to imagine such violence in a place as tranquil and quiet as this.

It would have been easy to loaf away the entire day

grow in abundance such as blackberry, strawberry, black-caps, salmon berries, the red cap berry (also known as thimbleberry), Oregon grape, gooseberry, Salal berries and red huckleberry.

After a pleasant picnic lunch on the beach, our next course took us through the canal which connects Bedwell Harbour with Browning Harbour, or Port Browning as it is now shown on the charts. Before the canal was dug in 1903, the strip of low land connecting the two islands was a favorite portage place for Indians. Later early island settlers remember hauling boats across between the two harbors.

The short run is most scenic, almost reminiscent of a short river trip. Narrowest part of the channel is about 75 feet and minimum depth at low tide is six feet, so most boats would have no difficulty making the passage. Sailboats are limited by a 26-foot clearance on the bridge at high tide. We experienced no noticeable current on an incoming tide. Again, that large scale chart adds assurance.

One of the finest anchorages in the Gulf Islands is Boot Cove on Saturna Island. This favorite cove of many yachtsmen, easy to miss because of its narrow entrance, is completely protected with plenty of depth

Stan Lettner's Bedwell Harbour Marina is a Port of Entry in the Canadian Gulf Islands and a popular rendezvous with complete facilities for the yachtsman. Moorage space was tripled in 1966

here but another spot we've passed up before beckoned us. We returned to the boat, upped anchor and headed back into Bedwell Harbour and Skull Islet, almost half way along the shore of South Pender to the canal entrance.

Although the clear water and bright sunlight made it reasonably easy to see the many rocks making up this reef, it was comforting to have the depth sounder on and that large scale chart (#3474) for quick reference.

This so-called islet lies across the outside of a small but picturesque bay with excellent beach. Beaumont Marine Park is located on the point protecting the bay and several Provincial Park anchor buoys are placed between the point and the islet. Oysters on the rocks, swimming, picnicing, camping, hiking and fine opportunities for picture-taking make this a favorite spot for boaters.

The two Pender Islands are known to naturalists as an excellent place to find most of the 22 varieties of moss which grow in the islands. Many of the wild berries also

Port Browning is a pleasant bay affording good anchorage. Shores are mostly quite steep and well wooded with very little beach area*

Saturna Island lies across Plumper Sound with Croker Point about 1½ miles from the entrance to Port Browning. Just inside Croker Point is the scene of the famous Saturna Island Lamb Barbecue, held on the first of July each year, Canada's Dominion Day. This event attracts more and more boaters annually. Games usually start at 11 o'clock with the lamb served about 2:30. If you've never attended, you've missed something, but tickets should be bought early to assure getting some of that luscious barbecue. They can be ordered by mail from the Saturna Marina, Saturna Island, B.C.†

Narvaez Bay, indenting the Eastern end of Saturna, offers only fair anchorage for a good southeasterly or easterly can make it a bit uncomfortable.

East Point, the most easterly part of the Gulf Islands,

*Port Browning Marina now at the head of the bay offers fuel and supplies.
†For barbecue tickets, address your requests to Saturna Community Hall, Saturna Island, B.C. VON 2YO.

was called Point de Ste. Saturnina on Eliza's original charts. Fishing is generally good in this area. Just around the point lies Tumbo Island with its satellite, Cabbage Island. These are off the usual waterways traversed by yachtsmen but are well worth a visit. They have an entirely different mood about them, one which will attract you for repeated visits to enjoy the coves and beaches.

Mr. Peter Georgeson of Saturna Island tells of a terrific battle which took place on the shore of Saturna, across the channel from Tumbo. A band of raiding Indians from the North attacked a local tribe and at the height of the battle the waters of Tumbo Channel were red with blood. Until just a few years ago human skulls and bones were often found scattered along the bank.

About a mile Northeast of Tumbo Point lies Rosenfeld Rock, named for the sailing ship *Rosenfeld* which was wrecked on the rock shortly before the light at East Point was established. She was loaded with coal and lay on the rocks for a year before she broke up. Islanders used

at a good rate, calling for extreme caution or negotiating only at slack water. The shorelines of all these small islands are composed of solid rock and large loose rocks backed by beautiful evergreens.

A small bay indents Samuel Island on its inner side and just beyond is Winter Cove, a favorite anchorage of many, leading to Boat Pass. Around a point and the King Islets Lyall Harbour has excellent anchorage, a ferry slip, government wharf and gas dock.

With all these bays and harbours so close at hand, a skipper has a wide choice for a suitable place to snug down for the night. Our choice was an old favorite, little Boot Cove just south of the entrance to Lyall Harbour. Its entrance is narrow but it soon widens into one of the most charming bays in the entire Gulf Island archipelago. On the right is a steep solid rock wall straight up from the water's edge. The left side isn't so steep, is well wooded, and settled here and there with houses and cottages, some on small coves with floats and boats. Minimum depths are

The Danginn, largest privately owned yacht in the world, anchors in Bedwell Harbour. Her 257-foot length dwarfs the shore boat, seen lying alongside

One of the twin beaches in Peter Cove offers an inviting spot to go ashore for a picnic or a hike. The cove is well protected to provide a delightful anchorage for a lazy afternoon or a snug berth for the night

the coal, built a cabin on the shore from salvaged lumber and hunters often sat on her decks to shoot ducks.

Heading northwestward from Tumbo Island, we came to Boat Pass, formerly called Canoe Pass and perhaps very appropriately, for it is a tricky pass, very narrow, with a rock just off the entrance and quite an overfall when the tidal current is running. It is an experience to go through but not recommended except at slack water and then only with extra care.

The Belle Chain Islets, parallel to Samuel Island, are a long row of small islets, rocks and reefs. Samuel Island extends from Boat Pass to form another pass at its other end which enters on either side of Curlew Island and Lizard Island. Horton Bay, protected by Curlew Island, is a snug anchorage, but the tidal currents in the pass boil through

one fathom. We anchored in 21 feet not far from three cruisers and a sailboat. A couple of log skids and a boom of logs added to the picturesque scene with the golden rays of a setting sun peeking in through the entrance.

After a luscious dinner of barbecued salmon, we loafed in the cockpit, listening to chords from a plaintive guitar in the sailboat blending with a frog chorus from the far end of the cove. Dusk faded to darkness slowly and with it the almost ever present reminder that this was true relaxation and peace, far from jangling telephones, speeding cars and the pressures of modern civilization. One occasionally hears talk about developing these islands. We, and many others, hope it's never done. They are just right the way they are.

PLACE NAMES AND THEIR SOURCES

BEDWELL HARBOUR — Edward Parker Bedwell, Second Master *Plumper* 1857-60, Master 1860.

BELLE CHAIN ISLETS — Isabel (Belle) Nagle, youngest daughter of Capt. Jeremiah Nagle, Harbormaster, Victoria.

BRUCE BIGHT (Saturna Island) — R. Adm. Henry William Bruce, *H.M.S. Monarch.*

ELLIOTT BLUFF (Saturna Island) — Lt. George Henry Elliot, Royal Marines, *H.M.S. Ganges,* flagship of R. Adm. R. L. Baynes.

GOWLLAND POINT (South Pender Island) — John Thomas Gowlland, Second Master *Plumper* and *Hecate.*

HORTON BAY — Robert John Horton, Hudsons Bay Co., for many years on boats and marine wharf duties.

KING ISLETS (near entrance to Lyall Hbr.) — Staff Commander John William King, R.N.

LYALL HARBOUR — David Lyall, M.D. — R.N. — Surgeon, *Plumper.*

MAYNE ISLAND — Lt. Richard Charles Mayne, R.N. of *Plumper* and *Hecate,* later became Rear Admiral.

MONARCH HEAD (Saturna Island) — *H.M.S. Monarch,* flagship of R. Adm. Henry William Bruce, third line-of-battle ship to arrive in these waters. On station 1854-1857.

NARVAEZ BAY (Saturna Island) — Formerly known as Deep Cove, renamed in 1905 by Capt. John F. Perry after Jose Maria Narvaez, sailing master and mate in command of *Saturnina.*

PAYNE POINT (Saturna Island) — C. F. Payne.

PENDER ISLANDS — Daniel Pender, Master, R.N. Second Master and later Master of H. M. Surveying Vessel *Plumper,* later Master of *Beaver.*

PETER COVE — Peter William Wallace (Q.V.).

PLUMPER SOUND — by Capt. Richards after his vessel *Plumper* in these waters 1857-61.

PORT BROWNING — George Alexander Browning, Second Master *Hecate,* Asst. Surveying Officer, *Beaver.*

ST. JOHN POINT (Mayne Island) — Lt. F. E. M. St. John, R.N.

SAMUEL ISLAND — Samuel Campbell, M.D.—Asst. Surgeon *Plumper.*

SATURNA ISLAND — In 1791 after Spanish naval schooner *Saturnina* (alias *Horcasitas*) commanded by Jose Maria Narvaez.

TAYLOR POINT (Saturna Island) — George Taylor, stone mason.

WALLACE POINT — Peter William Wallace, M.D., Assistant Surgeon, R.N. attached to *H.M.S. Satellite.* Medical officer in charge of H.M. Naval Hospital, Esquimalt 1857-65.

17
Cove Hopping Deluxe

Separated by a maze of intricate waterways, the British Columbia Gulf Islands beckon the yachtsman with a promise of ideal cruising conditions, near perfect climate, an ever-changing panorama of wooded slopes, hidden bays and protected coves, narrow inlets and distant mountain peaks.

Another clear, warm summer day greeted us as we upped anchor in Saturna Island's Boot Cove and pointed the bow across Plumper Sound toward Navy Channel. A slight morning breeze rippled the blue-green water but not enough to disturb the reflections along the shores of the light and dark greens of the forests, the yellows of dried grass on the hills or the browns and purples of bald rocks. The sun climbed higher in a clear sky with an occasional puff of a cotton cloud scattered here and there. The sharpness of the close-up scene was softened in the distance by a typical Northwest morning haze.

At the entrance to Navy Channel we swung to port for a look into Hope Bay. Although the chart shows an anchorage area south of little Fane Island, we weren't impressed by the protection offered. Smith's store in Hope Bay has a small float and provides gas, oil and groceries. Local knowledge no doubt permits passage between Fane and North Pender Islands but the chart showed enough rocks, shoals and foul ground to discourage our trying it so we swung around the outside.*

Running through some slight tide rips near Conconi Reef, we turned in for a look at a lovely little bay on North Pender just opposite the reef. The charts fail to give it a name but we were told locally it is known as Clam Bay. A nice beach runs around the bay with a house at the eastern corner and an old shack at the head.

Across the channel Mayne Island is well wooded, dominated by a 50-to-70-foot cliff and huge rocks lining the shore. Kelp marks the rocks and reefs extending out and around Dinner Point. The unnamed bay behind the point is a scenic spot for an afternoon siesta but offers no protection from westerlies. The same applies to Village Bay although the chart shows it as suitable for anchoring. A ferry slip at the head has no wharf, float or landing facility for small boats but the bay is scenically attractive.

We approached Helen and Collinson Points marking the entrance to Active Pass. One of the three major passes from the protected waters of the islands to the Strait of Georgia, it is aptly named, for it is perhaps busier than either of the others. It is on the shortest route between Vancouver and the Pacific and there is almost constant traffic of the smaller commercial and fishing, vessels as well as the B.C. Ferries. In addition it is a popular sports fishing area with many a record fish being taken around either entrance or inside the pass itself.

As fitting as it may seem, its name derived from activity in its waters. Originally called Plumper Pass, it is now named for a small wooden paddle-steamer built in New York in 1849 and first called the *Gold Hunter*. Sailing around the horn to San Francisco, for four years she carried California gold seekers from the Isthmus of Panama to the Golden Gate. Bought later by the U.S. government, she was renamed *Active* and under Lt. James Alden, u.s.n., assisted in the boundary survey at the 49th parallel in the Gulf of Georgia. On one of his passages in *H.M.S. Plumper*, Capt. Richards learned that *Active* had been the first steam vessel to navigate the pass and then and there changed the name to Active Pass.

Any small boat with a speed of less than ten knots will do well to negotiate the pass at or near the slack of the tidal current as velocities up to eight knots can be found on large tides. There are also rather violent tide rips in places, particularly on the flood. It is well to miss the big B.C. Ferries in the pass for they throw a tremendous wake. One can check by obtaining a schedule or by monitoring 2182 kc as the ferries radio when approaching the pass.†

Captain R. C. Mayne, for whom Mayne Island is named, in his book "Four Years in British Columbia and Vancouver's Island," writes of an experience in the pass. "On July 31st in company with *Termagant* and *Alert* as we steamed through Plumper Pass *Termagant* met with an accident which well might have turned out seriously for her. Rounding the point in the middle of the passage (Mary Anne Point) the current caught her bow and she would not answer the helm. For a moment she appeared to be going stern on to the rocks, when she suddenly veered around a little, but not in time to clear them altogether. The rocky bank against which she grazed was fortunately sheer and

*Smith's no longer supplies fuel.
†The ferries make their presence known to each other using VHF Channel 6.

Bonnie Lass of Victoria at anchor in Selby Cove

An inviting beach on Prevost Island's Ellen Bay

White Iris of Vancouver in Diver Bay, Prevost Island

steep; so that, although she heeled over so much that those watching her thought she must have capsized, she shot back into the middle of the stream, tearing up a tree with her fore-yard and throwing it over the yard-arm as though it had been a broomstick."

Georgina Point at the outer entrance to the pass is the only spot in the Gulf Islands where Captain George Vancouver landed. A boat party camped at the point in 1794 and in 1881 W. T. Collinson, a settler (for whom Collinson Point is named), unearthed an English penny of 1792 and the remains of a seaman's knife.

Mayne Island is credited with being the first place in British Columbia to grow apples. Mrs. Mabel Foster told the story of a Capt. Simpson who, ordered to the Pacific Coast for survey work, was given a dinner party in England before sailing. A lady jokingly slipped a few apple seeds into his waistcoat pocket, telling him to carry them to his far-off destination and there to plant them. Simpson forgot the incident until he arrived in the islands. When wearing the same waistcoat at a formal dinner the seeds were found, later planted on Mayne Island and produced the trees bearing the delicious King apples still growing there today.

Gas and oil are available at Mayne in Miners Bay inside Active Pass as well as at Galiano Lodge in Sturdies Bay at the outer entrance to the pass. This lodge is popular with yachtsmen who are welcomed by Allen and Vivian Clarke to enjoy the moorage, good meals, swimming pool, showers, laundromat, gift shop and cottages.*

Just around the corner a bit to the northwest, snuggled in behind Gossip Island, is Whaler Bay; southeast of Georgina Point a couple of miles and around Edith Point is Campbell Bay, both offering protected and enjoyable anchorages for the yachtsman.

Returning through the pass we left Enterprise Reef Light on our port and made a clockwise exploration of Prevost Island with its wealth of intriguing bays, coves and offshore islets.

This is Gulf Island cove hopping at its best. Each of these myriad bays and coves is delightful in itself, for each has its own mood and individual characteristics. On a warm summer afternoon after you've chipped enough oysters off the rocks for the evening meal and had a plunge in the crystal clear water to cool off, there's nothing better than to laze on a grassy plot in the shade and let the world stop.

Chewing on a blade of grass with the peaceful silence broken only by the chittering of birds overhead or the occasional scolding of a squirrel, you sense the history all around you. You almost catch a fleeting glimpse of a sailing ship — perhaps commanded by Eliza, Narvaez, Vancouver or Malaspina — on the spangled water outside the cove. Or a fleet of canoes unloads a band of dusky red men on their way to a potlatch over there on the point. Or an early settler fells fir trees to build his log cabin. Whatever your vision, it's peaceful; no pressures, no hurry, no demands. And you return to your ship renewed and refreshed.

As you round each finger point separating these bays with the protruding rock or islets off the point and their weather-bent evergreens forming an artist's dream, a new vista opens up with another invitation for your enjoyment.

The unnamed bay behind Portlock Point, though small, has plenty of water for anchorage. Diver Bay is impressive with rock-bound shores and sparse evergreens growing to

*Galiano Lodge, owned and operated by Roszanne Shuey and Sonia Maans, offers the same services minus the fuel dock.

the water's edge in places. The metal-roofed house at the head was obviously not deserted but there was no sign of life around.

Ellen Bay is lined with solid rock, back draped with madronas, firs and cedars. Two rocky points at the head protect a sandy beach and a comfortable red-roofed house in an ideal setting. We found 40 feet of water almost into these points.

Rounding Pt. Liddell we entered Captain Passage with the picturesque Asland Islands on starboard and the Channel Islands to port. Long, narrow Secret Island and a smaller sister parallel Prevost to form another interesting cove. We'd been told entrance could be made between the end of Secret Island and Glenthorne Point but we hesitated to try it. Swinging around to enter from the northwest we took another look from the inside and decided others could use that entrance if they chose but, for us, those three reefs across the entrance, clearly visible at about half tide, were something we'd rather not play tag with.

The cove, along with Annette Cove, Selby Cove and James Bay, all on the northwest end of Prevost Island, offer the yachtsman good protected anchorages with plenty of depth, although attention should be paid to the depth sounder and chart. There are shoal spots and an occasional rock to watch for. Although each one is different they share the common denominators of beauty, peace and quiet. James Bay is more open to northwest winds than the others, thus not as desirable for overnight anchoring.

The need to restock ship's stores made Ganges our next objective. Here is a village which will not only supply most of your cruising needs but will enchant you as well. It has long been a port of call for yachtsmen cruising the area and is now even more attractive with its new small-boat basin and moorages.

After cruising up the long arm of Ganges Harbour, split down the middle by the Chain Islands, a skipper formerly headed around in back of the spit for moorage. The new basin is to the left of the spit and is a welcome addition to the facilities at Ganges.

One can hardly be around Ganges or on Saltspring Island long without hearing about the Battle of Ganges Harbour or, as it was formerly called, "The Massacre of Admiralty Bay."

The actual eye-witness account by settler Henry Lineker sets the date as July 4, 1860. A Bella Bella canoe bearing a white man named McCawley, nine braves, three squaws and two Indian boys beached near his house. About 50 Cowichan Indians were encamped nearby. While McCawley was at Lineker's house, the Cowichans attacked the Bella Bellas and, after an hour's battle, killed eight of the visiting braves and took the women and boys prisoners. One Bella Bella escaped while the Cowichans had no casualties.

The intriguing part of the story is how it has grown through the years. One account has 30 Bella Bellas against 900 Cowichans and Saanich warriors turning the harbor crimson with blood and the dead and dying piled in heaps along the shores.

An even more exciting account had the Bella Bellas numbering 300 and the Cowichans 2000. By this time, the battle had become a full-blown naval engagement lasting eight hours as desperate struggles between canoes full of warriors took place up and down the harbor.

Another bit of early day history reported, matter-of-factly, in the Victoria Colonist for July 12, 1860, shows how

The bay behind Dinner Point on Mayne Island

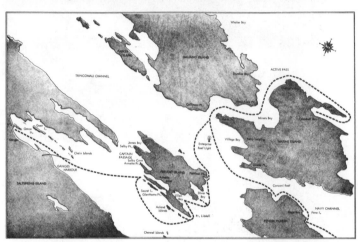
Mar-Jay-En behind a bight in Annette Inlet, Prevost Island

Smith's Store in Hope Bay, North Pender Island

At the head of the inlet behind Secret Island

precarious life was in this idyllic setting only a century ago.

"A few days after the Bella Bellas had been killed, two Cowichan Indians in a canoe were quietly fishing about 200 yards from the shore (having had nothing to do with the massacre), near them being a boat in which were two white men similarly engaged, when suddenly appeared, round a point of land a short distance off, several canoes filled with Fort Rupert Indians, who, on perceiving the fishermen, made directly for them.

"The Cowichans got into the white men's boat, evidently seeking protection, deserting their own canoe which went adrift. The Fort Ruperts dashed alongside the boat, and, seizing the unhappy redskins, five or six knives were buried in each, their heads cut off and the bodies thrown to the fishes.

"No violence was offered to the white men, who were terribly alarmed at the awful sight. Nothing was asked, no explanation given by the Fort Rupert Indians, who continued on their journey, taking the heads with them. The next day one of the heads was found stuck on a tall pole on a small island near Saltspring Island."

The June 12, 1862 Colonist further reported, "In June, 1862, the harbour was again the scene of Indian lawlessness, and this time of swift punishment. Early in this year the number of northern Indians congregated at Victoria had grown to such proportions, and they had become, through intemperance, crime and disease, such an intolerable nuisance, that the authorities decided to deport them to their houses, and the gunboat *Forward* was instructed to convoy them a portion of the journey.

"While the canoes, in tow of the gunboat, were passing the entrance of Ganges Harbour, the Cowichans fired at the Indians from the shore, some of the shots passing unpleasantly close to the gunboat.

"Capt. Lascelles stopped his vessel, cast off the canoes, sent an armed boat's crew on shore, who captured the rascals and brought them on board the gunboat, where they immediately received three dozen lashes each as a gentle reminder to keep their bullets at home for the future. It is recorded that the flogging exercised a very wholesome influence on other tribes along the coast, to whom the news was soon communicated."

Today the harbor is peaceful while the town exudes a provincial charm hard to match. You'll enjoy shopping in Mouat Brothers' General Store with fresh greens and meat on the lower level and canned goods on the main floor with the hardware.* Wide streets, vacant lots and a variety of interesting shops contribute to an atmosphere of a small village a generation or so ago with only the modern automobiles out of place in the scene.

There are any number of protected spots in Ganges Harbour or in nearby Welbury Bay to drop the hook for a quiet night or you can stay at one of the Ganges moorages as we did after enjoying an excellent family style meal ashore.

Now the food items are in the supermarket next-door.

18
Paradise Found

A group of sun-kissed islands rises out of the glistening sea like a cluster of vari-colored gems. These are the Canadian Gulf Islands, set between the southeast coast of Vancouver Island and the Strait of Georgia for man's amazement and enjoyment.

Moving across the international border into the Gulf Islands we have still another cruising paradise worthy of the yachtsman's full attention and with more attractions than he can ever adequately cover in any one normal vacation period.

After leaving Ganges we carefully explored more of Ganges Harbour behind the Chain Islands, a scenic and interesting portion of this bay, but where close attention is needed to chart and depth sounder to avoid the scattered rocks and shoals.

A swing into Welbury Bay and around Scott Point brought us into popular Long Harbour. Although the younger crew members were anxious to get into the Scott Point Marina swimming pool, we took a turn around the bay first. Here there are several excellent areas for anchoring or, if you stop at the marina, it offers an excellent area for dinghy explorations of clam beaches and meandering shoreline on a lazy afternoon.*

In addition to the heated swimming pool, the marina itself, operated by Mr. and Mrs. J. W. Dickie and Mr. and Mrs. R. Taylor, offers just about all the facilities, supplies and services generally found at these cruising oases except a restaurant. For a bit of after-dinner exercise, a hike along the trails winding among a variety of trees and rock formations is a pleasant and healthful evening activity.

Of particular interest to those with a flair for history is the old bench on the porch of the lounge. The brass plate tells us that it is made of teak from *H.M.S. Ganges.* Built in Bombay in 1821, she was on station in these waters as Adm. Robert L. Baynes' flagship 1857-60. The last sailing line-of-battle ship of the British Navy on active foreign

A romantic link with the past

service, she was broken up at Plymouth in 1930 and her teak sold for memorials such as this bench.

From Long Harbour it's only a short four-mile hop across Trincomali Channel, past Phillimore Point and Bob Emmanuel's little Julia Island into Montague Harbour, another favorite of Northwest skippers. This land-locked bay is a delightful spot for a night, a day or several days.

The Provincial Marine Park in the northwest portion of the bay provides mooring buoys, float and wharf, picnic and camping facilities and fresh water. Clams and oysters are available and on the other side of the hook is a fine sandy swimming beach while just along the shore a short way are Mushroom Rock and the Indian Caves.

With Parker Island lying across the opening, Montague is completely protected with plenty of room for good anchoring. The popularity of this enchanting bay is attested by the large number of yachts stopping there all summer. Sunny weather or foul, it's a *must* on any Gulf Islands cruise.

Leaving Montague Harbour our course took us northwestward inside Parker, Sphinx, Charles and Wise Islands, past the Ballingall Islets which are designated as a bird sanctuary, and along the steep-walled cliffs of Galiano Island. These solid rock cliffs rise from the water to as high as 300 feet in places, like the walls of a medieval fortress.

Galiano is considered by many to be the most scenic of the Gulf Islands. Sixteen miles long and from one to two miles wide, it has more shoreline in relation to land area than any of the others. The Bluffs, fronting on Active Pass, are dominated by the oldest and largest trees on the island and are covered with rock plants and colorful wild flowers.

65

*Scott Point Marina is closed to the public.

A beautiful beach just a short hike across the spit at Montague Harbour

Along the lower coastal sections rough rock formations meet the sea; twisting arbutus or madrona trees hang their copper-colored trunks precariously out over the water while flaming Scotch broom paints the hillsides with golden splendor and the incredibly swift humming birds dart among the flowers.

Retreat Cove, about half way up the island, is a small but irresistably charming litle bay which could be missed if one doesn't know about it. Retreat Island, lying in its mouth, gives good protection for anchoring with plenty of depth in the southeastern end and back of the island. The northwest end shallows a bit but is still good if one checks the tide tables and the water.

Entering to the right of the island there is plenty of room and a clear channel, but caution should be used when entering to the left of the island. A government wharf and float gives access to the road where a short hike will bring a reward of those small but luscious wild blackberries in season.

Continuing up Trincomali Channel, we leave Wallace Island and the Secretary Islands on our left for consideration along with Thetis and Kuper in a later chapter. To check on a couple of small coves on Hall and Reid Islands, we swung across channel thus missing two little bays we'd intended to explore on Galiano. On the chart Spotlight Cove and a larger indentation a little further up look intriguing. We'll have to explore these later.

Anyone looking for small, isolated coves away from the crowds will find the two little diadems of beauty on the east sides of Hall and Reid Islands worthy of attention. Be sure to watch the kelp for shoals and check your depths carefully.

Porlier Pass, Cowichan Pass or The Gap, as it has been called by some in the past, is another gateway from the islands into the Strait of Georgia. Liberally sprinkled with rocks, reefs and shoals, it requires close attention to navigation to negotiate but nonetheless it is an intensely interesting bit of waterway. Tidal currents run through the pass at up to eight knots. The lighthouse on Race Point makes a particularly good subject for camera fans and together with the wreck lying on its side on a rocky reef produce a sea-going atmosphere of saltiness.

Porlier is also a popular fishing area where July and August are the best months for the blueback salmon which run up to 50 pounds. Strip-casting for the fast coho in the tide rips is an exciting experience; grilse, the young salmon running up to two pounds, are caught in July, August and September.

Northwest of Porlier Pass is Valdes Island with even higher, nearly perpendicular cliffs than on Galiano along most of her western shores. About half way along her length the De Courcy Group of Islands lie parallel to form Pylades Channel between them. This group, consisting of Link, De Courcy, Ruxton, Pylades and a host of smaller islands and islets is alluringly fascinating to the yachtsman with its wealth of coves, inlets, passages and photogenic shorelines.

Probably the most popular and scenic spot in this area is Pirate's Cove This landlocked little bay, tucked in behind a couple of small islands and a mushroom-shaped headland on the southeast corner of De Courcy Island, is not only an ideal anchorage but a thoroughly enchanting place to laze away an afternoon or a week.

No official name for this cove is shown on the charts and, among yachtsmen, it had several names. Some years ago many called it Gospel Cove but in late years Pirate's Cove has been more generally used. This is probably the official name by now for it was the one used in all the negotiations when the British Columbia government made it a Provincial Marine Park late in 1965. Both Canadian and American yachtsmen were happy over the action to preserve this beauty spot for the enjoyment of boaters both present and future.

This can be a difficult cove to find unless you are acquainted with it A long ridge extends out from the top of the headland gradually getting lower until it becomes a submerged spit which runs to a point across from about the middle of the outer small island.

Never having been in before, we had been advised to hug the shore on the right as we entered. Upon checking the chart, we couldn't be sure whether our advisor meant to hug the right shore of the small island.

Spotting a boat fishing just northwest of the small islands, we swung in to ask directions from them. We were told to run outside the small islands until we saw some paint on the rocks up a way on the small island, then swing in between the spit and the island, keeping well to the right.

These directions were fine except that the tide was low and we ran too far to the right. We were nearly in the bay, proceeding very slowly, keeping a wary eye on the fairly flat rocks which could be seen to starboard in the clear water. Suddenly the ship came to a grinding halt, her bow firmly aground on a huge submerged boulder.

After a couple of tries at backing off, and fearful that our stern might swing inshore with damage to the propeller or rudder, we decided to wait for the incoming tide to lift us off. Our anchor was carried forward in the dinghy to give

Scott Point Marina in Long Harbour is a popular rendezvous

us something to work on should the incoming current swing us back toward the rocks.

It was only minutes before we were free with no damage done to anything but our egos. One friendly skipper, on his way out of the cove, consoled us with his invitation to "Join the Club" and his statement that no one could be considered an experienced yachtsman until he'd had the experience of going aground. Since then our feeling is that a just-right-of-center-channel course is called for.

Once inside the bay and safely anchored, we relaxed to enjoy a most pleasant afternoon A hike across the marshland at the head of the bay to one of the rockbound coves fronting on Ruxton Passage was great fun except for the huge swarms of mosquitos we stirred up in the marsh. The long flat rocks, eroded by the sea into many little hollows, the fingers of sand extending into the rocks and the beaches were full of marine life which delighted the youngsters.

the ruins for the money and other valuables thought to have been hidden. Nothing was ever found, however; Brother XII supposedly took his treasure with him when he hurriedly departed.

Such an enticing bit of history, which is really good for a story in itself, simply adds further interest to an already charming place, making a visit to Pirate's Cove and De Courcy Island along with the neighboring islands a featured highlight in any Gulf Islands cruise.

After years of cruising through Dodd Narrows on the way to Nanaimo, I had a secret ambition to negotiate the tricky False Narrows between Mudge and Gabriola Islands. I'd been told several times by different people that it could be done if due caution was observed.

The afternoon we planned to make the try we found the tide too low and a stiff breeze too strong to make it seem judicious so we postponed that adventure for a future attempt.

Montague Harbour is a snug cove on Galiano Island, a favorite spot for all boaters cruising the Gulf Islands

Another exploration trip along the southwest side of the cove proved fruitless even though an enjoyable expedition. We had read and heard of the rascally Brother XII and his religious colony which was established on De Courcy Island around the turn of the century. Somehow I'd gotten the idea that this settlement was on Pirate's Cove but was told later that it was on the other side of the island.

With a band of faithful followers, Brother XII set up a completely socialistic community with himself not only as spiritual leader but a virtual dictator. After relieving his flock of all their worldly possessions, he turned them to cooperative farming. For some time his venture went well, according to the story. He set up his favorite girl friend (or possibly she was his wife) as Queen. She, reportedly, was a mean witch who ruled with an iron hand. Eventually discord and dissatisfaction grew until rumors started leaking to Nanaimo and an investigation was started by the authorities.

Brother XII ultimately disappeared and the settlement was deserted. For many years, even after the buildings had completely deteriorated, people are said to have searched

Looking into False Narrows from the east, the south end of Gabriola Island presents quite a high, steep cliff which drops off further in with some beach showing at low tide. Both Mudge and Link Islands are fairly low on this side with some attractive waterfront and nice looking property.

Gabriola Pass is the narrowest of the three major gateways from the Gulf Islands with a tidal current of up to eight or nine knots possible on the spring tides. We hasten to add, for the benefit of the neophyte skipper, that a spring tide isn't one occurring in the springtime, but one of extreme highs and lows. A fast boat would have no great problem, but slower boats should run the pass during slack currents on the larger tides.

Another tidal note might clear up some confusion for the inexperienced boatman in these islands. It is so easy to think of the tide as flooding into a bay and ebbing out of it that many naturally think of a flood tide as flowing in through the passes and ebbing out to the Strait of Georgia. Actually, though, a flood tide flows in from the ocean through the Strait of Juan de Fuca and the Gulf Islands to the

Strait of Georgia. Thus it floods *out* through the passes and ebbs *in*.

The approaches to Gabriola Pass from Pylades Channel are both scenic and interesting. Possibly these coves and bays are considered a part of the pass but I like to think of the narrow section between Josef and Cordero points as the pass proper.

To the south on the north end of Valdes Island are two attractive little coves with Wakes Cove, behind Cordero Point, an especially charming haven. Many boats use this as a pleasant place to wait for favorable currents in the pass.

On the other side is Degnan Bay with an island in the middle of its entrance. Here is another well protected harbor for awaiting proper conditions in the pass or for spending the night.

Entrance should be made to the right of the island. Rocks and shoals extend south of the island and for some distance to the east so the right side of the channel should

be favored. Depths from half to five fathoms offer plenty of good anchorage with a wharf and float at the head of the bay.

Just outside of Gabriola Pass, nestled off a corner of Gabriola Island, are the Flat Top Islands, another popular rendezvous for both Canadian and American yachtsmen.

Wherever you go in these lovely Gulf Islands, you'll be enchanted by the pleasant passages between green forested islands with ever changing shorelines of rock or sandy beaches, exciting and scenic passes for fishing, myriad enticing quiet coves for exploring, hiking, clamming, oystering, crabbing, or just plain loafing, and plenty of protected bays in which to snug down for the night. The sunshine belt in this area gives promise of above average amounts of clear weather and warm water for swimming. The Gulf Islands are an integral part of the great Northwest cruising paradise.

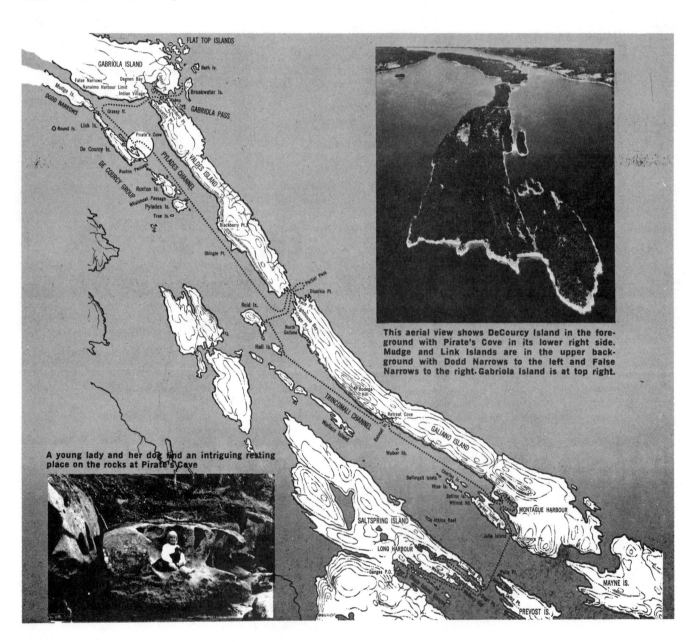

This aerial view shows DeCourcy Island in the foreground with Pirate's Cove in its lower right side. Mudge and Link Islands are in the upper background with Dodd Narrows to the left and False Narrows to the right. Gabriola Island is at top right.

A young lady and her dog find an intriguing resting place on the rocks at Pirate's Cove

19
Popularity Winners

Dawn comes early and dusk late during summer in the British Columbia Gulf Islands. An azure sky is a wide-vision screen for dream shapes of cotton clouds drifting hazily across from West to East. The world stands still with strife and discord far removed on a warm afternoon.

Shafts of sunlight thrust through the tall evergreens on the island shores to reflect sparkling paths on waters of the bay in a corduroy pattern. Life is good and you are king in this cruising paradise. Even the name "Silva Bay" imparts a bit of enchantment to the scene as you breathe deeply of the pine-scented air tinged with a suggestion of barbecuing oysters from the hibachi on a neighboring boat.

This favorite bay of both American and Canadian yachtsmen nestles in the lap of the Flat Top Islands which lie off the east end of Gabriola Island and northeast of Gabriola Pass. In addition to offering excellent anchorage and a choice of moorages, there is good fishing just outside and a wealth of oysters, clams, crab and shrimp.

Approaching this next highlight in our Gulf Island series, we came through Gabriola Pass on slack water. For a boat with plenty of speed this may not be necessary but many expert skippers advise it for tidal currents can run from 6 to 8 knots and a dangerous overfall can develop in this narrow pass. Remember, too, that here, as in the other passes through these islands to the Strait of Georgia, the flood flows into the strait and the ebb from the strait into the islands.

Emerging from the pass, we headed for the beacon on the western side of Breakwater Island's long tail. This heading gives plenty of clearance to the small islands with their many reefs to the southeast of Cordero Point and also avoids Rogers Reef on the left leaving the pass.

After clearing the reef, a 90° swing to port took us up the passage between Breakwater Island and the eastern end of Gabriola Island. For the driftwood fan, the outer shores of Breakwater Island are generally loaded with a wide selection of bizarre and oddly shaped pieces. Best approach by dinghy, however, or walk across the island for these shores are fraught with rocks, reefs and shoals.*

The Flat Top Islands, so called because of their fairly uniform heights with no peaks, present a maze of intricate, interesting and scenic waterways separating green-clad islands bounded by rocky and sandy beaches.

Names are always confusing in this group. The chart lists one set of names while Canadian and American yachtsmen use another set. For purposes of reference, we will use the charted names here, but in order that newcomers may converse with old timers, here are the local names.

Saturnina Island is called Eagle, Gaviola is Hen, Acorn is Southeast, Carlos is Salmon Rock, Vance is Indian and Sear is Passage.

There are three entrances through the islands to Silva Bay. Coming from Gabriola Pass, the shortest route uses the narrow passage between Gabriola and Sear Islands. It's easy to miss and a course favoring the Sear Island side is recommended.

Another entrance lies between Tugboat and Vance Islands and a third between Lily Island on one side, Carlos and Vance on the other. It's advisable not to enter between any of the other islands, as channels are shallow or filled with rocks. Large scale chart #3509 of the Flat Tops is a comfort to have aboard when cruising this area.

Silva Bay proper has anchorage depths of from 1-1/2 to 4-1/2 fathoms at low tide, and there are several moorages with a variety of services and supplies. Withey's,† for many years has been one of the better known shipyards in British Columbia. The Royal Vancouver Yacht Club has floats and an outpost on Tugboat Island.

No Gulf Islands cruise should miss the many charms and attractions of Silva Bay and the Flat Top Islands. Sea food gourmets will find an abundance of everything their tastes could desire.

Poking our bow out into the Strait of Georgia and finding nearly a flat calm, we elected to head for Nanaimo along the outside of Gabriola Island, through Forward Channel between Orlebar Point and Entrance Island and into Fairway Channel. This took us around Gallows Point on the south tip of Protection Island and into Nanaimo Harbor.

Nanaimo, northern terminus of many an International Cruiser Race and jumping-off place for the trip across the Gulf into British Columbia cruising waters, marks the northernmost point in this Gulf Island series. As an important yachting center, it not only provides a complete shopping center with all types of marine service, but is a most interesting historic town. There is much to see and do. Whether you are waiting out the weather for a Gulf crossing or cruising the Gulf Islands, a couple of days in Nanaimo are always well spent.

In approaching Nanaimo, no matter from which direction, it is well to have the large-scale harbor chart (#3558) and use due caution, with careful attention to buoys, lights and markers. Mud flats and shoals abound, making it easy for the first-timer to get into trouble.

---

*Breakwater Island is privately owned and access across it is prohibited. The shores are still public below the high tide line.
†Withey's is now the Silva Bay Shipyard operated by the Bentzen Brothers.

The downtown public government wharf and floats lie in Commercial Inlet, in behind the CPR dock. Nanaimo Yacht Club is located further north, opposite Bate Point at the entrance to Newcastle Island Passage.

Although the yacht club is most hospitable and welcomes visiting yachtsmen, many of whom have joined the club in appreciation of courtesies extended, it is not as convenient to downtown shopping as is the public float.

Theatres, many fine restaurants, Chinatown and the museum in the old block house are just a few of the attractions to be found in this town which began as a coal center. Then there's the fact that one always seems to meet boating friends at Nanaimo. We've never been in there yet when we haven't run across several old friends and made new ones.

This trip we enjoyed dining ashore with the Pete Coffins, there in their *Jimcin*, and the Walter Shearers who live in Santa Cruz, California, but do their boating in these waters flying the Tyee YC burgee from their *Sonora*. Later the Bob Spences arrived in their *Scotty Gal* and joined in our exploration of Newcastle Island.

This 720-acre island which, with its little sister Protection Island, protects Nanaimo Harbour from the wrath of the Gulf, has a romantic history dating back to the days when cruise ships and excursion boats of all kinds and sizes brought city people to its shores to enjoy its delights. The city of Nanaimo acquired Newcastle Island for park purposes some years ago. More recently it has been given to the Provincial Government and developed into a first-class Provincial Marine Park.

Only a few minutes' running time across the harbor there are mooring floats, good swimming, large open play areas, picnic spots with shelters, kitchen units and tables, trails leading to unusual rock formations, interesting beaches and breath-taking scenic points. In addition to Nanaimo residents who enjoy this park, more and more yachtsmen are including an afternoon or overnight stop at Newcastle Island.

The Nanaimo area offers still other attractions. Departure Bay, to the north of town, as its name implies, is the starting (or waiting) spot for that Gulf crossing. It has excellent beaches and is reported to be a good place to swim. Fishing is also good around the islands and rocks just outside in the Gulf. Big ones are frequently taken near Hudson Rocks, Five Finger and Snake Islands. Some Queen City Yacht Club members report good crabbing on the mud flats at the mouth of the Nanaimo River south of town at low tide.

Indian pictographs can be seen on the rocks about 500 feet south of Jack Point on the west side while Galiano Gallery in the vicinity of Descanso Bay provides a fascinating spot to visit.

Also known as Malaspina Gallery, this remarkable natural overhanging gallery of unusual rock formations is about 300 feet long and 12 feet high. It is situated at the water's edge, near Malaspina Point on the western end of Gabriola Island. The gallery was discovered in 1792 by the Spanish naval officers Galiano and Valdes who anchored in Descanso Bay with their exploring vessels *Sutil* and *Mexicana*.

The gallery is named after the commanding officer of the expedition, Dionisio Alcala Galiano, from whose sketch and report it was ultimately made known to Europeans. An original and interesting picture of the gallery is found in Capt. Malaspina's "Voyages" (page 200) edited by Lt. Pedro de Nova y Colson of the Spanish navy, and published at Madrid in 1885.

An inviting anchorage in the Flat Tops

Descanso Bay with its ferry slip is a scenic spot with its rocky shores but offers little of interest to the yachtsman.

Rounding the point from the bay, we entered Northumberland Channel with cliffs over 100 feet high on our port as we headed for Dodd Narrows and our return into the Gulf Islands. It's interesting to note that the British Columbia Pilot states "the tidal streams in Northumberland Channel are unusual as the set is continually eastward at a 1-2 knot rate at springs." If you have time to spare while awaiting slack water in the narrows, there is a measured mile just above the Narrows on Gabriola Island.

The running of Dodd Narrows shouldn't be undertaken lightly. Maximum current can run as high as 8 to 10 knots and all but the faster boats should plan to negotiate it at slack or near slack water. High water slacks are 17 minutes earlier and low water slacks are 25 minutes earlier than corresponding slack waters in Porlier Pass which are listed in the Current Tables. Duration of the slack is about six minutes.

When the tidal stream is running at strength, a tide rip in a well-defined curve is always to be seen outside the narrowest part of the narrows on that side toward which the tidal stream is running. The gradual disappearance of this tide rip is the sign of the slackening in the tidal stream. Passage can be safely made when it has entirely disappeared. For those who like large-scale charts, #3471 is excellent for Dodd Narrows.

A couple of other points to be remembered about these narrows: the flood current flows north, the ebb south; frequently log tows can cause trouble in this channel which is 75 yards at its narrowest point.

Once into Stuart Channel one can choose a course down the center, to the left along the De Courcy Group of islands or to the right behind Round Island. There are many good anchorages and moorages within easy cruising range including Boat Harbour, Kulleet Bay, Ladysmith Harbour, Chemainus, through Ruxton Passage to Pirate's Cove, North Cove, Preedy Harbour, Telegraph Harbour or Tent Island.

We chose Kennary Cove in Boat Harbour for a visit with the colorful Kendalls. This and some of the other interesting coves and harbors mentioned will be covered in the next chapter of Northwest Passages.

For a chart of the Flat Top Islands, see page 241.

Silva Bay in the Flat Top Islands offers ideal anchorage in all weathers

Complete facilities for yachtsmen are found at Silva Bay.

Leaving Silva Bay between Tugboat and Vance Islands

Bath and Saturina Islands guard the entrance to Silva Bay

Peaceful coves abound in the Canadian Gulf Islands

Heading out through Gabriola Pass

20

Pirates, Cannon and Coves

"Boo-o-o-m-m-m!" Reverberations hadn't yet begun to echo among the rocks on shore when a kersplash off our starboard bow sent spray over the deck. Momentary visions of a Canadian Coast Guard boarding were replaced with the remembrance that we were approaching Kenary Cove in Boat Harbor and were receiving a typical Kendall greeting.

Actually a cannon-ball-across-the-bow isn't exactly a typical greeting; it's used only occasionally and can be a salute meaning "Welcome, friend" or a warning for "stuffed shirts" to stand off. In our case we hoped it was the former and proceeded into the floats.

Northwest cruising isn't only the enjoyment of peaceful coves and quiet waterways among emerald isles set in a crystal clear azure inland sea. It's also the pleasure of meeting people, either old friends or newly-made acquaintances from other boats or ashore.

One of our pleasures is to stop for a visit with Ken and Mary Kendall. Born Arthur Lloyd Kendall, it's been just "Ken" for many years and Kenary Cove, now an official name, is a combination of Ken and Mary.*

Although there is a variety of interesting things at the Kendalls', perhaps one of the most intriguing is the Kendall philosophy, intriguing because he appears to live and think in a way many of us would like. Completely uninhibited, he dares to do and say what he likes.

A graduate engineer, he became a machinist because he couldn't stand being tied to a drawing board or confined to an office. He feels entitled to his piratical masquerade, pierced ears, gold earrings, his collection of big and little cannons, guns, swords and daggers, because of his six toes on each foot.

"All through history," he explains, "the extra finger and toe has been considered the mark of a pirate." He was born with six toes on each foot and six fingers on each hand but his father, a doctor who also had 12 fingers and 12 toes, removed the extra fingers when he was a baby.

He enjoys dressing the part of a pirate and, with friends and neighbors equipped with Kendall-made cannons and swords from the Kendall collection, reenacting pirate battles on the beaches. Another sport, which he allows causes concern from some, is cannon practice where balls are lobbed at the rocks on a distant beach from the 90-pound cannon he cast himself or the big 700-pounder which came from Sitka, Alaska.

Many yachtsmen have a Kendall-made cannon mounted on the bows of their cruisers. Don't get any ideas of ordering one, however, for Ken says he has more orders ahead than he can fill the rest of his life.

The signs one finds around the place are amusing, yet cause one to wonder about his welcome. You're hardly off your boat when a warning sign on the floats greets you and further up another one with a skull and cross bones reads PRIVATE PROPERTY!"We dislike having to post these damned signs, but we get so many Idiots, Bill Collectors, Revenours, Jehova Witless, City Slickers, and some just plain Bastards, that our Burial Ground is filling up too fast."

Other signs warn against the danger of stray gunshots or state, "We sincerely Hope That Anyone Removing Flowers, Plants, Moss, Or Anything From This Place Breaks Their Damned Neck."

Such signs do little to slow the stream of visitors coming year after year. Their guestbook logged some 2500 during the previous season. Ken admits it can all get a bit tiring at times. "We really don't want them," he says, "and there's really nothing here for them, but I like to study human nature and I sure get the chance."

Mary goes along with it all. She keeps busy with her housework, yardwork, cooking, preserving, freezing and canning. On occasion she'll sell homemade bread, jellies, clams or chowder and is compiling a cookbook which may contain her special grass salad or some of the 250 ways she has learned to disguise hamburger.

Yes, Pirate's Roost, as they call their place, in spite of what they say, holds lots of interest and settling there was no accident. In his search for an ideal home, Ken found something wrong with every place he looked. He wanted shelter for his boat, isolation for peace of mind, yet access to schools for the children. That left out islands — he's tried them and found them a false dream.

"So are the South Seas," he says. "We don't have insect pests here. Our only pests are stuffy people."

Stuffy people are the Kendall's pet aversion and Ken delights in "un-stuffing" the occasional "white pants" type

*No more high jinx! Both Mary and Ken have passed away.

yachtsman who puts into Kenary Cove in his big spit-and-polish craft.

Regardless of the signs, the disparaging talk about visitors, etc., we have a suspicion the Kendalls do enjoy at least some of their guests. Ken writes that he has a new dock almost decked in and even enclosed a membership card to his Boat Harbor Yacht Club. Under a royal blue swallow-tail burgee with a brass cannon on it, the card states the bearer "Has been elected to full membership and is entitled to the privileges of all club members at Kenary Cove." It's signed "Old Chief Six Toes."

We hope this means we're welcome back and that we aren't considered stuffy. If you're considering a visit to Boat Harbour, Canadian Hydrographic Chart #3453 has a good blow-up of this bay.

Continuing down the east coast of Vancouver Island we rounded Yellow Point with a wide sweep, remembering that years ago a Queen City YC Cruising Guide had warned that the rock off the point isn't in its charted position. We weren't sure whether this had been corrected and decided not to gamble.

Poking into Kulleet Bay we weren't too impressed with the protection offered although the chart shows it as an anchorage.

Around Coffin Point, Coffin Island, past Evening Bay and Sharp Point we turned into Ladysmith Harbour. Here's a long narrow arm with many attractions for the boater. There are several lovely coves for anchoring such as Sibell Bay, certain areas in back of the Dunsmuir Islands and Burleith Arm. There is famed Manana Lodge still further in where the yachtsman will find a cordial welcome from Rolly and Gladys Yoxall with their moorage, all the usual marine facilities and excellent meals served in a delightful rustic setting nestled amid tall Douglas firs with a striking view of the harbor.*

The town of Ladsmith now has public floats and offers all types of supplies, including an excellent bakery.

Oysters and clams are plentiful at almost any stage of the tide at several places in the harbour, but care should be taken not to trespass on private commercial oyster beds.

About five miles southeast is Chemainus Bay and the town of Chemainus. This is another popular spot with boaters. A government wharf and floats lead to the main street with stores and shops of all kinds, including another well-known home-type bakery and a meat market which specializes in good steaks and smoked meats. A tour of the sawmill is another attraction. Fishing in the area is good with Cohos, Springs and Bluebacks plentiful in season.

Across Stuart Channel just a bit over three miles is

*Though the Yoxall's are gone, this is still a good place.
†Conover Cove is now private.

little Tent Island, little in size but big in popularity. The Provincial Marine Park in the bay is a favorite with many boaters as a place to swim, picnic, camp or explore. The shoreline, varying from sandy to shell or rocky beaches backed by picturesque trees and a harborful of colorful boats with little dinghies darting in and out or a couple of small sailboats serenely spreading colorful sails all combine to offer the camera fan some fine possibilities.

Tent Island is good for an hour, an afternoon, a day or even an overnight stay on one of the park buoys if the wind isn't blowing. Our stay this trip was all too short, just long enough for the kids to check the warm swimming water against a promised return visit.

Swinging around the southern end of Tent Island, we turned north to enter Houstoun Passage on a big "S" course around Southey Point on Saltspring Island's northern tip. A generous sprinkling of rocks and reefs called for a slow bell in our exploration of Jackscrew Island, the Secretary Islands and Wallace Island.

In behind the long reef which lies southwest of Wallace Island we found plenty of water, although caution and close attention to the depth sounder were required as we poked the bow into the several scenic nooks and coves. A delightful resort in Conover Cove welcomes the yachtsman while the bay behind Panther Point on the southeast end of Wallace Island seems to issue a mute invitation to just come in and "set a spell" or drop a fishline.†

Our next objective was Clam Bay, one of two harbors formed between Thetis and Kuper Islands, and famous for its clam beaches. Our course took us up the northeast side

Looking out from Kendalls' Pirate's Roost, "Old Chief Six Toes" can keep a good watch for any unwelcome "stuffed shirts"

The little pass between the Secretary Islands is one of the many beauty spots enjoyed by boaters cruising the Canadian Gulf Islands

Manana Lodge in Ladysmith Harbour with its excellent meals and marine facilities, is popular with both U.S. and Canadian skippers

of Wallace and the Secretary Islands, between Norway and Hall Islands and between the Centre Reef buoy and Penelakut Spit.

Thetis and Kuper Islands are just barely separated by Boat Pass, a narrow channel which can be negotiated at high tide by small boats. Some blasting and dredging of the pass was going on but we weren't sure how much had been done so weren't willing to take the gamble of this short cut to Telegraph Harbor.

After digging a bucket of clams, we set out for Telegraph Harbor by circling Thetis Island. Cutting in between Pilkey Point and the reef which is charted as the Ragged Islets, we explored two covelets, one right on Pilkey Point and the other behind the point. These tiny bays along with larger North Cove and its high cliffs present still further evidence of the beauties and pleasures to be found in Gulf Islands cruising. North Cove is a good anchorage with protection from all directions except north or northwest.

Another good anchorage, perhaps not so well known, is to be found in Preedy Harbour. This bay, nestled between Crescent and Foster Points and behind a group of protecting islands and islets, has plenty of depth. The ferry from Chemainus lands here and there is a government wharf and float.

There are several entrances between the islands, but a liberal scattering of rocks and shallow areas calls for close attention to the chart and depth sounder. We entered close to Crescent Point and came out between the buoys which lie beween Dayman and Hudson Islands. We recommend Canadian Hydrographic Chart #3453 for these waters. If you've ever seen the so-called foul ground around Alarm Rock at the entrance to Telegraph Harbour at low tide, you'll be sure to give that light a wide berth.

Telegraph Harbour is perhaps one of the best known

Conover Cove on Wallace Island is a delightful spot with plenty of water

places in the Gulf Islands. Situated, as it is, almost in the center of this group, it lies between Thetis and Kuper Islands. With its dog-leg entrance, it is completely protected. Just a short hop from such shopping centers as Chemainus and Ladysmith and boasting two fine marinas, it is a regularly scheduled stop on most cruising itineraries in these waters.

Coming into the harbor by way of the dog-leg entrance, the Happy Landing store and marina are on the left. Operated by Happy and Fred Boughen, this facility has just about everything to satisfy the boatman's needs. There is a post office and the store is headquarters for those famous Indian-made Cowichan sweaters.*

Further in the bay, at the entrance to Boat Pass, is the Telegraph Harbour Marina operated by Norm and Marg Friesen. Here, too, the yachtsman will find complete facilities including a store and coffee shop. The Friesens are delightful hosts, anxious to make their guests' visit as pleasant as possible.†

Sometimes, at the height of the summer season, both marinas will be full. If you want to be sure of a berth, it's best to arrive early in the afternoon or call ahead for a

(Left) The cove behind Pilkey Point on the north end of Thetis Island is serene on a summer's afternoon . . . (right) the head of North Cove on Thetis Island provides good protected anchorage except in a north or northwest wind

*Happy Landing is now Douglas Ewart's Thetis Island Marina offering complete facilities.
†Alma and Luke Paquette, the present owners, now welcome visitors at Telegraph Harbour Marina.

Cruisers at anchor, a little sailing dinghy casually making its way around the bay, swimmers enjoying the
warm sun and water, a beach fire and picnic are all a part of the scene of enjoyment at Tent Island

reservation. Don't let this keep you from visiting Telegraph, however, for there is ample room for anchoring. Or if the weather is right, it's only a short run down to Tent Island.

Here's another of those places mentioned in our last chapter where the thoughtful skipper will reduce speed so that his wake will not cause damage or discomfort to the moored and anchored boats.

Telegraph is also popular for its abundance of clams and oysters and its warm water for swimming. And Clam Bay or Tent Island, also abounding in oysters, clams or good swim-

ming waters, are only "just around the corner" by dinghy.

We didn't cover a large area in this section of our Gulf Islands cruising or log very many miles, but this kind of cruising isn't measured by distance. Within this section of these delightful islands one can find spectacular scenery, quiet coves for isolation and relaxation, busy harbors and towns for shopping, good marinas with all the facilities and services required by boaters, plenty of fish, clams, crabs or oysters, excellent swimming and a wealth of interesting people.

Reefs along the southwest side of Wallace Island hide the entrance to inviting bays and coves

21

More Gulf Islands

Saltspring Island, Maple Bay, Birdseye Cove, Sansum Narrows, Genoa Bay, Cowichan Bay, Canoe Cove, Tsehum Harbour. What a wealth of memories these names conjure up for the yachtsman who knows them and what an intriguing invitation they offer for those who have yet to cruise in this delightful section of the Canadian Gulf Islands. Wide passages lead to narrower ribbons winding among and between green clad islands forming an ever-changing labyrinth, occasionally revealing a harbor, a bay or a friendly cove.

No matter where in the world a skipper may point his bow, he will be hard pressed to find any place which can surpass the green-mantled islands, the maze of sparkling waterways and the myriad other attractions contained in the vast cruising waters of the Pacific Northwest.

To conclude our exploration of these islands we left Telegraph Harbour behind and Tent Island on our port as we set a southeasterly course to the west of Saltspring Island. The Shoal Islands with their unusual rock formations were to starboard as we swung in for a look at what we thought was Vesuvius Bay but turned out to be an unnamed cove behind Dock Point. It is a lovely little bay with a beautiful home in a magnificent setting on the point.

Vesuvius Bay which, with Ganges, is one of the two main communities on the island, is served by a ferry from Crofton and has several shoreside facilities.

We didn't go into Osborn Bay across the way. The chart shows anchorage possibilities here, a wharf, Post Office, and the small settlement of Crofton, also the big B.C. Products Mill.

The channel ahead narrowed. We favored the Saltspring Island shore with its huge tide-scoured rocks providing a firm footing for the copper-barked madrona or arbutus, pine and cedar trees which marched from the high water mark up to 1500-foot Mt. Erskine.

Saltspring is the largest and most developed of the Gulf Islands, 17 miles long and nine wide at its extreme point with 45,000 acres. The Indians called it Klaatham — salt. Early maps showed it as Chuan Island, but the first settlers called it Saltspring because of the 14 salt springs, mostly near the north end. In 1858 Capt. Richards charted it as Admiral Island in honor of Admiral Baynes but residents persisted in calling it Saltspring and the admiralty finally capitulated.

Pioneers had to contend with bears, wolves, couger and elk. Surrounding waters are teeming with fish while the beaches abound in clams and some oysters. The island very early had a reputation for roasted clams and one pioneer minister wrote that the Indians were probably roasting clams on Saltspring beaches when Moses was writing the Pentateuch on Mount Sinai.

Island history is full of tribal Indian wars and the problems of settlers with the red man. Safety precautions for a lone fisherman in the 1860's are recorded by a gentleman named McKenzie who, in addition to his fishing gear, carried two rifles, two pistols, one axe, one naval cutlass to repel boarders and one small keg of rum, "to stimulate the spirits in the event of Indian attack." Conditions have changed since then and today's fisherman is assured these items are no longer necessary.

Saltspring has 11 lakes with trout and bass and surrounding waters are generally warm for swimming, especially at two lovely beaches in Vesuvius and Burgoyne Bays.

When Spanish officers Galiano and Valdes explored this area in 1792 in their ships *Sutil* and *Mexicana*, they carried instruments called eudiometers to test the air for possible presence of "noxious gases." Admiralty records in Madrid proclaim that the air of the island was properly analyzed and found pure.

Modern day yachtsmen do not need an eudiometer to test the purity of the air. Almost any ordinary nose will testify that the salty tang blended with traces of pine and wild flowers is pure and far superior to that found in heavily populated cities.

Maple Bay is perhaps one of the best known and most popular places in these islands. I'm sure that when I first saw it some 20 years ago, it was more attractive than now for it was less developed but it should definitely be included in any Gulf Island cruising itinerary.

In addition to being a delightfully scenic bay, it offers complete facilities for the yachtsman. Entering between Arbutus Point and Paddy Mile Stone, intriguing names to begin with, one sees first the Maple Bay Yacht Club and a*

*Maple Bay Yacht Club moved near the head of the bay.

wharf leading to the store and post office.

The rugged shorelines of the bay meander to the south into a hill-surrounded sheltered nook called Birds Eye Cove where yachtsmen from all parts of the west meet in fine weather to enjoy the fine facilities or in bad weather when Sou'easters or Nor'westers make small boating uncomfortable or even dangerous on the "outside." This cove puts a crowning touch on this beautiful bay.

On the west shore is Kurt's Marina operated by friendly Kurt Horn and offering moorage, gas, diesel, oil, water, ice, shore power, telephone, marine hardware, a grid, outboard mechanic, parts, bait, taxi service to Duncan and usually fresh salmon for those whose fishing luck ran out.*

Still further in is the Maple Bay Marina, a modern and complete installation with all facilities necessary for the yachtsman. The Bentzen brothers, Arne, John and Lief, have built a good reputation not only for the services they offer but also as outfitters for sailboats. Their float plane can deliver parts or a mechanic to a disabled boat in a matter of minutes. A 62-foot tug is on call at all times for rescue work. She has two masts with a 45-ton lift which can actually lift a sinking boat out of the water.

Another innovation is an overturned railroad barge which just barely floats above the water. It has proved valuable several times when boats which had hit logs came in only to find the marine ways in use. They were run up on the barge and were ready to be worked on 20 minutes after arrival.

The Mai Tai Restaurant, opened in 1965, has already been enlarged. With a tropical South Seas motif and excellent food, it is proving extremely popular with yachtsmen and adds to the attractions which make Maple Bay a top spot in the area.

Burgoyne Bay, indenting Saltspring Island, has a government wharf, offers good anchorage and boasts a lovely sandy beach along its south shore. Rounding Bold Bluff, we entered Sansum Narrows, a most scenic waterway with fairly steep forested sides and a couple of fascinating little coves which, understandably, appeared to be private.

This is a popular and productive fishing area with the heaviest concentration of anglers generally found between Sansum Point and Burial Islet. We managed to land a nice

20-pound salmon in about 15 minutes of trolling.

Through the Narrows and around Separation Point is Cowichan Bay with large mud flats at its western head. The village of Cowichan on the south shore near the mud flats has three gas docks, a marina, public wharf and float, stores and restaurant. Further east is the Lambourn Marina. This bay is another favorite and productive fishing area.†

To the north an offshoot of the bay is Genoa Bay, frequent terminus of the International Cruiser Race and on almost all Gulf Island Cruising itineraries. On entering be sure to remember that the beacon in the middle is not a center channel marker but warns of a reef and should be kept on the starboard hand. It's possible to go on the other side but many a boat has had its bottom raked by the rocks on that side.

Once inside there are well kept floats or plenty of room for anchoring. Captain Morgan's lodge was started on the site of an old sawmill on the point by Peter Morgan, an ex-submarine commander and one of the last remaining direct descendents of the famed Sir Henry Morgan. The lodge has now been closed although the moorages, gas dock and small store are still operating (1968) under a lease arrangement and the swimming pool was reported open.‡

The breath-taking beauty of the bay is enhanced by the historical lore. The little red school house, part of the sawmill village, still standing is used as a tool shed while some of the other buildings are part of the original settlement. Of interest are two piles of sawdust near the floats which have solidified into something nearly hard as rock and show where the old mill originally stood. Clam digging is a popular low-tide activity in the bay.

It could almost be called "The Forgotten Arm" — so many yachtsmen have been ignoring it through years of cruising in adjacent waters.

Saanich Inlet, the long arm which points southward for some 13 miles from the southern extremities of the British Columbia Gulf Islands and is just around the corner from the American San Juans, is a back door for Victoria. It has several interesting features to offer and definitely should be included sometime in a cruise itinerary in these waters.

Coming out of Maple Bay and through Sansum Nar-

Captain Morgan's Lodge, on the point between Genoa and Cowichan Bays has been closed

Some Royal Victoria Yacht Club members use this outpost at the head of Tsehum Harbour for summer moorage while others keep their boats here the year around

A cruiser leaves Genoa Bay for a bit of fishing just around the bend in Cowichan Bay

77

*Kurt's Marina became part of Maple Bay Marina.
†Lambourn Marina is no more.
‡Leonard Lambrecht, proprietor of Genoa Bay Marina, offers these services without the swimming pool. A cafe in the store has home cooking and baking.

rows, a course of 121° (M) toward Satellite Channel ran from Musgrave Rock to Wain Rock, missed Patey Rock by a good half mile and gave us a direct path into Deep Cove, the small bay on the northwestern tip of Saanich Peninsula.

Deep Cove turned out to be an interesting bay with a Government float but not really suited for an all-weather anchorage. One might feel a bit of quiet envy, however, for those fortunate enough to have waterfront property on this picturesque little body of water. Deep Cove was rewarding and we were glad we visited there.

Following the eastern shore of the inlet, Patricia Bay is next in order. This is practically a "Keep your bow out of here" area as the Canadian Department of Defense uses it for a large shore installation as well as restricting a mile-square area out in the inlet for aircraft maneuvers and practice. The yachtsman had best read his charts carefully and stay out of the restricted zone or he may get tangled up in some dive bombing tactics. The buoys are deceptively hard to locate but, once spotted, one can avoid trouble.

In clearing this restricted zone it is best to lay a course nearly to the west shore of the inlet. This gives one an opportunity to poke a bow into, or stop, at Mill Bay, the only real bay on the western shore. There is a Government float, marine gas station, resort, cafe and stores. A small marine ways and outboard repairs are also available.*

Another advantage of this course is that it is easier to clear the rocks off the point of Coles Bay, an east shore cove offering fairly good protection and a comfortable anchorage. Thomson Cove, a short way to the south, receives some protection from southerly winds from Henderson Point. Around the corner, Senanus Island stands as a sentinel guarding Brentwood Bay and Tod Inlet.

We throttled down for a slow bell investigation of the many features in Brentwood Bay, offering the yachtsman just about everything he might need in the way of supplies and services at a wide variety of places. The chart shows plenty of water behind little Daphne Island in the bay but, since the tide was low, we elected not to gamble and stayed on the outside as we headed for our night's anchorage in Tod Inlet.

A small cove opening up on our left looked inviting with two boats anchored side by side under the trees. Here we could see the Butchart Gardens float leading to a short walk which opens up the wonders of this famous complex of floral beauty and perfection. If you've never been there or have a hankering to see it again we highly recommend it and this backdoor approach adds a novel feature to your voyage in these waters.

Leaving a black can buoy marking a rock and reef to our port, we continued into Tod Inlet. We've been advised that from this buoy on out into the bay the salmon were biting but both evening and early morning tries were unsuccessful.

The afternoon sun lengthened the shadows of the dark evergreens on our right while those on our left reflected their brighter green in the cool blue mirror of water that was disturbed only by our lazy wake. The scene recalled memories of sylvan beauty from a previous visit to the lovely gardens above us, creating a feeling that this little cove was ours alone. It was almost like a

voyage of discovery and we wondered if Captain Vancouver felt this way when he put into some strange northwest bay for the first time.

This mood was partially broken as we rounded the ell of the inlet to see several boats at anchor at the head. On the north shore was a long float. A post office is reported up the road a bit but we didn't go ashore. The anchors and buoys appeared to be permanent ones and turned out to be privately owned.

In an effort to recapture that "aloneness" we came about, re-rounded the ell and dropped anchor in a little indentation we were sure had been reserved for our exclusive use. The hook was hardly down, our bearings checked, tide tables consulted and water depth measured before the kids had the dinghy in to set off on an exploration tour of their own.

High heavily forested walls of this miniature Princess Louisa precluded any view of a sunset but the peaceful quiet suggested early to bed and early to rise for that fishing at daybreak. We were snugged down for the night before darkness took over completely.

Around Willis Point, through Squally Reach and down Finlayson Arm to the southernmost tip of Saanich Inlet was almost anticlimactic after Tod Inlet although there was a boathouse, marine ways, store and motel on the west shore and a marine reserve offered camping and picnicking facilities on the east shore.

Yes, the "Forgotten Arm"—Saanich Inlet—should be remembered for some future cruise plan and Tod Inlet should be a "must" for those skippers seeking a secluded spot on the "under" side of Georgia Strait.

A sandy beach and a rocky point give the north end of Portland Island an almost tropical look

Skippers cruising Gulf Island waters are familiar with Fulford Harbour by name if not by personal visit for it is the principal reference point in the Canadian Tide Tables for this area. There is good anchorage up towards the head and fuel, store and post office are available as well as a ferry running to the peninsula.

Leaving Fulford Harbour we swung in behind Russell Island. The shoreline of Saltspring in here, clear around beyond Beaver Point, is laced with tiny coves, most of them guarded by rocks. It appears to be a fascinating place for exploration by dinghy or small outboard cruiser.

It's possible that the islands off the northeast and east of the Saanich Peninsula are frequently forgotten as part of the Gulf Islands but they definitely belong to the group. Little Chads Island, the northern satellite of Portland Island, is a picturesque little wooded isle, low level with a sandy point. In behind, a finger bay indents Portland Island which could offer good protection for small boats. The point,

78

with sand and rock beach, gives an almost tropical appearance, as do the points, rocky promontories and the Pellow Islets down the east side of the island. There's a chance here for some exotic photography.

In behind Reynard Point on Moresby Island is a bay which appears much more protected than shown on the chart. Several little coves on the north and east sides of Moresby invite exploration and perhaps a swim at their nice sandy beaches. There are several rocks all well marked by kelp along the shoreline and kelp seems to form a floating gate across the entrance to some of these little coves. But it can be passed and the rewards are worth the effort. This is for smaller boats, not the large cruisers.

Down near Point Fairfax is another nice beach although it is unprotected. We ran into tide rips after rounding the point and found nothing of interest along the high, forbidding and rocky southwestern side of Moresby, so headed for the southeast side of Portland Island.

This is the island presented by the British Columbia government to Britain's Princess Margaret during her 1958 visit. Here we found many rocks and small islets which called for proceeding under slow bell with close attention to chart and depth sounder. If one isn't in a hurry and likes to poke into interesting and scenic places, one will be well rewarded in this area. A beautiful sandy beach lies in back of little Brackman Island, but watch the shallow depths.*

Another pleasant sandy beach is southwest of Harry Point on Piers Island. Coming on around the island we saw several more beaches in between the rocks. Private homes and cottages dot the southern shores of this beautiful island. Knapp Island also offers equally good exploration possibilities but Little Pym Island has too many rocks and reefs to make it inviting.

Crossing Colburne Passage to enter Iroquois Pass and

The Mai Tai Restaurant, at the Maple Bay Marina, has already been enlarged and beautifully landscaped . . . the Tahitian decor inside and out, along with fine food and drink, make this a popular Gulf Island stopping place

Canoe Rock between Portland and Moresby Islands presents an interesting study at low tide

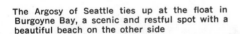

The Argosy of Seattle ties up at the float in Burgoyne Bay, a scenic and restful spot with a beautiful beach on the other side

The moorage in Genoa Bay is well protected and offers the yachtsman good shoreside facilities

*A provincial marine park, presently undeveloped.

the group of little islands between Coal Island and the peninsula, we were happy to have the new large scale chart #3455. It makes navigating these intricate waterways much more comfortable.

Our first stop was in Canoe Cove and See's Canoe Cove Marina, another fine facility for the yachtsman.* We were told that many boaters use Page Pass, but somehow all those rocks gave us the jitters so we went out between Fernie and Goudge Islands. In spite of the many hazards, this is one of the most strikingly beautiful spots in the islands and well worth visiting.

Tsehum Harbour, around Curteis Point, is a beehive of activity with Van Isle and Westport marinas all offering complete yachting facilities. Clark Brothers' Boat Works† is located here as well as Capital City Yacht Club and Royal Victoria Yacht Club's outstation. There are many shallow areas in this bay which could prove embarrassing to the first-time visitor, although the above-mentioned chart will help keep him out of trouble.

Roberts Bay, just around Armstrong Point, is fairly open, quite shallow and has little of interest to the yachtsman. Still further to the south is Sidney, a principal port of entry. Government wharf and floats give ready access to the town with a full complement of stores, facilities and services.

After replenishing ship's stores and getting a necessary haircut, it was too late to set out for any known anchorage. Rather than spend the night at the Sidney float, we headed down the coast a bit and dropped anchor in Saanichton Bay to enjoy a good night's rest among some of the local fishing fleet. It wasn't exactly a secluded cove, for the bright lights of the Canadian Industries Limited, across Sidney Channel on Jones Island, were on all night.

Heading around the long sand spit on the northeastern end of Jones Island, we were amazed at how different it looks from what one might expect from the chart. It appears much longer and narrower than shown.

Sidney Spit is a long, narrow strip of sand extending from Sidney Island. This is a favorite crabbing area and is a Provincial Marine Park with several mooring buoys. Although the beaches are inviting we didn't try the swimming. Caution should be used here for water depths are extremely shallow in places.

The other smaller islands of the vicinity, Forrest, Domville, Brethour, Comet, Gooch and Rum offer some interesting exploring with a few scenic little coves. Mandarte and Halibut Islands to the south have nothing of interest.

So our enjoyable cruise of re-discovering the Canadian Gulf Islands came to a close as we headed across the International Boundary for Roche Harbor.

Boats in the background are anchored in the head of Tod Inlet, one of the most delightful anchorages in the area, yet neglected by many northwest yachtsmen.

80

*Canoe Cove Marina is now managed by J. Simson.
†Clark Brothers Boat Works is out of business.

PLACE NAMES AND THEIR SOURCES

BEAVER POINT — Probably after the Hudson's Bay Co. paddle steamer *Beaver,* the first steam vessel on this coast. The 70-hp engines gave her a speed of 9¾ knots. The places named after this famous vessel were given at various dates, 1837-67, by officers of the H.B. Co., Capt. Richards and Capt. Pender.

CAPE KEPPEL — After R. Adm. the Hon. Sir Henry Keppel, K.C.B., later known as the "Father of the British Navy," by Capt. Richards, 1859.

CHADS ISLAND — After Capt. Henry Chads, HMS *Portland,* flagship of R. Adm. Fairfax Moresby, on this station 1850-53, by Capt. Richards, 1858.

COLES BAY — After John Coles, midshipman, R.N., HMS *Thetis,* on this station 1851-53. After retiring from the service he returned to Vancouver Island to take up land at Saanich in the vicinity of this bay where he resided until 1866. Member of the first Legislative Assembly at Victoria. By Capt. Richards, 1860.

CORDOVA SPIT (and Channel) — From the name Cordova being used in the early days of the colony of Vancouver Island, Puerto de Cordova being the name given by Sub-lieutenant Quimper of the Spanish navy, commanding the sloop *Princess Royal* on an exploring voyage in 1790, to the Harbour of Esquimalt.

COWICHAN BAY — From the name of an important tribe of Indians who resided in the Gulf Island area in large numbers and were divided into many small bands. Named by officers of the Hudson's Bay Company circa 1850.

DOMVILLE ISLAND — After Rev. David Edward Domville, Chaplain, HMS *Satellite,* by Capt. Richards, 1859.

FAIRFAX PT. — After R. Adm. Fairfax Moresby, by Capt. Richards, 1858.

FINLAYSON ARM — After Roderick Finlayson of the Hudson's Bay Co., who was one of their most trusted servants and was practically the founder of the city of Victoria. By Capt. Charles Dodd of the H.B. Co. steamer *Beaver,* circa 1845.

FULFORD HARBOUR — After Capt. John Fulford, HMS *Ganges* on this station 1857-60.

GOOCH ISLAND — After Thomas Sherlock Gooch, R.N. second lieutenant, HMS *Satellite,* by Capt. Richards, 1859.

JAMES ISLAND — Named by the early settlers, circa 1853, after His Excellency James Douglas, Governor of Vancouver Island. Adopted by Capt. Richards, 1858.

KNAPP ISLAND — After Kempster Malcolm Knapp, R.N., Naval Instructor, HMS *America,* on this station 1845-46, by Capt Richards, 1858.

MINERS CHANNEL — Named from the fact of the channel being used in the days of the Fraser River gold excitement, 1858-59, by the miners as a channel on their canoe journey from Victoria to the river. Name adopted by Capt. Richards, 1859.

MORESBY ISLAND — After R. Adm. Fairfax Moresby, Commander in Chief, Pacific station 1850-53, flagship *Portland,* by Capt. Richards, 1858.

OSBORN BAY — After Capt. Sherard Osborn, R.N., C.B., of HM paddle sloop *Vesuvius,* by Capt Richards, 1859.

PARKIN POINT — After Lt. George Henry Parkin, Third Lt., flagship *Portland,* by Capt. Richards, 1858.

PARMINTER POINT (Saltspring Island) — After Rev. Henry Parminter, B.A., Chaplain HMS *Ganges,* by Capt. John F. Parry, 1905.

PIERS ISLAND — After Henry Piers, R.N., surgeon, HMS *Satellite.* Dr. Piers was a brother Arctic navigator with Lt. Pym, after whom the adjacent island is named, by Capt. Richards, 1858.

PORTLAND ISLAND — After HMS *Portland,* 50 guns, 1476 tons, by Capt. Richards, 1858.

PREVOST PASSAGE — After Capt. James Prevost, HMS *Satellite* on this station 1857-60, by Capt. Richards, 1859.

PYM ISLAND — After Lt. Frederick Whiteford Pym, R.N., Lt. Cmdr. gunboat *Skylark,* 1856, accompanied Capt. Richards to the Arctic 1852-53. By Capt. Richards, 1858.

SANSUM NARROWS — After Arthur Sansum, R.N., First Lt. of HMS *Thetis,* on this station 1851-53, by Capt. Richards, 1858.

SATELLITE CHANNEL — After HM screw corvette *Satellite,* 21 guns, 1462 tons, 400 hp on this station 1857-60, also 1869, Capt. James C. Prevost, by Capt. Richards, 1859.

SHERARD POINT — After Capt. Sherard Osborn (see above).

SHUTE PASSAGE — After Capt. James Shute, Royal Marines, HMS *Topaze,* on this station 1859-63, by Capt. Richards, 1860.

SIDNEY ISLAND — Named Sallas Island by Hudson's Bay Co. officers circa 1850 and known by this name to the early settlers for years; changed to Sidney Island by Capt. Richards, 1859.

SWARTZ BAY — After a man named Swart who squatted in this area in the early days.

TOD INLET — After John Tod, a noted Hudson's Bay Company officer on this coast, by Capt. Richards, 1858.

TOM POINT (Gooch Island) — Named from the fact that, in the spring of 1858, the schooner *Violet,* owned and commanded by Thomas Phamphlet, generally known as Captain Tom, was becalmed off this point, when a party of surveying officers from HMS *Plumper* came off from the island and visited Phamphlet, hence the name "Tom Point".

VESUVIUS BAY — After HM paddle sloop *Vesuvius,* 6 guns, 976 tons, 280 hp by Capt. Richards, 1859.

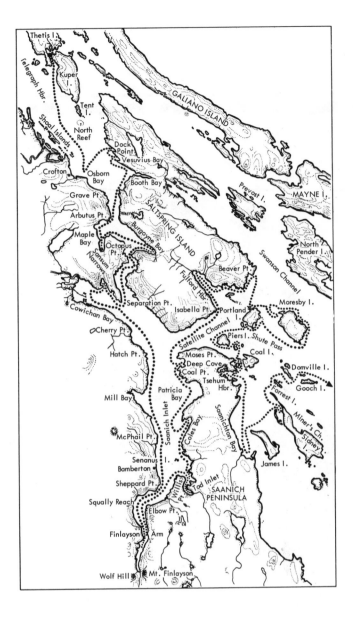

Part IV

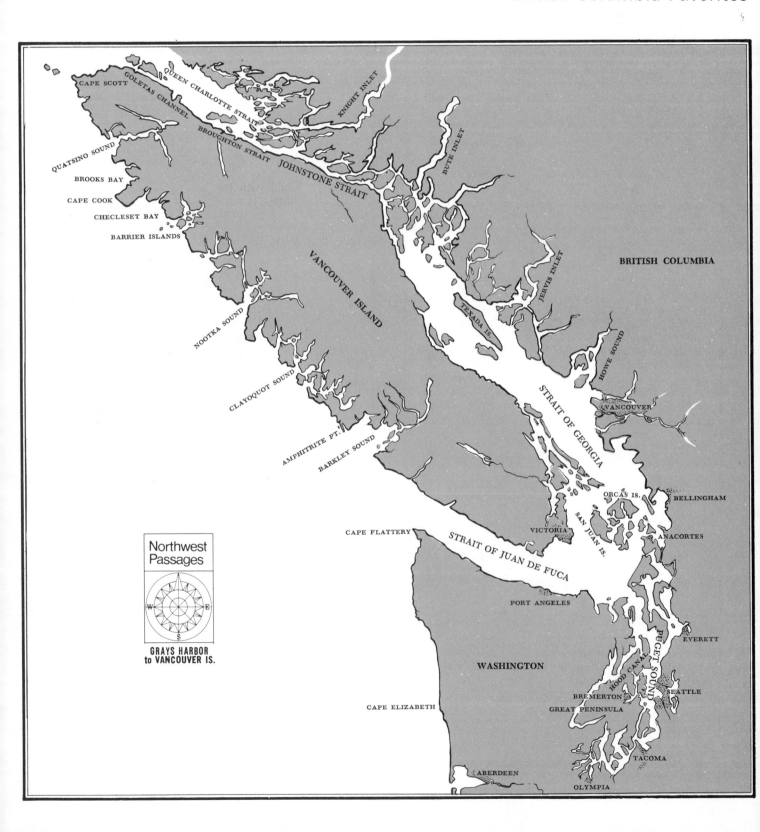

CAPE SCOTT
GOLETAS CHANNEL
QUEEN CHARLOTTE STRAIT
KNIGHT INLET
BROUGHTON STRAIT
QUATSINO SOUND
BROOKS BAY
JOHNSTONE STRAIT
BUTE INLET
CAPE COOK
CHECLESET BAY
BARRIER ISLANDS
JERVIS INLET
BRITISH COLUMBIA
VANCOUVER ISLAND
NOOTKA SOUND
TEXADA IS.
HOWE SOUND
VANCOUVER
STRAIT OF GEORGIA
CLAYOQUOT SOUND
AMPHITRITE PT.
BARKLEY SOUND
ORCAS IS.
BELLINGHAM
VICTORIA
SAN JUAN IS.
ANACORTES
CAPE FLATTERY
STRAIT OF JUAN DE FUCA
PORT ANGELES
PUGET SOUND
EVERETT
Northwest Passages

W E
S

GRAYS HARBOR
to VANCOUVER IS.

WASHINGTON
HOOD CANAL
BREMERTON
SEATTLE
GREAT PENINSULA
CAPE ELIZABETH
TACOMA
ABERDEEN
OLYMPIA

22
Rugged Alberni

Rugged virgin-timbered shores, snow-clad mountain peaks, several different kinds of fish, the scenic grandeur of primitive country, supplies and facilities readily available and fresh or salt waters to delight the heart of any boatman can all be found in one package.

Each year more and more small boatmen from farther and farther away are discovering the Alberni region of Vancouver Island.

An easy 52 miles from Nanaimo or 125 miles from Victoria over excellent highways, the twin cities of Alberni and Port Alberni nestle in a valley on the harbor marking the head of Alberni Inlet.

To the trailer sailor this region offers a variety of interesting choices. Two good launching ramps give access to the waters of the harbor from which he can cruise out Alberni Inlet to Barkley Sound, the Pacific Ocean and as much of the west shore of Vancouver Island as he cares to explore. Once outside the Sound, however, much will depend on weather conditions.

The entire 35 miles of the inlet provides top fishing for Coho or Tyee salmon with many of the huge fighting Tyee having been boated right in the harbor within sight of Port Alberni's main street. Another favorite spot is around Nahmint about halfway down the inlet. 40- to 50-pounders are not at all unusual.

Just about any type of supplies desired can be found in stores or modern shopping centers in the twin cities. It's a good idea to stock up here as many things are not available in the smaller communities along the way. For instance, many of the more remote fish buying stations have ice, but only the chipped or shaved type.*

Good docks, water and home-cooked meals are available at Nahmint Lodge. Ice, frozen herring, water and groceries can be found at Bamfield, located at the entrance to Alberni Inlet in Barkley Sound.

Natives and local fishermen all through the area are most friendly and hospitable. They will offer you their honest opinions on the best lure or bait to use, but few of them agree so you'll have to make up your own mind. Regardless of your choice, however, it's almost a certainty you'll get your share of fish.

Barkley Sound with its cruising, fishing and sight-seeing possibilities is not recommended for the small boatman if he comes up the outside of the island, but via the Alberni region it becomes easily accessible and promises never-to-be forgotten experiences and memories.

For those desiring fresh-water cruising and fishing the region offers two of the largest lakes on the island. Five miles northwest of Alberni is Sproat Lake with 140 miles of indented shoreline and waters of 72° temperature in the summer guarded over by snow-topped Mt. Klitsa.

An excellent concrete-ribbed launching ramp is located in the Provincial Park which also provides picnic facilities and a swimming beach.

Those with an interest in Indians and history will enjoy

From Port Alberni's municipal dock, looking down harbor, can be seen the opening to the 35-mile long Alberni Inlet leading from this inland seaport to Barkley Sound and the Pacific Ocean. Catching 50-pound Tyee salmon is not uncommon here.

the ancient Indian petroglyphs to be found in the park near one end of the lake.

The lake itself is roughly in the shape of a cross, the four arms each offering a variety of fishing and scenic spots to delight the boatman. Four resorts on the lake provide gas, launching and marine service as well as meals and lodging.

Sproat Lake is also the scene of an annual outboard regatta held each July.

Fishing is good for Steelhead, Cutthroat, Rainbow of Kamloops trout and here again local fishermen and natives are happy to furnish their well considered advice although about all they agree on is that there are fish in the lake.

Another five miles farther along the same road from

*The twin cities have become one–Port Alberni.

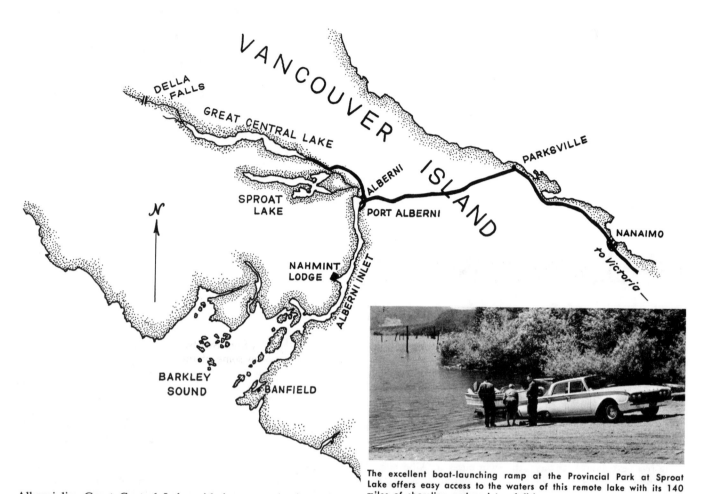

The excellent boat-launching ramp at the Provincial Park at Sproat Lake offers easy access to the waters of this remote lake with its 140 miles of shoreline and variety of fish.

Alberni lies Great Central Lake with its mountain-rimmed 22 miles of boating and fishing pleasure. If you're looking for a chance to stretch those sea legs a bit, an 11-mile hike from the head of the lake will bring you to Della Falls, the highest in North America.

Whether you cruise to relax, fish, explore, enjoy the scenery or a combination of these, you'll find them all, with perhaps a slightly different flavor, in this comparatively unknown frontier country.

More and more frequently the statement is heard that you haven't really cruised British Columbia waters until you've cruised in the Alberni region. Its sheer remoteness will be a barrier to many but for the adventurous soul with that ever-present drive to see the "other side of the hill," this area pays dividends to those ambitious enough to try it. Those who have gone once always leave with the promise to return when they can spend more time.

23
Barkley Sound

It was mid-afternoon of a bright July day. He stood bracing himself against the port rail as he watched the huge breakers dash themselves into grotesquely shaped fountains of spray on towering rocks along the shore. This was a change from the scene he had been enjoying for several leagues where the rollers had been chasing each other up a long sandy beach.

Life was good. He savored the salty tang of the air while drinking in the beauty of diamonds dancing in the sun on the wave tops and the dark green of evergreens which faded into the deeper hues of snow capped peaks in the background. Since leaving England in August and sailing more than half-way around the globe he'd spent a month in Nootka Sound. The trading there had been profitable and his original 3000-pound investment in the venture was well protected.

As his ship rose and fell on the swells, driven by a fresh nor'westerly, his thoughts turned to the lovely young bride he had brought along on this voyage. She had proved herself a good sailor and he was proud of her. He wasn't exactly sure why he had ordered an east-by-south course from Nootka instead of the more usual southerly or westerly ones. Perhaps it was an overpowering curiosity about the coast of this strange country or possibly, anticipating long weeks of sailing the open ocean, he wanted contact with land as long as he could have it.

Presently his attention was attracted to what appeared to be an opening in the shoreline ahead. The rising spume of surf on rocks jutting out from a point suddenly subsided and didn't continue for some leagues in the distance. Impatiently, he waited for the ship to come abeam of the point and what he now could determine was a group of islands.

The ship continued on her course until he could see an extensive body of water opening up to the northwest. Course was changed and the *Imperial Eagle* under the command of 25-year-old Captain Charles William Barkley entered the sound which he named for himself.

Barkley Sound is today one of those rare areas ideally suited for the cruising yachtsman yet still very much the same as it was on that day in 1787 when Capt. Barkley discovered it. Lying on the west coast of Vancouver Island about 20 miles from Swiftsure Bank or 36 miles from Neah Bay, it contains some of the most interesting and beautiful unspoiled cruising waters to be found in the Northwest.

It isn't the nearest or easiest place to get to from Puget Sound or British Columbia ports but, given a break in the weather, the skipper who tries it will find himself amply rewarded. Portland yachtsmen discovered it years ago; yet despite the long run out the Columbia River and the sometimes rough passage up the Washington coast, they go back year after year. Once seen, there's a magnetic attraction which insists on return visits for further exploration and enjoyment.

The outboarder can enjoy the charms of this distant paradise by trailering to Port Alberni and entering the sound by way of Alberni Inlet.

The yachtsman pays for his pleasures in this area, in the long and possibly rough passage to get there. He must be ever alert for the multitude of rocks and reefs. He must be willing to put up with chipped "fish" ice instead of block ice.

Whatever the problems, a western skipper's cruising experience is not complete until he visits Barkley Sound.

The 1964 Norpac was sailed in these waters for the first time, and many of those participating stayed after the racing for cruising. Others have scheduled future trips.

Like the San Juans, a count of islands in the sound will vary according to one's definition of an island. However, over 200 pieces of land surrounded by water can qualify in anyone's dictionary and there are enough rocks and islets to bring a total figure well over 1000.

Cape Beale marks the southeastern entrance to the sound. Barkley named it after his purser, John Beale, although a year later when Capt. John Meares was there he took credit for naming it. According to Mrs. Barkley's diary, there was no love lost between Meares and Barkley. She accuses Meares of confiscating her husband's charts and journals and, in several instances, crediting to himself information contained in them.

With a high regard for his young wife, Barkley used her three maiden names, Frances Hornby Trevor, in naming points in his sound. There is Frances Island, one of the first islands he saw as he discovered the sound; Hornby

Rock at one of the main entrances; Hornby Peak and Trevor Channel, a main channel leading to Alberni Inlet.

To two other main channels which divide the sound he gave names dear to him, Imperial Eagle for his ship and Loudoun for a former ship.

The sound can be roughly divided into three sections for purposes of description. The easternmost of these would take in everything to the east of an imaginary line running northeasterly up Imperial Eagle Channel. The chain of islands between Imperial Eagle and Trevor channels is known as the Deer Group.

This chain consists of Tzartus Island, the largest in the

Benson Island (center)
with Effingham Island
in center background

sound, and five fair sized islands with a host of smaller ones scattered around and between them. Aside from passages on either end of the chain, there is only one break where Satellite Passage offers navigable access between Imperial Eagle and Trevor Channels. Small boats with local knowledge can negotiate between some of the islands but caution should be used.

One such passage is Dodger Channel near the southwestern end of the chain. It was named by Capt. Pamphlett of the schooner *Meg Merrilies* when he ducked in to escape from a storm. Encountering Capt. Richards of H.M. Surveying Vessel *Plumper* in the channel, he remarked, "It is a fine place to dodge the weather in." Capt. Richards replied, "That is so and it will be forever known as Dodger's Cove."

About a quarter of the way up Trevor Channel on the east side are Bamfield and Grappler Inlets with a common entrance. In Bamfield the yachtsman can find protected anchorage and moorage as well as a customs clearing station, gas docks, groceries and a complete machine shop.

Bamfield is more of a scattered settlement than a town, with houses all around the inlet. It was originally named after W. E. Banfield (spelled with an "n"), who came here as a ship's carpenter on HMS *Constance* in 1846. The name accidentally became Bamfield (with an "m") due to some clerical error at the time a post office was established there.

The settlement first started when the Canadian Overseas Telecommunication Corporation was established with cables leading out to points all over the world. The abandoned buildings of the cable station still dominate the eastern side of the inlet although fishing is now the major occupation of most of the inhabitants.

Of particular interest is the variety of vessels used for fishing. Many of them have hulls dug out, Indian fashion, from cedar or spruce logs. With their tall trolling poles, tinkling gear and low freeboard they hardly look seaworthy enough for a lake, let alone the ocean; yet they may be seen all through the islands, as well as bobbing like match sticks on the high ocean swells. They also serve as a means of transportation around Bamfield Inlet. A trip to the store, post office or social event is made by boat rather than by car.

Grappler Inlet, while quite an extensive waterway, is shallow beyond Port Desire where there are several floats.

Trevor Channel, fairly well protected by the Deer Group Islands, offers several anchorages in addition to Bamfield and Grappler Inlets. Entrance Anchorage, between Helby Island and the Wizard Islet group, Roquefeuil Bay, Poett Nook, Sproat Bay and Christie Bay are all well protected.

Alberni Inlet takes off from the northeast end of Trevor Channel culminating at Port Alberni, largest town in the area where the yachtsman can fulfill all his needs. Shores on either side of the inlet are of rugged rocks rising abruptly from water's edge to the summits of mountains. Approaching the head the land flattens out.

Uchucklesit Inlet with good anchorage in Elhlateese Cove and Snug Basin offers an interesting side trip.

The middle section of Barkley Sound lying between Loudoun and Imperial Eagle Channels consists of the Broken Group, innumerable large and small islands with a generous sprinkling of small islets and rocks. A first glance at the chart might discourage a skipper from attempting to penetrate these islands, but a large scale chart and a bit of study mixed with caution will be well rewarded with some of the most enjoyable and scenic cruising he has ever experienced.

Evergreen clad islands, most of them looking exactly as they did to Capt. Barkley nearly 200 years ago, reflect their stately elegance in the clear blue-green mirror surrounding them. The muffled throb of your motor is the only sound to answer the cry of a sea gull or the satisfied-with-life song of a bird. The wavelets of your wake caress a sandy or pebbly beach or curiously explore between masses of driftwood on a more rocky lee shore.

Trees on the outer fringe of islands mutely tell of their struggles with storms of the Pacific while those in your protected anchorage illustrate their peaceful life by gracefully swaying their arms in a slow hula-like dance.

The fighting salmon, cod and sea bass challenge your skill while the crabs or shrimp argue over the entrance to your trap. Clams and king-size scallops are abundant and the skin diver returns from the depths with a sackful of abalone while the pungent smoke from the hibachi in the stern mingles with air so fresh it forces you to breathe more deeply.

1. Looking across Howell Island toward Effingham Island. The many small islets and rocks which make navigation hazardous add to the beauty of the Sound.

2. The entrance to Ucluelet Inlet sets a picturesque scene in the western corner.

3. Coaster Channel in the Broken Group is one of the passage through this interesting and scenic group of islands.

4. Rugged rocks guard the entrance to Effingham Bay, one of the best and most beautiful anchorages.

5. The hull of this 25-foot Bamfield Inlet fishing boat is carved out of a huge spruce log.

1.

2.

3.

4.

5.

You're in a world apart, a world so far removed from the pressures of civilization that you find yourself wondering if you should return to it. Here is solitude, peace, quiet and relaxation, all for the taking.

The chart shows the islands of this Broken Group arranging themselves in smaller groups like square dancers, with protected anchorages in their middle. Several navigable channels thread through the group with enticing scenic passes between islands inviting you to explore further. Some of the best bays are so well protected that care must be used in entering.

One of the finest anchorages in the group is found in Effingham Bay. Capt. John Meares describes his first visit there in 1788: "The long boat was sent to find the anchoring ground and returned to pilot us into a fine spacious port where we anchored in 8 fathoms water over a muddy bottom and securely sheltered from wind and sea. A large number of natives came off in their canoes and brought abundance of fish, among which were salmon, trout, cray and other shellfish with plenty of wild berries and onions. These people belonged to a large village situated on the summit of a very high hill. This port we named Port Effingham in honor of the noble lord of that title."

Another excellent anchorage is in the center of a group formed by Dodd, Willis, Turtle, Walsh and Chalk Islands.

Others can be readily found on the charts.

The third section of the sound includes islands in and to the west of Loudoun Channel. While exquisitely picturesque, these islands are more scattered and do not afford attractive anchorages except at the far northern end. Here several bays and Pipestem Inlet offer the yachtsman good cruising waters, protected harbors and interesting territory for exploring.

Ucluelet Inlet, running up in back of Amphitrite Point, marks the western boundary of Barkley Sound. Here the village of Ucluelet is a good shopping center for the yachtsman with floats, stores, gas docks and other services. Further up the inlet good anchorage is found.

Amphitrite Point was named in 1859 by Captain Richards of the *Plumper* after HM Frigate *Amphritrite* which was on this station from 1851 to 1857. In Greek mythology, Amphitrite was King Neptune's wife — the Goddess of the Seas. The name is appropriate for the point is surrounded by rocks and reefs. There are several small passages but they are treacherous and difficult to navigate in bad weather.

Barkley Sound, originally called Nitinat by the Indians, is almost a last frontier, beckoning the yachtsman to partake of its tranquil serenity amidst a pristine beauty of emerald isles like gems set in a crown of silver. Once he has been there chances are he will return again and again.

24
Gulf Crossing Stop-Overs

Even the saltiest skipper can have a first mate who is squeamish about crossing the Strait of Georgia. And who can really blame her, for "The Gulf," as Canadian yachtsmen love to call it, is a mighty temperamental bit of water which can kick up not only unpleasant seas but, at times, dangerous boating conditions. Yet it must be crossed in order to enjoy the infinite variety of the world's finest cruising waters to the north.

Probably the most used crossing is the stretch from Nanaimo to Welcome Pass. Nanaimo, of course, is almost a "must" on any northern cruising itinerary whether it be the northern terminus of a Gulf Islands vacation or a way point for those heading further up. It's a full fledged town with every possible facility and there's plenty of interest for all hands if weather demands a one or two-day wait for the crossing.

The usual course direct to Merry Island Light, or a bit more to the west to pass between Merry and Thormanby Islands, is about 15 miles of open water. Seasoned yachtsmen generally agree that a late afternoon or early evening crossing is most likely to find the best conditions.

There are those who like the far western route up the east coast of Vancouver Island but it's a long grind with very few suitable protected places to sneak into if the weather should turn bad.

A third and little used route not only offers the answer for that squeamish first mate but also provides some enticing cruising waters. Its principal merits are that it can be broken up into short hops without ever being exposed to more than six miles of open water at a time.

If all seems well in Nanaimo's Departure Bay, one can head out the channel, round the Horswell Rock Buoy and lay a course northwesterly toward the Ballenas Islands. If, after rounding Lagoon Head and proceeding a short distance, the seas are more than the first mate likes, the course can be changed to a westerly one to head into Nanoose Harbor. From here to another haven in the Ballenas Islands is only four miles, and from the Ballenas Islands to the south tip of Lasqueti Island is five and a half miles.

Lasqueti offers all kinds of harbors if needed or, if the seas look agreeable, there are only five miles of open water

from the southern tip of Texada Island to the Thormanby Islands or six miles into Smuggler Cove or Secret Cove. Yes, it's a little longer, but not much, and the added feeling of security for the first mate (and some skippers, too) can be well worth the extra few miles.

When we checked this route out we left Nanaimo in the morning. Once out in the Strait we found a good easterly already building up so we headed into Nanoose Harbor, so named for a band of Indians who once lived there. Even in the bay seas ran high but by getting in behind and up close to the breakwater, we found a comfortable anchorage.

About seven o'clock that evening winds died, so we snaked our way through the Ada Islands and made a flat water crossing to Squitty Bay on the southeastern end of Lasqueti Island with no need for a stop at the Ballenas Islands. We could have continued on to Secret Cove but wanted to explore the area more thoroughly.

Although Squitty Bay is not well known to many yachtsmen, it is a favorite haven for fishermen and a truly delightful spot. It's easy to miss as its entrance looks like another of the many rocky little bays and coves that make up this shore of Lasqueti. We took a range on the two points at the south end of the island and used the stop watch to make the 8/10ths of a mile to the entrance.

There is reportedly an underwater rock about mid-channel in the entrance. We were told this is not the rock shown on the chart and advised to leave the charted rock to port, staying close to it and skirting the southern shore. We did this on a slow bell and experienced no difficulty, although people we met in the bay said they always skirted the northern shore. We tried this going out and, again, had no trouble. Apparently the right thing to do is stay away from center channel at the entrance.

The bay itself is long (but not very long) and narrow. There is a government float with room for six or eight boats but the gas dock and store have been closed. The shore, like the entire end of the island, is rocky. Trees on the higher ridges lean to leeward, bent by the winds off the Gulf. A short hike will unfold many scenic vistas as well as plenty of photographic possibilities. We heard a rumor that the entire area had been purchased for private

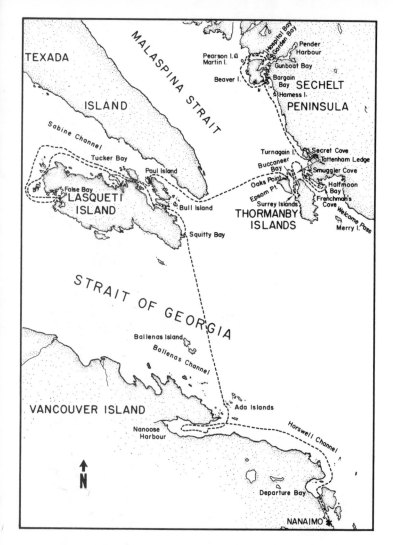

Tucker, secretary for many years to Sir John Jervis, Earl of St. Vincent, and Jedediah Island for Tucker's eldest son, Jedediah Stephens Tucker.

Aside from its possibilities as a storm haven, Lasqueti and the smaller islands around it are well worth a visit. Oysters and clams are abundant and the fishing is excellent.

When the southeasterly subsided we crossed to the Welcome Pass area. Yachtsmen are inclined to think of this as a way point when heading farther north or only as a likely place to wait for propitious weather for a southerly Gulf crossing. But there is plenty here for vacation of cove-hopping, loafing, swimming, fishing, oystering and clamming. Large scale chart #3509 should be carefully used in these waters.

The sloping sandy beach connecting the Thormanby Islands is excellent for swimming and picnicking although the harbor doesn't offer much protection except in calm weather. Tattenham Ledge stretches up from South Thormanby Island. There is a cut through it but, unless you have local knowledge of where it is, better be safe and go around the light at the tip of the ledge.

Frenchman's Cove, on the northwestern corner of Halfmoon Bay, is a delightful scenic spot. Care should be taken in entering and larger boats should use caution in anchoring if staying through a low tide. A favorite activity is the dinghy exploration of the labyrinth of channels among the rocks and islets. Many starfish of various sizes and colors are found here.

At the upper end of Welcome Pass on the peninsula is another favorite hideout with the romantic name of Smuggler Cove. There are several good anchorage spots among the rocks and small islands. Our preference is for one near the far end of the cove. A rock lying in the center of the entrance channel is covered at about half tide, so

Allen's Store in Secret Cove is a favorite source of supplies for yachtsmen heading both north and south.

favor the port shore on entering.

Secret Cove, less than a mile north of Smuggler Cove, is really a collection of several secret coves with the entrance around the south end of Turnagain Island. Here again a rock, a fairly large one this time, lies in center channel with a marker on it. Passage can be made on either side, but the favored entrance is midway between the rock and the shore of Turnagain Island.

With its several arms and little nooks, there are at least six good anchorage spots, all well protected. There is room in some for several boats to raft together or there are small bights with the seclusion of a one-boat anchorage. Oysters can be obtained and there is a fine clam beach on the east shore of the cove southeast of the store. The Secret Cove area also boasts a good parking lot where

use so it's possible it may not be available to yachtsmen in the future.

It was a good thing we had decided on a day or two to explore in this area, for a 25-30 knot southeasterly was whipping the Gulf into a fury. Even Sabine Channel between Lasqueti and Texada Islands was white with rolling breakers. Several small coves on Lasqueti, west of Bull and Jedediah Islands offered quiet anchorages but both Tucker Bay, further along on the north shore, and False Bay, on the west end, were receiving wave reaction from the southeasterly. There are large scale charts for both these bays; #3509 for False Bay and #3508 for Tucker Bay, and it's a good idea to have these aboard.

A store, post office and gas dock are at the settlement of Lasqueti in False Bay but there are no facilities in Tucker Bay. We found a lovely little cove near the northwest tip of Jedediah Island with its entrance opposite Paul Island and spent a peaceful night there even though the breakers were still churning up the channel around the corner.

Names and their sources are always fascinating to us. Lasqueti Island was named in 1791 by Spanish naval officer Jose Maria Narvaez who was in Lt. Eliza's expedition from Nootka. The Ballenas Islands were discovered and named in 1791 "Islas de las Ballenas"— Islands of the Whales — by the Eliza expedition. Sabine Channel was named in 1861 by Capt. Richards after Major-General Edward Sabine, R.A., president of the Royal Society and a well known scientist. Tucker Bay is named for Benjamin

90

guests driving up to meet a boat for a vacation period can park their cars.

Another feature of Secret Cove is the excellent marine facility operated by Fred and Joyce Allen. A government float with water and a complete fuel dock leads up to their fine store. Groceries, meats, drug sundries, marine hardware, fishing gear and tackle, frozen herring and ice are available. There are also laundry facilities and the cleanest showers we've found anywhere with a fresh floor mat for each shower customer. The Allens are friendly, bend over backwards to keep the store well stocked and have everything neat and clean. No matter where your favorite anchorage may be in the Welcome Pass area, you aren't more than a short run from a source of supplies at the Allens'.*

Dr. Byron Ward's Seaward anchors in Smuggler Cove on a peaceful summer afternoon.

For those who like an occasional meal ashore it's just a short hike up the hills to the Jolly Roger Inn, a rustic resort set in the trees overlooking the cove. We have enjoyed excellent breakfasts and dinners here.

There isn't much connection between yachting and horse racing yet, incongruous as it may seem, many of the names in the Welcome Pass area are the result of an interest by Capt. Richards and his crew in the sport of kings. The Thormanby Islands are named after the race horse, Thormanby, who won the Derby in 1860 while Richards was surveying these waters. Welcome Pass is so named on account of the welcome news of Thormanby's win. Merry Island is named after Mr. Merry, wealthy iron master and owner of Thormanby.

Although it may take some of the romance away from those who have visualized Buccaneer Bay as a former rendezvous of pirates, it's necessary to report that it, too, is named for a horse. Buccaneer was a contemporary of Thormanby. Other names in the area connected with the turf are Epsom and Oaks Points on North Thormanby, Tattenham Ledge and the Surrey Islands.

Five and a half miles farther up the coast is Bargain Bay. Exposed to both southeast and southwest winds, it doesn't offer much in the way of protected anchorage although the scenic beauty of its islands is great. It is also an excellent fishing spot with many "lunkers" being taken here each summer.

Just to the north around Beaver Island is Pender Harbor, a long inlet with innumerable bays, coves and anchorages. Fishing is excellent both inside the bay and outside around Pearson and Martin Islands. Those wonderful small shrimp are also available if you have the proper trap with 250 to 300 feet of line on it.

Pender Harbor has about everything the yachtsman could desire. Lloyd's store, on the neck of land to Garden Peninsula separating Garden and Hospital Bays, carries a complete line of fine meats, fresh and frozen vegetables

Looking out of the entrance to Smuggler Cove, South Thormanby Island can be seen, with Texada Island in the distance.

and fruits, hardware and ice. A fuel float is located next to the government floats in Hospital Bay. A hospital, hotel and tavern are also on the peninsula. Both private and government floats, marinas and resorts can be found around the perimeter of the harbor.†

For those in need of repairs on either boats or motors, the Garden Bay Boat Works, Ltd., on the eastern shore of Garden Bay has a marine ways and owner Denny Harling is an excellent mechanic.‡

As a provisioning point, a jumping-off spot for cruises to Princess Louisa, Desolation Sound or waters farther north, or a complete vacation area in its own right, Pender Harbor is such a well known and popular place that further details are superfluous. A word of warning might be in order, however, about taking a larger boat into Gunboat Bay at the head of the harbor. While there is adequate water inside the bay, the narrow, rather restricted channel into it is shallow and every year a few boats in search of clams or oysters have been caught by a low tide and forced to wait for the next high. Better check the tide tables carefully or else go by dinghy. Although we have not yet tried it ourselves, we have been told that it is possible to take a modest sized cruiser through Bargain Narrows between Beaver Island and the mainland, but only at high tide and if you need less than 13 feet of vertical clearance. Large scale chart #3510 will not only enhance your pleasure of exploring in Pender Harbor but will add to your feeling of security by clearly showing the shoal areas and water depths.

If your cruising itineraries haven't yet included some time spent around Lasqueti Island or in the Welcome Pass areas, we hope you will take the time some summer to enjoy them.

*The Allens sold Secret Cove Marina which has been enlarged and improved. The Jolly Roger Restaurant was destroyed by fire in 1976 but the Marina there is operating.
†The hospital was converted to the Sunshine Inn open in the summer.
‡Garden Bay Boat Works is closed but the adjacent Penga Marina offers repair facilities.

25
Sounding out Howe Sound

After a couple of "days out" in the stuffiness of civilization and big city life, it was good to be back on course again. We fueled, watered, iced, provisioned, showered, laundered and said farewell to friends at Royal Vancourver Yacht Club's Coal Harbour moorage. English Bay was calm, as though confirming the weather forecast for fair with light winds.

It was almost a right angle turn around Point Atkinson as we swung onto a 307° (M) heading to explore Howe Sound, an intriguing fragment of the sea too frequently missed by American yachtsmen. Canadian skippers, particularly from the Vancouver area, are well aware of the charms of this island-filled inlet so abundantly blessed by nature to provide all the elements of good cruising close at hand. They make good use of it.

The American, on the other hand, either heads for favorite areas farther up the Strait or, if he has been to Vancouver, is so anxious to get north that he by-passes a cruising experience which certainly should be included in some summer's itinerary.

It was the middle of June, 1792, when Captain George Vancouver explored the body of water which he named Howe's Sound in honor of Admiral Richard Howe, one of three brothers all of whom played an important part in early American history during Revolutionary War times.

The Sound itself stretches northward and northeastward from Point Atkinson on the east and Gower Point on the west. In the entrance are several islands and islets dividing it into main channels. From east to west there are Queen Charlotte Channel, Collingwood Channel, Barfleur Passage and Shoal Channel.

With Point Atkinson on our starboard quarter we could see across Queen Charlotte Channel to its western side starting at Point Cowan on Bowen Island. A short distance north is Seymour Bay with a government wharf.

We were careful to leave the Grebe Islets and nearby shoals and rocks well to starboard and soon had Passage Island, in mid-channel, on our port beam.

Names in these northwest waters are interesting things and sometimes confusing. Many geographical features were named by Capt. Vancouver and other explorers long ago. Today the names on some charts differ, depending on whether they are published in Canada or the U.S. and frequently a local name has been substituted and is better known than the one given on a chart. For our purpose here we will use names as shown on the Canadian charts with U.S. chart names in parenthesis.

The first of these is Eagle Harbour (Johnson Cove) which lay to our starboard on the mainland. Just above it is spectacular Fisherman Cove (Robson Cove), home of West Vancouver Yacht Club, Vancouver's largest marina and a popular spot for moorage, fuels, bait, tackle, repairs and just about anything the mariner would need.

Still farther up is Batchelor Cove (some call it Garrow Bay) which also has marine services and supplies.*

Rounding White Cliff Point, we swung to starboard, rounded Lookout Point, swung more to starboard to clear Tyee Point (Robertson Point) and enter Horseshoe Bay. Here is a complete community with government and private wharves and floats and everything from doctors to a beauty shop. Ferries to various points on the Sound make frequent departures from this bay which is just a comfortable drive from downtown Vancouver

On a westerly course to Bowen Island the number of craft of all kinds and sizes with fishing gear in use substantiated the report that fishing was good in these waters. Here we also got our first full-scale impression of this arm of an inland sea.

It might be likened to a prelude or overture to the symphony of scenic vistas which the yachtsman continually enjoys on all British Columbia cruises. Great numbers of rock-clad mountains are gathered in convention around the perimeter of a horseshoe bowl. The taller ones behind, with their snowy peaks seeming to blow smoke rings of fleecy clouds around their lofty heads, crowd the shorter ones standing with their feet in the sea. The dissolving snows rush in foaming torrents from the frigid summits in long white shafts or foaming cascades down the rugged sides and broken chasms in a relentless search for the sea.

The water, carpeting the floor of the bowl, is dotted with a variety of islands so shaped to provide the land dweller with many excellent plots for a home or summer cottage and the boatman with innumerable coves, bays and inlets for exploring or anchoring.

92

*This facility is closed.

Snug Cove (Wharf Cove) and Deep Bay (Lodge Cove) share a common entrance on the east side of Bowen Island. The island itself is most conspicuous with its own Mt. Gardner rising to a smooth, round, partly-bare summit of 2460 feet.

Snug Cove, while quite narrow, offers an excellent sheltered anchorage in about nine fathoms as well as a government wharf and floats. Fuels, an inn, post office, store, cafe, and repairs are available.

Deep Bay, with mostly private residences, is open to the southeast which allows swells to roll in while sunken rocks extend into the bay from its south shore. A short distance north of Deep Bay is Millers Landing where there is a government wharf and float during the summer season.

Continuing up the east side of Bowen Island we took a look at Cates Bay then rounded Finisterre Island to Hood Point, the northeastern extremity of the island. Here we passed many small bays and indentations with summer homes and private floats.

Bowyer Island, lying due north of Horseshoe Bay and northeast of Bowen Island has nothing to offer the yachtsman. Our good friend, Seattle garden expert Cecil Solly,* told us an interesting story about it. He says some years ago he was approached by a group of promoters who mistakenly took him for a millionaire in trying to sell him a lot on the island. As part of the sales effort he was taken on a tour of the property. High rocky shores make it practically inaccessible from the water except on a point on the south end. Towards the north end a hill rises to 660 feet with a clear lake on the very top and water cascading down the east side.

The proposal to turn the entire island into a very exclusive park-like home development, private golf course and all, for the very wealthy, eventually fell through. Mr. Solly was flattered to be considered in that class and happy he had a chance to see the island, even to the copper mines on the west side which some Spaniards are supposed to have dug years ago.

Our course continued north to Halkett Bay on Gambier

Government floats and marine park as well as anchoring buoys in Plumper Cove on Keats Island offer a snug harbor for the yachtsman.

Island, where we poked our bow in for a quick look then continued still farther north around Halkett Point and up the east side of the island to Brigade Bay (North Bay). Here we found only summer homes with private floats.

Pam Rock is a prominent islet 26 feet high nearly in mid channel between the mainland and Gambier Island with drying rocks extending about a quarter of a mile both north and south of it. Three quarters of a mile above it is tiny Christie Islet (Cynthia Island).

Anvil Island, so called by Vancouver because of its 2500-foot peak which resembles the horn of an anvil pointed upwards, lies in the northeast portion of the main Sound.

Montagu Channel, running up the east side leads to the long arm extending up to Squamish. Ramillies Channel separates Gambier and Anvil Islands.

Leaving Brigade Bay we set a course just off Irby Point which is quite cliffy and forms the southern tip of Anvil Island. We heard that there is a post office about a mile up the island from the point.

Montagu Channel brought us to Porteau Cove where a settlement on the mainland is now called Glen Eden Park.

The two Shelter Islands lie close to Keats Island and help form protection for Plumper Cove, just to the left, with its government park, wharf and float. Beyond can be seen Shoal Channel, between Keats Island and the point of mainland seen on right.

Snug Cove on Bowen Island offers the yachtsman a cozy harbor in a sylvan setting as well as facilities to supply his needs.

There is good shelter here with private dock and floats, fuels, store, cottages, showers and launching facilities.

Following the steep shoreline of the mainland, we entered the dog-leg reach extending some eight miles north and northeast. About four miles beyond Porteau Cove is Britannia, a Port of Entry mining town with two wharves, customs office and complete community to provide just about all needs.

After rounding Watts Point, Squamish came into view with a spectacular waterfalls cascading down the side of a mountain about a mile south.

This town, with its government boat basin, wharf and floats, have everything a yachtsman might need and has become the rendezvous point for Royal Vancouver Yacht Club's Annual Easter weekend outing. Members come by boat, air or road for a program of activities which includes skiing at nearby points, bus trips for sightseeing in beautiful Squamish Valley and Alice Lake, lunch at Paradise Valley Restaurant in the heart of the mountains, a special dinner and evening dancing.

Coming back down the inlet Woodfibre is a town opposite Watts Point in the angle of the dog leg. Although it has some facilities including emergency fuels, it is basically a company town for the large pulp mill and does not offer good overnight accommodations for yachtsmen.

Re-entering the main part of the Sound we left the Defence Islands to starboard and set a course of 222°(M) to clear Domett Point on the north end of Anvil Island and

*Deceased.

93

The Government wharf, floats and anchoring area at Gibsons give access to shops and services in this major center on Howe Sound.

Elkins Point, the northern extremity of Gambier Island. Southwestward, at the head of a bay is Elkins Point Landing, a summer resort with a government float.

Passing the northwestern corner of Gambier Island, Woolridge Island splits the waterway into Latona Passage on the east and Thornbrough Channel on the west. Our course took us past Longview with its logging pier, Seaside Park with a government float and Port Mellon. This is another complete community with pulp and lumber mills and an industrial harbour.

A mile farther south is Hillside with gravel pit, a sawmill and private floats.

We had to swing southeasterly then southwesterly to round Witherby Point. Williamson's Landing, two miles south on the mainland, has a government float and post office and a little beyond is a YMCA camp with a float. Across the Channel on Gambier Island is New Brighton with government wharf and floats, store and post office.

We wanted to explore the three finger bays indenting the southern shore of Gambier Island so we rounded the Grace (Twin) Islands off the southeastern tip of the island. This is a very scenic point with what appear to be both permanent and summer homes. So many places seen on Howe Sound are typical well ordered English country homes, trim and well manicured, with flower gardens, gravel paths, a small float with dinghy and a sailboat moored to a buoy. Carefully trimmed hedges form a guard line against the pine forest and even beaches and rocky shorelines look tide washed and scoured.

Gambier Harbour (Grace Landing) is a short distance up the inside. A government wharf and float lead to the store, post office and a campground located nearby. It is reported that visitors, especially ex-servicemen, are welcomed at Veterans Memorial Hall with special parties on Saturday night and a wet canteen. We made a good guess at the meaning of that last term but were unable to verify it.

West Bay is about a mile in length. In a small cove at the Western entrance is a summer resort and government wharf and float. It's well to pay close attention to the chart in this bay. A rock which dries at three feet lies in center channel and a shoal of drying rocks extend out from the east shore. The head of the bay is used as a log booming ground.

Centre Bay is a mile and a half in length with an average width of a half mile. Sparsely populated with four or five homes and a summer resort, it offers a picturesque and peaceful setting, spoiled somewhat by innumerable log booms. These booms have a value, however, for depths up to 40 fathoms preclude normal anchoring, and the logs offer a good tie for those wishing to spend some time in

the bay. A small island lying about half-way in can be safely passed on either side with a wary eye out for a drying rock off its southeast corner.

The third bay is Port Graves and is one of the principal anchorages in Howe Sound. Its shores are steep, mostly of solid rock and, like its sisters, lined with log booms. The water is considerably shallower with depths up to nine fathoms in the middle and the head drying at two feet. A short distance in on the left side is East Bay with a government float. Well-known Camp Artaban is near the head and boasts a government float.

To complete our circuit of this most interesting Sound, we cruised down the northwest shore of Bowen Island leaving Hutt Island and Hutt Rock on our port. In behind these is Mt. Gardner Park with a government float and a road to the park and across the island to Snug Cove.

Collingwood Channel leads out from the Sound to the Strait of Georgia with Bowen Island to the east. Bowen Bay offers no protection and in Tunstall Bay Camp Cates has a private float.

To the west is a group of islands unofficially known as the Ragged Islands to many yachtsmen, not to be confused with the Copeland Islands which are also called Ragged Island. Ragged, Mickey, Pasley, Hermit and Worlcombe are the principal islands although there are many smaller ones and the passageways between them are cluttered with rocks and foul ground. Without local knowledge any exploration should be limited to a small boat.

Barfleur Passage returns from the Strait to Howe Sound between this group of islands and Keats Island with little Home and Preston Islands lying close to Keats.

Keats is a fairly high island with a bare cliffy hill rising to 795 feet near its middle. Eastbourne is a summer camp with a government float near the southeast corner.

A dock, float and dinghy sailing were found at the head of Centre Bay, one of three inlets indenting the south shore of Gambier Island in Howe Sound.

Swinging westward across the north of Keats Island we could see where the ferry lands at Langdale on the mainland and just below it Hopkins Landing and Granthams Landing, both summer resorts with post office and government floats.

Still further south, protected by a high point called Steep Bluff is Gibsons Landing, shortened in recent years to Gibsons. Here the yachtsman can moor at the government wharf and floats or anchor out in about eight fathoms, while he takes advantage of a complete community of stores, services and repair facilities and the last government liquor store below Powell River.*

Although a large scale chart shows sufficient water for passage to the Strait, through Shoal Channel, shoals and rocks cause the Coast Pilot to warn that it should not be used unless the skipper is in possession of local knowledge. We know some skippers who use it, especially at high tide, but the best advice calls for plenty of caution.

*Henry J. Smith of Smitty's Marina Ltd. at Gibsons, says there are also liquor stores at Madeira Park and Sechelt.

Directly across the Channel from Steep Bluff is a settlement on Keats Island composed mostly of summer homes. There is a post office and government wharf and float.

Turning north, we skirted the partly wooded Shelter Islands which are almost joined together at low water. We gave wide berth to the rock off their northern tip then swung hard over to enter a serene little bay called Plumper Cove. We'd been told this offered a snug anchorage regardless of how hard the wind might be blowing in the Strait so it was chosen as our berth for the night.

Originally we had intended to do some fishing and oyster gathering but the day had been so full of sightseeing and exploring that we hadn't taken time out for these pleasant sports. Plumper Cove boasts a government marine park with both floats and buoys and anchorage in the middle in about seven fathoms. Our late arrival found both floats and buoys occupied so we dropped the hook.

After dinner we sat in the cockpit to watch the world change from light to darkness, a daily phenomenon experienced everywhere but which always seems more enjoyable, more vivid in coloring and more peaceful in mood to those in boats. We sat there long after the sun had set and beckoned its red, orange and purple crown to follow down behind the bluff on the point of mainland separating us from the mighty Strait of Georgia.

After checking the anchor and snugging down for the night, the thought persisted that our cruise on Howe Sound had been a most pleasant experience and that we would recommend it to our friends.

It was easy to understand why Canadians in general and Vancouverites in particular have chosen it for both permanent and summer homes as well as for close-at-hand cruising or sailing. We are certain many American yachtsmen would also enjoy its charms.

Howe Sound looking northeastward from Gibsons. Keats Island is in the foreground on the right and the southeastern tip of Gambier Island on the left.

26

The Skookumchuck
Violent Gateway to Serenity

"Its roar can be heard for several miles!"

"They're the most dangerous rapids in the area!"

"The lives of 27 people have been lost in that mean stretch of water!"

Those are some of the things a yachtsman is apt to hear about the Skookumchuck, or more currently, the Sechelt Rapids and is perhaps a reason why more skippers haven't discovered the delightful boating pleasures lying beyond in Sechelt, Narrows and Salmon Inlets.

Perhaps every one of those statements is true. But they are no cause for missing a trip into these waters. A little bit of simple addition and subtraction with figures found in the Canadian Hydrographic Service's Pacific Coast Tide and Current Tables will tell you when a safe passage may be made on slack water with no trouble or danger. If you're timid, it's a simple matter to check with fishermen or local residents at Egmont and vicinity to verify your figures.

Skookum, in Chinook jargon, means even more than "mighty," "strong," "powerful." Chuck is water or body of water. Skookumchuck is definitely strong or mighty water when four times each lunar day, as the tide rises and falls, an immense amount of water must drive into or out of these inlets at 10 to 12 knots through that narrow neck of a channel. The result is a magnificent surge of force and violence that stirs the imagination to contemplate but holds one spellbound while watching giant whirlpools, ominous boils and eight to ten foot outfalls plunge and seethe in the mad, inexorable drive of water searching for more room.

After the emptying or filling has taken place a period of calm and quiet prevails for approximately nine minutes when even a canoe would find a placid lagoon. The whole trick and secret for the navigator is to establish when those nine minutes will occur and to plan passage, according to the speed of his boat, during or within 15 to 30 minutes before or after.

Skookumchuck Narrows is actually the first three miles of Sechelt Inlet which opens up about one mile SE of Captain Island where Agamemnon Channel joins Jervis Inlet. The lower end of the narrows is obstructed by rocks, islets and shoals in an 1800-foot-wide channel to form Sechelt Rapids.

We left a pleasant moorage at Larson's Resort in Pender Harbor early in August. Swinging wide around Daniel Point to give plenty of clearance to the reef lying off it, we headed almost due north and later northeasterly for the nine mile run up Agamemnon Channel. Some skippers anchor in Green Bay, a small indentation of Nelson Island on the left about four miles up the channel, and make their start from there. Earl Cove, on the right toward the upper end, is the terminus of the road coming up from Langdale and Pender Harbor and is where the ferry takes off for Saltery Bay. Earl Cove and Agamemnon Bay do not afford much protection for overnight anchorage.

A turn to the SE and we are into Skookumchuck Narrows. The three Sutton Islets in center channel have safe passage on either side although the skipper should be aware of two rocks which are awash at low tide a bit southeast of Egmont Point and a rock lying a short way off the tip of the southeasternmost Sutton Islet.

On the right side going in, opposite the Islets, Johnny and Dorothy Bosch, well known in the area, have established the Egmont Marina and Resort. They didn't open until after we were there so we are indebted to Spencer and Ollie Hall of Sausalito, California, for help in this portion of our narrative.†

The Halls were spending their first summer in British Columbia waters cruising in their *Sea Bell*. Coming into Skookumchuck, they wanted to get a little local knowledge to help double check their figures on the rapids. The *Sea Bell* was nosed in toward a little dock where a couple of men were working and Spence hailed them for permission to tie up. While fenders were being placed and preparations made for landing, Spence could see the men busily sweeping off the float.

The joys of cruising in northwest waters are not limited to majestic scenery, meandering passages separating towering mountain peaks, colorful rocky shores or sandy, tide-scoured beaches fading into the vari-shaded greens of forested glades. The people one meets during such cruising are equally delightful and friendships

96

*Larson's Resort is closed.

†This marina is now operated by the Mullers.

(Left) Photographs have a way of making water appear flatter than it actually is. In this picture of the overfall in Sechelt Rapids it is 8 to 10 feet from the upper water level to where the rushing torrent breaks into a back swirl of angry violence at the bottom. (Right) Swirling eddies, upsurging boils, ominous whirlpools and cresting breakers are all a part of the wild torrent of water that passes through Sechelt Rapids four times each lunar day. This picture shows only a portion of the seething confusion of the rapids and was snapped a good hour after the maximum velocity.

thus made are remembered even longer than nature's settings.

With the *Sea Bell* secured and permission granted for a night's layover, Johnny Bosch introduced himself and Jack Clark, his friend and neighbor from across the water. Johnny, a Holland Dutch logger, knows the area like a life-long native. In addition to the usual gas, oil, diesel, outboard fuel, water, kerosene and Standard Oil products, Johnny's new place has cabins with a history. Originally built for war housing in Vancouver, they were later barged north to a lumber camp. Still later Johnny bought them, barged them to his place on the narrows and set them up on shore. Spence admits they look a bit rough on the outside but reports they are beautiful inside with electric refrigeration and all the comforts of "city livin'."

The Boschs also offer guided tours through the rapids, into inlets, up to Princess Louisa or around to Powell River. Their son, Dorn, is an excellent boatman and frequently runs the charter boat or takes out fishing parties.

Introductions over, talk turned to the saltchuck, fishing, cruising and anchoring possibilities and the hundred and one questions a skipper new to an area can ask of local experts. Even before dinner was started Mrs. Bosch sent down some venison and a loaf of just-out-of-the-oven home made bread—the best they'd ever tasted, according to the Halls.

It isn't hard to understand why the Halls stayed around for a week instead of overnight. Each day brought some new adventure or the discovery of more new friends. One of the first adventures occurred when Spence needed a haircut. Johnny allowed as how he could stand one, too, so they crossed over to Jack Clark's. Jack reminded them it was Sunday and he'd have to charge twice as much. Before the operation could begin, however, Mrs. Clark insisted a cup of coffee was in order. Several cups of coffee later, after an hour of talk about the saltchuck, the business at hand was attended to with Spence first up. He says Jack did a fine job of haircutting but when the money was offered he refused to take anything.

"You don't understand how we live up here," he said. "We swap things among each other and any of us calls on the other for skills they may have."

"That's all very well, but I won't be around long enough to swap anything or to offer any service in return," insisted Spence.

"Oh, that's all right," Jack returned. "Just send us a Christmas card."

Spence saw it was useless to argue so, on a return trip later, he left a carton of cigarettes for Jack and his wife.

When the week's stay was over the Halls had been taken on car rides to adjacent lakes, through the rapids in Johnny's 18-footer with two 40-hp motors, on several fishing expeditions with Charles Bradbury of Vancouver, Bill Blakely and Freddy Vaughn and had invited Johnny and Dorothy to cruise the inlets with them.

Other new friends included Mrs. Day, an early pioneer who came across the plains in a covered wagon and proves her interest in Indians with a large collection of artifacts; George Stanton, a retired geologist who loves to talk rocks, display his collection or give a lantern-slide-illustrated lecture on the subject; and Jack Longsdale who came to the region 40 years ago to become a trapper for the winter and is still there. He's married to an Indian princess named Margaret. Although some ninety years of age, she carries her water from a spring, is well educated and crosses the narrows in her canoe at will without benefit of a tide or current table other than her own knowledge of nature's ways.

The Halls are thrilled over their summer's cruising and can hardly wait for another summer to arrive so they can return for more. They are convinced that northwest waters offer not only the finest cruising in the world but the friendliest and most cordial people anywhere.

As to Johnny Bosch's advice, he says give all chartered and known rocks a wide berth in any inlet and when going through any rapids for the first time, go against the current. By doing this, if you've misjudged times, you can always turn around, come out and wait. If you're wrong and going with the current, this isn't always possible and could lead to disaster.

Old time yachtsmen have known Egmont as a small place on the left, or north side of the narrows coming in. The general store, gas float, and docks burned down a few years ago and have not been rebuilt. The Canadian charts show Egmont (P.O. and store) in Secret Bay on the right or south shore and now this is definitely known as Egmont with a store and gas dock. The big rock or reef in the middle of the bay as well as rocks in front of the oil dock are well marked. There is a government wharf leading up to the store and Post Office.

We made a stop here to double check our slack water figures with some fishermen on the dock and were gratified to find our calculations correct. Further verification came from Ted Phillips on *Sea Spray* and Milt Benson on *Cle Illahee*, both of Bremerton YC, who were tied to the Egmont float.

There are two ways to arrive at the time of slack water. The British Columbia Pilot says that high water slack occurs 1 hour and 12 minutes after the corresponding slack in Vancouver's First Narrows. Low water slack is 1 hour and 35 minutes later.

The Canadian Tide and Current Tables says to add 1 hour and 45 minutes to the turn of tide time at Point Atkinson and then add 5 minutes more for each foot of rise or 7 minutes more for each foot of fall of tide at Point Atkinson.

We worked it out both ways and found they both came out fairly close but chose the latter method to run on. It worked out this way on August first:

After converting from Standard Time as shown in the tables to Daylight Savings Time we found tides at Point Atkinson of 2.6 feet at 09:48 and 11.9 feet at 17:22. 17:22 + 1:45 = 19:07. The difference between the high of 11.9 and the previous low of 2.6 gives us 9.3 foot rise. Multiplying this by 5, we get 46½ minutes to add to 19:07. This is 19:53½ or the time of slack water at the rapids.

Sechelt Inlet with its two connecting arms. This scene looks north from Sandy Hook or Four Mile Point, just above Porpoise Bay at the bottom of Sechelt Inlet.

We decided to allow 15 minutes for any deviation so arrived just above the Sechelt Islets, or Earle Islets on older charts, which dot the rapids, at 19:38. The water, although still eddying and boiling slightly, looked safe enough so we went through without any trouble. It was our first experience, exciting for the few minutes of the run, but after it was over we thought only how foolish we had been to be concerned. A later look at the rapids when they were running full bore returned our respect for them but we learned that careful figuring can eliminate any element of danger. Our calculations for getting out worked just as well. Recommended courses through the Islets are shown on the accompanying chart.

Leaving the rapids where the inlet opens into a broader expanse, we set a course to the left of Skookum Island (also known as Bowlder Island on some old charts) and headed for Cawley Point keeping eyes peeled for the rock off the western end of the island and shoals to the north. Storm Bay was our predetermined anchorage for the night.

After the tensions of figuring and running the rapids, the glassy smoothness of the blue-green water reflecting the browns and greens from the forested mountain sides and picking up the golds and reds of the waning sun

Steep, rocky cliffs, forested at lower levels, and snow-capped mountains form the walls of Narrows Inlet in this picture approaching Tzoonie Narrows.

produced a welcome spirit of peace and calmness almost impossible to describe. Passing between Highland and Sockeye Points we got a preview look up Narrows Inlet with its shaded reaches extending an invitation to enter.

We resisted the temptation, knowing that on the morrow we'd have a chance at exploration. Our course was set for the head of Storm Bay where the chart shows a symbol designating a good anchorage. Just inside Cawley Point we passed a small island on the right with a couple of cruisers at anchor in a beautiful little cove behind it. A quick turn of the wheel after a hurried glance at the chart for rocks and shoals brought us into one of the most delightful spots we've ever dropped a hook. The cruisers turned out to be Dan Martin's *Dan-Mar II* and Charley Anderson's *Lazy Gal*, both of Seattle's Queen City YC.

The sylvan beauty of the woods surrounding the cove met the rock bound shore at the high water mark. Tremendous rocks piled on each other like blocks from a child's fallen castle. They were smooth from the endless comings and goings of the tide and, at lower levels, were covered with oysters. The First Mate's description of "intimate beauty" fits the spot exactly. On a plateau above the bay a couple of deserted houses gave evidence of previous enjoyment of the cove and the remains of an old dock on top of the rocks suggested a fisherman's abode. A sign inside one of the houses, written in pencil, invited anyone who wished to use the premises but re-

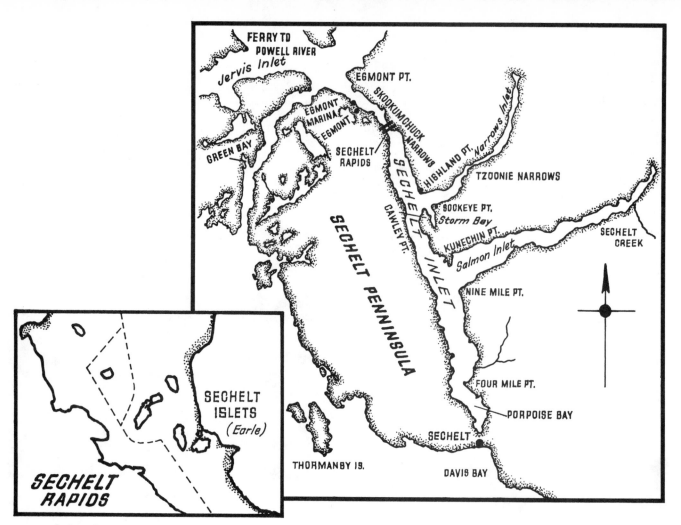

SECHELT
ISLETS
(Earle)

SECHELT
RAPIDS

quested that they be kept clean. It was signed by John Bosch.

A restful night in a secure anchorage readied us for anticipated exploration the next morning. Just around the corner to the northeastward is the reach known as Narrows Inlet. Rounding Sockeye Point was like lifting the covering from a three-dimensional painting of one of nature's masterpieces. Cruising onward, slowly, so we could take in every dramatic detail, we were reminded that someone had compared this inlet with Princess Louisa and we couldn't help but agree. It was the same narrow slit in the mountains, a valley carpeted with water, between majestic peaks, some of them snow-capped. Perhaps they weren't quite as high or quite as steep but the comparison is a good one, nevertheless.

About a third of the way in, the eight-mile length almost closes up to form Tzoonie Narrows, a hundred yard wide passage where the current can run up to 3 or 4 knots. Because of the deep water—45 fathoms in some places—Narrows Inlet does not offer good anchorage. Some skippers solve this, however, by tying to log booms or by using two anchors—one off the stern until it catches on the steep underwater bank and one off the bow onto the shore. We didn't have time to try it, but sea-run cutthroats are reported plentiful beyond Tzoonie Narrows and can be caught with worms and small spinners.

Salmon Arm, to the south, takes off in the same general direction and is similar except for being wider and with a total length of 12½ miles. Care should be taken

to stay well out from the spit or delta at the mouth of Sechelt Creek. Good anchorage can be found in the little cove just west of this spit or at the head of the inlet.

The chart shows a falls at the head but a hydro-electric plant is now there. Floats are marked "No Dockage" and "Don't Use." However Johnny Bosch claims they really don't mind if you get permission and stay just overnight.

With fresh water pouring into the head, trout fishing is good.

Sechelt Inlet continues SSE ending in Porpoise Bay where a ¾ mile hike will take you to the town of Sechelt. For the trailer-boater who wishes to cruise the inlets from the south and miss the rapids, launching can be effected at the Government wharf or from Sandy Hook, marked as Four Mile Point on the charts. We found the wharf at the head of the inlet in poor condition and dirty, not a particularly attractive place to moor.

Extensive logging is done from the camps which can be seen on the shores of all three inlets and all waters abound in Salmon, Cohoe, and Cod with oysters, clams and crabs there for the taking in many places. A good side trip can be made to Clowhom Lakes beyond the head of Salmon Arm and there are many interesting shore hikes. Watch should be kept, however, for the numerous bears that frequent the area during the berry season.

Returning to Storm Bay, we rejoined the *Dan-Mar II* and the *Lazy Gal*. We make no claims of discovery but no one had ever mentioned the rock formation on the

100

left hill when approaching. It forms a remarkable likeness of a smiling Indian face.

All of us made our way to a small cove behind Rapid Islet, lying along the west shore about mid-way between the rapids and Skookum Island. Here we found secure anchorage by putting out both a hook and tying to trees on shore. In a couple of fast outboard runabouts we ran in behind a little hook just below the rapids, got out on the rocks and watched the water put on its show. We stood on rocks forming a point around which the cascading torrents snarled along the shore then deflected their brute force toward mid-channel into an 8 to 10 foot overfall. The falls, fairly smooth on top and in the downward plunge, dissolved into a seething, swirling fury of upsurging boils and huge whirlpools at the bottom and for at least a quarter of a mile beyond. The tremendous push of tidal power in this mad confusion resulted in a crashing, reverberating roar that out-thundered any Wagnerian masterpiece. It was terrifying while it was exalting. No skipper or crew would care to even think of going through the rapids at its maximum velocity, but all should have the opportunity to thrill to this burst of power by doing as we did or by mooring at Egmont or across the narrows and hiking the mile or two down the trails to the narrowest point.

The Skookumchuck can provide a never-to-be-forgotten experience, fascinating your souls with its turbulence or quietly and smoothly introducing you to another wonderland of cruising pleasure. The rapids demand respect but there need be no fear with proper planning and your trip into the inlets will prove a most rewarding cruise.

27

Jervis – Passage to Enjoyment

Although his father wanted him to become a barrister-at-law like himself, John had other ideas. With a love for the sea and an attraction to the navy, he became an able seaman and, with natural ability, attention to duty and a series of brilliant successes, advanced himself to become an admiral, an earl, first Lord of the Admiralty and finally, Admiral of the Fleet.

Admiral Sir John Jervis, Earl of St. Vincent, never saw the inlet which Capt. George Vancouver named in his honor but some 175 years later Northwest yachtsmen are intent upon enjoying its many charms.

Jervis Inlet, or "Jarvis" as the English pronounce it, shows on the chart as only that portion of the inlet from the Gulf of Georgia, along the north shore of Nelson Island to where Prince of Wales Reach begins. From Vancouver's Journal, however, it can be assumed that he intended the name to include the entire inlet clear to its head and probably Hotham Sound and Agamemnon channel as well.

Pender Harbor with its many protected anchorages, moorages, resorts and sources of supplies is a natural jumping-off place for cruising in Jervis Inlet. Agamemnon Channel provides the shortest approach with comfortable, hazard-free cruising through its 9-mile length with an average half-mile width.

Because of distant destinations, most skippers hurry through this channel with hardly more than a glance at the chart and thus miss a delightful little cove worthy of attention. Green Bay offers a secluded and protected spot to drop the hook for lunch, an afternoon snooze or an overnight stop. Beware, though, for this peaceful and quiet beauty has its price. Extremely careful watch must be kept on water depth and tidal heights. There is a shelf of smooth, more or less flat rocks in the inner portion of the bay. Local knowledge is required to get around it but the acquisition of this knowledge is one of the fun-challenges of cruising and the effort is well rewarded.

By leaving Pender Harbor on about a westerly magnetic heading and rounding Cape Cockburn, one comes to the main entrance to Jervis Inlet. Here is a favorite area for many yachtsmen with its host of attractive anchorages.

Billings Bay indents Nelson Island with Hidden Basin affording anchorage. A small islet in the middle of the entrance channel is connected on both sides to the shore and dries at 3 feet of tide, so entrance and exit must be made at or near high tide. Once inside there is plenty of water up to 18 fathoms and an excellent harbor.

Blind Bay is the name given to a sizable bit of water lying between Nelson Island and Hardy Island. With its many islands, islets and coves it has been a popular area for many years. A delightful anchorage is in a small cove on Hardy Island in behind Fox Island. When we visited here in the 'forties the property was owned by California people. From floats in the cove a trail led northwestward across the island for a half-mile to the house with its outdoor fireplace and tidal swimming pool. Friendly deer came out of the woods to eat from our hands. Tom, the caretaker, demonstrated how he had trained a brilliantly colored tropical bird to dance.

All of this is gone now. The house burned down, leaving the lonely fireplace to stand guard over the empty pool and a deserted orchard. The island has been bought for a tree farm but the trail is still there and offers a good opportunity for leg stretching and driftwood hunting along the northwest shore.

Several other little bays and coves cut into the south shore of Hardy Island to provide intimate anchorages almost among the trees.

Across Blind Bay behind a group of small islands is Ballet Bay. Although not as isolated and secluded, here is another fine anchorage. While most of the place names in these parts were given by early Spanish and British explorers and later cartographers, Ballet Bay was more recently named.

It was in the early forties that Harry and Midge Thomas bought property on the bay. Their daughter, Andree, a leading dancer with the Ballet Russe de Monte Carlo, was enchanted with the spot. With its ever-changing scenes of the seasons, the tides, the graceful swooping of the seagulls and the backdrop of snow-capped mountains she likened it to the Ballet. The name became popular and today the charts officially recognize her Ballet Bay.

Cruising northeastward up Blind Bay it narrows as Hardy Island and two small islands off its tip almost touch the shores of Nelson Island to form Telescope Passage leading out into Jervis Inlet. Here are more coves which seem to invite anchorage and an exploration trip ashore. The passage itself is navigable but care should be used. A rock near mid-channel has bent or ruined props and shafts of quite a few unwary pilots in a hurry.

Across the entrance to Jervis Inlet is another haven although not as desirable. Thunder Bay is well protected from westerlies but is fairly open to the easterly winds although the peninsula in back of Thunder Point affords some protection.

Just around the corner from Telescope Pass is Vanguard Bay on Nelson Island. Although fairly open, it affords protected anchorage by choosing the proper shore. Some years ago a marina and real estate development offered good facilities at the head of the bay. This is inactive at the present but a caretaker maintains the floats and permits moorage there for a nominal fee.

A trail of some 850 feet leads to West Lake where there is a dock and float for swimming.

North of the eastern end of Nelson Island is Hotham Sound, extending northward for nearly 8 miles. Two bays at the head of the Sound plus a few scattered small bays offer fair anchorages but are greatly overshadowed by the beauty and protection afforded by the Harmony Islands along the Sound's eastern shore.

These islands are small and will not accommodate many boats at anchor, however, if one is fortunate enough to find a spot, it will be an enjoyable and snug berth. Several times when we found the island's facilities filled to capacity we left Hotham Sound and rounded Foley Head to anchor in Dark Cove. Little Sydney Island protects the cove and makes it a comfortable haven.

Another good possibility, a little further, is Johnnie and Dorothy Bosch's Marina just inside the entrance of Sechelt Inlet. Here is moorage, fuel, supplies, ice and fishing equipment. Sechelt Inlet just beyond with its roaring Skookumchuck Rapids and many other attractions has been covered in an earlier chapter of Northwest Passages.*

Heading northward, Jervis Inlet turns into a series of reaches to form a reversed 'S.' Royally named, they are progressively Prince of Wales Reach, Princess Royal Reach and Queens Reach.

Many people, including native Norwegians, say that the inlets of British Columbia are more spectacular and beautiful than the fjords of Norway. Geologists claim that long ago this inland coast extended clear to the Pacific where an outer range of mountains met the sea with a great valley between them and the next inner range of even higher mountains. Sometime before the last glacial period some giant upheaval of the land mass tilted and partially sank the coastal range, leaving the higher peaks to form Vancouver Island and the thousands of other islands now dotting the vast inland sea which stretches from Puget Sound to Alaska.

The steep cliffs of Princess Louisa dwarf 120-foot-high Chatterbox Falls which in turn dwarfs the boats below.

*Egmont Marina and Resort is now operated by the Mullers.

This peaceful anchorage in the Harmony Islands of Hotham Sound is a favorite of many Northwest yachtsmen.

The sea rushed in to meet the inner mountain range, filling the valleys and entering ancient canyons and river beds, thus making the inlets and reaches we know today. Sheer cliffs, bronzed with moss and tinted with green of scraggly firs, drop to the water's edge and continue down to depths of several hundred fathoms. Anchorage is practically impossible but in many places a ship can be moored alongside the cliff.

Cruising up the winding reaches of Jervis Inlet one has the feeling of being in the giant gorge of some mighty river. Mountains with snow glistening on their peaks and ribbons of white water cascading down their faces reach up into scattered cotton ball clouds leisurely floating in the blue sky. Rounding a bend of the inlet from one reach to the next, the mountains soon hide the water left behind and pry open yet another passage ahead. The awesomeness of the magnitude and splendor in this stupendous scene of nature tends to put one in another world, far removed from the foibles of mere man and his frantic civilization.

There are few good stopping places after entering this portion of the inlet. Vancouver Bay, about half way up Prince of Wales Reach and Deserted Bay at the top of Princess Royal Reach offer rather indifferent anchorages, and a scattering of logging camps along the shore will sometimes provide moorage in an emergency. Generally, though, the trip is planned to go all the way in a single run. Tidal currents in the inlet are generally light, being controlled by the winds.

The head of Jervis Inlet looks today as it looked to Capt. Vancouver on that Monday, June 18, 1792. He describes it as "terminating in a swampy low land producing a few maples and pines. Through a small space of low land, which extended from the head of the inlet to the base of the mountains that surround us, flowed three small streams of fresh water apparently originating from one source in the N.W. or left hand corner of the bay, formed by the head of this inlet; in which point of view was seen an extensive valley that took nearly a northerly uninterrupted direction as far as we could perceive and was by far the deepest chasm we had beheld in the descending ridge of the snowy barrier."

Aside from the spectacular beauty, yet considering the lack of comfortable anchorages and other facilities, one might ask what there is to attract yachtsmen to cruise through these three reaches of Jervis Inlet. The answer, of course, is perhaps the epitome of cruising and scenic beauty anywhere in the world — Princess Louisa Inlet.

Unfortunately for him, Vancouver bypassed this lovely inlet although he noted the entrance in his jounal. He wrote, "About two leagues (six miles) from the head of the inlet we had observed, as we passed upwards on the northern shore, a small creek with some rocky islets before it, where I intended to take up our abode for the night. On our return, it was found to be full of salt water, just deep enough to admit our boats against a very rapid stream. . . . From the rapidity of the stream and the quantity of water it discharged, it was reasonable to suppose, by its taking a winding direction up the valley to the N.E. that its source was at some distance. This not answering our purpose as a resting place, obliged us to continue our search along the shore for one less incommodious."

Princess Louisa Inlet has been completely and thoroughly covered through the years in SEA but, because of the many new boaters being added to the roster each year and because the superb attributes of this inlet can never be adequately described, it is easy to extol its virtues over and over again.

Of course the Indians found and enjoyed it first. In 1908, John S. McMillan, founder of Roche Harbor, records a vacation cruise here and notes their enjoyment of the scenic wonders including "Bridesveil Falls," the name then used for what we presently know as Chatterbox Falls.

It was in 1919 that James F. "Mac" Macdonald first saw Princess Louisa and decided it was so so beautiful he must have it. It was 1927 before his dream was realized and, through a Crown Grant, he purchased the upper part of the inlet. A lovely log cabin on the flats to the right of the falls was built which subsequently burned as Mac was bringing his bride to his paradise.

After a day's run, there's plenty of time to enjoy dinghy sailing between Hardy and Fox Islands.

For many years Mac welcomed visiting yachtsmen to the inlet and extended the hospitality of "his" property. Somehow, though, it wasn't "his." More and more he came to feel that Princess Louisa was too lovely, too majestic to be owned by one person and that he was merely holding it "in trust" for all to enjoy. The idea grew in his mind and, with the laudable purpose of preserving his beauty spot, untouched by man's "development" for future generations, he made the decision to donate the property to Northwest yachtsmen.

To administer the gift and see that Mac's wishes were carried out, The Princess Louisa International Society was organized in 1953 with both Canadian and American

A cruiser heads for
Princess Louisa Inlet in
Prince of Wales Reach with
snow-capped mountains
on all sides.

The Sea Ranger, home port Kirkland, Wash., drops
the hook to enjoy afternoon in a cove of Hardy Island.

yachtsmen making up the board of directors. For a $2 annual membership or a $30 life membership, yachtsmen from both sides of the border joined the organization. The money was used to build and maintain moorage floats and shore-side fireplaces.*

As the years passed it became apparent that the Society wasn't able to do an adequate job in keeping things up, so in 1964 it was decided to deed the property to the British Columbia Parks Department. It was to become a Provincial Marine Park with all of Mac's dreams and stipulations to be carried out. The Society continues as advisor and to investigate and recommend new sites for Marine Parks.

So — Princess Louisa, in all her glory, continues to attract over 1200 visitors each summer and will continue to do so for the foreseeable future.† Mac still acts as unofficial host from his houseboat behind the moorage floats and each week his bright red canoe carries him down the inlet to Malibu where he imparts the legends and ceremonial dances of the local Indians to the youth attending the Young Life Camp there. Now in his 80th year he expects to be back again this summer from his winter sojourn to Mexico.†

The entrance to Princess Louisa, watched over by the Malibu Lodge (originally a plush resort), is also guarded by Malibu Rapids which Vancouver thought was a river. With currents up to 9 knots on spring tides, the rapids with a bend in the middle are best negotiated at or near slack water. High and low slacks occur respectively 8 minutes and 36 minutes after the corresponding highs and lows at Point Atkinson.

As one enters the inlet after running the rapids it is like raising the curtain on one of nature's most exciting and gorgeous stages. Our language doesn't contain enough superlatives to describe it. Many have called it a magnified Yosemite carpeted by the sea. Cruising into this canyon between mountains well over a mile high one has trouble accommodating to the perspective. The high peaks reflected in the still water seem to double their height and it is difficult to tell where the water ends and the greenclad cliffs begin their sheer ascent. Yet somehow heights aren't noticed so much in the nearness of the walls on each side. A cameraman is hard put to catch the entire vista or even a believable portion of it in his lens.

In the early summer months, uncountable waterfalls tumble down the rocky cliffs only to lose themselves in the trees. Later in the year after some of the melt from the snow fields has run off the number of falls diminishes, but these are always enough to add their charm to the picture.

Of course Chatterbox Falls at the head of the inlet is the crowning glory of the entire scene. Although one can see from back in the inlet the river from which the water for the falls comes, it appears to suddenly burst out of the wooded hills. Trails lead from the moorage floats up to the head of the falls. It's a thrill to stand there and watch the torrent hurl itself over the precipice. In spite of Mac's frequent warnings and signs imploring people not to go past the fences, many lives have been lost by those disobeying the warnings. The best and only advice is to heed the signs and not venture onto the rocks beyond the fences.

Besides the floats there are also anchorage buoys available. A ledge extends out into the inlet in front of the falls offering the only place to drop an anchor. There need be no fear of swinging for the current from the falls always keeps the ship headed towards it.

The sun sets early in this deep canyon but it's pleasant to sit in the cockpit and watch the night approach through the dabs of crimson on the snow-capped peaks and the purple shadows below. Thousands of yachtsmen, their crews and guests concur with Mac when he says, "In Princess Louisa I find a peace that passeth understanding."

One may range further — even around the world — but it is unlikely that he will find anything to surpass, or even equal the enjoyment to be found in Jervis Inlet crowned, of course, by the incomparable wonder of royal Princess Louisa.

*Currently $5 annual membership or $30 life membership.
†11,000 visitors were logged in 1977. Mac's last summer there was in 1972.

28

The Lore and Future of Princess Louisa Inlet

by Bob Walters

Louisa is the regal one of all fjords. She is Nature's great perpetual endowment to western pleasure boating. And she is going to be kept that way. To the many visiting yachtsmen who have made it up there through the decades, her magnetic attraction is pure, old, natural charm that outranks Victoria's ivied Hotel Empress or the empire visit from the Queen and the pipers in Stanley Park on Dominion Day.

She is indeed a princess. The only inlet that the explorers felt worthy of naming after royalty — Princess Louisa, as euphonious a pair of words as ever rolled off a cruising chart. Yachtsmen have been flocking there in increasingly greater numbers from June into September with boats from beyond the Canadian borders outnumbering the provincials. These same yachtsmen and their guests can never quite believe her serene beauty, her granite magnitude and always-changing blue and green colorings. They are not conditioned to what they comprehend on the first visit and are hard put to believe it all the second time, the fourth or the tenth.

This is the cruising destination one always begins laying plans to return to. The acceptance of her unspoiled charm is immediate and lasting. She establishes this impression at the very first because she stands so regally tall to the more distant horizons that she does, in fact, create her own juncture between water, sky and mountains. And when you cruise tight to the granite cliffs you are lucky if you don't develop a crick in the neck from looking up to the tops of the spires of this cathedral.

It is these very granite-faced and wooded heights that create the unusual atmosphere and *feel* that are conveyed to the sensory perceptions. It is a *feel* that cannot be adequately described for you. When it is hot, there is the anomaly of the feeling of coolness. When it is bright on one side, it is dark black-green on the other. Here, too, where cold salt water and chill glacier water mix, the swimming water in July and August, a few hundred yards from the greatest falls in British Columbia, is in the delightful 70-degree range. If you have ever tried a mountain lake where

The inlet's head viewing away from falls toward one jog.

snow is still visible on peaks, you'll know why some say this, in itself, is the greatest phenomenon of all. The Indians named it *Suivoolot* — sunny and warm. And the anomalousness continues through many subjects: natural formations of face and animal "carvings" on the granite walls that are almost as spectacular as man's creations at Rushmore; water distances so deceiving to the practiced eye that one learns to allow for his personal optical deviation.

For here, far inland, is an almost completely closed body of salt water five miles long, less than a mile wide at its greatest and a thousand feet deep. It has more placidness than almost any major mountain lake and yet its ocean water flows constantly with the heavy tides of the region. But, inside, the currents are almost nil despite the seven- to nine-knot Malibu Rapids at the entrance.

Being virtually at sea level yet inland among huge mountains not only adds to all of the wonderments, but lends itself to some standard jesting. It goes something like this: A lady guest visiting for the first time, and lost in all of this geographic grandeur, will often comment on the exhilarating qualities of the air. The phrase "mountain air" is then dropped into the conversation by the perpetrator and the power of suggestion is further added by comments about thinness of the air at this altitude. The visitors often agree and come back with remarks akin to that made by one lovely lady who had lost sight of the route from which she came, "Yes, I have noticed a little dizziness. Altitude always affects me that way." It is a kind prank because even those who chuckle at it, fully appreciate that the Inlet creates strange illusions.

Adding considerable depth to the pleasures of a cruise to the Inlet, is the winding course that takes one 50 nautical miles inland from Pender Harbour and

The 120-foot falls . . . top of granite cliffs climb out of range of camera . . . Ted Conant's Dorado from Southern California is near trees.

other points of Jervis Inlet — and return several days to a week later. Draw a line two to four miles on each side of this natural estuary that rivals the great canals of the world and the mighty peaks rise 3600 feet to 7800 above you. It is what is known as "close enough to touch." And the names along the route are so loyal to the empire and royalty, beautifully so: Prince of Wales Reach, Princess Royal Reach and Queens Reach. Lovely names like that make winter cruising-nostalgia what it is. The sun never sets on the British Empire. It cannot officially set on the Inlet. The cliffs are too high and shadows come early. But it can be said without exaggeration that your cruising log book will never be complete if you haven't relaxed through a couple of sunups and sundowns while moored near mellifluous Chatterbox Falls.

The art of comparison is just one more form of enjoying nature and carries no depreciation of the *other* wonder of the world. The gorgeous Valley of the Yosemite is constantly compared to what yachtsmen see at the Inlet. Here is Louisa, five miles long and at sea level; Yosemite, 4000 feet above sea level with the valley floor seven miles long. Tuktukamin cliff near the head of Louisa is 5300 feet; the granite

Mac celebrated his 89th birthday in 1978.

cliffs above Yosemite are listed at 3500 feet. The granite head escarpment called "One Eye" at mid-inlet is 7300 feet above the water level of the inlet and its appearance has been compared to the Half-Dome of John Muir's great discovery. Louisa's Chatterbox Falls is 120 feet from top to high tide; Yosemite's falls are much higher — still the 120 feet is impressive. But comparison is not the point, except to establish the *nth* wonder of the world that can't be reached by wheeled vehicles, only by pleasure boats and an occasional float plane.

The yachtsmen's associations with the Inlet are always shared equally with the acquaintanceship with a great man and friend to all including the tribes of earlier days — James F. Macdonald (note the different spelling). The mere use of "Mac" establishes his identity to all. Through 38 summers he has been the guiding spirit of the Inlet with all of the wisdom, the kind that can be compared to that of a great and likable bishop with his flock. He is friend, historian, philosopher, raconteur excelling in the Indian lore of the region, general counsellor, welcomer, guidance counselor by natural instinct to the youth who gather easily around him, and a memorable entertainer with folk and native dances and customs.

Yet he is never The Keeper of the Keys. Visitors are always welcome and always were when this was his property. Somehow, in his presence, people of all ages carry on as they should. Many, many men who have known him well and favorably over the years have individually expressed why he is the true patriarch of the Inlet. All compliments end up at the door of the word *unobtrusive*. He dispenses hospitality to all, he sets the tone of dignity, but is never under foot. He moves on without appearing to so do. A long-time friend of his, H. W. McCurdy of the famous yacht *Blue Peter*, wrote this about Mac for this article: "During the winter of 1937-38 we (The McCurdies and Macdonald) traveled to Tahiti and lived in grass shacks near each other. Because of his world-wide travels he is at home wherever he hangs his hat. If I were to go around the world with only one friend accompanying Katy and myself, that friend would be Mac. He has the happy faculty of always being at hand when you want him and not being around when you wish to be alone, unobtrusive and never underfoot, the ideal traveling companion."

Mac recently celebrated his 79th birthday. He carries the build and the appearance of an athlete much younger. He swims daily at Princess Louisa in the summers and in Mexico in the winters. His winter home is Acapulco where each day he journeys to a little island where he unfolds his desk, his reading matter and his chessmen. The others will eventually gather and the chess club meets el beacho.*

The story of the two — The Inlet and Mac — begins in 1919 shortly after he doffed his infantry captain's uniform. He boated to the Inlet. He had traveled the world and no place to him was like it. Then came six years of prospecting in Nevada. Without sight of tree or water he longed more for Louisa's waterfalls and forests. He made his stake in 1926. In 1927 he took up the property at the Inlet's head. It was "wild land", never surveyed by the government. He built his famous, lovely log home in 1928. It burned in 1940. He had left it shipshape and spotless near the falls to return with his bride. As they rounded the point to face the distant cabin by the falls, it burst into flames and was quickly reduced to ashes. Combustion of waxes and varnishes on the dry log walls was probably the cause.

At first some thirty or forty boats a season would arrive. The Inlet was a long way from Seattle and Vancouver for the boats of that era. Besides, there were fewer boats. And now today, with several contributing reasons to the popularity, a thousand boats a season will spend from three days to a week and upward at the head of the Inlet.

In 1953 the non-profit, non-private Princess Louisa International Society was formed to keep the Inlet in perpetual trust so that it would and will always be there for yachtsmen to enjoy. In voluntarily passing along his portion of the Inlet property, Mac stated this to SEA & PACIFIC MOTOR BOAT at that time: "In giving my property to the boating public I feel that I am completing a trust. It is one of the most spectacular beauty spots in the world. To me it is Yosemite Valley, the fjords of Norway and bits of many other places all wrought into the background of our Pacific Northwest conifer forests.

"It should never have belonged to an individual and I do not want it ever to be commercialized. Loggers, trappers, Indians, fishermen and the many yachtsmen have always been welcome to any hospitality that I had to offer. I have a deep feeling that I have been only the custodian of the property for Nature and it has been my duty to extend every courtesy. Now I turn it over to representative yachtsmen in a group from each side of the international line. Turning it over in perpetuity as an international project that you, your children, your children's children, ad infinitum, all may enjoy its peace and beauty."

It was agreed that Mac would always have his place near the falls where he could moor the houseboat *Seaholm* which is summer home to him. None would ever have let it be otherwise.

Now, the next chapter in properly maintaining the physical property is being written (see inset story of the change-over).

Among the cascading, glacial waterfalls (until mid-June at least sixty tumble into the Inlet) Mac has told his stories of honest lore. They are many. There is the one of why the Suivoolot was tabu for the Sechelt Indians for many earlier generations. And the great tale of Chieftains' Rock. Mac told it to this visitor one time as we drifted directly below this fissure arising perpendicular from the water to a shelf 150

feet overhead. The young Indians had to climb it with a heavy rock strapped to their backs. It was a show of manhood and sad was the plight of the less husky. Then there are his demonstrations of the fire ceremony to prove the young braves' mental stamina in the face of severe pain.

Echo Rock and the ledge where dwells Old Man Echo is another of Mac's memorable stories. The echo from this ledge is true to pitch. Quartets in the quiet of the evening have bounced off some of the finest barbershop harmony ever over the water.

And then there are the fascinating figures that can be seen on the granite cliffs in the gathering shadows — The Egyptian Princess (Mac's regal favorite), and Dopey, Mike the Logger, The Phantom Ship, Dillinger, the Indian horsemen, George Washington and others.

Stories, tales, grandeur, finding new "carvings" in an unusual light, campfire sessions, camaraderie between yachts. This is what they have all over the years. It is impossible to mention many and hardly fair to mention a few. John Barrymore and Dolores Costello used to annually renew friend-

Thea Foss (former Infanta) in one of her many visits to the Inlet.

Mac, the legend-spinner, calls into the echo ledge and fascinates a lad with the tale of Old Man Echo . . . the base of Chieftain's Rock is to port (see story references)

ships with Mac. They came aboard *Infanta*, a name that, by coincidence, means "princess." The famous yacht now frequently enters the Inlet as *Thea Foss* at the hands of Henry Foss and others of the famed towing family from Tacoma. Mac points out that not only has McCurdy's *Blue Peter*, in addition to some of his previous boats, been a many-time visitor, but he has now known four generations of McCurdies at the Inlet. And four generations of the Allen Engles aboard *Neoga.* The late Allen was one of the trustees for the Inlet Society. Charlie Frisbee with *Alatola* often pointed her bowsprit into the stone gullies and, with an improvised hose, filled his water tanks with pure glacial water. And the memories go on. Tony Jensen skippering in Ronald Coleman and Bill Powell. "Doc" Harvey, another trustee, with *Kittiwake,* and others of his earlier yachting years. Bill Boeing, the founder of the flying boat firm, with *Taconite.* Col. Blethen of Seattle Times fame. Roy McCumber. Max Fleischman with *Haida.* The Sangsters and *Twin Isles* annually move Mac's home up from Pender Harbour. And on it could go. Mac loves to recall the time that Mack Sennett and a band of bathing beauties stopped en route to Alaska to film one of his famous reels. He became so excited over the Inlet that he shot thousands of feet of film with the girls, using the Falls and other areas for background. His pilot stopped him saying that there would be a dozen Louisas in Alaska. Mac saw "Alaskan Love" some months later in San Francisco and prominent in the scenery were the bathing girls at Chatterbox Falls.

And today over forty years after he first saw the fjord, Mac says that he can only repeat that he still thrills to its beauty which is ever new and always changing. It is here that he hopes to continue his summer routine for many years to come, putting on his fire ceremony for the Malibu kids and continuing the yarns of the region for it is here "that I find a peace that passeth understanding."

Mac in the Northwest enroute to the Inlet for the summer of '65.

Not far from the entry at Malibu Rapids.

29

Savary –
An Island with a Savory Aura

"About sunset on a summer afternoon we sailed betwixt the main and this verdant isle, which I named Savary's Island. Here we landed and made camp on a delightful plain with a fine, smooth beach before it that rendered the situation most desirable and pleasant and of a beauty such as we have seldom enjoyed."

So wrote Capt. George Vancouver on July 1, 1792 in his dispatches to His British Majesty, King George the Third.

Since then, particularly during the first half of this century, many world-known travel authorities have written about Savary Island. Almost without exception their use of adjectives has been in the superlative: the best, the greatest, the most, unsurpassed. In writing about Savary Island the use of superlatives is definitely a "must."

Lying near the north end of the Strait of Georgia, Savary is approximately 11 miles up from Westview and four miles out of Lund, the northern terminus of the highway up from Vancouver. Most yachtsmen cruising in British Columbia's inland coastal waters pass by Green Point, the eastern tip of Savary Island, on their way north to Desolation Sound and beyond. Few stop, however, thus missing one of the gems of this area.

Known as British Columbia's South Sea Island, it is as if one of those fabled islands of the southern seas had been magically transplanted to the Gulf of Georgia. The long reefs with their breakers, blue lagoons, nodding trees, dazzling sunlight on the sparkling sea and miles of silvery white sand on the curving beach, shady woodland trails bordered by tall lacy ferns, glorious sunsets, nights of moonlit loveliness all combine to bring the glamor of the tropics to this paradise island.

Savary is crescent shaped, about five miles long from east to west and between ¼ and ½ mile in width. Between the points of the crescent on the north shore is a long, shallow, sandy beach of white and gray sand. Here the water is generally quiet and smooth and, even at high tide, bathers can wade out for several hundred yards. On the south beaches, more exposed to the vast expanse of the Strait, long rollers break on the shore for the enjoyment of surf bathers.

The big surprise awaiting swimmers at Savary Island is the temperature of the water. It's hard to believe that any salt water in this area, which is usually on the chilly side, could be as warm and pleasant as bath water, averaging a comfortable 72°. The reason for this phenomenon is that the tides coming in from the ocean around the northern end of Vancouver Island meet those coming in around the southern end at this point. Consequently these waters are very little disturbed and the result is the warmest water anywhere in the Pacific Northwest.

Savary is also different in formation from any other island between Vancouver and Alaska. It is simply a long clay ridge covered with a sandy loam. Owing to the warm nature of the soil and its sheltered position, the flora is different from that of the rockbound coast and other islands. Many of the flowers and creepers which grow in great profusion are, as a rule, found only far to the south and berries and wild fruits are abundant. In addition to usual fir, hemlock and shore pine, there are groves of arbutus and other flowering trees while along the southern ridge is a forest of yew trees. It takes six people touching finger tips to gird the trunk of North America's largest arbutus treet growing here.

One spot on Savary may be like a desert while a few hundred yards away there is a dense growth of tall ferns, moss, salal and wild flowers. Peach and other fruit trees flourish and there is a wealth of wild blueberries, huckleberries and blackberries.

All of this offers sanctuary to deer, some of them quite tame, and a wide variety of birds. Bald eagles are a familiar sight while bird watchers can delight in the swallows, humming birds, thrush, sparrows, woodpeckers, kingfishers, screech owls, great blue herons, sandpipers and sea birds of various kinds including loons and seagulls.

Fishermen and those interested in underwater life will find plenty of salmon, lingcod, rockfish and flounders along with herring, perch, dogfish, hake, huge sculpin, small grass eels and skates. Starfish are plentiful and an abundance of oysters can be chipped off nearby rocks or gathered from the sandy beaches. Clams can be "raked" or easily dug by hand with a bucket full of small butter clams commonly dug from a two-foot area. Seals frequently come in for a look at the humans and occasionally killer whales can be seen cruising by.

Any island with natural attributes such as these is attractive but Savary has still more. An atmosphere of history pervades the place, highlighted by tales of coastal Indians using it as a principal summer meeting spot and fortifying Indian Point, the western tip, against marauding bands from other tribes. Vast middens of empty clam shells have been found at various places on the island. A later discovery turned up specially laid rocks. Their use is a mystery, but it is believed that this was either a ceremonial site or possibly a form of steam bath.

Later there were white settlers with their children or grandchildren presently living in the hundred or so homes along the shores or in the forests. Names such as Keefer, Mace and Ashworth are prominent in the island's history and one can occasionally dig out memories of "Gulf" ships that used to call or the putting out of a lantern on a cold winter night to guide some skipper through a howling sou'easter.

The yachtsman visiting Savary Island today will no doubt be greeted by Bill Ashworth who, with his wife, Marian, operates the Royal Savary Hotel. Bill will probably be clad in typical South Sea Island or beachcomber attire — shapeless slacks, an open shirt and barefooted. If you can find him when he isn't busy acting as host, bell boy, boatman, mechanic or bartender, he will be happy to relate how his father, a newspaperman, came to the island in 1910 to cover a murder story. Falling in love with the place, he bought property near Indian Point and built a huge house. In 1928 the house was turned into the present hotel.*

Bill might also tell the story of buried treasure, about a man named Green who, in 1898 at the height of the

Sailfish, the sail/power catamaran designed by Bill Ashworth for his own use, serves as water taxi, supply boat or ski boat.

Yukon Gold Rush, ran a trading post on the east end of the island. He traded with prospectors on the ships going to and returning from the Alaskan gold fields and the Indians living on the other end of the island.

One dark night two white men who lived at the Indian village with their Indian wives set out for the trading post intent on robbing Trader Green. They succeeded all too well, Green was murdered, his money stolen and the building burned to the ground.

It wasn't long before the Royal Northwest Mounties were on their trail. Before the men were arrested, tried and hanged for murder they managed to hide the money and never revealed the hiding place. From that time to the present the fortune has never been found. It is generally believed it was buried on or near Indian Point, and to the visitor, it's an intriguing idea to hunt for this buried treasure.

Bill is justly enthusiastic about the hotel's "sand" golf course laid out on the hard white beach. Here guests use a 2, 3 or 4 iron as they enjoy a unique version of the game, many of them barefoot, and there are no green fees. There is also a tennis court and badminton court. The island now boasts an airstrip for private fliers.

Boating visitors are always interested in Bill's boat Sailfish, a catamaran hull with both sail and a powerful outboard motor. He designed and built it himself and uses it as a supply boat or water taxi for frequent trips to Lund, as well as a ski boat.

*Bill and Marion Ashworth sold out in 1975. The new owners are John and Sally Smithers.

The Royal Savary Hotel . . . south seas hospitality and informality in a northwest setting.

While the Royal Savary Hotel isn't set up with marine facilities — there isn't even a dock — most yachtsmen who visit the island like to schedule a dinner ashore. Following an afternoon of swimming and sunbathing around Indian Point, they anchor in front of the hotel, well out to avoid grounding on the long sandy shelf. Bill is always happy to point out where the deeper water begins.

Any thought of extra effort in going ashore by dinghy is soon forgotten in the enjoyment of an evening at the Royal Savary. As you sip a tall, cool one in the Clam Diggers Club Room the informal "Mood of the Pacific" is set amidst the fish nets, shells, an old dugout canoe, comfortable Chinese wicker chairs and bar stools topped with cushions Bill has beachcombed. The room is done in natural wood in the design of a stockade.

After an excellent meal served in friendly family style, visitors are urged to stay for an evening of fun. Despite the fact that life on Savary is relaxed and easy-going, the sandy beaches aren't "rolled up" at dusk. One may enjoy dancing, a card game, clam-bakes or wiener and marshmallow roasts on the beach, a good book from the diversified library or a gab session in the large living room before a crackling fire in the huge fireplace with Bill spinning yarns about past or modern adventures. Sometimes a dinner of baked or planked salmon with roasted oysters is served outside in the barbecue area. Strangely enough, there are no mosquitoes on Savary.

Sometimes, along about midnight, Bill will shut down the lighting system — a generator run by an old one-lung diesel engine with its slow ker-chug-ker-chug muffled in the woods behind the hotel. Candles then appear to add to the mood of rustic remoteness and romance.

Perhaps the waters inside the hook of Indian Point wouldn't be considered the best of overnight anchorages. Unless the wind is blowing, however, or predicted to blow before morning, it's a good enough gamble to lay there for the night. If one should get caught, it's only four miles to Lund.

Although history is definite that Capt. Vancouver gave the island its name, the source of the name is a bit clouded. One story has it that it was given in honor of the celebrated secretary of the first Napoleon; another says it was given owing to the peculiar odor of the clams which the Indians dried in great quantities on the shore.

We're inclined to accept the former claim, but regardless of the source of its name, any yachtsman heading for northern British Columbia waters will enjoy a stop to savor the delights of Savary Island.

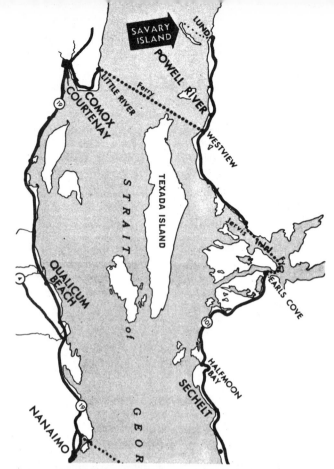

Even at high tide there's plenty of sand, and the sloping beaches permit bathers to wade out for several hundred yards.

The beach at Savary Island is a pleasant place to set up camp.

Savary Island's Indian Point has one of the finest sandy beaches in all Northwest cruising waters.

112

30
Malaspina Inlet

Beloved by those who know it is a rock-strewn and island-dotted arm of water extending southeastward from Desolation Sound, and consisting of three separately named inlets, known as Malaspina Inlet.

It is another of those hundreds of off-the-main-course reaches, full of inviting coves, good anchorages, plentiful seafood and soul-satisfying scenery making up these finest cruising waters in the world of the Pacific Northwest.

A Spanish navigator, Captain Alejandro Malaspina, spent the summer of 1791 in the coastal waters of British Columbia and Alaska as part of an around the world Spanish scientific and exploring expedition. He left his name in several places on charts familiar to northwest skippers. Besides the inlet, subject of our present consideration, there is Malaspina Strait lying between Texada Island and the mainland and extending the length of the island; Malaspina Point marking the northwestern point of Gabriola Island opposite Nanaimo; Malaspina Peninsula forming the body of land between the inlet and the Strait of Georgia.

It was a bright August morning when we swung our bow out of the double harbor at Westview. A course of 288° M. took us up past Powell River on the starboard and Harwood Island on the port, between Mystery and Atrevida Reefs and Mace and Hurtado Points. Water in the Strait was so calm that even the First Mate could relax enough to enjoy the millions of diamonds dancing from ripple to ripple against a backdrop of huge, fantastically shaped rocks and overhanging evergreens making up the shoreline.

Repulsing an urge to explore the inviting wide sandy beaches of Savary Island or to have lunch at the Royal Savary Hotel, we maintained course and sped up Thulin Passage, through the interesting Ragged (Copeland) Islands and around Sarah Point at the tip of the peninsula, the entrance to Desolation Sound.

Entering this delightful area, so full of intriguing attractions for boaters and belying Vancouver's name for it, memories turned to many familiar spots only a short distance away — Cortes Bay, Squirrel Cove, Refuge Cove, Prideaux Haven with its charming Melanie Cove, and, further up, Pendrell Sound, Waddington Channel and Walsh Cove leading to still more storied cruising waters beyond.

After the turn at Sarah Point we made out Zephine Head, the point of Gifford Peninsula which forms the northeastern boundary of Malaspina Inlet and which is almost an island except for the 500-foot-wide neck connecting it to the mainland between Portage Cove and Wooten Bay. The V of our bow wave curved to the right as we swung into a course of 66° M. toward the actual entrance to the inlet. At this point we switched to chart #3573, a large scale chart of the inlet.

Although Malaspina Inlet had been one of several major objectives on our itinerary, somehow we had neglected to obtain this large scale chart. It was only at the insistance of our good friend Dan Martin to loan us his copy that we had it aboard and we were hardly past the entrance before we were most happy to have it.

This points up something all old time cruising yachtsmen know and one of the reasons why cruising is such a popular activity. Skippers, as a whole, are the best sports in the world. They are always anxious to share whatever they have — knowledge, gear or whatever — to help the other fellow enjoy himself as much as they do.

Getting back to the large scale chart, a word of caution. After considerable navigating from a chart where the nautical mile is something just short of an inch, a switch to one with six inches representing a mile necessitates a rather sudden change in perspective. You find yourself passing a certain point, rock or island almost before you have it spotted on the chart.

We started off by calling this inlet "a rock-strewn and island-dotted arm of water." Actually this applies only to about a third of it, the part officially called Malaspina Inlet proper, connecting with Desolation Sound and the only entrance, is the upper left arm of the Y, Lancelot Inlet is the upper right arm and Okeover Inlet is the base.

Lancelot and Okeover Inlets provide plenty of deep water with no serious hazards. Only Malaspina is crowded with islands, rocks and shoals providing an outstanding stretch of fabulous scenery but requiring close attention on the part of the skipper. You must traverse this arm to get in but don't let it bother you too much. A channel, averaging 800 feet in width and well defined on this large scale chart, has been swept to a depth of 24 feet, so, with care, there is no need to deny yourself the rewards lying inside. Tidal

113

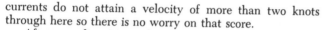

Isabel Bay within Malaspina Inlet (upper left) has good anchorage. It varies in depths, with some shoal area. The best part is back of Madge Island where the boat in the picture (lower left) is anchored. The anchorage runs from 15 fathoms to six at the southern end or to 4½ at the west of Madge Island.

The entrance to two-mile-long Theodosia Inlet (right) that takes off from the north tip of the Inlet was cloud-shrouded this day. Cruisers know how very hot it can get in this portion of the sheltered inlet on most days of the summer season. The anchorage at Theodosia has from 3½ to 9 fathoms of water, is in the center and is somewhat limited.

currents do not attain a velocity of more than two knots through here so there is no worry on that score.

After rounding Myrmidon Point we headed just inside Hare Point, leaving Beulah Island and Josephine Island on our starboard hand and giving plenty of berth to the small island and rocks northwest of Josephine. Cavendish Rock is the next consideration. By heading on Thorp Island and favoring the Josephine Island side we had no problem here. Cross Islet and Rosetta Rock extend fairly well to the middle of the inlet so we bore well over to the Thorp Island side on our starboard until we were clear of Rosetta Rock then swung to a heading on Neville Islet to avoid the rock southeast of Thorp Island.

Sound too complicated? It really isn't. With the large chart, the swept channel and a fair amount of attention, islands and rocks are easy to identify or locate and there is no problem clearing them. After coming abeam of the northern tip of the Cochrane Islands, we kept pretty much mid channel past Kakaekae Point, bearing to port to stay about 500 feet off Scott Point.

In originally planning to visit Malaspina Inlet we hadn't chosen any predetermined anchorage. The chart showed so many interesting coves that we were sure we'd have no trouble in finding a suitable place to drop anchor. Here, again, another helpful skipper turned up with a tip. Our friend and Port Madison neighbor, Dexter Dimock, had tied his *Foible II* alongside a few nights previously and highly recommended Isabel Bay as an ideal anchorage.

We decided on this as a base of operations so proceeded past the entrance of Grace Harbour and Moss Point, staying well to the right toward the Ibister Islands to avoid foul ground in the cove between Moss Point and Selina Point. We ran between Selina Point and Lion Rock, which was easily visible, rounded Edith Island and Stopforth Point to enter Lancelot Inlet. Our objective, Isabel Bay, was just a short distance farther up to our left.

Polly Island, lying at the left of the main entrance to the bay, has a rocky shoal extending out into the entrance calling for a wide turn to give a clearance of about 600 feet to the tip of Polly Island. Larger Madge Island lies in the northern part of the bay with its northern half sourrounded by shoal water to the shore of the mainland. Any part of the bay provides good anchorage in about 15 fathoms but best spots are in the southern tip in six fathoms or to the west of Madge Island in four and a half fathoms. We chose the southern tip with a cautious eye on our scope so we wouldn't swing on a large rock which is well charted.

Our hook was hardly set before the kids were demanding the dinghy for an exploration trip. An hour later they were back with reports of a rocky shore overrun with oysters and an alleged "haunted" house which later proved to be an abandoned fisherman's or trapper's shack. In the meantime our crab trap had been set nearby.

Now it was the skipper's turn in the dinghy while the small fry tested the water for swimming and found it excellent. Some photography was called for with more of nature's wonders and beauty spread around us than could possibly be caught by a single film. The day was still bright and clear with an afternoon sun warming the air to a lazy 75° and just beginning to lengthen the reflections of pine covered hillsides and cotton-fleece clouds in the blue-green of the water.

Trying a dozen angles to find one which would best include as much as possible of the gorgeous scene in one picture was a fascinating challenge. Finally, as good lighting began to fade, we realized the tide was rising rapidly. Grabbing a bucket we scurried for shore, just in time to collect a pailful of oysters without having to get our feet wet.

That night we feasted on seafood: oysters, clams and crabs in several different and delectable dishes. Never was a better meal served in a more quiet and peaceful setting. We had the entire bay to ourselves until late in the evening when a small cruiser anchored in behind Madge Island.

Lancelot Inlet extends north with Wooten Bay at its head. Good anchorage can be found here in seven to ten fathoms and it is here that one may hike across the narrow neck of land to Portage Cove on Desolation Sound. Cruising down the east shore, we rounded Grail Point and the Susan Islets to enter Theodosia Inlet, another small arm extending a couple of miles to the northeast. The narrows at the entrance are shallow with a minimum of one fathom at lowest normal tide. The only rock in the narrows is well charted and once inside, the water deepens to six to 18 fathoms in the first mile but dries about a mile out from the head. A small picturesque island lies to the left just inside after passing through the narrows.

Coming out of the inlet we rounded Thymme Island off Bastion Point and swung right into Thors Cove with its little islet. With Thymme Island to the northwest and a small peninsula forming a natural breakwater to the south, here is another bay offering an ideal anchorage with a western outlook.

Cruising south past Bunster Point and Hillingdon Point on our port we entered Okeover Inlet which ex-

tends southeastward almost five miles. Its eastern shore is completely free of any danger with depths off it of 40 fathoms two thirds of the way in. Approaching the head we passed a large oyster farm on the left, one of the few evidences of civilization we saw along the shores of this remote waterway. At the head of the inlet is Freke Anchorage, another interesting spot to drop the hook and go ashore to explore the ruins of an Indian village which once stood just south of the flats at the head of the inlet.

Cruising up the west shore, we found a government float and dock nearly two miles up from the head. This marks the terminus of a road connecting to the road which runs up the Malaspina Peninsula from Powell River to Lund. A mile further up the west shore is Penrose Bay, still another little cove inviting you to anchor for a night of quiet relaxation or a few hours' layover to swim, gather oysters, dig clams, catch crabs or explore ashore.

The western shore, unlike the eastern, has several rocky and shoal areas but all are well charted and no cause for concern.

The Coode Peninsula with Coode Island off its northern tip extends two miles to where Okeover Inlet joins Malaspina Inlet. Trevenen Bay runs down behind the peninsula for about one and a half miles. With widths up to nearly 1000 feet and depths to 12 fathoms, this is another bay offering a fascinating haven to the adventurous yachtsman.

As we headed out of this fabulous waterway we poked our bow into the last, or perhaps it should have been the first, of its many bays and coves. Grace Harbour is a favorite rendezvous for many northwest yachtsmen and runs northly for a mile up from Malaspina Inlet. Little Jean Island lies about mid channel near the entrance. It should be left on the port hand on entering with any exploring behind it relegated to a dinghy operation. This bay offers good anchorage and, like most of the others in the inlets, all that a boating family could ask of a pleasant spot to spend a night or a week.

Available references do not show that these combined waterways we call Malaspina Inlet were ever actually visited by the man whose name they bear and present day yachtsmen couldn't care less. They do know, however, that for a cruising objective which offers just about anything a skipper and his family could want for a day or for a full vacation, Malaspina Inlet is up near the top of the list. If you've been there, you'll no doubt go back again. If you haven't—try it, you'll like it!

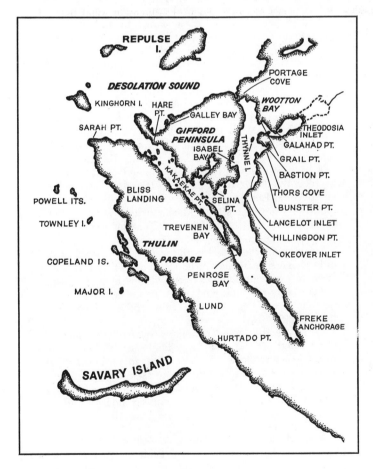

31
Desolation Sound
Is Not Desolate

It is ironic that an area which boasts the magnificence, the glory and grandeur of a mirror sea with arms entwining myriad islands of all sizes and surrounded by troops of mountains rising straight from the water with their ranks growing ever taller to the snow-clad peaks that meet the sky should bear the unlikely name of Desolation Sound.

Modern day cruising yachtsmen have an entirely different outlook from that of Captain Vancouver who wrote variously of the area in June and July, 1792, "The night was dark and rainy.... At break of day we found ourselves surrounded by a detached and broken country, whose general appearance was very inhospitable. Our residence was truly forlorn; an awful silence pervaded the gloomy forests, whilst animated nature seemed to have deserted the neighboring country, whose soil offered only a few small onions, some samphire, and here and there bushes bearing a scanty crop of indifferent berries. Nor was the sea more favorable to our wants, the steep rocky shores prevented the use of the seine, and not a fish at the bottom could be tempted to take the hook.

"This afforded not a single prospect that was pleasing to the eye, the smallest recreation on shore, nor animal nor vegetable food, excepting a very scanty proportion of those eatables already described, and of which the adjacent country was soon exhausted after our arrival. Nor did our exploring parties meet with a more abundant supply, whence the place obtained the name of Desolation Sound."

Today generally considered one of the most delightful cruising areas in Northwest waters, Desolation Sound is becoming increasingly popular. More and more skippers every year venture further and further north to taste its delights. Quite possibly the isolation, the lack of man's development of the rugged terrain, the very things which displeased Vancouver, are what make it appealing today as we seek to get away from what we call "modern life."

In considering this area we are actually embracing somewhat more than Desolation Sound proper. Using any one of a half dozen delightful bays or coves in the Sound as a base, there is a good summer-full of fascinating and beautiful cruising with innumerable inviting anchorages within comfortable cruising radius in all directions.

Coming up from the south through Thulen Passage

we have the Copeland Islands on our port. Locally known as the Ragged Islands, there are several isolated protected coves in this group. Plenty of opportunity here for some interesting exploring or a private overnight anchorage.

Around Sarah Point is the entrance to Malaspina Inlet with several excellent bays in which to spend a night or a week. Our favorites are Isabel Bay and inner Grace Harbour. You may find company or you might have the whole anchorage to yourself.

Northeastward of the entrance to Malaspina and around Zephine Head are several popular anchorages in Desolation Sound proper. Behind a spit on the southeast side of Mink Island is Mink Cove, a lovely bay highly recommended by Jan Koren who likes to anchor his sloop *Chinook* there. If your charts show this as Repulse Island, don't let it worry you. Originally named Mink Island, it was recently changed to Repulse Island by government chart makers. Local inhabitants were so upset by this that a petition was circulated and the official name is again Mink Island. A bit further along is Tenedos Bay with several good places to drop a hook.

Through another bend in the waterway, nestled behind and between several islands, lies Prideaux Haven, probably known to everyone who has cruised this area. Consisting of four wonderful anchoring spots, it has become the final objective of many a vacation cruise and a way-point for others going further.

There are the main anchorage between the mainland and Eveleigh Island, the long finger of Melanie Cove, Laura Cove and finally, for the most adventuresome, the shallow cove in behind Copplestone Island. Featuring fine anchorages, excellent swimming and plenty of oysters, Prideaux Haven's popularity is understandable and you are almost certain to find someone here you know or, if not, to make new friends.

Alan Morley, British Columbia writer, who claims to be the second and last Hermit of Prideaux Haven, tells of Mike Schuster, the first Hermit. He says that Mike lived at the head of Melanie Cove for 40 years on an orchard-ranch he built by himself. On stonewall terraces 10 to 12 feet long, and five or six feet wide he planted apple and cherry trees. An enormous domestic blackberry vine was trained over a trellis near the mouth of the little creek.

116

The four acres of orchard were surrounded by a split cedar fence with poles extending another six or eight feet and strung with old fishnet to keep the deer out.

The living room of his little white house was heated by a stove made from an old oil drum. A carpet six inches deep was made of layers of deer, bear and cougar skins underlayed by Vancouver newspapers dated in the early 1890's. The ceiling, made of canvas nailed above the rafters, bulged low between them from a huge nest made by generations of packrats.

Mike was a cultivated Austrian immigrant who had read much and traveled extensively. As a handlogger he was known as a skilled and daring man in a most dangerous occupation. Working alone at a job usually requiring two men, he felled the huge trees and struggled to

Squirrel Cove is a long-time old favorite of cruising families. Its proximity to one of the shallow inlets into Salt Lagoon provides some with prowlin' sortees. Refuge Cove, directly across Lewis Channel, provides a supply center.

"run" them down the hillsides to the salt chuck with Gilchrist jacks. His real avocation, however, was hospitality.

When Morley took over the ranch after Mike's death in 1921, he found in one of the three rooms a cider press and a score of large wooden barrels with the aroma of hard cider and blackberry wine. He tells how Mike filled his larder with deer shot from his doorstep, goats taken from the mountainside above and fish from the haven.

Most of the two generations of yachtsmen, loggers and fishermen who anchored in the cove stopped by for a visit with Mike and enjoyed a taste of venison, bear or goat from his oven or a glass of wine or cider from the big barrels. Among his innumerable friends and visitors were the American author Stewart Edward White and actor John Barrymore.

Although Mike shot what game he needed for food, he had a great love for the creatures of the wild. Morley relates how one of them paid a great tribute. When he was reading by the stove one evening he felt a tug at his trouser leg. There was a weasel, obviously following an old custom of begging for a handout of chopped bacon or cold meat. After the shy, sinister little assassin of the forest got used to him, he resumed what must have been regular calls, even climbing up on his knee to get the food.

Prideaux Haven was recently deeded to the University of British Columbia by Reed Hunt to preserve it as a public anchorage and as a part of British Columbia's natural heritage. Morley says, "I hope the university will not find it necessary to 'improve' it. Let the boats come and go, and as the last ripples of their rising anchors fade away, leave the haven and the cove to their unspoiled loveliness, quiet and at peace as they have always been." To which we add a fervent amen.

It was when leaving Prideaux Haven that we met Dick and Alma Lewis, their teenagers Ron and Aldean and guests Chet and Phyllis Ulin in their *Erlyndee* headed for Toba Inlet. Dick, a past commodore of Olympia YC, invited us to join them. It's always pleasant to explore unknown waters with folks who have been there before so the invitation was eagerly accepted.

The day was clear and warm with cotton puffs of clouds nestled around the snow capped peaks of the higher mountains. The bow wave of *Erlyndee* just ahead of us curled lazily, making it appear that the boat was cruising on a sea of gray-blue #50 lube oil. After passing between Channel Island and Brettell Point the beauty that is Toba Inlet opened up before us.

Toba, like so many of the fjord-like inlets of this country, is a deep valley carpeted with milky, glacier-fed water from the many falls that cascade down the almost perpendicular walls from the mile-high peaks behind. Ever changing vistas of spectacular scenery lure the photographer into a feeling that each shot is the ultimate yet the next one is always better.

If you're expecting fancy moorings at Toba's head, you'll be disappointed. A log boom in a little bight along the north shore just short of the head looks pretty good after checking the 40 to 65-fathom depths in unprotected water.

The *Erlyndee's* small boat took us to the head of the bay for a look at the old Indian cemetery. A verdant growth of underbrush had taken over but Dick finally spotted a large wooden cross and, after much knocking down of weeds and ferns, we located many of the stones and wooden markers. Oldest legible inscription we found was on a stone marked, "Joseph of Toba Inlet. Died August 22, 1905, aged 90 years."

Across the mouth of the river we enjoyed exploring the remains of an old logging camp. Decaying buildings and rusting bits of old machinery scattered around in the underbrush which had taken over silently described a bit of history.

Fishing at Toba's head, usually good, proved disappointing, although we trolled until dark. None of several boats caught anything that evening.

Coming back from Toba one has a variety of choices. You can come down Pryce Channel, go up Ramsay Arm to try for a mess of prawns, and then through North Passage to Calm Channel to head for the Yacultas or the Hole in the Wall. Another possibility would be through Deer Passage for a wealth of exciting cruising in the Sutil Channel area. Fanny Bay or Redonda Bay offer likely stopover points. To return to Desolation Sound you can come down Waddington Channel between East and West Redonda Islands.

This route turns up some more favorite anchorages. Walsh Cove, snuggled in behind some small islands, is an ideal spot to anchor with good swimming and an abundance of oysters. Doctor Bay, a little further down the east side of West Redonda Island, although not as picturesque, offers protected anchorage.

Dick Lewis' Erlyndee (left) of Olympia cruises up to the fjord-like waters of Toba Inlet. always a majestic vista of great forests, a touch of snow still remaining from winter. At right, the many falls of Toba Inlet come out of the mountain side. Many approaches bring one to Toba via either Pryce or Homfray Channels.

Pendrell Sound, nearly cutting East Redonda in half, features more oysters than we've ever seen in one area. The shores are literally lined solidly with them from high to low water marks.

Coming out of the lower end of Waddington Channel where it joins Desolation Sound a delightful little cove indents West Redonda on the starboard. Known to many as Marylebone Bay, some charts show it as Roscoe Bay. Swimming here is reported to be tops in exceptionally warm water. Caution should be used entering this bay at low tide as a rocky reef extends across the narrow entrance channel about half way in. Rock grass showing at water level provides a good warning signal for all but the shallowest draft boats.

Skirting the southern shore of West Redonda Island one comes to Refuge Cove on the southwest corner. For some years Mr. and Mrs. Norm Hope have operated the store here, and it has become a major supply port for this area. The post office, telephone, lines of groceries, fresh meats, hardware, ice and general store items, plus the fuel dock and moorage all made this a frequent stop for yachtsmen.*

Unfortunately, on March 31, 1968 a fire started in the basement of the store building and living quarters. The Hopes had only 30 seconds to get out before the whole structure was gone.

The facility at Refuge Cove pictured prior to the 1968 fire is being rebuilt and is serving visiting boats. This is a favorite supply center for the whole area, a great cove in itself, and a place to visit with other cruising boats as they put in for fuel and supplies. A "crossroads landing" would properly fit Refuge.

While the disaster is lamentable, we doubt that it can dull Norm's roguish sense of humor. There was the time that he bet a yachtsman that he could get at least three salmon off the end of the float in five minutes. Norm won the bet by going out to his fish-buying shack at the end of the float and taking three fish off the ice. Then after the bet was paid, he presented the salmon to the loser.

Up Lewis Channel about four miles from Refuge Cove is the entrance to Teakerne Arm which branches into a Y at its head. The southern end of the Y is a holding area for logs. At the end of the other twin head is a float apparently used for fueling the logging tow boats. Here an ever-flowing fire hose provides good clear water from Cassel Lake in the hills above. While we filled our tanks the distaff members of the crew had a fine time washing their hair in the soft water.

Directly across the Channel from Refuge Cove is Squirrel Cove, still another scenic bay on Cortes Island. With its several islands and connecting salt water lagoon this has been a favorite spot of yachtsmen for many years. Through a narrow rocky cut, water flows into and out of the lagoon with the rise and fall of the tide forming a small rapids which the youngsters delight to "shoot" in a dinghy. The lagoon also provides an opportunity for some interesting dinghy exploration.

This lagoon is one place where the chart makers really goofed. They show it as the extension of an arm of Von Donop Creek from the other side of the island. Actually it is entirely landlocked except for the connection to Squirrel Cove.

Approximately six miles down Cortes Island and around Mary Point is Cortes Bay. A good anchorage, moorage, fuel dock and general store make this another desirable and convenient spot to put in the ship's index of Cruising Ports of Call.

Yes, Desolation Sound, in spite of its depressing name, and Vancouver's disparaging remarks about it, has much to offer the yachtsman. It may take more than one visit to enjoy all its and the surrounding area's many attributes. The sparkling waters lapping the rocky shores of forested islands or of sheltered coves, the comfortable swimming, the clams, the oysters, the crabs, the prawns, the salmon, the barbecue on the beach, the late summer sun closing an eventful day with a vari-hued painting hung in the sky behind the grandeur of majestic mountains, all combine to create memories to savor before the fireplace on a blustery winter night and inevitably draw one back to this cruising paradise again and again.

118

Refuge Cove General Store is now managed by Ken Ferguson and Norm Gibbons.

This limited chart portion does not cover all points in the story. It's a vast region of inlets and havens, yet a 20 N. mile half-arc, swung from Desolation S. takes it all in. Toba Inlet (not shown) runs inland NW from the juncture of Pryce and Homfray Channels. The idyllic Prideaux Haven group of island-bound harbors is NE of Mink I. (Repulse) at Homfray's lower end; The famed Yaculta Rapids is north of Raza on a heading of approx. 297; Hole in the Wall is westerly from Raza; Squirrel Cove and Refuge Cove are active harbor-opposites at lower Lewis Channel; Walsh Cove is at the N E point of W Redonda I. channels, harbors, islands and mountains.

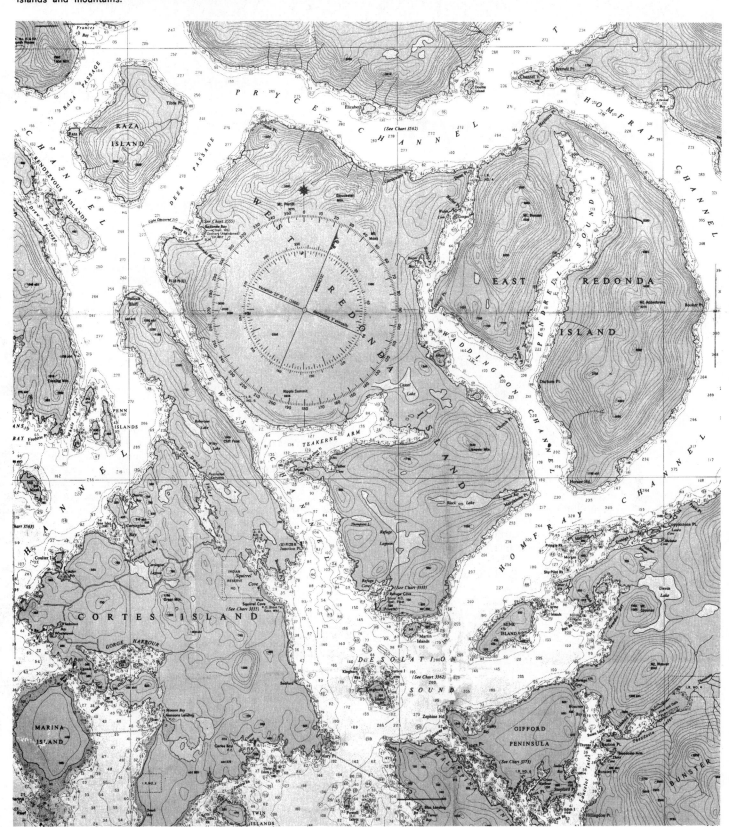

32

Quiet Isles with a Bawdy Past

The splash of the anchor followed by the rattle of chain disturbs the quiet solitude of the cove. As you pause to drink in the sylvan beauty of this pocket in British Columbia's inland cruising waters, it's hard to visualize a past of bullets, violence and killing.

Part of the joy of cruising is meeting new friends and listening to their stories; tales which bring alive the rocks, the trees, the water and the shoreside trails to give added interest to each day's adventures.

We headed out to explore the offerings of Sutil Channel. Leaving Cortes Bay on Cortes Island, we said farewell to the general area of Desolation Sound and ran inside the Ulloa Islands to round Sutil Point. It's a good idea to watch the chart carefully here and not cut any buoys, for a reef and many rocks extend well beyond the point.

Coming up the west side of Cortes Island we headed for Manson's Landing to renew acquaintance with lovely Hague Lake. We were first introduced to this lovely little lake with its warm blue water and white sand beach some 20 years ago. It's well worth the mile-long walk from the float for a swim and bit of sun bathing. If you are looking for an anchorage for the night, there's a nice little cove just north of the landing a bit.

It's only a short piece around to the narrow entrance to Gorge Harbor. Here there is a small government wharf, several small coves for isolated anchoring and a store, fuel dock and moorage floats at the Gorge Harbor Marine Services. Gorge is a delightful place which shouldn't be missed. But keep a wary eye on a large scale chart to avoid the many rocks and reefs. We watched as one cruiser struggled into the float after badly damaging both props and rudders by getting too close to one of the islands.

A pleasant Gorge interlude is a visit to Harlequin House where Mrs. Duncan Robertson serves tea, hot rolls, cinnamon rolls, jelly, jam, pie and ice cream for a modest fee. Another is to search out Bernie Allen, old-time settler in the harbor and hear his stories of by-gone days. Gorge abounds in oysters and clams and all-in-all is a most delightful place.*

From Gorge Harbor it's only a short hop around the corner to Whaletown Bay where Bergman's Store is the principal source of supplies for this area. It's well stocked with general merchandise and there's a post office and fuel dock. In negotiating the narrow passage around Marina Island's Shark Spit, be sure to mind the markers and beacons, and stay on the proper side. It's easy to get in trouble if you don't. Some charts show Marina as Mary Island but Marina seems to be the more modern name.

The name Whaletown isn't just a fantasy. Back in the days when whaling was a big industry, this was where the whalers put in with their catches. An important rendering works was located across the bay from the store and one of the huge kettles is being saved by local residents as a reminder of the past.

Continuing up Sutil Channel through Plunger Pass, there are several bays and coves of interest on the west side of Cortes Island with Carrington Bay the largest. These all offer good spots to drop anchor.

Still further along is a lovely inlet called Von Donop Creek. No one seems to know why it's called a creek. It indents the island deeply and its several anchorage possibilities are favorites with many Northwest yachtsmen. It's a good idea to check charts and tide tables here for there are some areas where the unwary could wake up to find themselves high and dry.

Jim Layton, known to some as the Von Donop hermit, lives at the head of the inlet and is noted for his garden. On what is a small island at high tide, fenced in against the deer, he grows a variety of vegetables, many of which would be prize winners at a county fair. Jim is proud of his garden and insisted we take back to the boat a bag full of beautiful cabbages, cucumbers, string beans and tomatoes.†

The Layton house is comfortable, rustic and in a lovely setting. A look at his visitors' log reveals many familiar names of skippers who have called on him through the years. One might wonder if he wouldn't get tired of so many interruptions but we got the impression that he enjoyed having the yachtsmen drop in on him and he's always ready to tell where the best oysters, clams and crabs are to be found or to point out the location of the spring with its sweet, cool water. Even though he is called a hermit, he isn't too often alone and has made several trips to England to visit his family.

120

*Mrs. Robertson no longer owns Harlequin House.
†Jim Layton is gone and his house reported burned down.

Remember that charts showing the salt lagoon as running down to connect with Squirrel Cove are in error. There is no such connection.

From Von Donop Creek we swung over to investigate the Penn Islands and then into the several coves making up Evans Bay on Read Island. Here are several interesting places to drop a hook. In the southwest corner of the bay is a small government float. The store and post office are closed.

Our next stop was at Hill Island where Mr. and Mrs. C. H. Mitchell have developed as unique a marina as will be found in the area. It's small, that's the way they want it, but it's beautifully kept. With room for only 12 to 14 boats, you'll have to get there early to secure a moorage.*

Floats covered with white canvas, a rustic sun deck, a barbecue-picnic area front the "Chart Loft," a gathering place with fireplace and artistically designed lamps. The Mitchells, former Californians, moved to the Northwest to get away from the rat-race. They spend their off-season time in fixing up and building their island paradise which they enjoy sharing with others.

Trails have been cut with such picturesque and intriguing names as Cape View Trail, Water Tank Road, Power House Road and Sunset Ridge Trail. The hiker is well rewarded on any and all of these trails with rustic seats and benches from which to enjoy the variety of magnificent views.

There are a few housekeeping cabins and rental boats available; fuel, fresh eggs, ice and fishing tackle are for sale. For the yachtsman looking for something just a little different, a stop at the Mitchells' Hill Island should be included in the cruising itinerary.

Just west of Hill Island, in Burdwood Bay on Read Island, we met Mr. and Mrs. Les Stubley and from them heard tales of a lively past history of the island. Les is a one-man chamber of commerce for Read Island as well as its historian. He not only gave up his time to tell us the stories but even took us on a tour to point out where some of the events occurred.†

As you come into the Stubleys' you see just north, up the shore a way in another little cove, what appears to be a large white abandoned house. Les tells that in a by-gone day this was a hotel owned and operated by a man named Wiley. Complete with bar, game room and frontier-type dancing girls, it was a popular weekend gathering spot for loggers from the camps on surrounding islands.

Captain Manson, for whom Manson's Landing was named, is said to have operated his boat as a ferry between the camps and the hotel, always collecting the round trip fare in advance as he knew everyone would be broke by the return trip.

Hotel owner Wiley ran a wide open place. His one interest evidently was making money without regard to the means. Les says that he frequently sat in on card games. Several times, during a losing streak, he'd bet the hotel and lose it. Strangely enough the winner would always be found next morning out in the woods shot to death.

The story goes that Wiley had been a member of the notorious Dalton gang of desperadoes. When the police finally began to break up the gang, this man fled across the border, changed his name to Wiley, and, possibly with others of the gang, settled on Read Island.

By the time his own end came, he must have had

In a Gorge Harbor cove, Westerly, Klahanie and Vamos raft up for a go at clamming and then a restful night before sailing on.

*Hill Island has been sold and is privately owned.
†Les Stubley is deceased.

some pangs of regret over his life of crime. Feeling he didn't deserve a decent burial, he asked that he be placed face down in a rock crevasse on the shore and cemented over. Les says that this was done, with Wiley's name spelled out in small rocks atop the cement. However, the grave is not located where many claim it to be, but on the shore of one of the coves of Evans Bay.

The hotel was later used as a school house and boys amused themselves during rainy day recesses by digging bullets out of the wall in the old bar room.

Jim Layton's place at Von Donop Inlet is separated from his island garden, but at low tide it is connected.

Von Donop Inlet offers innumerable secluded spots for anchoring with oysters, crabs and clams in abundance.

On a sunny afternoon, sitting in comfortable rustic lawn chairs in front of the Stubley house, we watched the youngsters trying to make friends with a tame deer as Les told another historical yarn of Read Island. He called it the Mad Mutt story.

It happened in 1893 at a Read Island logging camp during a party when five loggers drank 16 bottles of whiskey in 24 hours. One of the loggers named Harry had a dog and was always boasting about the dog's ability as a guard. Mike, a big Irish logger, scoffed at the claim whereupon Harry put a $10 gold piece in his waistcoat pocket and placed it in the middle of the floor. Ordering the dog to guard it, he said anyone who could take it could have it.

Mike strode up to the dog, hit him and ordered him to get away. As he picked up the waistcoat and pocketed the money, Harry drew his six shooter to kill the dog. Mike stopped him, saying, "Big man, huh! Only good when you've got a gun."

Harry invited him to get his own gun and they'd see who was good. As Mike turned, Harry shot him in the back. Grabbing his dog, he held the others at gun point while he backed out the window shouting, "Don't anybody start anything. I rode with Jesse James so this isn't the first man I've shot and I'll shoot anyone who tries to stop me."

The story has two endings. Both agree that, with the police hard on his trail, Harry couldn't shoot anything to eat or build a fire. In a small boat the authorities cruised Ramsay Arm, Calm Channel and Bute Inlet. Several days later a wisp of smoke was spotted on the side of the Downie range. One ending relates how Harry had killed and eaten the dog and finally shot himself. The other says the policemen waited on a trail coming down the hill until Harry showed up, arrested him and jailed him for life.

Still another tale of violence has to do with the murder of Charlie Baker, partner with John Westcott in the Read Island Store. Baker's body was found in his skiff floating in the channel. It was many months before the police investigation brought to trial a Mr. Scanlon.

Apparently the morals of some of the islanders weren't all they might have been. The prosecutor's case was based on testimony by Scanlon's wife, but her reputation was such that the jurors refused to believe her story. Scanlon was acquitted. Full details of the case are not such as can be told in a family journal, but Les is always happy to relate them to a good listener. He admits the names used are not the real ones.

So, as you enjoy the peace and quiet of some friendly little cove, remember that it may not always have been that way. From the times when the fierce northern Haida Indians came south in their big canoes for bloody raiding parties, through the period when early white settlers were practicing their particular brand of culture, down to the present times, these islands have had their share of excitement. Knowing the history and background of a place makes cruising there that much more fascinating and the only way to know is to search out and make friends with people like Les Stubley, Jim Layton, Bernie Allen and many others who love their places and like to talk about them.

Continuing on down Read Island's shore we rounded the southern tip to head for Quadra Island. Open Bay and Hyacinthe Bay are fairly open to the southeast. Heriot Bay is more protected and has a government wharf and float. We didn't go ashore but a store and postoffice are reported there. It is here that some of the people from islands in the area keep a car so they can come by boat and drive across the island to Quathiaski Cove for the ferry to Campbell River for supplies, medical or dental attention and other "big city" features.

Just below is Drew Harbor, protected by Rebecca Spit which is a Provincial Marine Park. Taku Resort is on the west side with a store, lodge and cottages. The harbor itself offers good protected anchorage.

The days spent in the Sutil Channel area were most enjoyable and interesting. The wealth of bays, coves and islands present the cruising family with a wide variety of choices for anchoring, exploring, crabbing, clamming, oystering and relaxing. And we found all the people we met extremely friendly. This portion of our cruise will be long remembered and re-lived many times.

All is peaceful now around what appears to be an old abandoned house, but years ago Wiley's Hotel on Read Island was the scene of plenty of action when loggers came for a week-end of revelry.

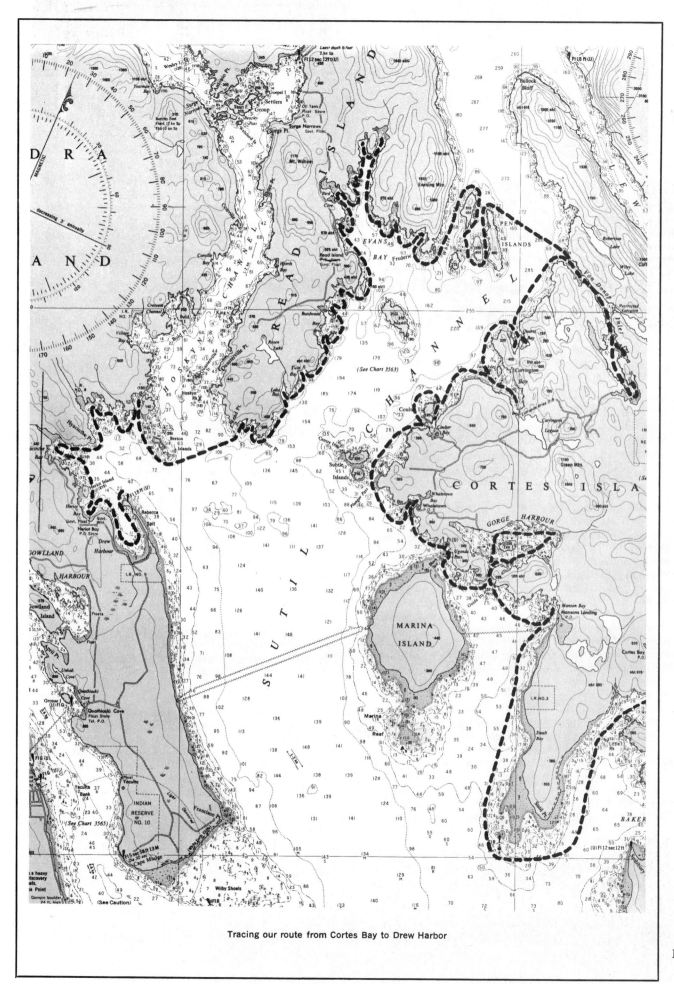

Tracing our route from Cortes Bay to Drew Harbor

33
Circling Quadra Island

With literally hundreds of cruising areas scattered generously in the waters nestled between Vancouver Island and the British Columbia mainland, the cruising yachtsman never has a problem of where to go. The innumerable arms, inlets, bays and coves dotted with islands of all shapes and sizes offer a cruising paradise second to none.

Perhaps not quite as well known and popular as the Desolation Sound and Sutil Channel areas, the waters surrounding Quadra Island, in the same latitude to the west, have the same attributes and attract more and more boaters every year.

Shaped somewhat like a turkey leg, Quadra lies east of Vancouver Island and is surrounded by Sonora, Maurelle and Read Islands. The passageways and channels between them provide scenic and fascinating cruising with plenty of safe anchorages and a bit of challenge in various rapids.

Leaving Sutil Channel we headed south to round Cape Mudge on Quadra's lower tip. Shoaling and rocks call for standing fairly well off. A buoy marks Wilby Shoals which, if you stay below it, provides a safe course although several cruise books show courses between the buoy and the land.

A word of caution is in order on entering Discovery Passage. With a flooding tidal stream and southerly or southeasterly winds, there is a heavy race off Cape Mudge which can extend clear across the entrance and be dangerous to small boats.

The town of Campbell River, in addition to being famous as a fishing rendezvous, is an important source of supplies and city-type services for a large section of the surrounding area. There are both public and private moorages, stores of all kinds and a hospital. The world famous Painter's Resort and Tyee Club are located here.

As you cruise in Discovery passage you are "on parade" for Campbell River shoreline residents and tourists who delight in boat watching. Just over a mile wide, this busy marine route of the inside passage to northern British Columbia and Alaska is a constantly changing picture of ocean-going freighters, passenger ships, tugs, barges, sleek yachts and tall-masted seiners, trollers and gillnetters.

Much of Campbell River's fame as a fishing center is due to two things: the big fighting spring salmon that often top the scales at better than 50 pounds with a record of 77 pounds, and the Tyee Club.

Although fishermen from all over the world came here even before the turn of the century to try for the mighty salmon that each summer head for spawning grounds in the Campbell River, it was 1924 when a group of anglers organized a club along the lines of the famous Tuna Club on Catalina Island. The purpose was to conserve and standardize spring salmon fishing in B.C. Organizational meetings were continued until 1927 when a formal charter was granted.

Rigid rules and regulations were adopted and it was agreed to name fish weighing over 30 pounds "Tyee." Light tackle was specified and rowing was essential to the sport. Buttons would be awarded; bronze for 30 to 40 pounds, silver for 40 to 50 pounds, gold for 50 to 60 pounds and a diamond button for a fish over 60 pounds. An annual championship button and the title "Tyee Man of the Year" was to be awarded to the fisherman landing the largest salmon.

The club has focused world-wide attention on this area with hosts of noted sportsmen and famous personalities coming to try their hands at the sport. Best fishing is usually in August.

Across Discovery Passage, northeastward from Campbell River, is Quathiaski Cove with good anchorage, government wharf and float, stores, post office, fuel and ferry service to Campbell River.

To the north is April Point. The fishing resort here is a favorite of many yachtsmen, offering moorage, fuel, water, power, ice, meals, tackle, laundry and showers. They boast that 1500 salmon were caught off the outer float, using the spinning method. In the arm behind the resort is good anchorage and a float.

We spent an afternoon and evening fishing from April Point across to Duncan Bay but it was a poor year and we weren't successful although Leon and Peg Judy landed a modest sized salmon.

Gowlland Harbor lies to the north protected by Gowlland Island. Although entrance can be made around the south end of the island at high tide, extreme caution should be used as the waters are full of rocks. Preferred entrance is around the north end of the island. There is good protected anchorage in this harbor although the government float shown on the chart and in several cruise books was in disrepair and apparently abandoned.

Gowlland is a pleasant harbor with several scenic little islands and is a popular waiting spot for slack tide at Seymour Narrows. Menzies Bay, just below the narrows, and Brown, Plumper and Deep Water Bays to the north are also good places to wait for favorable currents.

Seymour Narrows, about half a mile wide at its narrowest point, should be run only at slack or near slack. Through this hour-glass opening flows much of the northern tidal water on its way from and to the Strait of Georgia. Twice each lunar day the surge and ebb of the tide fills and empties tremendous amounts of water to raise and lower the level of the strait and all of the many bays, coves, arms, inlets and channels from six to eighteen feet.

The inexorable rush of all this water through this narrow restricted channel produces currents up to 15 knots with giant whirlpools, boils and overfalls. Although one may see fishboats running the narrows at all stages of the tide, the pleasure boat skipper is well advised to be guided by the current tables in making his passage.

The southgoing tidal stream also surges past Race Point at a rate of 6 to 10 knots at times. The resultant heavy overfalls and eddies against a fresh easterly or southeasterly wind make this race very dangerous for small boats.

A major menace to navigation in Seymour Narrows was Ripple Rock in the center of the channel. Then in 1958 two and a half million pounds of explosives and the biggest man-made non-atomic explosion in the world blew the top 40 feet off the underwater twin peaks in a dramatic removal of the hazard.

Continuing up Discovery Passage, we rounded Bodega Point and the group of islands in Kanish Bay to a pleasant overnight anchorage in Granite Bay. A quick look at the chart discouraged an exploration of the cove marked "Small Inlet" off the northeastern end of Kanish Bay. We heard later that, although the entrance is narrow and shallow, inside depths to six fathoms offer good anchorage. Perhaps an exploration by dinghy first would be advisable.

Leaving Kanish Bay we cruised inside Nixon Island and around Granite Point to enter Okisollo Channel bordering the north and northeast of Quadra Island. Here is a most pleasing waterway with a goodly scattering of interesting islands, numerous secluded coves and bays and upper and lower rapids. Except for an occasional boat passing, one feels far removed from civilization, cruising on placid water in total silence. The islands or groups of islands seem suddenly to detach themselves from what appeared to be a solid shoreline.

Running between the Okis Islands and Haro Island, we poked our bow into Barnes Bay for a quick look at what appeared to be a good anchorage. We went on to pass Walters Point and enter Owen Bay leaving Grant Island to starboard. Charts and cruise guides show a government wharf, store and post office but we learned that the store and post office hadn't been in operation for 10 or 12 years.

After landing at what we thought was the government float we were told that it was now private. Seeing another float in the southeast part of the bay, we came upon Walter Lumsden working on a boat and asked if we could moor

Beazley Pass of Surge Narrows between Peck and Sturt Islands is the favored route of most skippers. Currents up to 12 knots mean running at or near slack is recommended.

there. He said we were welcome. The right part of the float was his and the left was public. He also told us that the first float where we had landed was, in truth, a government float in spite of what we had been told.

Mr. Lumsden, a Scotsman, enjoys visiting and told how he had been around the world three times, spending time in Australia, New Zealand and Fiji. His wife died some years ago and he spends his time designing and building boats. He and one other family are now the only ones in the bay.

Okisollo Channel's Lower Rapids are below the Okis Islands while the Upper Rapids are between Cooper Point and the islands to the south of Owens Bay. Both Upper and Lower Rapids run up to 9 knots on spring flood and ebb tides with a heavy overfall on the ebb below the Upper Rapids.

Just below the Upper Rapids, between Springer and Etta Points is the Hole In The Wall. This four-mile-long channel runs between Sonora and Maurelle Islands to connect Okisollo Channel with Calm Channel to the east. This narrow passage between high cliffs rising to peaks up to 1735 feet is one of the most scenic spots in these waters. With rapids in the narrows at each end, many yachtsmen hesitate to go through but close attention to the current tables will prove rewarding. The rapids at the southwestern end are the dangerous ones with spring tides running up to 12 knots on the flood and 10 knots on the ebb. The flood, joining currents from the Upper Rapids, can break into dangerous eddies that extend into Okisollo Channel.

One of the most beautiful and intriguing areas in these waters is the Octopus Islands group. Days can be spent exploring the many interesting coves, fishing or just lazing around enjoying the peaceful setting. Anchorage can be found in Bodega Anchorage north of the Octopus Islands, in Waiatt Bay or in one of the protected bights north of the bay. Oysters and clams add another attraction to this delightful cruising area.

Some three miles to the southeast Okisollo Channel ends at Surge Narrows. Here again is one of nature's beauty spots not too well known by many Northwest yachtsmen. The narrows proper, between Quadra Island and Antonio Point on Maurelle Island, attain a velocity of up to 12 knots on spring flood tides. Attention to the current tables is recommended.

There are three possible courses through or around the islands called the Settlers Group; however most skippers prefer Beazley Pass between Peck and Sturt Islands, keeping a wary eye out for Tusko Rock. Fishing in this

Dodman's Store and fuel float are located on Read Island just opposite Beazley Pass of Surge Narrows.

Boat Passage of Whiterock Passage between Maurelle and Read Islands has been dredged to a low water depth of 6'.

Southwestern tip of Read Island, with Hoskyn Rock to the right, is at entrance to Hoskyn Channel.

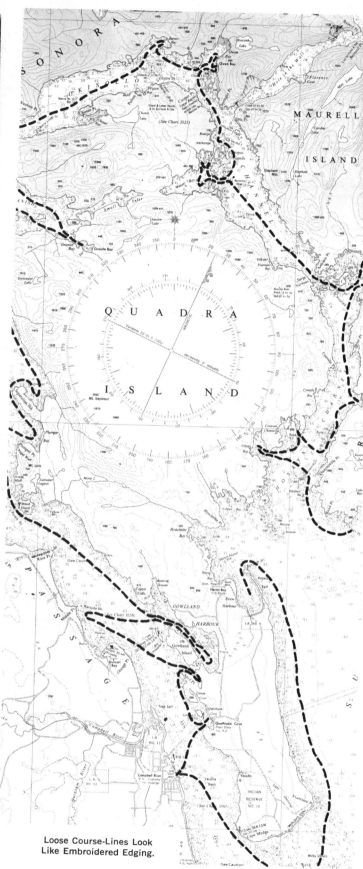

Loose Course-Lines Look Like Embroidered Edging.

Hjorth Bay on Read Island's west side offers protected anchorage.

area is usually good. The first mate landed a beauty here.

The settlement of Surge Narrows is to the east of the Settlers Group on Read Island. Mr. and Mrs. George Dodman operate a general store, fuel float and post office and are enthusiastic boosters for the many attractions of the Surge Narrows area. They report that the government float and fuel float charted in the little bight just north of Surge Point is no longer open.

Mr. Dodman also pointed out that Boat Passage of Whiterock Passage has been dredged to a depth of six feet at low tide and is now passable. Two ranges, one a bow range and one a stern range, facilitate passage. Plenty of caution, a depth sounder and a slow bell are called for to avoid the rocks and reefs. Better yet, get George Dodman to draw you a little sketch and describe the proper use of the ranges. This passage is a convenient short cut to Calm Channel.

Continuing south in Hoskyn Channel there are several coves worthy of consideration. Along Read Island's western shore we found two cruisers rafted together in the bight behind Sheer Point. A little further along is lovely Hjorth Bay and still further are a couple of small coves behind the King Islets as well as a bay below Dunsterville Point.

On the other side of the channel there is a bight behind Conville Point. Just below is Conville Bay. Fairly protected anchorage can be found behind Bold Island. Village Bay is all right in good weather but somewhat exposed to southeasterly winds.

This brings us back to our point of departure in our circumnavigation of Quadra Island. Discovery Passage, Okisollo Passage and Hoskyn Passage with their wealth of islands, bays and coves, good fishing, exciting narrows and rapids, quiet and peaceful anchorages and superb photographic possibilities offer the cruising skipper, his family and guests just about all he could desire for a few days or as long as he wants to spend. The area is another gem in the crown of this great Northwest cruising paradise.

34

Alaska Beckons

Wwhat's a cruiser race to Alaska? It can be cold, uncomfortable and challenging. Everyone on the bridge was silent. The steady rhythmic swish-swish-swish of the windshield swipes marked a steady beat like a metronome to time the pulsing of the motors. The four men huddled deeper into their jackets as the raw, dank cold of the fog outside penetrated the curtains to do battle with a trickle of warm air coming up from the hatch of the cabin forward.

The navigator rubbed his hands together to warm them while giving his attention first to the chart on the table before him, then to study the radar screen, occasionally peering out through the arc made by the swipes. That was useless. No landmarks were visible in the fog and semi darkness of early morning. He went back to the radar.

At the wheel the helmsman kept his eyes on the compass. He must hold the boat on its course of 318° for the shores on either side of the passage were rocky. He was so intent on steering a straight course that he was unaware of the numbness in his fingers gripping the wheel or of the small droplet that hung from the tip of his nose.

Although it wasn't a duty, the observer joined the skipper in staring ahead in an effort to spot drifting deadheads through the gray-white curtain that surrounded them. The eyes of each swung with the swipes, trying to catch a quick glimpse through a bit of clear glass before it became misted over again.

It wasn't raining, yet rivulets of water ran off the tip of each swipe as it reached the end of its sweep. A tiny stream wound down the inside of the center windshield — the result of a leak where the wiper shaft went through the wood. The fog was so thick it turned to water on contact with anything.

After another look at the radar screen, the navigator applied the dividers to the chart, scribbled some figures on scratch paper and broke the silence by announcing to the helmsman, "We're okay. You're on course, dead center in the channel. We just passed Baudre Point and I can make out Asher Point coming up."

Silence again, except for the swish-swish of the wipers, as the tenseness relaxed. Enough warmth was oozing up from the hatch now to cloud the windows on the inside.

The skipper turned on the windshield fans while the observer wiped the side windows. The navigator jammed his hands into the pockets of his jacket searching for warmth while the helmsman flexed his fingers, opening and closing his fists one at a time, still staring intently at the compass.

"She'll be lifting soon," the skipper said, matter-of-factly. "The breeze is picking up and should blow it off within a half hour." He slid in beside the helmsman. "Here, I'll take the wheel. You go down and see if you can stir the girls into starting breakfast."

What's a cruiser race to Alaska?

It can be piling out of a cozy bunk in the cold gray darkness of early morning; fumbling with the wet stiff lines to cast off from the nightly raft-up of boats or from the floats of a fishing village; feeling a way through the murky haze to find the buoy or point designated as the starting line for a day's first racing leg and hoping the combination of boat and crew can outwit the currents, wind, fog or rain for a better score than yesterday.

It can be gloriously bright sunshine reflecting green, forest-clad hills with the backdrop of purple snow-capped mountain peaks into the labyrinth of sparkling waterways forming the highway of the sea which is the famous Inland Passage to the storied land of the north.

It is cruising through enchanting passages which wind through a myriad collection of islands and peninsulas, inlets and straits, where the land and the sea meet again and again in a kaleidoscopic jumble that gives British Columbia some 16,900 miles of coastline and Alaska more than double that figure.

It is traversing nearly virgin territory with very little evidence of civilization and the realization that you have been preceded by Haida, Tsimshian and Kwakiutl Indians whose totems silently log your passage. Polynesians and Orientals are said to have cruised these waters. History is a bit more specific about Sir Francis Drake having been here in 1759, Juan de Fuca, the Greek, possibly in 1592, Bering and Chirikof, the Russians, in 1741, followed by Perez and Quadra of Spain, Captain James Cook and Captain George Vancouver of England. Today this fantasy of unspoiled seascape and landscape appears much the same as it did to these earlier sailors.

What's a cruiser race to Alaska?

It can be warm, relaxing and enjoyable.

Racing was over for the day. The skipper plopped down in one of the big comfortable deck chairs across the back of the raised cockpit. Resting his feet on a folding canvas stool, he pulled his navy blue yachting cap over his face to keep the bright sunshine out of his eyes and sighed contentedly. In a moment he was asleep.

After setting up a course to the bay where the boats would rendezvous for the night, the navigator busied himself with the day's racing fiures. The women came on deck from the cabin to busy themselves with applying sun-tan lotion and fingernail polish, writing post cards and "oohing" and "ahing" at the beauty of a narrow waterfall which fell down the mountainside on the starboard in a series of silvery ribbons as it plunged from terrace to terrace and split into three iridescent veils before joining the sea.

The ship's give-away observer was back aboard and joined the group lazing in the cockpit by pulling another deck chair out into the bright sunshine. Gentle snores from the skipper emphasized the relaxation everyone was enjoying.

The helmsman's wife screwed the cap on the tube of lotion, placed it on the table, leaned back in her chair and stretched her arms out to take advantage of the tanning rays. "The scenery is beginning to look more like I expected Alaska to look," she observed.

"Yes, it's more like the pictures," said the skipper's wife.

"So far it's been beautiful but not much different than the San Juans or Gulf Islands. Now the mountains are higher and more rugged with the snow on top much closer to us."

"It's even more spectacular than the pictures," added the observer's wife.

All fell silent as they watched a large brightly colored butterfly flit around the deck. A moment later their attention was drawn to half a dozen seagulls describing graceful flight patterns as they soared, glided and swooped lazily above and behind the boat.

Suddenly the navigator called back. "Look at the entrance to that bay over there," he said. "Isn't that where we got that 35-pounder two years ago?"

The skipper's wife swung her foot around to kick the stool out from under the sleeping skipper's feet. "Dear, there's the place we caught the big one last time. Let's try it again."

"Humf! How's that? Whadja say?"

"Come on. Let's try some fishing."

There was a flurry of excitement as poles were pulled down from their brackets, herring dug out of the deep freezer, and the boat swung around toward the entrance of the bay. Bait was put on the double hooks and four lines were in the water before they reached the spot.

With one motor stopped and the other throttled down to a good trolling speed, a run was made across the bay's mouth. The skipper took the wheel, headed along the steep wall of the shore then made a short U-turn to head back in the opposite direction.

The turn was hardly more than completed when the "Zing-g-g-g" of a reel was followed by a scream from the helmsman's wife.

"Ooo-o-o — I've got one!"

The others reeled in while the boat was stopped and the observer raised a deck hatch to get out the landing net.

Jerry Bryant's Alexa plays tag with an iceberg in Endicott Arm

A peaceful setting and a convenient float provide an ideal rendezvous in Hobart Bay

Plenty of oysters, clams, fish and crabs are always a part of a cruise/race to Alaska. Here a couple of crew members of Dr. Mitch Bilafer's Doressa of San Francisco get ready to cook their crabs

A park of totem poles and a tribal house is one of the attractions at Wrangell

"Careful now, Honey," advised the helmsman. "Don't give him any slack."

Suddenly the singing of the reel quit. The helmsman's wife pulled up on the pole which bent almost double. She managed a few cranks on the reel, another pull-up of the pole and another crank or two before the big lunker took off again, the reel screaming merrily.

All at once the screaming ceased, the line went slack and the excited girl yelled, "I've lost him!"

"Reel in! Reel it in!" shouted her husband. "He's probably just gone down or headed back toward the boat."

She reeled slack line for what seemed minutes before there was a violent jerk and the line was humming out again.

Three times the helmsman's wife fought the fish in, pulling the pole up, reeling in the few feet gained and repeating the operation. Three times, before it was anywhere close to the boat, it took off on another headlong run seaward. The others lined the rail, shouting advice and encouragement to the tiring girl.

Again there was a slackening in the line. Out in the distance the water splashed. A magnificent King Salmon stood on his tail and tried to shake the hook clear.

"There he is!" shouted the navigator.

"Fifty pounds if he's an ounce," guessed the skipper.

Another long, tedious reel-in, the fish resisting every foot of the way, brought him alongside. They could see him just below the surface still fighting the hook but definitely tiring. The observer had the net over, ready for a landing when the water erupted into a fountain of foam.

"Watch out!" yelled the skipper, "He's headed under the boat. Put the tip of your pole in the water and walk around the stern to the other side."

By the time this operation was completed the fish was headed for the rocks along the shore. Patiently, almost gently, the girl worked the fish back toward the boat. It swam lazily broadside for a moment. A quick flash of the net, a mighty heave and the sun's rays flashed off the shining silvery sides of the salmon as it thrashed about in the net on the deck.

The helmsman's wife collapsed into a deck chair. The scales showed 48 lbs. 10 oz. A pound and six ounces short of the skipper's estimate, but there was enough so every boat in the fleet had a sizable salmon steak or two that night.

What's a cruiser race to Alaska?

It's days of pitting navigational and piloting skill against the elements, interspersed with fascinating side trips, either conducted or private, for sightseeing, exploring and picture-taking, followed by nightly rendezvous where boat hopping, a card game, a song fest, a beach fire, yarn swapping and good fellowship prevail.

It's coming out of a narrow passage into a larger body of water to discover a pod of whales surfacing, blowing and jumping out of the water as if putting on a special show for the visitors' benefit. It's watching half a dozen porpoises play tag around the boat with the bow as their home base.

The first boat came into the bay about mid-afternoon, dropped anchor and had its dinghy in the water and a crew of young explorers ashore before the next boat came in to tie alongside. It was a beautiful clear afternoon with heat from the sun belying that the 56° parallel of latitude had just been crossed an hour before.

The anticipation of lazily lounging on the deck, soaking up sunshine while drinking in the scenic beauties of this lovely bay with its fir-lined shore and complete isolation, was cut short by an announcement from the racemaster. He told of a winding trail that followed the creek back into the forest and up the hillside. He told of the possibility of sighting bears as they fished the creek for the spawning salmon headed upstream.

Bella Bella is a popular place to re-fuel and restock ship's stores

It was only minutes before the placid waters of the bay were dotted with shoreboats headed for the mouth of the creek and loaded with cameras and fishing gear.

The skipper had been there before, so elected to stay aboard as did the girls who were tired from a too-early rising that morning. The navigator, helmsman and observer were anxious for the trip and promptly lowered the dinghy from its stern davits.

A landing was made on a gravelly point thrown up by the rushing waters of the creek across its mouth where it joined the saltchuck. The outboard was pulled up and the boat made fast to a large rock well up shore against a flooding tide.

In spite of the remoteness of the area, the trail appeared well worn. It followed the creek for a way until the waterway formed a big "U" to backtrack a bit between wide sandy beaches. At strategic spots along the beaches eagles stood in statuesque poses, waiting for a fish bound upstream that suited their fancy.

After the path entered the deeper forest, it was frequently crossed by game trails leading to the water. Even though the hikers were traveling in shade the warmth of the day called for the shedding of outer garments. The sun seemed to be drawing a moist warm mist from the damp matting of undergrowth up through the trees overhead.

At one point on a curve of the trail the foliage opened up to form a lacy frame revealing the flat area below and the picturesque cut in the distant shoreline where the creek entered the bay. Both the navigator and helmsman dropped back to snap pictures of nature's gorgeous painting.

Before long the trail paralleled the creek again. There, on a sandy point on the other side stood a large black bear. He had just emerged from the water with his fish and was shaking himself. Either his nose or his ears warned him of the approaching hikers for he gave a disdainful snort and lumbered into the woods with his fish.

Where the trail started uphill just below a cascading waterfall, the party stopped. The stream was a solid mass of "humpies" ranging from a foot to two feet in length. They appeared to be just loafing in the stream as if awaiting courage enough to take off into the stronger current and fling themselves upward in the falls. The group stood enchanted and amazed as they watched the valiant efforts of the salmon fighting their way up river, overcoming all obstacles to reach the place of their birth.

The trail continued to climb until it reached a rustic lookout cabin where the hikers could sit on benches while they watched the fish negotiate another falls upstream or keep a lookout for more bears fishing downstream. The salmon continued their inevitable journey to the spawning portion of the river but the bears, evidently sensing the presence of humans, failed to show up. The party headed down trail and back to the boats.

What's a cruiser race to Alaska?

It's the grandeur of majestic glaciers grinding their slow, inexorable way down the mountainsides to the sea. It's the fantastically and beautifully shaped icebergs, sculptured in iridescent blue ice as if for a fancy float in a parade.

The first icebergs appeared as the boats approached Glass Peninsula. They were small and dirty looking, somewhat of a disappointment to those making their first trip. "Don't waste film on these," suggested the skipper, "They'll get bigger and better as we get further in."

Approaching the finish line of the first leg of the day's race just outside Holkham Bay, the navigator displayed the chart and pointed out the fork formed by Tracy Arm to the

north and Endicott Arm to the southeast. According to the racemaster's itinerary, time out would be taken between the two race legs for share-the-ride trips up Tracy Arm or to Ford's Terror down Endicott Arm.

Cruising slowly among the icebergs in Endicott Arm, the skipper explained the danger of these tremendous floating islands of ice. "With 75 to 90 percent of their bulk below the surface and with any number of odd shapes, it's easy to see how they can be a real hazard to a boat," he said.

Just then the helmsman called attention to one of the other boats circling a big berg and rocking it with her wake. The crew watched, enthralled, as suddenly the huge chunk of ice seemed to rise up in the water. It wavered a moment and then turned over with a resounding splash to reveal a long rough point which before had been just under the water.

"See what I mean?" said the skipper.

What's a cruiser race to Alaska?

It's trips ashore to visit fishing villages you've heard of from other yachtsmen during a bull session in front of the yacht club fireplace or aboard someone's boat in a snug anchorage on a frosty winter night. Villages such as Butedale, Klemtu, Bella Bella and Namu move out of the realm of fancy to become real places as supplies are bought in the general stores and the boat is refueled while the crew watches the fishermen work over their nets on the floats.

Larger towns, too, turn into reality as Prince Rupert, Ketchikan, Wrangell and Petersburg offer the crews a night of shore leave with the ladies donning skirts and the men blue blazers with their yacht club burgees decorating the breast pockets. Here again, more shopping, sightseeing, and a dinner dance at the local Elks Club changes the pace once more in a whirling two weeks that serve up something new and different every day — and often many times a day.

Semi-familiar place names change to living bays, inlets, lagoons, passages, channels, reaches, narrows and sounds, impressed firmly in memory for all time.

And then there's the Grande Finale, the parade of boats up Gastineau Channel to Juneau, the awards banquet at the Baranof Hotel, walking the narrow un-planned streets to souvenir and specialty shops, taking in the "musts" such as the famous piano and songs of Juneau Hattie or the taste of the old wild west days at the Red Dog Saloon.

What's a cruiser race to Alaska?

It's racing and cruising with people having a common interest, many of whom are strangers at the start but before the event is ended all are friends and a new camaraderie has been established. That feeling of "one for all and all for one" helps smooth the rough spots — the loan of a needed part, a boat with radar slowing pace to help others through the fog, sharing fuel with someone who runs short, and a hundred other such acts which create and cement friendships.

What's a cruiser race to Alaska?

It's the experience of a lifetime — not to be missed!

Nobody had more fun or saw more sights than the crew of the Bessie, slowest boat on the race. Here part of the crew returns from a sightseeing trip around Swanson Bay in the canoe which was carried in addition to a dinghy and two bicycles.

Morning fog lifts as the fleet puts into Butedale for refueling

35

Highway of the Sea to Alaska

A laska beckons to the western yachtsman. What adventuresome skipper has not heard or read of the spectacular labyrinth of narrow waterways winding through rugged ranges of naked cliffs or amidst lofty vistas of green clad hills or scattered islands set in an opalescent sea?

He no doubt harbors, consciously or unconsciously, a dream of someday steering a course along that Highway of the Sea which is the famous Inland Passage to the storied Land of the North.

There may be a bit of hesitancy about planning such a cruise for he perhaps has also heard or read about surging narrows where rapids attain a velocity up to 24 knots, or of open stretches of the great Pacific with its giant waves, or of passages clogged with icebergs. He's still intrigued, however, even while recognizing the need or advisability of some local knowledge.

The perfect answer seems to be for the first-timer to enter the Alaska Cruiser Race, a predicted log event staged every other year by the International Power Boat Association. As Racemaster Frank Morris says, "This isn't a predicted log race as most of us think of one but a family type fleet cruise with some navigational competition thrown in."

A day's run could include a couple of legs of predicted log racing, time out for a side trip to some spot with an extra bit of scenic wonder or a waterfall or roaring rapids, a bit of salmon fishing, perhaps a shipwreck party on the beach, oyster hunting or clam digging expedition, or an evening rendezvous with your choice of group singing, a card game or swapping sea stories.

Actually, the Alaska Race is a sort of personally conducted tour by a veteran skipper who has cruised these waters many times and plans the entire event before starting. It is the perfect opportunity to make a first-time Alaska run, not only with expert guidance, but with a real fun group of yachtsmen. And—those who have gone before seem to enjoy a repeat performance.

Racing legs are sometimes interspersed with "free runs" through exotically beautiful areas, into such off-the-course places as Endicott and Tracy Arms and Ford's Terror with their spectacular icebergs, glaciers and

waterfalls. Through tricky passages and rapids a pilot boat leads the way. These free runs are before, after or between the legs of the predicted log race so the skipper and crew do not have to be concerned with strict attention to course and speed but can relax and enjoy the sights. Still further latitude is allowed by permitting a boat to stop at any time during a leg to fish or explore on its own.

The 1966 Alaska Race started on July 11, following the International Cruiser Race. Divided into two sections, the first ran from Entrance Island, just outside Nanaimo, to Prince Rupert and the second from Prince Rupert to Juneau, each section taking about a week.

Of 21 boats representing ten yacht clubs from the San Francisco, Portland, Puget Sound and Vancouver, B.C., areas, 16 participated in the race while five were along "just for the ride."

Courses ran through enchanting passages, channels, reaches and narrows with their swirling whirlpools and rushing currents. Night stops during the first section of this race-cruise were made at Refuge Cove, Cracroft in Port Harvey, Port Hardy, Codville Lagoon, Swanson Bay, the inner harbor at Kumealon and finally at Prince Rupert, the Halibut Capital of the World.

These bays and coves as well as many others we poked our bows into for exploration have a sylvan peacefulness, many of them with silvery ribbons of cascading water drawn irresistibly from higher elevations to plunge headlong down a vertical hillside or to laze through limpid pools before finally emptying into the salt chuck.

The evening rendezvous was something to look forward to when everyone relaxed from the tensions of racing, navigating narrow passages through fog, threading through a maze of gillnets or just plain weariness induced by a daybreak start of the day's run. Boat hopping is popular with crews becoming better acquainted and sharing the thrills and excitement of the day with each other.

A special noon-time stop at Sointula on Malcolm Island was a highlight of the trip. At this Finnish community of several hundred people many of the crew members took advantage of the hospitality extended by a group of local citizens under the leadership of Barney Prestie. Cars were provided for trips from the two boat basins to markets or the Sauna Baths.

A cruise to Alaska may not be all milk and honey. Weather plays a big part in this untamed country and can be almost anything—but mostly unpredictable. Placid water can sparkle in bright sunshine while snow capped peaks glisten against a clear blue sky. Fog and a misty drizzle can last for days or may merely drape the morning hours while the afternoon comes forth in a dazzling party dress. Gales and driving rain can force the skipper to seek a sheltered nook for hours or even days.

The gods were with us on our cruise, however, with smooth seas on all open ocean crossings and only a day and a half of rain. Fog was evident only in the morning most of the time with afternoons clear and warm.

Sitting on deck at an evening rendezvous in a quiet, scenic bay we could see the straggling streamers of fog sneak in around the tops of the peaks huddled together in bulky, jagged silhouette. In the early morning about sunrise or shortly after, the streamers are still snuggling around the hilltops but as the morning progresses, the fog drops to water level to make navigation difficult until it burns off around noon. At such times a good compass and carefully plotted courses are "musts" and, of course, radar can be most helpful.

Whatever the weather, a cruise to Alaska is an exhilerating experience. One tends to play down or forget weather conditions, in favor of the majestic surroundings of apparently never-ending passages, channels and inlets with rugged hills dressed in their green trees, rising from the water against a backdrop of snowcapped peaks highlighted by an occasional shimmering blue-green glacier. Islands, winding passageways, hidden bays and inviting coves beg to be explored. The beauty and awesome scenery continues each day defying verbal description and one wonders if even the camera can record it adequately.

Any avid boatman who gathers with others of the clan at favorite anchorages or at bull sessions in the yacht club cocks a keen ear whenever Alaska cruise stories are told. Part of the thrill of his first cruise there is becoming intimately and personally acquainted with places whose names he has heard.

Places such as Port Hardy, Namu, Bella Bella, Klemtu and Butedale are converted from mere names to living towns, each with its own particular charm. Minstral Island, Queen Charlotte Strait and Sound, Millbanke Sound and Chatham Sound turn from dreams into reality. Particularly anchored in memory are the beauties of narrow and rocky Reid Passage, enchanting Jackson Passage, an intriguing waterway narrow and rocky at its opening with many scenic little bays along its course, and the indescribable beauty of 50-mile-long Grenville Channel.

Arrival of the fleet at Prince Rupert was, in the minds of many, a major accomplishment. What perhaps had seemed awesome to the neophyte before he started was now commonplace, almost the same, yet with some differences, as cruising the San Juan or the Gulf Islands.

Anan Creek, emptying into Anan (Humback) Bay, presents an interesting picture from the trail leading upstream.

Arrangements for an Awards Party had failed to materialize but an impromptu affair was staged at the Prince Rupert Elks Club. Who would have ever thought that a group of cruising-racing yachtsmen from a variety of yacht clubs would find themselves celebrating the halfway mark of their race in an Elks Lodge.

Perhaps it wasn't so strange after all. As everyone who ever took the Power Squadron Piloting course knows, Elks are tied to boating through the little memory trick of relating B.P.O.E. to buoys—"Black-Port-On-Entering" or "Black-Port-Odd (numbers)-Entering." In Prince Rupert ties between Elks and yachtsmen were strengthened as Exalted Ruler Pat Deane and some of the boys of Lodge #342 saw to it that the Benevolent and Protective Order of Elks brought the fleet safely through a crisis.

The affair was a happy combination of serious awards presentation, fun and good fellowship. In addition to the trophies for race winners of the first section, special prizes went to skippers, observers, crew members or guests who did something outstanding during the week which others could appreciate or enjoy.

Examples were prizes for best exchange observer, most helpful boat, best racing log, and good seamanship. Fun prizes were also given for such things as "no mistakes" to a boat that didn't race, for hitting the biggest log, for a happy ship, for the biggest fish, for best behaved wife and children, etc.

Such is the camaraderie to be found on a race-cruise of this kind where the feeling "all for one and one for all" grows with each passing day. The first section was finished—a great success—a never-to-be-forgotten experience. The second half and the grand finish at Juneau lay ahead.

Twisting through sheltered fiords and channels bordered by green-timbered slopes of coast mountains, we continued our cruise on the Highway of the Sea.

On this, our first adventuring into these waters, there was a growing and inexpressible anticipation as we left Prince Rupert on the second half of the race. Soon we would cross the International Boundary to enter our 49th state, Alaska, the storied land of the midnight sun with its heritage of robust history and romantic legend.

Even the name intrigues the imagination. Alaska comes from the Aleut word Alaxsxaq meaning "The Great Land" a definition most befitting this area.

It was another day of early rising as we rolled out of the bunk at 4:30 to find dull, leaden skies exuding a fine mist filtering through a blanket of fog which had already slid down the surrounding hills to water level. Following a warming breakfast we felt our way through the fog to the next basin to board Bill Killam's Porpoise III as observer for the day's run. Departure was scheduled for 6:00 A.M.

Digby Island, lying across the mouth of Prince Rupert Harbour and protecting it from the wrath of the Pacific pouring through Dixon Entrance, offered two courses to the starting line off Tugwell Reef. While some boats chose to round the south end of Digby, Bill elected to go thru Venn Passage to the north of the island.

Proving a right to his reputation as one of Canada's top skippers, Bill exhibited as neat a bit of navigation and piloting as we've seen by taking Porpoise III through the pea soup fog to a point exactly between the two markers at the entrance to the passage.

During the run through narrow and rock-cluttered Venn Passage we were kept busy watching the depth sounder and peering through the fog in search of the frequent markers in the tortuous channel but not too busy to realize that, without the fog, this would be a waterway of incomparable beauty. We regretted that the fog precluded any photography.

With Mac Bowell's Camiram III and Mitch Bilafer's Doressa following close astern, Porpoise III approached Metlakatla Bay, the end of the Passage and the entrance to Chatham Sound. We could pick up the light on our port and finally located what looked like a black buoy off our starboard bow. We were sure we were in center channel. Suddenly a large bed of kelp appeared off the port bow. Bill immediately cut down on the throttles but it was too late. There was a grinding crunch as he disengaged the gears.

Wild gesturing warned the boats following of the danger so they were able to avoid the reef.

It didn't take long to discover that our port propeller was too badly bent to use. Bill wavered between going back to Prince Rupert for a haul-out or proceeding with the fleet on one engine. The decision made to continue, we took a test run with the Camiram III to establish speed on one engine, refigured the first leg and radioed an amended predicted log to the judges.

At the end of the leg our estimated speed of 8.5 knots proved far from accurate as we logged better than 37 minutes fast. A quick recalculation of the leg showed us running near 10 knots. The second leg from Tree Point to Ketchikan through the nearly unpronounceable Revillagigedo Channel was run at 10 knots but we were still 10 minutes fast.

An example of the good sportsmanship and spirit of helpfulness prevailing on a cruise/race of this kind was demonstrated when Mitch Bilafer radioed from his Doressa that he would be in Ketchikan sufficiently ahead of us to line up a shipyard with ways clear to haul us out. As good as his word he spent considerable time going to four yards before he found one which would take us if we got there by 5 o'clock.

It was 4:30 when we transferred back to our home ship, Miss Kathy, in the channel at Ketchikan and Bill took Porpoise III on for a change of propeller and shaft.

Ketchikan, known as the Salmon Capital of the World, impressed us as a fishing village grown into a modern town. Another fabulous banquet at the Ketchikan Elks Club was the highlight of the evening marking the end of the first day of the second half of our trip. It was here that we were all inducted into the Order of the Alaska Walrus and presented with a certificate and lapel button.

Tuesday dawned partly cloudy with some sun leaking through. Watching a faster-than-predicted tide race past the harbor, we delayed our departure until 7:50. The day's run featured a school of porpoises which played tag around the boat for 15 or 20 minutes with our bow as their home base.

Our course took us up Clarence Strait, into Ernest Sound and through Seward Passage to Anan Bay, marked Humpback Bay on some charts. Here was another hauntingly beautiful harbor providing a cozy anchorage and an unusually interesting side trip.

Anan Creek empties into the bay after a devious run down the mountainside. A well-kept trail following the creek is frequently crossed by wild life trails used by deer, bears, and other animals on their way to the water. We had an ambition to get a picture of a bear fishing in the creek but we were too late in starting our hike and those ahead of us had scared them away. All we saw was one big bruin as he left the creek to head into the woods.

The creek was literally a solid pack of humpback salmon making their way upstream to spawn, fighting up the rapids and hurling themselves upward in the falls. A rustic observation house provided an opportunity to rest and watch for bears or see the struggling masses of fish. On the return trip we were fascinated by the many eagles swooping down to lift a salmon from the swirling rapids or waiting patiently on a sand bar at the mouth of the creek for one that struck their fancy. It was a fairly long hike but well worth the effort.

Wednesday was our day to observe aboard George Steiner's *Gem*. We hoped their luck would be better than the day before when, leaving Ketchikan, they had picked up in the props, of all things, a sleeping bag. Attempts to clear them only wound the shreds of the bag tighter and they had to go on the ways to cut it out.

We were now getting well into the long coastal arm of the Alaska panhandle with some 11,000 islands appearing to account for more land mass than the mainland. From the many pictures we have seen of Alaska we were looking for waterways bordered with high snow capped mountains, their black or purple ruggedness rising nearly perpendicularly from the water's edge. Thus far we could distinguish almost no difference from the general scenery found in the San Juan and Gulf Islands, delightful channels winding gracefully through a maze of green clad islands.

A change was gradually taking place now as we churned ever northward. Mountains, which had not yet taken off their white nighties of fog with filmy streamers of lace hanging down to their feet, were growing taller. Misty fiords with steep walls, cascading water falls and a cooler crispness to the air were all contributing to a subtle change marking the engaging charm which is Alaska.

While making our way up Blake Channel and Eastern Passage the morning fog lifted enough to reveal the imperishable beauty of these narrow waterways leading to Wrangell. We were lucky, for the curtain dropped again and some of the later boats had trouble on the mud flats off the mouth of the Stikine River.

Wrangell, one of Alaska's oldest towns, has a character all its own. It was here we found some of that traditional Alaskan hospitality and warm friendliness. A stop at the cannery where we purchased five pound cans of dry-pack shrimp was followed by a walk through a park of totem poles and an Indian tribal house to the inner boat basin. A later walk through muddy streets took us to a supermarket as huge and modern as found in any metropolis.

Pulling out of the harbor, we watched a fisherman unloading huge wire baskets of Dungeness crabs at the cannery. The unloading was completed by the time we came alongside and an offer to buy a few crabs was turned down. The fisherman reached into the cockpit and tossed three huge beauties to us which he had planned to take home. Offers of payment were refused with, "Guess that's the least we can do for state-side visitors."

The run up lovely Wrangell Narrows was a memorable one. In addition to the incomparable beauty of the

Ketchikan, Alaska's southernmost major city, holds a friendly welcome for all ships.

scenery, there was the thrill of meeting the two tremendous passenger boats *Prince George* and *Malaspina* in the narrowest part. Gordy Shotwell's *High Cotton*, immediately ahead of us, was so dwarfed by the giants that she looked like the smallest dinghy.

Another impressive feature of Wrangell Narrows was the excellent system of markers. With these large markers, brilliant orange paint, lights and ranges, it would be virtually impossible to get into trouble, providing, of course, one chooses the right stage of the tide.

The day's run ended at Petersburg, a town that seemed geared primarily for the fishing industry with sports fishermen preparing for the big annual Salmon Derby at Juneau. Once again the Elks Club was host for dinner and dancing.

Tidal currents called for a later start Thursday so we enjoyed the luxury of the bunk until 8:30. Leaving Petersburg at 9:40 we watched the sea and the sky meet along the rugged coast to decide on the mood for the day. The fog lifted and, as the sun burst through to reveal the panorama of mountains, the spectacle became three-dimensional with depths of from perhaps 50 to 100 miles.

Skirting the northeast shore of Kupreanof Island, the course in Frederick Sound rounded Cape Fanshaw to turn north and bring us into Hobart Bay. A warm, sunny day together with a short run and an early arrival in a bay with unmatchable scenic beauty put everyone into a gay mood. A fisheries department float provided a chance for all boats to be together. Boat hopping, shore side hikes, clam digging and picture taking kept all hands busy.

When the *Gem* arrived late from a fishing stop-over, cheers were loud and long as Marian Steiner displayed her big King salmon. Arguments over the fish's weight were rampant with the claim of 56¼ pounds being discounted by experts who said it couldn't be over 42 pounds. Whatever it really weighed will probably never be known but it was big enough to provide one or two nice large salmon steaks for every boat as Marian generously divided it among the fleet.

A driftwood beach fire with hot dogs, marshmallows and songs highlighted the evening after a gorgeous sunset.

Friday was a memorable day for several reasons. It was our first clear, bright morning. We could see a few mountain tops with a white frosting of fog running down their sides, but the crisp air promised a lovely day.

As we left the bay the sea was smooth, like oiled steel with the surface disturbed only by the wave of lacy phosphorescence cast aside by the bow. Sea birds either stood on their tails before a quick jack-knife dive below the water or made a double line of expanding dimples as their wings drummed water and air in an effort for speed and altitude.

Suddenly a huge curved knife rose from the depths to cut the water. A moment later the gleaming back of a whale rolled lazily above the surface. Before long there were whales on all sides of us, rolling slowly, spouting fountains of steamy mist into the air, or jumping nearly clear of the water to stand on their noses before submerging again. It was an awesome and exciting display.

Later in the morning we sighted our first iceberg as we came up on Glass Peninsula. The first ones were small but as we approached Holkham Bay they grew larger.

A turn into Endicott Arm brought Sumdum Glacier into view and more bergs of fantastic and beautiful shapes, sculptured in iridescent blue ice as if for a fancy parade float.

Most boats took time out from the race, some turning left for a trip to the glacier filled fairy land of Tracy Arm, others continuing up Endicott Arm for the spectacular sights in Ford's Terror.

It was here that one of the classic quotations of the trip was spoken. Taking advantage of the "share-the-ride" program to Ford's Terror, Don Shotwell had anchored his *Martina* in Sumdum Bay only to return and find her aground on a tide which ebbed more than anticipated. Don Smith, race computor, remarked, dryly, "That was some dumb anchorage."

On the afternoon leg up Stephens Passage to Taku Harbor the jagged mountains, many of them sheathed in glaciers, grew higher with more snow-capped peaks. Here was the scenic splendor of Alaska we had been looking for.

Taku Harbor is a well sheltered anchorage but lacking the remote wildness found in some of the bays where we had spent nights. On one side of the bay was the headquarters of the late Father Hubbard, Alaska's famous flying priest, while at the other end was a fisherman's home and float. A community float for fishboats also gave evidence that we weren't far from civilization.

Saturday was another warm clear day with the morning given over to much cleaning, shining and polishing as ships were dressed for the short last leg of the race and the grand parade through Gastineau Channel to Juneau.

The welcome in Juneau was a fitting climax to a great event. Everyone from Mayor Lauris Parker to the docking committee directing us to our berths in the moorage basin went all out to greet us with true Alaskan warmth. Even the weather warmed to a high of 85°.

The Awards Banquet at the Baranof Hotel Saturday evening, with emcee Frank Field and Racemaster Frank Morris passing out innumerable awards in addition to the race trophies, was enjoyed by all.

Trophies for the Prince Rupert to Juneau leg went to Don Bancroft, first in *Alaska Hunter*, Dewey Estey, second in *Miss Kathy* and Jerry Bryant, third in *Alexa*.

Overall honors for the entire race from Silva Bay to Juneau went to *Alaska Hunter* in first place; *Alexa*, second; *High Cotton*, third; *Miss Kathy*, fourth, and *Doressa*, fifth.

We were all further honored with the presentation of handsome certificates proclaiming us members in the Totem Igloo of the Mystic and Auroral Order of Alaska Cheechakos.

The race itself was ended but the event was far from over. Some had to hurry back. Others tarried to enjoy the sights and fun of Juneau, make a visit to the famous Mendenhall Glacier and Chapel by the Lake or cruise further on to Skagway and the rail trip through White Pass to Whitehorse.

On the return cruise the fleet split into small groups according to time available. Fishing, exploring and sightseeing in places missed on the way up allowed a relaxing contrast to the pressures of racing and gave everyone the oppurtunity to enjoy more fully the wonders and beauties of this Highway of the Sea which is the inland passage to Alaska.

136

Approaching Endicott Arm, the iceburgs frequently reminded one of specially constructed floats for a festival parade.

Juneau, Alaska's capitol, presents an interesting picture snuggled at the base of a mountain.

Petersburg has a large and convenient Boat Basin with plenty of room both for boats and yachts.

The Tribal House dominates the center of Totem Pole Park at Wrangel.

137

Part V

The Inland Empire and Other Stories

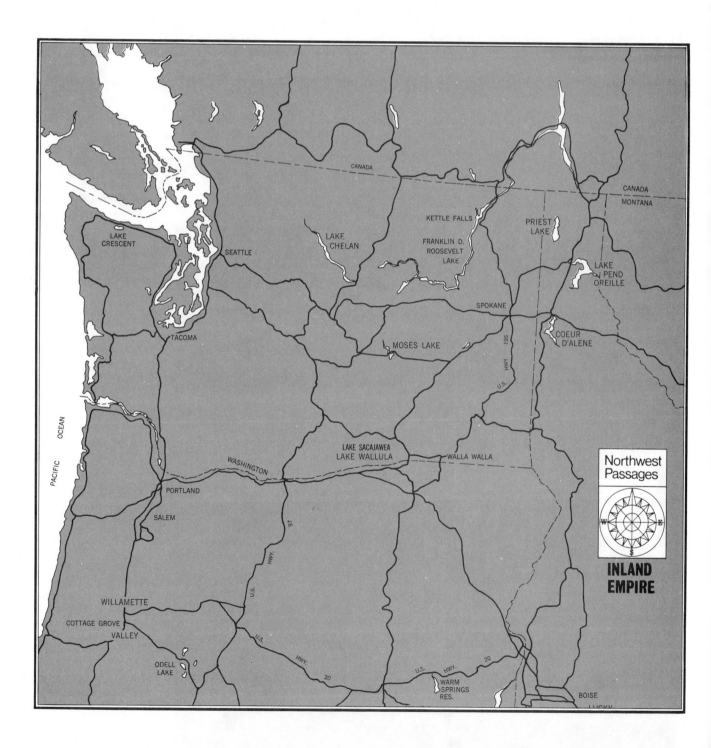

36
Boating Blooms in the Desert

A comforting breeze cooled the heat of a bright sun shining down from a sky flecked with transient puffs of white clouds. A group of outboarders, their boats pulled up on the sandy beach, were enjoying lunch in the park while skippers of larger boats cruised sedately to a club rendezvous and young people skimmed gaily along on water skis. The sail boat, just catching the wind as it rounded the head of the island, looked lonesome and serene.

The artist could have found this scene in any of hundreds of locations in the Pacific Northwest. Actually, the setting is the middle of the desert in eastern Washington.

Boating in the desert? Ah, but yes! With the new dams on the Columbia and Snake Rivers backing up waters to create lakes the population of the Tri-Cities area has taken to the water like the proverbial duck. Sagebrush and mesquite may still be part of the backdrop scenery but more and more new skippers are learning rules of the road, buoys, markers, lights and other aids to navigation. Boat registrations in the area have grown to well over 7500.

Interest and enthusiasm? Yes, again! Just talk to almost anyone, members of the Pasco Chamber of Commerce; men in the business end of boating such as Dale and Kay Metz of Kennewick's Metz Marina. Check in, too, with John F. Neuman, first commodore of the Clover Island Boat Club or any of its members. These and many others are a "Boating in the Desert Chamber of Commerce" with nautical stories and salty language that matches any that can be heard in seaport cities.

A drive down streets or alleys turns up boats on trailers in yards and driveways or confiscating the garage at the expense of the family car.

The Tri-Cities, Pasco, Kennewick and Richland, are situated where the Yakima, Snake and Walla Walla Rivers join the mighty Columbia and the reservoir back of McNary Dam forms beautiful 60-mile-long Lake Wallula with its more than 280 miles of shoreline and six convenient parks.

In 1962 Ice Harbor Dam, the first of four on the lower Snake River, was dedicated and has already formed another recreational area in Lake Sacajawea, 32 miles long, covering 9200 acres with 80 miles of shoreline. As the other dams are completed more lakes are forming

and boaters will have slack water navigation 325 miles from the Pacific Ocean to the mouth of the Snake and 140 miles up the Snake to the Lewiston, Idaho, Clarkston, Washington area.

The $122 million Ice Harbor Dam, boasting locks with the highest lift in the world at 103 feet, was started in 1956 and dedicated in May, 1962. The new lake behind it offers many miles of sandy beaches, interesting coves and bays with parks, camping areas, trees, rest rooms, docks and launching ramps.

Ice Harbor's name goes back to the 1860s when the Snake became the water trailway to upstream gold diggings in Idaho. Fort Walla Walla on the Columbia below the mouth of the Snake was the "jumping off" point with the goal Lewiston, Idaho, a bonanza boom town 140 miles upstream. Stern-wheelers, flatboats, and tiny river craft would lay off the mouth of the Snake in early spring, waiting for the ice-flow hazard to end. A few adventurous souls maneuvered their craft into a small kidney-shaped bay on the south shore of the Snake thus gaining a few precious miles' advantage over the waiting horde downstream. That tiny haven became known as Ice Harbor.

Calling themselves the Sunshine Capital of the Pacific Northwest, the Tri-Cities area, with an average yearly quota of 280 days of sunshine, is fast becoming a Palm Beach of the north. Situated in one of nature's peculiar "Banana Belts" it offers a mild climate even in wintertime.

A population of 8700 in 1940 had grown to over 100,000 in 1960 and the growth continues.

This recreation area, generously blessed by nature and developed by man, now adds to its many features a new series of attractions in boating, water skiing, racing, fishing, camping and sight-seeing. And this is just the beginning. Dale Metz doesn't hesitate to prophesy that Lake Sacajawea and the lakes which form behind the other dams will become the largest recreational region in the Northwest.

Although a majority of the boats now registered are outboards, the trend is to bigger boats and inboards. As more parks and shoreside facilities become available more skippers want to do more cruising.

In addition to the larger boats that make the trip up the river from the Portland vicinity and those trailered over

139

Whether boating for the afternoon, a weekend or an entire vacation, there are many protected bays, coves and docks where the skipper can pull in.

The Fleet takes off for a cruise on Lake Wallula, one of the large reservoir lakes formed by dams on the Columbia River, and one of the boating oases in eastern Washington's desert.

from the Yakima neighborhood, boaters are attracted from a radius of 100 miles to Lake Wallula and Sacajawea. Add all these to residents within only a few minutes of the water and it's easy to see why the boating boom figures are increasing rapidly.

Seven yacht clubs are presently in the area but more are bound to come. Each of the Tri-Cities has one with Kennewick's Clover Island Boat Club the oldest and one of the most active. Docks and moorages were built by members in regular work parties. The Cloverettes, their women's auxiliary, provided food for the workers and put on money-raising breakfasts. They also have a fine launching ramp which is used by trailer boats from all over the Northwest.

The Walla Walla Yacht Club located on the Lake Wallula gap, boasts a clubhouse, moorages, launching ramp and other facilities. Another active club is the Blue Mountain Yacht Club located in the Pasco Yacht Basin.

Furthest down-river organization in this area is the Mc-Nary Yacht Club with 90 members, some of whom live 70 miles away. Then there is the Tri-City Power Boat Asso-

ciation and, finally, the dry land group in a little town 36 miles N.N.E. of Pasco, The Connell Boat Club. Coordinating boating and club activities is the Mid-Columbia Yachting Association with another ardent boatman in the person of Lee Dickinson as secretary.

A 40-foot Patrol vessel is based at a new Coast Guard station on the end of Clover Island and serves boaters from The Dalles up where navigation is restricted at the Hanford Atomic Works on the Columbia and up to the head of Lake Sacajawea on the Snake. There are also three Coast Guard Auxiliary Flotillas active in the area.

Both state and counties have been generous with parks available to the mariner. Ranging from a few acres to the 40-acre 4½ mile long Columbia Park, they provide almost everything a skipper could desire including free boat docks, free launching ramps, camping and picnicking sites, swimming areas and basins with life guards and changing rooms, rest rooms, showers, laundry facilities and drying lines.

Claiming a boat registration second only to Seattle's, these desert boatmen boast they'll soon be first. With their enthusiasm, they just might do it.

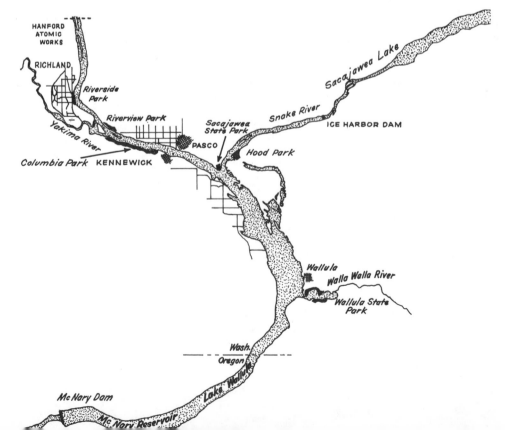

37

Eastern Washington's Greatest Cruise

Although it was mid-July and had been hot in Spokane, the 6:00 a.m. air at eastern Washington's Kettle Falls had an invigorating briskness reminiscent of north woods camping trips.

The surrounding hills, their tops blurred by a slight early morning haze, were reflected in the mirror-smooth lake. I say "lake" because the greater portion of our trip was on lakes which are part of the Columbia River, one of them formed by Grand Coulee Dam. Franklin D. Roosevelt Lake begins at the dam and runs east and north almost to the Canadian border and offers the boatman some 130 miles of scenic cruising water. A pamphlet on this area complete with map and a listing of 35 points with the facilities available at each can be obtained from the National Park Service. The Arrow Lakes, Lower and Upper, still a part of the Columbia, extend north for some 120 miles in British Columbia.

Our trip actually began the previous December when Bill Crossett, owner of Spokane's Village Store Marina, and the writer put our heads together to add to SEA's material on the wonderful cruising waters in his area and Bill provided us with a boat for a trip through the Arrow Lakes. My wife, our son David and daughter Valerie made the trip, too.

There were several places we could have launched and Kettle Falls was chosen. It is a fine marina, operated in the summer by William H. Brauner, providing an excellent launching ramp, groceries, ice, snack bar, boat rental, gas, oil and some marine hardware.

Our craft was a 25-foot Thunderbird fiberglass tri-hulled cabin cruiser, powered with twin 75-hp Evinrude motors which allowed us to average a high cruising speed of 27 knots. We made good use of this power when bucking the rapids in the narrower stretches of river for we carried a larger than average crew. Besides my family, Bill Crossett and his son Jerry were along.

We who cruise in salt water are accustomed to different water levels with the constantly changing tides but we never expected the 70-foot differential in river heights between winter and summer. At this time it was just starting down from its highest point, dropping about a foot a day. According to our skipper this was still a bit early in the year for the trip as there was considerable drift in the water. Even a small one-inch-thick branch can play havoc with a fast-turning prop and we were glad to have two extras along, for we needed them both.

There are plenty of places where it is impossible to avoid whirlpools. We were advised to steer the V of he bow right into the boil when bucking the current. This not only lessens the pull but you stand a better chance of cushioning what can be quite a drop in level when entering a 20-foot whirlpool and can surprise you if you aren't prepared for it.

The waterway narrows from Roosevelt Lake, a short distance north of Kettle Falls, and meanders up past Northport Trail, several small communities and Kinnaird to Castlegar. Kinnaird is behind a hill and isn't seen from the river. It was interesting to note how sparse the vegetation is for quite a way below Trail. Bill explained the growth is poisoned by fumes from the smelter at Trail.

The first real thrill in fast water came traversing the Little Dalles just below Northport, where, as Bill says, "The wide Columbia narrows down, turns on her side and really rolls." Although he admitted there was not too much actual danger, he still insisted we all wear life jackets whenever we hit the "boils."

We were glad to have a locally experienced skipper with us when we crossed the Canadian border at Waneta. There is nothing—not even a dock or sign—to indicate the Canadian customs and immigration. We pulled up to the steep rocky shore a short distance below a power dam at the confluence of the Pend Oreille and Columbia Rivers, and with fenders at the waterline, made fast to a big boulder. It was a rough climb up the rocks and a short hike along the railroad tracks to the small border station where we went through the necessary formalities. The 6 to 7 knot current held our craft snugly against the bank until we returned and found the kids having a gay time chunking rocks into the water.

The heaviest water encountered on the trip was at Tincup Rapids just below Castlegar. There are range and navigation markers in most of the bad spots which, when you become used to them, are invaluable, but to the first-tripper, they would be easy to miss. Too frequently they consist of logs or poles which sometime in the dim past have been

141

Dock with double launching ramp at Nakusp

Launching the trimaran at Kettle Falls Marina

Smith's Marina at Syringa Creek in Lower Arrow Lake

The venerable lodge buildings at St. Leon

painted red and white or black and white but some of the paint has worn off and it is often difficult to identify them.

Castlegar marks the entrance into Lower Arrow Lake. We beached on the left side just above the ferry landing and taxied the mile to the town for provisions. Everything one might need is available—meat, groceries, beer, liquor and ice. We got our ice at the meat department of the grocery store. A launching ramp and gas dock is about a mile upriver on the opposite side. Anyone wishing to trailer up this far should cross over the river on the free ferry to get to the ramp.

Our next stop was at Syringa Creek where Bill and Dorothy Smith operate a fine marine service with gas, groceries, ice, marine supplies, sandwiches and coffee bar.

From here north to Edgewood, Lower Arrow Lake glistens in pristine beauty without even an access road to her shores whereby man can come to spoil her with his civilization. The mouths of many small creeks offer interesting and scenic side trips or stops for lunch or camping or picture taking. We stopped for some leg-stretching on one picturesque sand bar which is a favorite rendezvous of the Spokane Outboard Club. Although fairly well flooded, with the river as high as it was, still we could readily understand its popularity and the kids had to try out their bathing suits in the sun-warmed waters backed up behind the bar.

There is gas at Edgewood and Needles as well as launching ramps, also a ramp at Fauquier, across the river. At this point a road crosses the river which follows north to Nakusp in Upper Arrow Lake.

Lower Arrow Lake narrows to river again at Burton. In this area we proceeded on slow bell. The head of the lake is shallow with frequent sand bars and the water is murky from melted glacial ice, making it impossible to see below the surface.

Here again some tricky piloting was required as we negotiated more rapids. Our skipper stayed well to the left until he had the range lined up, went almost to the opposite shore and then left again around the bend, keeping to the right as the bank drops off sharply while the other shore is rocky and shallower. He cautioned that this is one of the places where it's easy to lose or bend a prop.

In the river between the two lakes above Burton there are many sand bars and islands. Bill's local knowledge required steering slightly to the right of center and he warned about getting too close to either end of the islands. They're like a big diamond and extend some distance under water thus forming a dangerous shoal.

On curves he cautioned us always to keep to the outside and ordered a sharp lookout for even the smallest drift in the boils of the rapids.

At Nakusp we found another town complete with everything the boatman might need including motel and restaurants. Gas can be obtained by walking up to town or phoning to get a gas truck to come down to the dock. It's always well to remember that most stores and many businesses in the area are closed Thursday afternoons and Sundays. Some of them also close on Saturday afternoon.

Upper Arrow Lake is much like her southern sister except the hills and mountains are higher with some of their peaks wearing a mantle of snow the year around. Again no roads even closely approach the lake from Nakusp north to Arrowhead at its northern tip. In a few spots old logging

Early morning reflections in the Columbia

roads and trails exist but transportation is entirely by water.

In spite of its remoteness, which gives the feeling of exploring a place for the first time, this was a popular pleasure area for man many years ago. Vestiges of two resorts, famous in the early 1900's, can still be seen today. St. Leon, about half way up the lake, with its hot springs back in the woods a ways, and Halcyon Hot Springs, a few miles north, offer the boatman fascinating stopovers.

Before it burned down in 1968, the old hotel at St. Leon was a marvel. An unforgettable evening could be enjoyed around the old square piano in the corner, harmonizing with other guests.

Those interested in the history of the region used to spend evenings with Ed Gates who operated St. Leon. Well educated and a civil engineer by profession, he had chosen to live and work in this far away place. He had said he wouldn't think of going back to the racing-about modern day civilization. As you watched him assist the girls in the big kitchen serve you an old fashioned ranch type breakfast, family style, you understood what he meant and were just about convinced to stay there, too. It's unfortunate the venerable old lodge is gone. The memory will remain of those pleasant evenings around the fire or sitting on the porch watching the multi-colored sunset fade behind the snow capped mountains across the lake.

The resort building at Halcyon has burned down. We viewed the crumbling remains of the many pools and baths on the hillside and poked around in the old bottling shed, where we collected a variety of labels formerly used for different types of curative mineral waters.

Another feature of Upper Arrow Lake which struck us was the similarity of the general scenery to more familiar cruising waters in northwestern British Columbia. There were several times when we remarked how much the water and mountains looked like many stretches in the Canadian Gulf Islands and the various reaches we have explored.

If you want still further exploration, a trip upriver from Arrowhead to Revelstoke, some 25 or 30 miles, offers an exciting and scenic cruise.

The Arrow Lakes provided a thrilling and memorable trip and whetted our desire for more of this inland cruising. Bill says we "ain't seen nothing yet," and goes on to describe the wonders of lakes such as Kamloops, Shuswap, Okanagan, Slocum and Kootenay, all in the same general vicinity of British Columbia. They're all accessible by good trunk roads and offer the sailor with a trailerable cruiser, who doesn't mind driving a ways, an opportunity to enjoy cruising some of the finest waters in the world.

For those able to allow a week to two weeks for the trip, they will enjoy launching behind Grand Coulee Dam. Before them, then, stretches 400 miles of adventure. For reduced cruises, of course, it can be Kettle Falls, Northport, Castlegar and others with launching sites.

A full trip from Grand Coulee properly begins with a visit to the dam itself. The free tour and lecture are very interesting and give a fine appreciation of the immensity of the project that helped create this giant combination of lakes and river resembling an "L" from the reverse side. It is about 36 miles from North Marina at the Dam to Fort Spokane where you turn the "L" from running east to a directly north course.

The country on this part of the cruise is semi-arid. The black lava cliffs, towering to 1000 feet along the south edge of Lake Roosevelt, are spectacular. Once you turn north, trees begin to appear. Kettle Falls, where we began our cruise, a popular place with many, is about 90 miles from the dam.

The month of August is a very popular time for the cruise because the river is down but the current is also less. The few rapids are short and less troublesome yet, the experts agree, there is enough water to cover most submerged hazards.

There are really no worthwhile trips where the good skipper shouldn't carefully plan and prepare. The same goes for the Arrow Lakes classic. We certainly can recommend it to all good boatmen. We have been there. We aim to return.

143

38

Gem of a Boating Lake – Coeur d'Alene

Boating and Lake Coeur d'Alene are almost synonymous. Since the beginning of white man's history and for unrecorded centuries of the redman's life boats have played a major role on the silver-blue waters of this gem of a lake in the Gem State of Idaho.

Noted as one of five most beautiful lakes in the world, Coeur d'Alene is 33 miles east of Spokane. The Catholic priest, Father Pierre-Jean De Smet, first white man to stand upon its shores in April, 1842, fittingly described it as, "lying in a sea of forest — a magnificent forest of pine, fir and cedar with a backdrop of towering mountains, ridge rising above ridge, robed with snow and mingling their summits with the clouds."

As with so many Northwest names which were derived from the Indians, Idaho comes from the Shoshone EE-DAH'-HOW, "Behold the sunlight coming down the mountains." Coeur d'Alene, pronounced Core-da-lane, boasts of being the only town in the U.S. with an apostrophe in its name. It is the name given by early French traders to a friendly tribe of Indians because they were shrewd traders and refused to sell their furs for a few trinkets, thus they had sharp pointed hearts or "Heart of an Awl." With a population of 15,000, the town is 2,157 feet above sea level.

The shores of Lake Coeur d'Alene are dotted with marinas, docks, gas floats, launching ramps, beaches, resorts, lodges, camp grounds and motels. In spite of these abundant facilities for boaters, there are many places around the lakes that still retain a look and feeling of the undisturbed outdoors in a wilderness setting. There are no mosquitos nor poisonous snakes in the area and it is known as one of the best havens for hay fever sufferers. It can truly be called a trailer boater's paradise.

Winding between timber-clad hills, the lake is 22 miles long with over a hundred miles of shoreline, 41½ square miles of area and many bays and coves. Three rivers, Spokane, Coeur d'Alene and St. Joe, extend from the lake and each is navigable for some distance.

It wasn't so many years after the Indians' canoes had given way to the white man's boats that the lake's water commerce grew to such an extent that it was the scene of more steamboating than any other lake, salt or fresh, west of the Great Lakes. Ruby El Hult in her fascinating history of the lake and rivers, "Steamboats in the Timber," says it was the little Lake Erie of the West; its rivers, miniature Mississippis of the West.

The steamboats are gone now, relegated to the pages of history, but excursion boats and a mailboat ply the waters of the lake along with a host of pleasure craft. Coeur d'Alene is a boating lake, a "fun" lake, one to be seriously considered by the trailer-boaters or by those who would like to enjoy its pleasures in a rented boat.

It was early on a Friday evening when we cast off from the float at Coeur d'Alene. Wally and Betty Vawter and Max and Jean Emerson were our cruise guides for the excursion. Wally's 20-foot Uniflite *Vawterloo* has 150-hp inboard power with outdrive, as did Max's Skagit 20-foot *Sittin' Pretty*. Norma and I were in a 24-foot 185-hp Owens Express Cruiser from Earl Trudeau, owner of Trudeau's Marina in Spokane.

As Wally led the way down the east shore with Harrison as our destination, the mood of the lake quickly captured us. We could visualize some of the historic steamboats, their whistles echoing from the forested hills or a tiny tug with its brails of logs stretching out behind. Even the names along the shore had a ring of the past, Squaw Bay, Driftwood Bay, Gang Point, Black Bay, Powderhorn Bay.

The Idaho lakes have always rated at the top for anyone who has visited them. They are a great water playground for the Spokane Outboard Club and its members believe that the West's trailing boat skippers should again be reminded of the attractions of these beautiful lakes in the Panhandle, a descriptive term for this state that is derived from its unusual geographic shape. Their enthusiastic invitations to do a new series on this region was accepted.*

Harrison has good public docks, moorages, gas dock, stores and restaurants. Seeing it today we found it hard to believe that, at one time, it rivalled Coeur d'Alene as a big sawmill town. A serious fire, the decline of the lumber business and the end of the steamboat era have reduced it to a sleepy little village with only exciting memories of a wild and bawdy past.

After spending the night at Harrison we left early Saturday morning for a conducted tour part way up the Coeur d'Alene River with its series of small lakes. This was indeed

144

Such scenes as this gave inspiration to early pioneers to name their river the "Shadowy St. Joe."

a revelation to this salt-water, inboard cruiser skipper. Wally and Max decided that, perhaps with my inexperience in these waters and a borrowed boat, the larger Owens should be left in the lake, so we split the family between the two smaller boats.

It wasn't long before I realized the wisdom of their decision. Here was a type of boating entirely different than anything we'd ever experienced before. At the mouth of the river the green water of the river merges with the blue water of the lake. At places the cottonwoods and silver beaches on both banks almost form arches overhead and behind them can be seen flat meadows of green leading back to the darker green of the forested mountains. This portion was reminiscent of Louisiana Bayous.

For a distance of about 12 miles up-river from the mouth eight small lakes lie on either side, connected to the river by narrow, tortuous and sometimes shallow channels. Fishing is good in these lakes although a couple of them are privately owned with beautiful homes dominating delightful little coves.

During our exploratory side trips into a few of these lakes I was glad not to be at the helm. We learned about boat gymnastics as well as some of the advantages of the inboard/outdrive installation as we met with logs and trees lying across the channel. Our skippers were adept at "jumping" these obstacles, cutting the throttle at just the right moment for the prop to kick up and then getting it back down to continue with hardly a drop in speed.

Another interesting trick was used several times when the boat would ground in the mud at a turn in the channel or the entrance to a lake. The outdrive unit was raised to a point just below water level. Revving up the motor and shooting a geyser of spray high into the air, there was enough propulsion to move the boat into deep water.

Our exploration of Blue, Black, Medicine, Cave and Killarney Lakes was a fascinating experience, taking up the entire morning.

A return to Harrison for lunch was followed by a cruise to the south end of the lake past more places with colorful names such as Deadman Gulch, Shingle Bay and Red Cut to St. Joe Gap, a channel which is actually the mouth where the St. Joe River enters the lake.

Here is another interesting bit of waterway. Just before the St. Joe River runs into St. Joe Gap to flow into Lake Coeur d'Alene it runs through Chatcolet Lake, not into and then out of the lake but *through* it, between banks built up through centuries from sediment and now grown up with cottonwoods, bushes and slough grass. This phenomenon of a river flowing through a lake, its current independent of the lake waters on either side, was noted in one of Robert Ripley's "Believe It Or Not" features.

The St. Joe River is rich in beauty as well as history. In the higher swift-water part of its 125-mile course it flows rapidly over a gravelly bottom between mountains. In the last 30 to 40 miles its channel is so deep, reaching 200 feet in places, that it slows to become nearly still with the magnificent foilage of the cottonwoods and willows lining its banks mirrored in the moss-green waters. It it this feature of brooding, shifting reflections which has given it the lovely and appropriate local name, "Shadowy St. Joe." Even the mountains five and ten miles away are reflected in places along with the lacy trees.

As we made our way up its placid waters we could see the valley, wide at first between river and mountains with the level meadows looking like great green fields, narrowing until the mountains embraced it towards its source. The lower canal-like portion has no falls or rapids to an elevation of 2200 feet above sea level making it the highest navigable river in the world.

We were soon ready to agree with someone who said this river was certainly the most crooked in the world. This adds to its beauty, however, as its bends, twists and turns continually opened up new vistas and our churning wakes broke the mirror smoothness into curling rollers which caressed the shores. At some places we almost felt as though we were running through the Florida Everglades.

About eleven miles up-river we came to a fork where the St. Maries River joins the St. Joe. Here the old town site of St. Maries still has a few ancient buildings. Further up the St. Joe the towns of Ferrell and St. Joe have all but disappeared, the victims of vanishing sawmills, decreased lumbering and a disastrous fire. Reduced logging still goes on but it is a far cry from the hey day this area knew around the turn of the century.

145

The river narrowed and shallowed as we cruised still further with swirls of current showing up here and there. Again we had reduced our little fleet to the two smaller boats. As the skippers became more alert to shoal areas and boiling rapids we wondered how much farther we could go. Finally, some 40 miles from the mouth we pulled into a tiny little cove where we tied up to overhanging tree branches and went ashore for a short walk to an enchantingly beautiful waterfall.

Our return trip down-river gave us another chance to drink in the beauties of the Shadowy St. Joe and perhaps dream a little of the days gone by when timber barons and

Builders of a highway along the lake's shore left this waterway tunnel into a cove off Wolf Lodge Bay which otherwise would have been isolated.

Wally and Betty take their boat out at the ramp on the Spokane Outboard Club's SOC-PROP outpost on the Spokane River not far from Coeur d'Alene.

lusty loggers made a roaring history in this region. For boaters contemplating a trip to the area we can only advise that enjoyment will be increased many-fold by reading Ruby El Hult's "Steamboats in the Timber" before making the cruise.

The only hazards we encountered in the river were several large deadheads. Some of these were butts floating on the surface, others were of telephone-pole size, waterlogged to the point where they floated vertically or had one end stuck in the mud, but looked just like the butts. The possibility of hitting these at 20 knots was a constant concern of our skippers.

Shadows began to lengthen as we turned from the river into Lake Chactolet and headed for the floats at Heyburn State Park. We were impressed with the many excellent public docks and floats all around the lakes and rivers. Our guides explained that, in order to bring their boats to Idaho lakes, they must pay the boat tax for the privilege. This money is used for installation and upkeep of these docks, floats and other marine facilities.

A barbecue dinner ashore that night was an Epicurean delight. We learned many valuable tricks in the use of foil as Betty and Jean made use of both charcoal and wood coals to prepare gourmet dishes fit for any banquet table.

Our final day on Lake Coeur d'Alene included a cruise up the west shore of the lake with looks into many of the bays and coves. After returning the Owens to Rockford Bay we drove back to Coeur d'Alene to split up again and go aboard our guides' boats.

We still hadn't explored the northeastern arm of the lake that terminates in Wolf Lodge, Blue Creek and Beauty Bays so a course was set in that direction. In Wolf Lodge Bay we ran into another novelty. When a road was built along the north shore of this portion of the lake a fill cut off a small bay on which is located the Shady Rest Motel and Restaurant. What appears to be a large corrugated drainage pipe runs under the fill connecting the bay to the lake. Max's *Sittin' Pretty* ran through the tube to show us how it's done but Wally's *Vawterloo* was too high to make it.

Beauty Bay is aptly named and is said to be one of the most photographed spots in the Northwest. It is a favorite place for boaters who know the lake and a "must" objective for first-time visitors.

Swinging back westward once more we stopped at Arrow Point then headed northwesterly for a run up the Spokane River which is navigable for some 20 miles to Post Falls. This is the more civilized of the three rivers which are considered a part of the lake. Instead of flowing into the lake as do the others, it flows out, winding its way westward through Spokane to end up joining the Columbia. It has a quiet beauty all its own with many homes, both summer and permanent, along its shores.

Just a short ways up-river from its lake entrance is located the Spokane Outboard Club's outpost which they call SOC-PROP. A large roofed-over shelter, rest rooms, camping area and launching ramp make it a valuable part of the club's assets.

Wally pulled his boat out here while Max returned his to his summer moorage at the Yacht Club Sales & Service Marina between the entrance to the river and Coeur d'Alene.

As the river seemed to run into the setting sun we reluctantly said farewell to our guides and hosts as well as to a lake which will always have a favored spot in our log of cruising memories. On the morrow we would head for more Idaho lake cruising on Pend Oreille and Priest Lakes.

There are spots on the St. Joe River reminiscent of the Florida Everglades, with luxuriant growth overhanging the quiet waters of the river.

While we swung in to explore Beauty Bay, Max and Jean took time for a bit of fishing.

Our three-boat fleet ties up at the Heyburn State Park floats on Lake Chactolet for dinner ashore and a peaceful night.

Coming down river at a fast pace, deadheads such as the one at right were an ever-present hazard which kept skippers on the alert at all times.

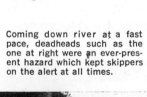

Scenes such as this hidden waterfall are the reward for a brief excursion ashore into places available only to the boater.

39
Idaho's Pend Oreille and Priest Lakes

Lakes have character.   Each of the three lakes we cruised in Idaho's Panhandle has a different character, all its own. While we called Coeur d'Alene the "Fun Lake," we might designate Pend Oreille the "Serious Lake." Not meaning to imply that one can't have fun on Pend Oreille, with its host of attractions for the boater, but its mood is entirely different.

Pend Oreille (originally spelled Pend d'Oreille, and pronounced *Pond-a-ray*) derives its name from an Indian tribe to which early French traders and trappers gave the name because these natives wore large pendant ornaments in their ear lobes. Formed somewhat in the shape of a question mark, the lake is one of the biggest bodies of fresh water in the U.S. With a length of 43.2 miles and a width of 6.25 miles it has 111.3 miles of shoreline and its greatest depth is 1150 feet.

There are several small towns ringing the lake, all with eating, sleeping and docking facilities. Hope, on the eastern shore, and Clark Fork, just up the Clark Fork River, are small pioneer towns established when the Northern Pacific Railroad's main line followed the watergrade through the Bitteroot and Cabinet Mountain ranges in the 1880's. Largest community is Sandpoint on the northwest corner of the lake. Small boats can be launched from any of the more than 20 resorts around the lake while larger craft can launch at Sandpoint, Garfield Bay, Bayview and Hope.

The first white man to see Lake Pend Oreille was David Thompson, an explorer and map-maker for the old Northwest Fur Company, who paddled his canoe down the present Rock River from the north and across to the eastern shore of the lake a bit below Hope where he built Kullyspell House in 1809.

This rough fort was the first fur trading post in northwestern United States, even predating Astoria on the Columbia River by two years. A short time later he established Saleesh House near Thompson Falls. These posts didn't last long, however, and in 1811 were moved to Spokane because the Indians in these parts only wanted to fish, pick berries and visit. Kullyspell House was destroyed by fire in 1834 and nearly faded from memory until 1923 when an 84-year-old Indian, who remembered seeing as a boy the blackened

chimneys standing in the forest, located the exact site of the fort.

Hosts and guides for our cruise of Lake Pend Oreille were Bill and Ruth Crossett, who operate Spokane's Village Store Marina and who "just happened" to have a 32-foot Tollycraft Explorer Sedan moored at Bayview. They, like our other hosts, are members of the Spokane Outboard Club and were most anxious to show us the beauties and attractions of some of their favorite cruising waters.*

After loading our gear aboard we cast off from the marina dock at Bayview and headed across the lake where the shore was almost perpendicular for hundreds of feet. Bill told us there was a herd of mountain goats living amidst the rocks, brush and trees on this steep hillside. Although we cruised slowly with all eyes searching, we failed to see a single goat.

Swinging up the east shore of the lake we were struck by the rugged, majestic beauty of the steep hills and mountains, some still with a mantle of snow on their shoulders, and the deep blue of the water. While there are some roads serving parts of the shoreline, there are stretches where the only access is by water. Perhaps, as a hangover from the lusty early days of logging and steamboating, some of the shoreside establishments make no secret of their business and a large sign or the word "BAR" spelled out in rocks on a sloping shoreside bank proclaims their·wares.

As we turned eastward, at the beginning of the question mark's curve, Bill told us we were entering favorite trolling grounds which extend on east and north to the north end of the lake. Along with beauty and pleasant bays and coves for cruising enjoyment, fishing is one of Pend Oreille's principal attractions. It was here that Wes Hamlet caught the world's record Kamloops, or giant rainbow trout which weighed 37 pounds. A 32-pound Dolly Varden taken in these waters also still holds the world's record.

There are 21 varieties of fish in the lake including unusually fine bass, perch, whitefish, bluegills and crappies. However, aside from trying for the big trophy fish, the Kokanee, a 10 to 12-pound Blueback or land-locked sockeye salmon that abounds in great numbers is the most popular. Beginning in February or March these Kokanee are in large schools. Hundreds of boats hover over these schools to hand-

148
Now the Spokane Yacht Club.

line them with bait. Later the schools break up and, as the fish scatter to all parts of the lake, they are taken by slow trolling. The Kokanee is generally regarded as the finest of all panfish and is delectable when smoked. Because of their large numbers, fishermen are permitted to take 50 Kokanee a day. One and a half million of these fish were hooked in the lake during a recent year.

The fishing season is open the year round for all varieties except trout which may be taken from May 1 to November 30. A season non-resident license costs $15, with a tourist seven-day license for $5 or a one-day tourist license for $2 the first day and $1 a day thereafter. Children under 14 fishing with a license holder do not need a license.*

Bill told us the best time to try for the king-size Kamloops rainbows or the large Dolly Vardens is October or November. He said May and early June also offer a better than average chance, although fishing may be slowed in these earlier months by the spring run-offs of melting snows in the mountains.

We'd have loved to try for one of those big ones but time was limited and we had lots to see. We continued northward, past the group of scenic islands toward the upper end of the lake, and then westward to Sandpoint. Here are stores, restaurants, motels, marinas and other boating facilities.

Until 1952 Sandpoint marked the head of the lake, but in that year Albeni Falls dam was completed 25 miles down the Pend Oreille River. This raised the river to the lake's elevation of 2062 feet above sea level and extended the lake another 25 miles westward.

As the afternoon waned we headed east along the south shore of the upper hook of the lake for Hurschell's Lighthouse on Ellisport Bay. Here we enjoyed an excellent meal and bedded down for the night at Al and Vi Atherton's comfortable Lake Aire Motel right next door. Al, an old-time yachtsman, also rents boats and operates a charter fishing boat. He gave us some tips on fishing the lake which we plan to keep to ourselves until we can try them out on a future trip.

A heavy fog slowed down our cruise the next morning but it lifted by noon as we swung into Garfield Bay on the west side of the lake. This is another favorite spot for boaters with moorages, marinas, resorts and stores.

Apparently trying to make up for its absence in the

Granite Creek flows into Pend Oreille on the east shore

morning, the sun turned on its full power to create a glorious afternoon. A swim seemed in order so Bill headed the Tollycraft for a lovely sandy beach and nosed her into shore. The water was cool at first but delightful after we got wet.

We explored the western shore of the lake, went back to look for the goats again, without success, took a look into Idlewild and Buttonhook Bays at the south end of the lake and, as the sun neared the horizon, returned to the Bayview moorage for another wonderful meal at the popular Golden Hind right there on the lake.†

Our visit was all too short but we were glad to have made the acquaintance of Lake Pend Oreille. This inland sea in a setting of green forests and rugged mountains is ever changing, ever beautiful. It absorbs the cares of man and imparts its serenity to him. We agree with the Indians that it is a great place for recreation, relaxation and genuine western hospitality.

White sand beaches extend into the forest at Priest Lake

Next morning found us at Bob Nieman's Priest Lake Marina where Jerry and Carolyn Crossett, who work with his father at the Airway Heights Marina, met us. They were trailering a 19-foot Traveler Neptune with OMC 150-hp inboard/outdrive.

Priest Lake and its connected Upper Priest Lake, tucked into the panhandle's northwest corner, could be called the "People's Lakes." Offering, as they do, every kind of water fun, they really belong to the people — all people. Jerry told us that years ago the U.S. Government leased waterfront property to applicants on long-term leases. A few pieces were sold but most of the land was leased. Now the leases have been cancelled and most of the sandy and forested shores of the lake are government property — or the people's property.

Lodges, resorts and motels are scattered here and there with plenty of campsites available even on the islands. Boats of all sizes can be launched at Bishop's Marina, Coolin, and Priest Lake Marina, Kalispell Bay. Smaller boats can be launched from most of the lakeside resorts.

In contrast to Pend Oreille's often steep and rugged shorelines, Priest Lake has more low-level waterfront although this is backed by hills and mountains. Its 26,000 acres of crystal-clear water wash many miles of wide sandy beaches fronting the stately pines and their carpet of brown needles. There are enough beaches so the boater can choose

*Currently a season non-resident license is $20 and a seven-day license is $7.
†The Golden Hind Restaurant has moved.

either the companionship and gaiety of those more populated or seek out the quiet serenity of one accessible only by boat.

Leaving Kalispell Bay, Jerry pointed the Traveler's bow between Papoose and Kalispell Islands, two of three wooded isles that dominate the middle of the lower part of the lake. Our wake rolled into a graceful arc as we turned southeast for a look into Cavanaugh Bay then headed north along the east shore, past Eight Mile Island and into Pinto Point. Here the lake narrows, to widen again after passing between Twin Islands.

Our course continued into Huckleberry Bay, around Canoe Point and into the north end of the lake along more sandy beaches and green clad shores with snow-capped Chimney Rock looking down benevolently from the horizon high above.

Swinging into a narrow winding channel which reminded us a bit of the Coeur d'Alene River, Jerry told us it was known by the non-nautical name of "The Thorofare" and connected Priest Lake with Upper Priest Lake. Several small arms drifting off from the Thorofare into the swamp grass to wind into the evergreens offer an intriguing invitation to explore them, but a canoe would be required for such an adventure.

As the channel widened into the upper lake, we were greeted by a vista of unspoiled beauty. Still almost as nature constructed it centuries ago, man has not yet "developed" it and its pristine attractions are available for the enjoyment of boaters only.

We selected a cozy little cove with a white sand beach for lunch which was followed by water skiing with Jerry, an expert skier, giving tips and demonstrations to the youngsters.

On our return trip back through the Thorofare and down the west shore past more spectacular yet serene scenery Jerry briefed us on the fishing in Priest Lake. Trophy fish are the 30, 40 and 50 pound lake trout or Mackinaws with the record thus far 54 pounds 5 ounces caught in 1964. There are also the big Dolly Vardens, the delectable Kokanee, native cut throat trout, eastern brooks and large mouth bass. Best times for "Mack" fishing are in the spring and early fall.

After a sumptuous family-style dinner at the Kaniksu Resort we continued along the west shore, took a look at the south end of the lake and returned to the Priest Lake Marina just as summer's late dusk settled over this lovely lake.

Our tour of the principal lakes in Idaho's panhandle was regrettably at an end. It was a delightful experience and we can heartily recommend any one or all three lakes for the consideration of trailer-boat skippers looking for new and interesting Northwest waters in which to wet their hulls for a weekend or a full-blown vacation.

Twin Islands rise in the northern part of Priest Lake

Cruising along the shore of Lake Pend Oreille turns up mile after mile of sheer beauty

40

Snaking down the Snake River

"We'll be going through fast white water in rapids that are tricky but not *too* dangerous. You will be in groups of five boats, each group with an experienced leader. As we go along you'll learn to know the Snake and its pattern with the rapids having a definite look as they fall over rims and rush over bars."

It was Cruisemaster Wally Vawter giving final instructions at a skippers' meeting at Kiwanis Park in Lewiston, Idaho, just before the start of Spokane Yacht Club's annual cruise up the Snake River.

Wally continued, "The best way to keep out of trouble is to try to keep the boat level. Think ahead and know what you're going to do before you hit a rapids. After you're in, it's too late to change your mind. When a boat starts to slide, it's like a car on a slick road, it keeps sliding and all of a sudden you find yourself in the rocks or on the shore."

This is the club's most famous, most thrilling cruise. Through deep rock canyons with frequent pure white sand beaches, 90 miles of the Snake's white water races, seethes and boils in some 99 rapids strewn with rocks between Lewiston and Hell's Canyon Dam which was dedicated in May, 1968.

In addition to the Spokane YC members, the fleet included guests from the Yakima Valley Outboard Club and the Hells Canyon Boat Club for a total of 23 boats. The Yakima contingent represented the entire membership of the Avocado YC, a club within a club which requires that members must have an avocado and white Fiberfoam boat with MerCruiser outdrive unit. The present three members are Louis and Barb Irwin in *Bobby Lou*, Stan and Ginny Sinclair in *Gin Sin* and Ben and Willy Worthington in *Wanderlust*. Avocado Commodore Ben Worthington says there will soon be two more additions to their club.

Spokane members have held this cruise annually since 1951. With today's larger boats and more powerful motors, the cruise up the Snake is a far cry from earlier days when it was made in 14' and 16' boats with 25-hp motors. It's still an adventure, however, and, for anyone with a yen for a challenging experience, it shouldn't be missed.

By late Friday afternoon, Kiwanis Park on the bank of the Snake was filled with cars and boats on trailers.

That evening the Hell's Canyon Boat Club entertained the cruise participants at their clubhouse on the Clarkston side of the river. Cast off time was scheduled for 1300 Saturday.

Lewiston and Clarkston, on opposite sides of the river, are named for the explorers, Lewis and Clark. Lewiston was originally founded in 1860 as a way station and supply point for gold seekers and packers. First recorded commercial navigation of the Snake was in July, 1860, when Tom Beall of Lapwai and a crew of Indian companions had a fleet of two 32' x 7' bateaux and a lighter flagship. First steamship was the *Colonel Wright* in May, 1861. Since then many famous steamers have made navigation history on the river.

As we left the landing at Lewiston those of us making the trip for the first time may have had a few qualms as we watched the first boats being grabbed by the current in the river. Although the Snake is wide and fairly placid here, there is still a good flow of water down-river and seeing a boat swept sideways before it got speed up, plus thoughts of roaring rapids to come, might cause the neophyte to question his judgment in deciding to make the trip.

Some confidence was restored when we saw our leader, Captain Charles P. "Shorty" Miller, a licensed and experienced river pilot, take off in his 16' open Skippercraft with a 60-hp Johnson Sea Horse Outboard and then regarded the *Vawterloo*, sturdy 20' Uniflite Cabin Cruiser with MerCruiser outdrive of our hosts Wally and Betty Vawter.

The first few miles were uneventful with wide open green fields, sandy beaches and civilization on both sides of us. A look ahead showed the flatness along the river giving way to ever growing hills. The first rapids a couple of miles above Lewiston were the Slaughterhouse Rapids. These and the next several more were mild and negotiated without trouble or incident.

Both Wally and Betty were fountains of historical and interesting information. They pointed out many places including The Swallow's Nest, a famous landmark and a swallow's haven; Paul Bunyan's Fan, rock formations which seem to be in ribbons and change colors with the

White water! It's a real thrill to run a rapids with the boat bucking in the seething currents.

seasons; The Rock of Gibraltar which appears to be a duplicate of the insurance company's famous picture; old Zig Zag Trail of Indian days; and Whiskey Gulch, famous in early days for a still which turned out whiskey noted for high quality and cleanliness and thus used for medical purposes.

Continuing up-river our introduction to rapids was a gradual sort of thing, each apparently getting progressively stronger with more white water. The river outside the actual rapids, on either side of them, would remind Northwest skippers of Deception or one of the other passes at maximum current with boils and confused water similar to tide-rips.

Most of the rapids are well marked with one or more sets of ranges. Wally said it's a good idea to stay on the ranges otherwise it's easy to go on the rocks. Capt. Shorty Miller deviated from this advice in a few instances where he said the ranges weren't in exactly the right place. This further emphasized that it's a wise idea to follow a competent guide until one knows the river well.

At mid-afternoon the fleet stopped on a sandy beach at Buffalo Eddy for a bit of leg-stretching and exploring. For hundreds of years Indians from tribes in Montana, Idaho, Washington and Oregon areas congregated here for pow-wows and ceremonials.

We inspected the ancient Indian writings and pictures on the rocks. There are many of them and, although they are so old that even the oldest Indians of the last century didn't know their age or meaning, these petroglyphs are still clear and easily distinguished. You get a feeling of smallness and insignificance on one hand yet, on the other, an expanded consciousness as your eyes range from the blue sky above to the rocky hills which were growing higher and rougher with each mile, to the hurrying river with its roaring, spuming rapids and then consider that a former man has left a record of his being there thousands, perhaps even millions of years ago.

Leaving Buffalo Eddy, arrangements were made for us to transfer to the lead boat for an opportunity to learn more about snaking the Snake as well as points of interest from Shorty Miller. It was a thrill to watch him handle that 16-footer through the roaring, frothy white water of the rapids. One hand on the wheel, the other on the throttle, he seemed to "feel" the currents and

guided the boat through just the right spot at exactly the right angle.

He appeared to know each of the rapids personally and explained their character as we went along. At Fisher Rapids he said, "This is a fast one. You hug the sand bar and then swing out at the upper end." At Capt. Lewis Rapids, "This is rough most of the time. It's one of the more hazardous because of the big swells and a boulder right in the middle."

Shorty was also filled with historical information. He pointed out Capt. John's place and the spot where he used to run a ferry across the river. Where the Grande Ronde River enters the Snake he showed us the early Indian congregating place and campground and told about a stone oven on the beach which is supposed to have been used by the Indians to smoke their fish. At Nigger Head Rapids there was an old cabin which belonged to pioneer miner Jim Chapman.

It was here that we learned about sturgeon for this is one of the better areas for them. The Great White Sturgeon, a carry-over from the Mesozoic age some 200 million years ago or perhaps even as far back as the Devonian age around 350 million years back, is a huge bottom-feeding fish. The U.S. record is pegged variously at 9½ to 10 feet, while reports from early mining days record up to 14 feet and weight up to a ton. Legal limits for sturgeon are between three and six feet. It is intended that those under three feet be left to grow up and those over six feet left to breed and reproduce.

A variety of wild life may be observed while cruising on the river. In addition to sturgeon the Snake and its tributaries abound in steelhead, small mouth bass, sizable native trout, channel catfish, crappie and, of course, these rivers are a principal spawning ground for the Chinook salmon. The area has an abundance of game birds, including the lordly Canadian Honkers. Deer are plentiful in Idaho along the river from the mouth of the Salmon River to Brownlee Dam and there are elk on the Oregon side of the Snake. Otters playing on a sandy beach are a frequent sight.

Wild Goose Rapids, caused by a huge mineral fault under the river, is one of the more boisterous and calls for careful attention. After leading the first group through, Shorty turned back to be sure the others made it safely. Turning in mid-rapids, being tossed one way and thrown back another caused a few missed heart beats but by this time we had full confidence in our helmsman.

When we reached Bear Bar Shorty called for another stop on this beautiful sandy beach to give the rest a chance to catch up. Don Baker, former commodore of Portland's Tyee YC and now a member of Spokane YC, was having some trouble with the big outboard on his Tollycraft so time out was taken for a check-over.

Shortly after leaving Bear Bar we crossed the Washington-Oregon border on the right. A little further along was Cache Creek Island, a bird paradise and large nesting spot for geese. There is hazardous water both above and below Cache Creek and around a bend is Cougar Bar Rapids rushing through a 30-foot channel, the narrowest on the lower Snake, and dangerous at low water.

Coming up on the mouth of the Salmon River, called the "River of No Return," there was turbulent water with no particular pattern which whirled, boiled and roared for a mile below the confluence of the two rushing streams. Care had to be taken so as not to be dashed into the bluff.

A bit above the entrance of the Salmon is the site for the High Mountain Sheep Dam proposed by Pacific Northwest Power Company and Washington Public Power Supply. The letters PNP-HMS are painted in white on the rocks. The Mountain Sheep Creek Rapids are considered dangerous for small boats if proper care is not taken. They are narrow and several large boats have been wrecked here in days gone by.

Eureka Bar, just below the mouth of the Imnaha River, had been pre-selected as a possible overnight camping spot. A rock cairn marker is the only sign of an early day settlement here. Steamers delivered freight and old time plans called for a post office, store and stamp mill but the loss of machinery in the wrecking of the *Imnaha* in Mountain Sheep Rapids in 1903 ended the mining venture and doomed the settlement. Because of higher water than expected there wasn't sufficient beach for such a large party to camp so the fleet returned to Bear Bar for the overnight rendezvous.

Boats lined the beach, some bow in, some stern in and some broadside. While stakes and rods were driven in and rocks carried down to tie to, Spokane Commodore Phil McCauley broke out two "sand anchors" which he had made from plans he found in SEA. They consisted of a steel disc 8″ to 10″ in diameter. To an eye bolt in the center of the disc was fastened a piece of chain about two feet long. The disc was buried in the sand two feet or so deep and the boat's mooring line tied to the end of the chain. It proved a very effective and simple anchor, one which any boater who uses sand beaches would find handy to have aboard.

It was a revelation to note the ingenious methods and equipment devised by these boaters to contribute to convenience and comfort. Lacking the deck and galley space of larger cruisers, they use the beach for their lounging and cooking. Chairs, tables and a variety of charcoal barbecues, hibachis and rotisseries were broken out. Steaks were broiled, roasts barbecued and other meats cooked. Holes were dug in the sand, lined and covered with foil for baking potatoes and vegetables cooked in containers fashioned of foil.

John Waters had trouble with his fire which he had built too close to the edge of the beach. Apparently some extra water had been released from the Hell's Canyon Dam

upstream causing the river level to rise. John was kept busy constructing dikes around his fire to keep it from being drowned before dinner had been cooked.

Following what, in our case, was a gourmet dinner with the Bakers joining the Vawters, a contest with prizes was staged among the young folks for the most and biggest driftwood for a campfire. Cruising yarns were followed by a campfire songfest with the canyon cliffs echoing the music up and down the river. As all hands turned into

The fleet takes a break for some leg stretching and exploring at Buffalo Eddy.

their bunks or sleeping bags on the sand a tremendous silence lay in the darkness.

Sunday morning the sun rose in a clear sky to usher in a beautiful but hot summer day. Shorty had promised to guide a small group of boats further up the river. Piloting John Waters' 20′ Fiberfoam runabout with MerCruiser stern drive unit, he led five boat loads of the more adventurous. The others stayed at Bear Bar, relaxing and enjoying the sunshine. Still plagued with motor trouble, Don Baker joined us in the *Vawterloo* while Betty stayed on the beach.

We passed Eureka Bar and entered the Imnaha Rapids below the mouth of the Imnaha River. A terrific current coming out makes these rapids long, fast and rough. Two of the smaller open boats turned back here leaving three still in the convoy.

The Imnaha River mouth is one of the beauty spots on the Snake River, especially when the water is high. Rich ore was found in this area in early days resulting in the writing of considerable mining history. Wally told of an old mine shaft on a ledge which contained a rich vein of ore. Flooding of the shaft caused by a blast resulted in the abandonment of the mine. Mining generally failed because of the lack of transportation.

Wally guided the *Vawterloo* with a firm hand as he followed closely in Shorty's trail. The rapids in this upper section of the river are treacherous, fast, sometimes shallow, sometimes through very narrow channels with high swells. At several points it seemed we could almost reach out and touch the underwater rocks on both sides of the swerving boat. It required tricky maneuvering of the wheel and throttle as well as careful attention to the range markers and Shorty's trail ahead. We could see rings still embedded in rocks which had been used as late as 1932 for ropes to help tow various craft through the more turbulent rapids.

We stopped to study a sign at Nez Perce Crossing which read, "Near this point in June, 1877 Chief Joseph led his people across the flooding Snake River into Idaho. They left their homeland to seek escape from General Howard. 6000 head of cattle and horses were forced to swim across with only slight losses. People and supplies were crossed on horsehide rafts towed by swimming horses under young braves. After three months of outfighting his pursuers, Chief Joseph was captured in Bear Paw Mountains of Montana only 30 miles from sanctuary in Canada."

Our extra Sunday morning cruise went up river to Pittsburg Landing, a little sandy beach, which had once been a townsite deep in the craggy canyon of the Snake at the foot of beautiful ranch country.

Worrying a bit about their gas supply with more used than planned on this extra trip, both Wally and John decided to put into Copper Mountain where Capt. R. B. Rivers, who operates the river mail, passenger and freight boat, maintains a camp for the overnight stop on his excursion trips. Gas is a rare commodity along the Snake so we were fortunate to be able to buy some from his drums on the river bank.

The return trip to Bear Bar produced a couple of added thrills. Coming through a rapids, just as Wally advanced the throttle for an extra surge, the motor coughed, slowed and lost power. He managed to keep it running enough to maintain a semblance of steerageway to get through the rapids and put the bow on a sandy beach. A changed element in the filter remedied the trouble although it happened twice more and the filter had to be cleaned and replaced.

Another time we were in the middle of a rather rough rapids when the boat took a sudden swerve and there was no steering response to the wheel. We whirled and tossed while Shorty came back to give us a tow line. It didn't take long for Wally to discover that the long nut connecting the steering cable to the outdrive unit had worked loose. It was quickly fixed while we berated him for purposely loosening it to provide a little extra excitement. Remembering the worried look on his face and the sweat on his brow there in the middle of the rapids, we decided to accept his claim of innocence.

By the time we got back to Bear Bar many of the boats had already left on the return trip while the crews of those

still there were well roasted in the bright sunshine which produced many sunburns.

Our return trip was uneventful. By this time we were accepting as commonplace the rapids, which seem to occur at about every turn of the river's tortuous course. Riding with the current gave us a faster yet different ride. Pilots had to be just as attentive to the ranges and boat handling as on the outbound trip.

Capt. Shorty Miller, experienced river pilot and leader of the cruise, takes John Water's 20' Fiberform through boiling rapids on the Sunday a.m. "extra" trip further up the river.

Upon docking at Lewiston we learned that one group which had left Bear Bar early had been led by someone who knew the river but ran at too fast a pace for all of the boats to keep up. A substitute leader, not so well versed on the river, took five boats on the wrong side of an island. They all hit rocks and bent or broke props or struts.

Thus the casualty list of five, plus Don Baker's recalcitrant motor, was not too serious. We had gone up and back through 76 of the 90 navigable miles of a surging, boiling, agitated river which through the centuries has cut the deepest gorge on the North American continent. The walls of Hell's Canyon, a few miles above the head of navigation at Johnson Bar, average 6600 feet with one point between Kinney Creek and Granite Creek where the canyon depth is just under 8000 feet.

We had enjoyed a pristine beauty and a power that thrills even those who have made the trip before. Wally had said at the pre-cruise skippers' meeting, "through fast white water in rapids that are tricky but not *too* dangerous," and he had been right. Snaking the Snake with the Spokane Yacht Club was a never-to-be-forgotten experience.

41

The World Famed Columbia River Chinook Salmon

"Fish on!" It's your pole that's bending almost double in its holder. You grab for it. The skipper throws the engine out of gear and shuts it off. Joe and the skipper reel in while you bring up the tip of your pole to be sure the fish is still there. He is.

You start reeling, being careful not to tighten the drag. But the line goes out against the drag. You brace your feet with one knee against the side of the boat as it rolls in the ocean swell. That morning breeze is still chilly but suddenly you're glowing and warm. It would be easier to bring this fish in if you could shed your heavy jacket, yet you realize that's impossible now.

Finally the fish stops his headlong run. Working pole and reel together you manage to gain nearly 50 yards of line on the reel before he starts another run. Your heart sinks as the spool gets smaller and smaller. Is he aiming to cross the Pacific?

Joe sits on the engine box, jealously watching you fight. The skipper has the landing net even though you aren't nearly ready for it. Your audience grows as a couple of outboards off to port come in closer to watch.

Now the second run ends and you anxiously work the fish back toward the boat. About half way he breaks water to do a sort of dance on his tail.

"It's a big one," yells the skipper. "Keep your line tight!"

Two more runs are shorter as you feel him beginning to tire. You are tiring, too. The muscles in your arms and back, even in your legs ache but you must keep fighting. The line on the reel tells you you're gaining on him. If only you could get rid of that heavy jacket! You can feel the sweat running down the middle of your back.

This time you get him almost alongside the boat and you get a good look at him as he takes a roll. The skipper has a net over. The fish has other ideas. He heads down and under the boat. It takes a bit of fast and fancy maneuvering to work the tip of your pole across the transom and around to the other side as the fish heads shoreward. At least you kept him from tangling the line in the rudder or propeller.

A shorter run this time and the reel-in is easier. Careful, now! Work him in slowly. A little closer in, toward the net.

There! He's netted, he's aboard and Joe clubs him smartly across the head to still the threshing.

You heave a sigh of relief as you gaze contentedly at 43 pounds of Chinook salmon, a real lunker, before stuffing him into the sack of chipped ice.

It takes only a moment to recover. The aches are gone and, if you're tired, you forget it as you join the others in hooking on another herring and getting your line back into the water.

That's fishing on the Columbia Bar, a sport that has been popular for several decades but in recent years has attracted more and more fishermen until today as many as 3000 boats may be out at one time. Over 300,000 fish were boated last year in a season that runs from July through September and sometimes starts in June.

In earlier years fishing at the mouth of the Columbia River was done mostly within the river, in the McGowan Hole, around Sand Island, and out as far as Peacock Spit. Astoria, Warrenton, Skipanon River on the Oregon side and Ilwaco, Chinook and McGowan's Tent City on the Washington side were the principal bases. Trolling was the popular method, and artificial plugs the bait.

Today the scene has shifted out across the bar with trolling and mooching about equally popular and herring the accepted bait. There are still some who stay inside the bar, many getting good results. But with the advent of larger boats and more powerful motors, the "outside" seems to be attracting more and more anglers.

It's impossible to say what this fishing phenomenon should be called — way of life, craze, religion, fever or phobia. Whatever it is, the area is well geared for it. Although the season is actually open 12 months, the spring, summer and fall months reach a climax in August with boats of all sizes from large yachts to 14-footers descending from Washington, Oregon, British Columbia, Montana and Idaho and as far away as California and Nevada. Of course the bulk of them come from western Washington and Oregon but a check of boat trailer licenses on the parking lots reveals large numbers from the other western states.

The little part of Ilwaco on the Washington side with a permanent population of 650 has become the main base for these sport fishermen. The moorages handle over

1000 boats. Ilwaco, named for Elowahka Jim, an Indian who lived there, is concerned with the business end of this fishing extravaganza while its neighboring communities of Holman, Seaview and Long Beach with their many restaurants, motels, resorts and places of amusements might be called the living-dining-bedroom of the area.

In May the sleepiness of winter awakes to near carnival mood as early fishing enthusiasts arrive. The "Strip," between the large parking area and the waterfront, is a beehive of activity with its bait and tackle shops, ice-houses, charter boat offices, launching hoists and hot dog stands. In the town itself fish canneries and fish cleaning, icing and storage establishments prepare for the onslaught of thousands of fishermen. It's a wild, hilarious, yet deadly serious atmosphere where fish is king.

The same thing, to a lesser degree, takes place at Chinook, with its boat harbor, the two harbors of Astoria, and the marinas in the Warrenton and Skipanon River areas. Many of the larger cruisers from Portland and vicinity take summer moorage at the Astoria Yacht Club. Trailerboats, both outboard and inboard/outdrive, launch at all of these areas with the bulk of those fishing across the bar using the Ilwaco facilities because of the shorter distance and protected water almost to the main entrance of the river. There is also a good launching ramp at Fort Canby State Park in behind Cape Disappointment.

Is crossing the bar dangerous? It can be extremely so. Or the bar can be as easy and safe as any other water depending entirely on conditions and the yachtsman's attention to certain rules. One look at a chart of the entrance, which marks the final resting place of 170 ships which failed to make it, gives a skipper plenty of cause to follow the rules in order that his ship not be added to this "Graveyard of the Pacific."

The U.S. Coast Guard maintains lifeboat, radio and helicopter stations on both sides of the channel. During the fishing season there are usually six or seven Coast Guard boats augmented by a like number of Coast Guard Auxiliary boats on patrol. This is pitifully few when one considers there may be up to 2000 boats fishing at the height of the salmon run. Best advice to the fisherman is to heed their counsel. There's never a dull moment for the Coast Guardsman in this area.

The first requirement is close attention to tide and current tables. During summer months it is usually safe to fish the *incoming* tides and to go in and out of the river on these tides. One should never attempt to traverse the bar, either in or out, on a strong ebb tide. On these tides the current can reach a velocity of six to eight knots, too much for a small boat to buck along with the steep seas that can build up over the bar with a brisk northwest wind.

Another hazard can be fog which may come in the early morning and lift by midmorning; however, it may not lift at all. At other times a fog may come in swiftly. The Coast Guard issues a small chart showing magnetic compass headings and distances between the Columbia Lightship, channel buoys and known check points.*

This chart also marks dangerous areas such as Peacock Spit, Clatsop Spit and other shallow or hazardous areas where the yachtsman could get in trouble. Basically, however, if the skipper follows the rules, paying close attention to the tides, and uses proper caution, he will have no trouble getting to and from the most fabulous fishing grounds in the West.

And, for those without a boat of their own, or a friend with a boat, there are some 125 charter boats in which you can spend the day fishing for $18 to $20 with everything furnished; less if you bring some of your own gear.†

In the Pacific Northwest almost everyone with a boat fishes for salmon. We've dropped a line in many of the popular spots from Olympia, up through Puget Sound, the San Juan and Gulf Islands, northern British Columbia waters and all the way to Juneau, Alaska. But we had never tried Columbia River Bar fishing. We'd heard so much about this that there was no hesitation in accepting an invitation to sample the fishing in these waters.

The current changed from ebb to flood at about 10 a.m. and we had agreed to meet at the boat at 8 o'clock. This would give us plenty of time to pick up bait and ice and get out to the bar at slack. The August morning was partly cloudy with a crispness in the air that presaged the approach of fall.

Skipper Bill Johnson of Portland was at the Ilwaco basin early, taking the curtains off his 24-foot Sea Skiff. He moored the boat there all summer for as much fishing as he could get in and for Coast Guard Auxiliary patrol work on a regular schedule. The previous night's heavy dew had left everything covered with a blanket of cold wetness. Top and curtains down and stowed away, deck swabbed and windows dried. The boat was ready. Bill checked his tackle box to be sure he had sufficient hooks, sinkers and leaders.

Boats head out to "make the tide" across the bar

A couple of beauties ready to be eaten, iced or canned

Who caught that one? The big job at the end of the day is for each fisherman to identify his own catch

*A bar guide for the Columbia River Entrance is available free from the 13th Coast Guard District boating safety branch in Seattle or from their safety detachments that travel throughout the district.
†Today's charterboat prices are considerably higher! In 1968, when this was written, a family of four could eat for $35 a week.

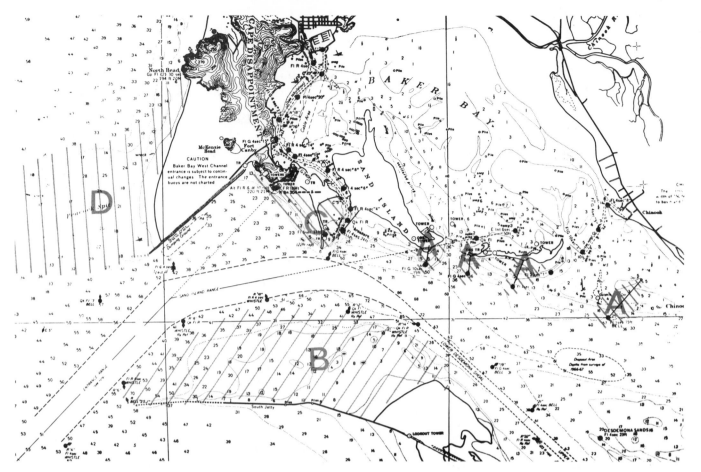

"You never can tell," he said. "Sometimes a dogfish or shark will snap a leader before you can shake him off. These salmon have needle-sharp teeth, too, which can fray a line or bend a hook by the time you have him boated."

Next it was back up the gangway to "The Strip" where we picked up a couple of packages of frozen herring and two large plastic-lined bags of chipped ice. Bill had already stowed aboard a carton of "makings" for lunch.

After a short engine warm-up we cast off to head out the well-marked figure S channel in back of Cape Disappointment, past Fort Canby State Park's launching ramp and behind Jetty A to the main stream of the Columbia. Although this is protected water, the wakes of a hundred or so other boats with a departure time about the same as ours kept the narrow channel well roiled.

Once around the end of Jetty A, Bill revved the motor up as he headed out the main river channel for the bar. We could see the line of even-numbered red buoys marking the left side of the channel and the odd-numbered black ones marking the right. Further to the north beyond the buoys, was the North Jetty and behind the left row of buoys, the South Jetty.

Bill explained that, in addition to the bar itself, shallow banks of sand lay along these jetties and how, if a boat didn't stay in the marked channel, it could swamp or capsize if it should lose power in the strong currents and steep waves over these shallow spots.

The bar, with a low water depth of around 40 feet, was tossing up some turbulent, high seas as we crossed. The skipper's calm face and confident look was reassuring. Soon we were in deeper water where the ocean swells lengthened out to give a more comfortable ride.

After a couple of miles on a southwesterly heading to-

ward the lightship, Bill cut the throttle to trolling speed and we baited up. He demonstrated the way to put the two hooks into the herring so it would "swim" properly about six feet behind a four-ounce weight. We checked them in the water for action.

"How deep?" was the next question.

"That's a good part of the secret of catching salmon," said Bill. "You never know at what depth they're feeding. It may be 20 to 30 feet down, 50 to 60, or it may be near the bottom. Once you locate them, then that's the depth to fish. Let's start at 30 feet."

Bill got the first one, a nice 15-pound Silver. Before an hour was up we had two apiece, each a Silver and a small King, or Chinook, as they are called there. We trolled for another hour or so, expecting any minute to get our third fish to limit for the day.

"Guess we've run out of them," Bill observed. "Let's try it a little deeper."

After reeling in to check our herring, we let 60 feet of line out. By this time we, along with a good segment of the fleet, were four or five miles southeast of the lightship. The clouds had transformed themselves into a scattering of white cotton puffs decorating the hills along the rugged Oregon coast. The sun had warmed the air to a just-right summer day. The sea rolled quietly in gentle swells. Everything was perfect except we weren't catching those last two fish.

We fished for another hour, working our way back north and trying different depths, all to no avail. Bill suggested we cut the motor, eat lunch and try mooching.

This is letting the boat drift, the currents taking the line out. If the water is still, one must give the bait some motion by moving the pole but there was enough wave action to keep the boat and thus the poles moving just about right.

We ate lunch, relaxed in the sunshine and talked about the Columbia Bar and its fabulous fishing. Bill pointed out that fishing was done as far as 12 miles south, and north to around Long Beach.

Suddenly the whine of a reel brought us back into action. We both grabbed for our poles. Bill had the fish on. He worked it carefully in by the boat, but before we could net it, it took off again for another run. The second time in we boated it, a nice 18-pound Silver.

We fished without results until time to head back and try our luck for an hour on the bar before tide change. Quite a few boats were working along the inside of the North Jetty. We joined them, taking several runs parallel to the jetty. We also criss-crossed the channel several times. We were sure we were going to get that last fish, for several times the herring was "stolen" off the hooks.

Now the channel was filled with returning boats and Bill had a real traffic problem. He was just about to call it quits when the fish hit. With the turbulence building rapidly on the bar, and surrounded by boats, we made quick work of boating that fish. It meant a chance of losing it but we were lucky and got a nice 13-pound Chinook aboard to limit for the day and head back to Ilwaco.

Next day called for a six o'clock departure. The morning was bright and clear. The bar crossing on a slight ebb current was calm and uneventful and we again headed for a fleet of boats fishing southeast of the lightship.

Everything went well from the start. We had four fish aboard by ten o'clock. At this rate we'd have no trouble limiting in time to make the noon slack on the bar.

We were just boating our fifth fish, a 32-pound Chinook beauty, when we realized that both the wind and the sea had made up considerably. A decision was made to try for a while longer for that last fish.

As the wind continued to increase, and the seas grew rougher, Bill had to give all his attention to handling the boat. Although we still had over an hour to go, we decided it was good judgment to head back in case the bar should be kicking up. We were pitching and rolling so much that it was tricky getting our lines in and the gear stowed. Bill did a good job of quartering the steep waves which by now were white capping and breaking over the bow.

It happened suddenly. One minute we were in bright sunshine, the next a curtain of thick white fog descended on us from the north. We were still too far south to see the line of channel buoys leading into the river mouth but Bill managed to get a bearing on a familiar shore mark and set a compass course before we were completely enveloped in the fog.

Bill had an intense look about him but didn't appear particularly worried as he fought the wheel in the mountainous seas. Most of the 1500 boats out were also heading back and we could hear a cacaphonic band of fog horns all around us. Visibility was down to 15 to 20 feet, calling for a close lookout in all directions just to stay clear of other boats. We reduced speed to five knots. Although Bill tried to keep his compass course it was hard to do and we just stayed with the fleet.

After what seemed hours of wondering if we'd make the bar on time, the fog lifted momentarily and we were able to pick out the end of the South Jetty and 2SJ Bell Buoy. From there on the fog thinned so we could follow the buoy line into the channel. By the time we were half way into Cape Disappointment and Jetty A we were in sunshine again although the curtain of fog still hung out there across the bar and out in the ocean.

The radio was filled with requests for help from lost and stalled boats and we could see the Coast Guard boats heading out to assist and towing in disabled craft. A trip later that afternoon up to the Cape Disappointment Lighthouse and radio station gave us a chance to talk to the Coast Guardsmen and see their radio log. It had been a busy day for them as they performed what to them is routine duty but to the thousands of fishermen is a valued and appreciated service. They are there to advise and help. The least the boater can do is to follow their advice and the rules set up for the safe enjoyment of this great fishing area.

We didn't get our last fish that day but it still had been a great weekend with a good sampling of the sea and weather conditions which can face the fisherman in this area. Three days are more than enough to "hook" almost anyone on the wonderment, the thrills and fever of fishing the Columbia Bar. What's more it can be enjoyed without having to buy a license.*

And, as if the fishing itself, the vacation resort atmosphere, the many excellent facilities taxed to capacity aren't enough, there is more. Astoria has its annual regatta while Ilwaco, Chinook and other communities conduct their fishing derbies which attract even more enthusiastic anglers.

Every fisherman has his favorite fishing spots, his favorite type of fish and his favorite ways of catching them but he just hasn't lived until he's fished the fabled Columbia River Bar. It isn't *just* the fishing — it's the whole mammoth carnival of fishing, boating, regattas, guests, vacationing, cruising and meeting friends from all over the West. It's fun!

*A salmon card is required for each fisherman.

42
Westport's Where the Action Is

Dingy clouds covered the sky. Early morning was dark and colorless but spirits were high in the Front Street restaurant as Dr. Ed and his "harem" finished breakfast preparatory to a day of salmon fishing at Westport. A keen excitement was evident among the girls as they trooped down the gangway to the float where *Bingo* was moored. It was "Fishing Day," when Dr. Ed Nowak, a Seattle oral surgeon, closed his office to give his wife and staff a try at the wily salmon at one of Washington State's best-known fishing spots.

Dr. Ed is an ardent fisherman who has his own boat but, like many others experienced in ocean fishing, he knows that fishing at Westport is best done in a regular charter boat with an experienced skipper to negotiate the tricky bar. As Capt. Paul Mankin backed *Bingo* out of her slip and threaded his way through the protected harbor, Jim, his son, deck hand and bait boy, assembled poles, attached gear and baited the hooks with herring. *Bingo* crossed the bar in relatively smooth waters at 7 o'clock. By 7:30 Dr. Ed had the first fish on, a nice 14-pound King Salmon.

Although there was little wind, a typical ocean swell came in from the northwest. The gentle roll of the *Bingo* was just enough to bother Karen. She wasn't seasick, she said, just had a squeamish stomach. It ended suddenly when the reel on her pole, in the holder on the rail, sang out indicating another fish hooked. By 8:15, with Dr. Ed's help, she had boated a 19-pounder. Action really started then with a double-header at 8:25. Karen got another which ran 14 pounds while Mrs. Nowak brought in a 10-pounder.

The bar starts at black buoy #9 and extends out beyond an imaginary line between the ends of the north and south jetties. The *Bingo* was fishing outside, between buoys #6 and #8 in 42 to 46-foot depths. The herring bait was on double hooks on 20-pound test leaders with 4 ounces of lead weight and about 20 to 25 feet of line out.

Several "shakers" were hooked during the morning. These are undersized salmon running below the 20-inch legal minimum and were promptly returned to the water.

There was another double-header at 9:10 with Evelyn getting one off the stern and Mrs. Nowak hooking hers on the starboard rail. Evelyn had hers boated by 9:25 while Mrs. Nowak, with the doctor's help, got hers aboard by 9:30. At 9:40 Evelyn tied into another beauty which she landed in 12 minutes to make a total of seven fish before 10 o'clock.

The ocean was dotted with fishermen, most of them concentrating their efforts in the vicinity of buoys #6 and #8 and just outside the bar. There were charter boats, large yachts, smaller yachts and innumerable outboards and inboard/outdrives. Although visibility was good and the wave-activated horns on the buoys were monotonous with their throaty "Maow-Maow" sounding like the bawling of a sick cow, it was easy to imagine that this would be a most welcome sound in the thick fog which can roll in to harass the fisherman.

The skipper told about another favorite spot called the Goldfish Bowl, an area some seven miles beyond the last buoy with depths of 160 to 180 feet. Here big Ling Cod and Red Snappers are caught as well as Silver Salmon. The name of the spot comes from the red-gold color of the Snappers.

His description was interrupted by more action as another of the girls hooked a big one but lost it by not keeping the line taut. Betty got one on and succeeded in boating it after a 15-minute struggle. After a lunch of Mrs. Nowak's luscious beef stew with plenty of meat, the *Bingo* was headed toward the north jetty. Mrs. Nowak got a big one on which she turned over to Dr. Ed for landing. He proceeded to lose it.

Ocean fishing along Washington's coast has long been a popular sport with such spots as the Columbia River Bar, LaPush and Neah Bay having a history dating back to Indian days. Westport, however, is more of a "come-lately" area as far as sportfishing goes.

Commanding the northern point of the 18-mile sandy shore of a Pacific peninsula, Westport's growth has been exciting. At the turn of the century whaling ships, clipper ships, schooners and steamboats stabbed their way to Aberdeen through a 30-foot channel which ran through what is now the center of town. In 1906 the completion of the South Jetty saw the moving of the channel, the gradual wave-driven accretion of sand assisted by the

The Westport harbor has nearly wall-to-wall boats before the fleet takes off for the fishing grounds.

hand of man with his mammoth dredges. It was then that Pt. Chehalis was born, creating a sheltered cove to protect an ever-growing fleet of vessels.

History records that Ed Kaakinen, founder of the now famous crabbing industry, was offered Pt. Chehalis in the early 30's by its owner, Aberdeen tug fleet owner Dick Ultican, for the sum of $150. He refused to take it, saying it wasn't worth that much. Today it couldn't be bought for $10 million.

Sportfishing by local residents in small boats probably started in the 30's. As a center for sport salmon fishing, Westport began its phenomenal growth about 1950 when large fleets of outboard kicker boats discovered this wealth of the sea. Commercial fishermen were taking sportfishermen out in their boats. Around 1954 an impetus was given to bring in more exclusive charter boats. Small cruisers were rebuilt with a large cockpit to accommodate six people.

As the sport mushroomed, specialized charter boats began making their appearance in 1956 and '57. This was partly the result of the public law #519 passed in 1957 which forced all charter boats to conform to certain Coast Guard specifications.

The charter fleet has grown year by year until today nearly every other place of business in town seems to be some kind of a charter service. Early charter boats designed by Seattle Naval Architect Edwin Monk have served as a basic pattern for the present fleet. The boats, costing in the neighborhood of $50,000, are mostly owned by private individuals who skipper them themselves or lease them to the skipper. They are operated through the charter offices which take care of reservations and other details.

There are 28 charter offices operating fleets out of Westport with 20 of them banding together for mutual cooperation in the Westport Association. Our skipper's *Bingo*, 43' x 14' x 5' 7", powered with a 260-hp Volvo Penta diesel and built in Seattle by Con Youngquist, is part of the 15-boat fleet of Salmon Charters headed by Del Fender.

With a season running from April 15 to the end of October and really booming from mid-June through September, many skippers keep busy the rest of the year at a variety of occupations including teaching, plumbing, truck driving, insurance selling and operating a radio station.

One thing they must have is experience. A charter boat skipper must put in an apprenticeship of two years as a deckhand or crewman on another boat. Then he must pass a Coast Guard examination for a license to operate a boat carrying up to six passengers. After two years on this limited license he can apply for a full license entitling him to skipper a boat with 12 people aboard, three fish on at once and no deck hand.

In talking with Chief Rowland Miller Jr. at the Westport Coast Guard station about the hazards of the bar, it became evident why sportfishermen would prefer to depend on the experience of a charter boat skipper. In addition to the bar itself, there are four dangerous shoal areas.

Inside the bay, on the right leaving Westport, is Outer Whitcomb Flats. Over this shoal water area, where it's easy for a boat to drift while fishing, sharp breakers up to six feet in height can occur if a swell is running.

Heading out to the bar is the Middle Ground where breakers up to 12 feet can form. On the bar the outward end of the South Jetty is submerged for 3000 feet and only shows at low tide. Breaking seas and submerged rocks make this an extremely dangerous area. Waters around the end of the North Jetty are also dangerous because of the shoal water and breakers which are almost always present.

Chief Miller also pointed out that many small boat operators are unaware that, at times, a run-out tide of 11 feet in six hours can cause a current up to six knots. When this strong ebbing current meets the ocean swell over the bar, severe breakers are formed which are extremely dangerous and unsafe for small craft. Fog is another hazard to consider. It can come in quickly and catch the fisherman unaware.

(Left) Evelyn hooks a big one while the skipper gives advice and stands by with the landing net. (Right) The end of a perfect day.

Captain Mankin stops the boat and leaves the bridge to get a landing net and help one of the girls land her salmon. Many Westport Charter boats are similar in design to the Bingo.

Fishing is done either by trolling or mooching. Trolling rods, usually in two sections, are graded according to the weight of the tip with six to ten ounce rods the most popular. Bait is fresh or frozen herring, spoon, plug or fly.

Although the salmon in this area are not the largest — a 45-pounder is a good sized fish here — they seem to be more numerous than in many other places in the Northwest with several races of Kings and Silvers returning to these waters during the season to lie offshore until they head upstream to spawn.

Westport is a typical small resort town having a definite western flavor with colorfully named restaurants such as Sourdough Lil's, motels, an aquarium, gift and souvenir shops and establishments for the cleaning, icing or canning of the fish.

Although charter boats are the big business, there are still many smaller boats, outboards and inboard/outdrives, trailered in and launched either at the town's launching ramp or the two lifts. Chief Miller estimates approximately 300 trailerboats a day come in at the peak of the fishing season. He says that, although this type of boat causes most of the "business" for him and his men, they are a much better and safer boat than the old, small, low-transom outboard boats of earlier years.

With Westport's sportfishing business grown to boom proportions, action is beginning to develop across the mouth of the harbor on Pt. Brown where the Ocean Shores Marina had some 10 charter boats operating last season. Some of these were new boats while others had moved over from Westport. The marina also boasts a restaurant, fuel dock, tackle shop, marine hardware store, paved launching ramp with parking space for boat trailers and a moorage basin protected by two rock jetties which eventually will hold up to 200 small boats.

For the novice fisherman, the non-boat-owning fisherman or the boat owner from other parts of the country who wants to have a try at the Northwest's famous salmon, charter boat fishing provides the perfect answer. Costs run about $15 to $18 a day per person for the boat, with tackle and bait available at a nominal fee. The charter fee includes cleaning the fish, plastic bags for carrying them and hot coffee.*

One might wonder how, with some 200 charter boats carrying an average of ten people per boat and 300 small private boats averaging two people per boat for a total of better than 2500 ardent fishermen out at one time during the peak of the season, the poor fish ever has a chance. Still they seem to keep coming and the fishermen keep coming after them.

*Expect to pay more today! When this was written bread was 29¢ and milk 27¢.

43
Outboard Cruising

Just for fun, try naming an outboard cruising and trailer-boating region comparing to it. There isn't a skipper's logbook big enough to hold his list of different Northwest harbors and islands after a couple of seasons of exploring. Peaceful waterways winding among forest-clad islands; wild white-water rapids rushing through deep gorges cut in majestic mountain ranges; fantastically-carved icebergs broken from centuries-old glaciers as they meet the sea; remote inland lakes stocked with fish; the tides of open salt water; an unbelievable variety of scenic beauties — all this goes to make up the chapters of the small-boat skipper's logbook.

Thousands of small cruisers visit this land o'plenty waterways on each side of the western international line, moving directly over the saltchuck from home ports stretched from Olympia to Vancouver and above. Others trail their boats from distant ports. Because of its mobility, the outboard or inboard/outdrive trailerable boat offers its owner a versatility denied the larger-boat skipper and

the fixed-port skipper. The small boater can save many hours of water travel to reach a favorite area by utilizing the highways. His is the specialized approach.

In the Northwest cruising possibilities are unlimited. More launching ramps, lifts and other facilities are added each year to open up more cruising areas than any one person could cover in a lifetime. There is the great inland sea comprising Puget Sound, the San Juan Islands and the coastal British Columbia waters that reach out to Alaskan waters. The innumerable lakes of British Columbia, Washington, Idaho, Montana and Oregon offer attractions which alone would take many years of cruising to cover.

The Columbia River invites exploration from its source in mid-British Columbia, through the delightful Arrow Lakes, Franklin Roosevelt Lake, Wallula Lake, down its tortuous course to its mouth where it meets the Pacific and produces some of the best salmon fishing in the world. Then there are the many tributary rivers, some with lakes

(Left) Minstrel Island, adjacent to outstanding salmon fishing and excellent crabbing.

(Center) Tahsis Inlet on the outside of Vancouver I., a Washington outboard cruises along . . . Inland or coastal, launching ramps "bridge" fine highways and great waterways . . .

(Right) Savary I., where the waters are warm and the beach gently sloping.

Gone exploring. Anchor down in Blind Bay, Jervis Inlet; the inflatable dinghy was used to go ashore.

Miles of San Juan Islands cruising.

formed by dams; others with sandy beaches for lunch or overnight stops. The Snake River alone can keep a boater busy for an entire vacation.

The wonderful thing about it all is that, with the mobility of a trailerable boat, all or any portion of these rivers desired can be cruised according to time available.

In the protected salt waters of western Washington and British Columbia the small boater finds an almost unbelievable wealth of cruising possibilities. Starting with the southern tip of Puget Sound at Olympia and running to Prince Rupert there are literally thousands of miles of shoreline, innumerable islands, bays, coves and passages in this inland waterway. From shores lined with beautiful homes to wild, untouched country looking exactly as it did to Capt. Vancouver nearly 200 years ago, the boater can pick and choose his favorite areas and put into the water wherever fancy dictates.

North of Puget Sound these inland waters group themselves into natural areas, each having its devotees who go back year after year or, after having explored one for a time, move northwestward each year. There are the San Juan Islands and the Canadian Gulf Islands, readily accessible without having to cross much open water. Across the Strait of Georgia are several cruising areas which are becoming increasingly popular with the small boaters: Howe Sound, Sechelt and Jervis Inlets and, of course, Princess Louisa Inlet. Any of these can be enjoyed by trailering along the British Columbia coast to the launching facility nearest to the desired area.

Still further up are Desolation Sound and the waters to the west. The more adventurous go on into Toba, Bute, Loughborough and Knight Inlets and clear to Queen Charlotte Strait. Beyond is the enticing inland passage to Prince Rupert with hundreds of interesting attractions including quaint fishing and Indian villages, and loggers camps on floats. Then, of course, there is southeastern Alaska with the rugged beauty of the Northland extending

up to Skagway or Glacier Bay and fascinating stops at Ketchikan, Wrangel, Petersburg or Juneau.

With small boats making up around 70 percent of the Northwest's boat population, there are many outboard and small boat clubs, most of them offering a well organized cruising program. Many owners, however, prefer to cruise alone or in company with another boat or two.

Perhaps the largest and most active group is the Northwest Outboard Trailer Sailors, with an active membership of about 120 families. Based in Portland with a branch in Eugene having 40-50 families, members range far and wide throughout Oregon, Washington and British Columbia. They have had organized cruises as far away as Princess Louisa Inlet.

Favorite cruising areas are not always close to home. Wally and Betty Vawter of the Spokane Yacht Club trailer their 20′ Uniflite *Vawterloo* long distances. "I don't think we could call any one place our favorite," Wally says. "Lake Coeur d'Alene with its three rivers rates high and we always make and enjoy the club's Snake River Cruise. We haven't yet tried the salt water but just as soon as time permits we'll be over there to taste of the San Juan and Gulf Islands."

Bill and Ruth Crossett with son, Jerry, and his wife are partial to Pend Orielle and Priest Lakes in Idaho. But it's still hard to outrank a cruise through the Arrow Lakes," says Bill.

Al and Beverly Mason with their 12-year-old Jim and 10-year-old Candy admit they are "loners." In their 23′ Tollycraft they like to explore. "This summer was our fifth afloat and we haven't even begun." Beverly was enthusiastic. "We trailer to Anacortes for launching and have spent all of our time so far in the San Juans and Gulf Islands. We like to get into every cove we can find and spend lots of time fishing, going after clams, oysters, crabs and shrimp. We also swim and water ski. Oh sure, we want to go on north; but there are so many islands and we don't want to miss any."

"A big boat is fine, I guess," mused Chuck Laird of Vancouver as he lolled on the sand of Savary Island after a swim. "Only trouble is we can't afford one. Alice and I like our little Sangstercraft and I'll bet we see more on our holidays each year than the guy with the big boat. We put in at Lund, go faster and can get into more places for far less money. Our favorite place? Oh, I don't know. Ask Alice. She lays out our cruises."

Alice was hesitant. "It's hard to say. Isabel Bay in Malaspina Inlet or Squirrel Cove, I guess. Still there's Walsh Cove and Prideaux Haven and that little bay on Mink Island. We like them all. There really isn't just one favorite."

The owners of a Fairliner at Big Bay were more definite. With a boy and a dog and a boat loaded with fishing gear it was obvious that they like to fish. "Yeah, it's a long way to come but we've tried lots of places and these Yacultas are the greatest."

The opinion was different at Minstrel Island. Here three boats, all with outboards, one from Oregon, one from Washington and one from British Columbia, had just returned from a fishing expedition to Rivers Inlet. "If you want to get the big salmon, you've got to go where the big ones are and that's the place," said one of the skippers. "Aw, it was a little dusty coming back across the open water in Queen Charlotte Sound, but with three of us together we felt safe enough if anything should happen and it really wasn't too bad."

At Effingham Bay in Barkley Sound on the outside of Vancouver Island it was Ted and Jean Thompson of Tacoma with two toddlers in a Reinell. "Certainly this is our favorite cruising area," Ted explained. "This is our third year here and it can't be beat. We drive to Port Angeles, ferry to Victoria and drive to Port Alberni for launching. No bad water to cross and these islands are the greatest. It's also fine for SCUBA diving."

So it is in the Northwest. No matter how many you talk with there is a wide divergence of opinion as to a "favorite" spot. All of which is good since there is no concentration in one place and there are plenty of places, at least for awhile yet.

It would almost seem that to be a successful and happy small boater, one would have to put up with a certain amount of discomfort. Not so! There is a knack which one soon requires. Lacking the room and convenience found on larger boats, the small boater becomes somewhat of a genius in making himself comfortable, inventing or copying someone else's ideas for utilizing every inch of the boat for stowing equipment and gear. He also learns new techniques of cooking in cramped quarters or on the beach. Don't think for a moment, though, that he doesn't eat well. Some of the finest gourmet meals we've been privileged to enjoy have been prepared on a small alcohol stove or in foil over a fire on a sandy shore.

"Foil and charcoal have probably done as much to advance the popularity of small boats as fiberglass and improved motors," says Jean Emerson. She and her husband Max, trailer their *Sittin' Pretty* from Spokane all over the Northwest wherever the mood takes them. John and Pat Waters with their family, also of Spokane, never hesitate to trailer their 20′ Fiberform wherever "the action is." "Although ours is an open boat," says John, "we have a top for it and we're always comfortable."

Some people are more creative and inventive than others but trailer boaters are a sociable group with everyone willing to help the other fellow. In the usual boat hopping one picks up all kinds of ideas and hints. A cleverly placed shelf or holder, a new way to stow something out of the way, an innovation in food storage or preparation, new gadgets or one made from something else. And everyone's anxious to demonstrate or discuss the things that have made his boating more enjoyable.

There is no question that the small boat has come of age, that it is here to stay and will continue to grow in popularity. With the addition of new and improved facilities throughout the continent and more to come in years ahead, there are almost no limits to cruising capacity. The mobility of the trailer-boat provides a versatility that opens up an endless variety of areas. Comfort, convenience and safety have been established.

44
Knowing How to Read Charts

Cruising both power and sail boats occupies a tremendous amount of the boating time of western skippers. Right now thousands of them are pointing their bows out to sea where knowledge of course and coastline under all circumstances is of greatest importance. Other multitudes are pointing bows through sparkling inlets, narrow entrances and playing the edges of passages at near slacks in the movement of otherwise dangerous waters.

The seasoned skipper knows what he is doing, knows his equipment is right and knows the exact water or geography all round him.

But what of those who have recently acquired their first boats? They, too, have been dreaming and will be heading for these same fabled cruising waters. It is to these latter that we address what we hope might help them toward more enjoyable and perhaps safer approaches to their great adventures.

Of all the tools the skipper has acquired to help him in cruising, perhaps the most valuable is the chart. Certainly it is primary. The navigational chart, like anything else, is simple enough if one studies it. It actually contains more information than could be guessed on first glance and, properly used, will enhance your knowledge, your seamanship and thus your enjoyment of cruising.

Charts are not the same as maps. They need study. One of the first things to note is whether the soundings, or water depths, are in feet or fathoms. The legend will tell you and a quick check of this item may save you the embarrassment of tossing your anchor into what you thought was 20 feet of water when actually it was 20 fathoms or 120 feet. Or, if it were the reverse, a low tide in the wee small hours of the morning could leave you high and dry.

Besides the water depth there are other valuable symbols such as M, Cl, S, or Rk to tell you whether the bottom is mud, clay, sand or rock.

Another aid to keep you out of trouble when near a shore line is the depth-contour line. This is a series of dots or dashes or both to indicate the limits of a certain depth. A series of single dots, evenly spaced, denotes six feet or one fathom, dots in groups of two denote 12 feet or two fathoms and so on up to six fathoms when a series of three dashes is used. The 10-fathom line is a combination of dash-dot-dash, 20 fathoms is a dash and two dots, etc., up to 50.

A sounding with a bar and a dot over it indicates that no bottom was found at that depth. A number underlined in the vicinity of reefs, or rocks exposed at low water, shows the height of the obstruction above the low water. Soundings shown are always at low water so, at other stages of the tide, you have an additional depth.

Appropriate symbols will also warn you of other dangers to navigation such as low and sunken rocks, foul bottom or wrecks. On the plus side you'll find many aids to navigation. Buoys are shown by little diamond-shaped symbols with the type labeled as "nun," "can," "whistle," "lighted" and "bell." The color is also shown and the little dot shows where the buoy is anchored to the bottom.

The Hydrographic Office shows the predictions on the direction and velocity of current on some charts. Remember these are only predictions; don't rely too much on them. General directions of the set of the current are marked by arrows. The flood tide or incoming current is marked with an arrow having feathers on one side of the shaft. The outgoing or ebb tide is shown by an arrow without feathers. A good trick to remember these is, "flood tide — feathered."

Still further helpful information can be obtained by attention to the kind of type used in certain places. When lettering is in regular or vertical type, it indicates that the object named is always above the surface of the water. If the name is in *italics* it shows that it is always below the surface.

In addition to information about the water, charts also tell you something about the surrounding land. The coast lines are clearly and sharply defined and colored differently to distinguish them from the water. The heights of the shore

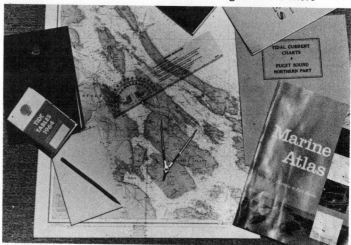

are plainly shown, whether high or low, with heights above the water given in feet.

Light houses, radio beacons, ranges, lighted-and-day beacons and other prominent or useful objects are plainly shown to help you in your navigation.

Harbors and bays are generally shown in great detail with cable areas, anchorages, rocks and foul ground carefully marked. On the land, prominent buildings, towers and church spires are shown to make it easier to locate yourself or to take bearings.

It's always a wise practice to draw your course on the chart lightly in pencil whenever in unknown waters. Observe the chart for landmarks ahead such as islands, buoys, lighthouses, hills, docks, bays, inlets and kelp beds (which can be mighty important) and note them as you pass.

The straight lines extending up and down the full length of the chart are the meridians of longitude. The lines running across the chart are parallels of latitude. They are important in navigation as they run true north and south and true east and west, thus helping to determine direction.

Longitude is marked off in degrees, minutes and tenths of minutes in the top and bottom margins of the chart. Of much more importance to the navigator are the scales of latitude found in the left and right margins of the chart, marked in degrees, minutes and tenths of minutes. Each minute of latitude is equal to one nautical mile, thus the scale can be used to measure distance. *Just be sure you never use the scales at top and bottom for this purpose.*

On the Mercator charts generally used for navigation, the scale of latitude or nautical miles will vary slightly the father north you go. If you want accuracy, therefore, always measure your distances on the scale as nearly parallel to your course as possible. On large-scale charts such as harbor charts and the like it is usually easier to use the scale of miles or yards found in the legend of the chart. Again, it is much more accurate to use a pair of dividers for measuring distance rather than other methods used by some skippers.

In measuring a course through a channel or other area where it is broken into a series of short legs, here is a method to make it easier: measure the first course line with the dividers. Then, using the end of that first course line as a pivot, carefully swing the arm of the dividers in the opposite direction of the second course line. Using the arm of the dividers away from the course line as a pivot, widen the dividers to the length of the second course line. Next, using the arm of the dividers at the end of the second course line as a pivot, swing the dividers in the opposite direction of the third course line. Using the arm of the dividers away from this course line as a pivot, widen the dividers to the length of third course line. By continuing this process to any desired point, you can then measure the entire distance on the latitude or mileage scale. You'll find this a much easier method than measuring and adding a series of short courses.

If this all sounds a bit confusing or difficult, stop right now, get out your divider and a chart and go through it step by step. You'll find how simple it really is and how much time it can save you.

On your chart the publishers have thoughtfully placed a number of large circles known as Compass Roses at convenient places. These are divided into 360° with North at 000 or 360°, East at 090°, South at 180° and West at 270°. The Compass Rose is used to determine the direction in degrees of whatever course line you may draw on the chart.

To chart a course, a straight line is drawn from one place to another, indicating where you wish to go. The direction of this line is then transposed by means of parallel rulers, a navigational protractor or any of the other devices now on the market, so that it crosses the exact center of a Compass Rose. Where this transposed line crosses the perimeter, you can read the True direction of the course line.

Remember, this is a "True" course. Since you are probably using a magnetic compass, we must now convert this to a "Magnetic" course. On all charts of Pacific Coast areas, Magnetic North is East of True North. This angular difference between the two poles is called "Variation" and you'll find it recorded in degrees in the center of the Compass Rose. Variation is different in different localities and even changes very slightly year by year.

This all means we must convert our True course to a Magnetic course to coincide with our magnetic compass. To do this we simply subtract the amount of the Easterly variation. Thus if our True course is 150° and the variation is 22° Easterly, the Magnetic course, which we would steer, is 128°. Or, if the True course were 007° or 367° (007 plus 360) and variation was 23° Easterly, the Magnetic course would be 344°. The Compass Rose also shows the Magnetic Variation, either in an inner circle or with the Magnetic degrees shown at the perimeter. This means you can determine a Magnetic course from the Rose without having to subtract the variation.

At this point the subject of "Deviation" also comes into the picture. This so-called compass error is caused by the magnet of the compass being subjected to attraction by metal parts of the boat such as engines, tanks, wiring, etc. If you've had your compass "swung" or adjusted, the amount of this influence will be found on the Deviation Card. This can vary according to the ship's heading and must be figured in a final course.

In steering a course, it must always be remembered that tools, light meters, kitchen utensils, even a can opener or beer can could throw your compass off, so keep anything of this nature well away from your compass.

Both the United States and Canadian governments have expended countless hours of work to give you accurate charts to aid you in your piloting. Avail yourself of the latest issues, study them carefully and use them. They were prepared especially for you, the skipper, and they will help to make your cruising safer and more pleasurable.

Note: We'd like to include a plug for the PACIFIC BOATING ALMANAC (Pacific Northwest edition) published annually with tide and current tables, U.S. Coast Pilot, and a detailed list of all marine facilities and the services offered. Available at book, marine and sport stores.

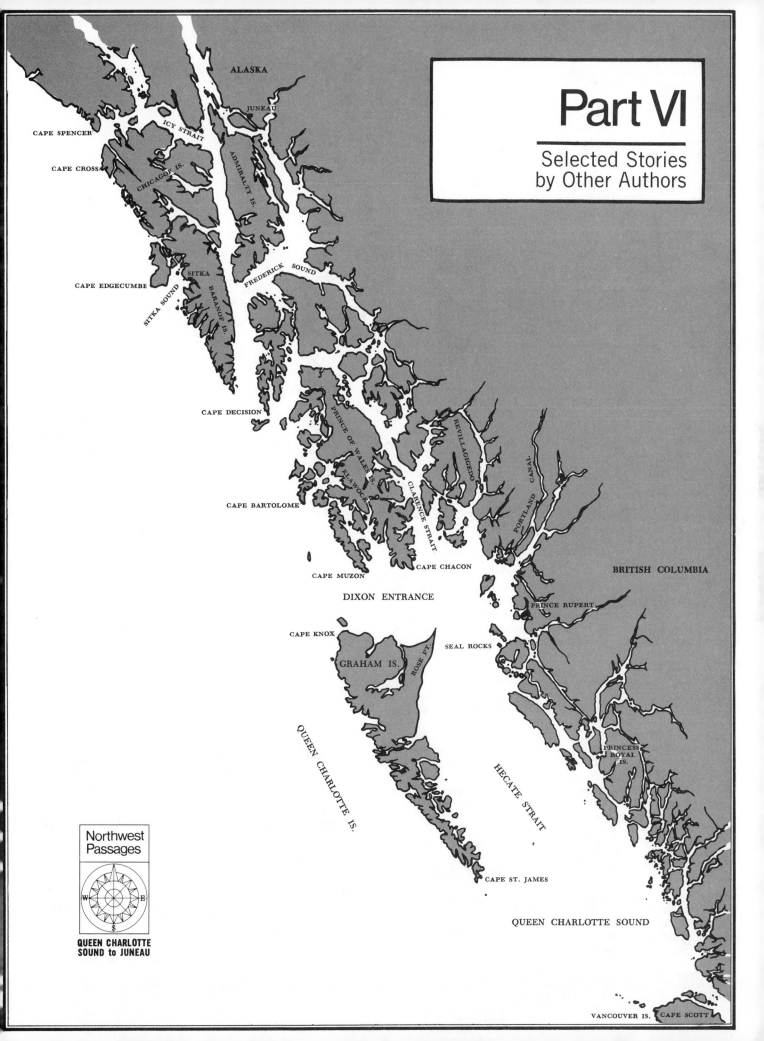

Part VI

Selected Stories
by Other Authors

ALASKA

JUNEAU

CAPE SPENCER

ICY STRAIT

CAPE CROSS

CHICAGOF IS.

ADMIRALTY IS.

SITKA

FREDERICK SOUND

CAPE EDGECUMBE

SITKA SOUND

BARANOF IS.

CAPE DECISION

PRINCE OF WALES IS.

REVILLAGIGEDO

PORTLAND CANAL

CAPE BARTOLOME

KLAWOCK

CLARENCE STRAIT

BRITISH COLUMBIA

CAPE MUZON

CAPE CHACON

PRINCE RUPERT

DIXON ENTRANCE

CAPE KNOX

SEAL ROCKS

GRAHAM IS.

ROSE PT.

QUEEN CHARLOTTE IS.

PRINCESS
ROYAL
IS.

HECATE STRAIT

CAPE ST. JAMES

QUEEN CHARLOTTE SOUND

Northwest
Passages

W   E

S

QUEEN CHARLOTTE
SOUND to JUNEAU

VANCOUVER IS.   CAPE SCOTT

45
A Happening at Port Townsend

A "Happening" in Port Townsend which is of interest to all Northwest yachtsmen was called to Sea*'s attention by James M. Bryce of Seattle.*

He writes, "All who know Port Townsend, the quaint old port of entry, know it is worth going ashore to visit. There are the beautiful old homes and buildings; even a real castle and now, a gourmet treat, John and Dorothy Conway's 'The Farm House.' It overlooks the Strait of Juan de Fuca from high up and is but a short taxi drive from downtown. Reservations are necessary but these can be made by ship-to-shore radio. Yachting attire is always welcome. My inability to write prompted me to ask Mr. Conway to set in words his idea of the 'happening' for Sea *readers. This is his answer."*

When we built our second home on the shore of the Strait of Juan de Fuca outside the main part of Port Townsend and remodeled a hundred-year-old farmhouse on the property, we said, "Now what shall we do with it?" An old friend, James Beard, a well-known gourmet, said, "Why don't you open a restaurant? You've always wanted one." As a University professor with an interest in food, I wasn't sure I was qualified, even though I'd been feeding varying numbers of people for years. So I compromised by offering to cook a series of dinners for the benefit of the local Summer School of the Arts.

I found I wasn't prepared for the wonderful bonus . . . the compliments, the thank-you notes, letters, presents and telephone calls from grateful guests. We consider them our personal guests, try to meet them at the door, either my wife, Dorothy, myself, or both of us, introduce ourselves if they do not know us, talk to them at dinner, sometimes join them for dessert or coffee if we have time, or take them next door for a look at the view from the deck of our own house. We generally feel we have made genuine friends of them.

People experienced in the restaurant business told me that if I served fish I must always have two entrees. I tried it with just the salmon and found that even people who do not like fish like our salmon. We set the grill up on the porch, cut the salmon into steaks or fillet it, marinate it and put it on the charcoal grill. It is fresh from our "front yard," the Strait.

I use my Japanese way of cooking it, called miso-yaki: first a marinade of wine, soy sauce, garlic, fresh ginger and miso, a fermented soy paste which resemble peanut butter. People tell me it is the best salmon they ever ate. Sometimes we bake the salmon whole, all 25 pounds of it in one piece, with bread and herb stuffing. Lately we have been serving it cold, in aspic. So this is always the Friday entree.

Sometimes in winter, we might serve other seafood: Dungeness crab (we can see the Dungeness spit from our window) or the wonderful local oysters from Mats Mats Bay. If there is any salmon left I serve it on Sunday to give those diners a chance to order it if they prefer it to the fowl on the menu. Sometimes it gets made into salad. When we serve it in aspic we serve it with a special garlic mayonnaise and garnish it with lemon and ripe olives.

Saturday night the entree is in the red-meat category: standing rib roast, boned leg of lamb either grilled in Greek style with green pepper and eggplant, or rolled and cooked in white wine and lots of garlic and ripe olives. Sometimes boeuf Bourguignon or Carbonnade Flammande, beef cooked in beer with lots of onions. The gravy is wonderful in that dish.

Sunday is usually Chicken Teriyaki day since our guests prefer it cooked that way. We serve a thigh and a half a breast to each diner. The chicken is marinated in wine, soy, garlic, sugar, fresh ginger and we cook it either on the grill or in the oven, basting it during its final stages with honey and soy under the broiler. During fall and winter months we sometimes serve turkey but always try to have fish for those who love it.

Vegetables seem to be a bug-a-boo of friends in the restaurant business. One young man said he never serves vegetables because they always "come back." They do need special treatment but when they are well-cooked, the carrots in bourbon, peas in the French style, Italian beans in sour cream, Blue Lake beans in a wonderful Japanese sauce based upon sesame seed wine and rice vinegar, they eat them, often asking for second portions. One lady said to me she hoped I'd omit the potatoes from her serving. When I said we seldom served potatoes she was delighted. Occasionally we do offer tiny potatoes dressed in finely chopped onions, butter and paprika and done under the broiler. They love them that way. Guests seem delighted not to be offered the standard so-called 'baked' potato which has been steamed in foil and dressed with sour cream, bacon and onion.

Serving only 70 people, I can treat food in special ways not possible with larger businesses. Often cooking larger quantities works in our favor such as with roasts. If you serve first-class meat cooked at low temperatures in large units such as a 20-lb. standing rib, it is much better than can be done at home in smaller cuts. Some foods are more difficult in larger quantities, and must be cooked in several small batches so they will not be over-cooked in holding. Food held on steam tables is bound to lose much of its flavor.

Perhaps our home-made soups served with toast-rounds done with Parmesan cheese make the greatest immediate impression. Soups are always slow-cooked on our wood range right out in plain sight. I learned from the Chinese to mix the meats in the soup base . . . lamb with beef, chicken with beef, veal with chicken, chicken with clams. One guest asked how I made the Scotch broth and when I told her I always used Scotch in it she wouldn't believe me, and still thinks I was kidding her. I always include some sort of liquor in the soup, either sauterne, brandy or Scotch. The alcohol cooks away but the flavor it imparts cannot be equalled. Sometimes I serve a delicious iced borsch with sour cream and in winter will serve a potage, either lentil with sour pickles and frankfurters, potato and leek, or bean.

The salad table, too, makes a lasting impression. Salads vary with the season and our patrons serve themselves. We usually feature about eight salads plus a few relishes such as olives, pickles, and sauerkraut. Our salads are made of many things: rice, lentils, cauliflower, cabbage, carrots, lettuce, raw mushrooms, zucchini, cucumber. The combinations of vegetables and fruit with various dressings intrigue the palate. For instance, cucumber with shrimp and a Japanese sauce of saki, rice vinegar and fresh ginger is very popular as is the rice salad in various combinations of vegetables and dressings, sometimes with shrimp, sometimes with salmon, often with curry. Our apple salad was invented for the Farmhouse and must be served each day because of the requests. It is a combination of apples, green peppers, pickles, peanuts, grapes, pineapple, raisins, preserved ginger and a special Farmhouse dressing containing tomato. We sometimes feature a special Chinese salad of stripped and shredded chicken with agar-agar. It has its own dressing and we get many calls for it. One special salad must not be forgotten: sliced beefsteak tomatoes dressed with Cognac.

Desserts are usually simple: champagne sherbet with pink champagne poured over it, French vanilla cream with a liqueur sauce, fruit and cheese, pumpkin chiffon pie with candied ginger and lately my wife has been making a delicious Armenian cake.

Patrons often know the kind of entree which will be served. The rest of the meal comes as a series of surprises. When veal is plentiful, we might do Vitella Tonnata, a combination of veal with tuna, an unlikely combination, but it's a classic dish and very delicious when served cold.

Eventually we hope to serve our own baked bread so that the house will be fragrant with the odor of bread baking in a wood range. I do not know of a more wonderful odor.

Winter sees us open only on Saturday for dinner, and an occasional Sunday brunch, the latter featuring a special version of Fritatta. Many casseroles are used during these months. We have large Italian ceramic casseroles and some Belgian enamelled iron ones. We prepare dishes from the Provincial French repertory with slow-cooked beef and chicken dishes with vegetables, to be eaten before the fireplace or stoves by candlelight.

The main part of the Farmhouse was built about 1865 and housed an English bride who came around the Horn bringing with her a small potted holly tree. The tree is now higher than the house and contains assorted quail, grouse, Chinese pheasants, salamanders, rabbits and other fauna. The house has had at least three additions, two of which we have made to accommodate our guests. There will be one further addition when we remodel the main room of the old house into a 'winter' room with a very large Tudor-style fireplace. Across one end it will have its own spit for the roasts and there will be two tables inside the fireplace.

The furnishings for the Farmhouse were bought mostly in Seattle when we learned that a famous old house was

Conway's Farmhouse at Port Townsend

to be razed. We bought the furnishings and refinished them. It is the very best oak furniutre that Grand Rapids could turn out in 1905. Some of the pieces look hardly used, others show their age. The wood range and wood heating stove with their nickel trim are much admired. The Tiffany dome hanging over the main dining table seems very right for the house.

One of our additions is a garden room whose tables are covered with black leather, and there are white bentwood chairs and a fairly bright green carpet. It reminds me of an English morning room when the sun streams in and the Scotch broom is solid gold at the window or the enormous wild currant is a riot of pink blossoms. The grounds have old fruit trees and we have added others along with many fig trees. We will eventually serve our own figs. Last year I planted sun flowers because I think farmhouses need them. We grow our own garlic. We have our own cherries and the most wonderful strawberries I have ever seen come from nearby Sequim.

I had a feeling we should do something about holidays for those people whose families are gone. It's difficult to have a proper Christmas dinner on the leg of a turkey. So we decided to open for Christmas, Thanksgiving and New Year's Day. Then we added Chinese New Year at which we serve northern Chinese food, not the Cantonese food of the Chinese restaurants. This day was so popular last year we had to double our celebration and hold it over the second week. Now we are adding Buddha's Birthday and Indian Independence Day, both days featuring curries and sambals.

We intend to add others appropriate to seasonal dining. We have had one request for Russian food, so I suggested celebrating the return of Peter the Great after his sojourn as a carpenter, the death of Rasputin or the Storming of the Winter Palace. A Russian friend is doing appropriate research now on the subject. I would also like to celebrate St. Swithin's day, because I like the name and because I like any excuse for roast beef and Yorkshire pudding. My family is from Yorkshire and I was raised on beef and Yorkshire 'pud.' Everywhere we go we bring back something in experience. I learned about the finest Japanese cooking for instance, in the kitchens of an exclusive Geisha house in Tokyo.

Looking over our guest book we find signatures from most of the countries of the world from Greece and Turkey to the Malay Straits and India. How they find us, we don't know, although I've always said people will go anywhere for good food.

I don't want to expand beyond the capacity for which I can cook myself. With a little help I can do for 70 now, and I will be able to take care of the additional places in a new room. But that is positively the last addition!

We plan to have our own sauerkraut, pickles, jams and jellies and eventually our own bread. I will not have a deep fat fryer on the premises so no one ever gets stuck with 'French' fried potatoes. If I ever offer anything fried it will be delicate Japanese tempura.

And so we go on from season to season, varying food with the weather. We are rather off the beaten track but we continue supplying the best food in the best way possible. Long ago I hoped to learn the very finest way to prepare each item, and then I learned there are several 'best' ways for each, so we vary the method as well as the item. As we try new things we either keep them in our repertory or discard them when we learn better ways.

The Farmhouse itself has a special happy quality about it and it makes everyone feel perfectly at home. We will continue to foster this feeling because these people are truly our guests and they usually end as our friends.

Note: Dorothy and John Ashby Conway have been operating the Farmhouse for over 15 years. John Conway retired from the University and devotes all of his efforts to quality dining with unique ever-changing menus. "We have proved that our original idea was sound, our patrons appreciate one menu at a time, freshly prepared from scratch," he said recently after reviewing this article he wrote some 10 years ago. "We appreciate the opportunity of changing menus monthly before anyone gets bored preparing them." The Farmhouse is open only weekends, Friday, Saturday, and Sunday and in summer on Thursday. It is closed in December and January. Reservations are necessary. Two guest moorings in Port Townsend are available to visiting yachtsmen. Their phone number: (206) 385-1411.

46
Cartography
by R.E. McKechnie M.D.

When was the first chart made of the Pacific North-west and who made it? This is a good question and hard to answer. Our coastal area was undoubtedly a busy one long before Captain Cook landed in 1778. There is evidence of a race which peopled the Pacific Coast 15,000 to 25,000 years ago, possibly the oldest inhabitants of our continent. And they undoubtedly used our waterways. Our present-day coast Indians began the first of their three great migrations from Asia about 6000 years ago and they, too, used our waterways. About the time the Romans were leaving England (407 A.D.), the Chinese were traveling by boat to our Pacific shores and had established the King-dom of Fusang (see Chart No. 4); the Land of Wan Shan (the Land of the Masked Bodies) and Land of Ta Han (Great China). These various kingdoms are described in the written records of Old China and apparently the trade routes and settlements were well developed.

More recently Thor Heyerdahl of *Kon Tiki* fame has suggested that the Polynesians traveled past our coast on their long intercontinental journeys. We know that the Haida Indians from the Queen Charlotte Islands paddled great distances in their slim canoes to trade off the mouth of the Columbia River with the Hawaiians, who were there to catch salmon.

These people left no charts. Thus, the charts we have today are of relatively recent origin. The earliest charts were commonly engraved by hand and printed laboriously sub-sequent to the return of a voyager from distant lands with his homemade charts complete with detailed observations about the places he had visited. Because navigation aids were crude, the exact location of a vessel charting an area was not always certain and this resulted in many in-accuracies. Superstitions of the time, blood-thirsty natives, fear of the unknown, famine and disease undoubtedly colored the imaginations and thus the reporting of those early explorers.

In addition to these factors there was the well-known human tendency to prevaricate and some of the reports and charts were downright bar-room tales. To complicate the issue still further, there was also the cynic and the practical joker who added his bit of untruth. Inevitably, in those days of poor communications, some of these false legends became accepted as genuine.

The chart of Admiral de Fonte (No. 2), showing the mythical Northwest Passage as a fact, is an example of a prank that became a legend. Many expeditions attempted to follow this chart, both in the Atlantic and the Pacific. Great sums of money and many lives were lost before the chart was proved false by Captain Vancouver and some of his contemporaries.

We have selected several charts as classic examples of the early charts of our coastal area. They illustrate the conflict of fact and fiction with the gradual emergence of truth as the area became better known.

Chart No. 1. This chart was drawn and printed about 1665 by an English cartographer by the name of Dudley, who lived in Venice. Most of the previous charts of the Pa-cific Northwest showed California as an island and land in the region of our coast as *terra incognita*. One or two Venetian cartographers obtained information about the Spanish explorations of the Mexican Pacific coastal area and compiled a land chart that was pretty good for the time.

Dudley decided that he would publish charts of this area also, one of the final ones being the one which is shown here. It was said by some of his critics that he dis-played one of the most remarkable geniuses for invention ever displayed by a cartographer. Perhaps half of the names on the map were given by him. Others were stolen from earlier, but not necessarily authentic, charts. Dudley in-vented the *Bay Porto de Nova Albion* and stated that the English explorer, Sir Francis Drake, had found horses there — an important observation if true. The anchors shown in some of the bays purport to show the anchorages of Drake and some of the Spanish explorers.

Chart No. 2. This chart is an example of the fallibility and gullibility of the human race. The story behind this and several other similar charts *(Chart No. 3)*, each pur-porting to show in its own way a passage from the Atlantic to the Pacific Oceans, stems from the stories told by Admiral Bartholomew de Fonte, who vividly described his passage between the two oceans in a magazine called *Monthly Mis-cellany or Memoirs for the Curious*. His curious tale ap-peared in the April and June issues of 1708 and were generally attributed to the imagination of the author of the magazine, one James Petiver. Because of the fanciful-

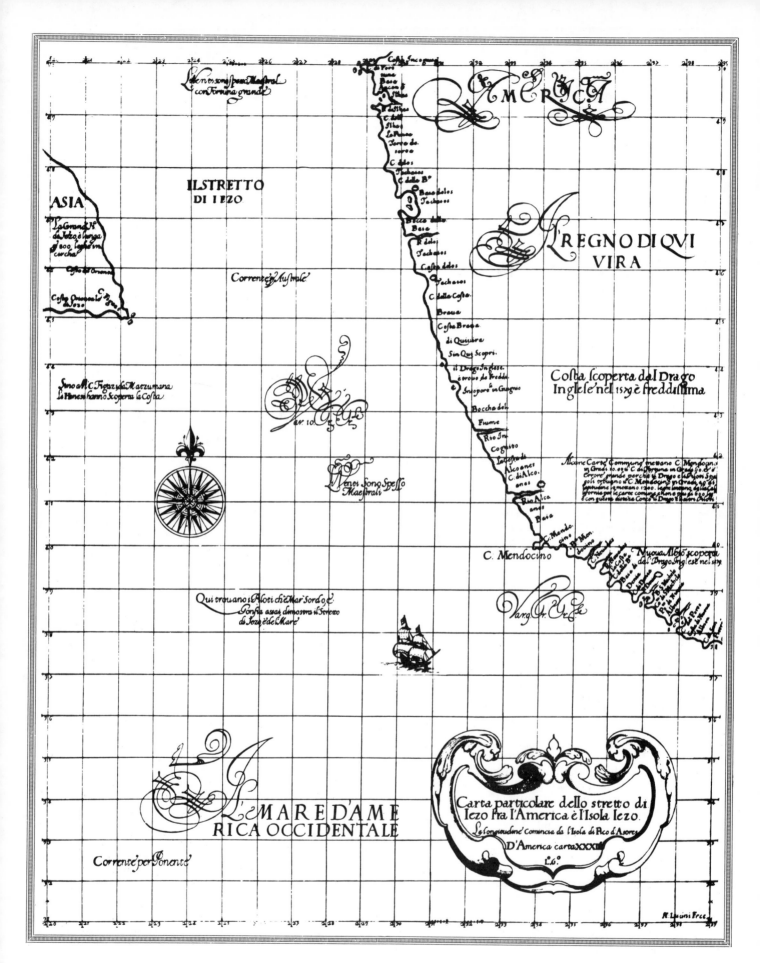

CHART NO. 1 — Straits of Iezo. Printed by Dudley in Florence, 1660

172

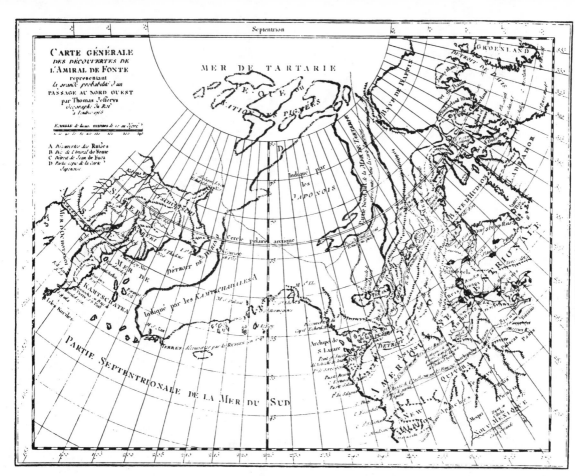

CHART NO. 2 — The Discoveries of Admiral de Fonte, indicating the great possibility of a Northwest Passage. Printed by Thomas Jefferys, Geographer of the King, London 1768; translated into French by M. de Vangrondez and engraved in Paris, 1772.

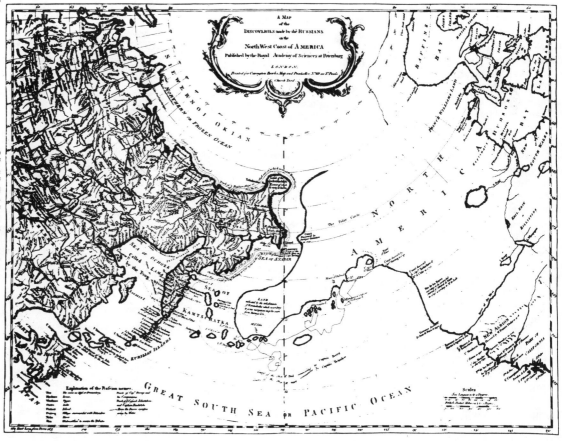

CHART NO. 3—A Map of the Discoveries of the Russians on the Northwest Coast of America. Published by the Royal Academy of Sciences of Petersburg. Printed for Carrington Bowles Map and Printseller, No. 69 in St. Paul's Churchyard, London, 1780.

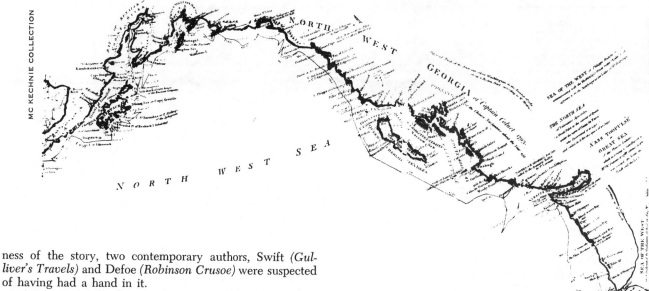

CHART NO. 4 — Chart of the Northwest Coast of America and North-east Coast of Asia explored in the years 1778-1779. Prepared by Lt. Roberts under the direction of Captain Cook. Published by Wm. Feden, Geographer to the King, Charing Cross, London, July 24, 1784. Second edition published January 1, 1794.

ness of the story, two contemporary authors, Swift *(Gulliver's Travels)* and Defoe *(Robinson Crusoe)* were suspected of having had a hand in it.

As time went on the yarn became a story and the story became a believed legend and certain navigators claimed to have sailed through what was now generally known as the Straits of Anian. The name Anian was given under rather unusual circumstances. It all started with a report by Marco Polo (1295 A.D.), who, on his return from Cathay, described a long salt-water passage with the Chinese province of Anian at the southeast end.

Later, Gastaldi (1562) a noted Italian cartographer, decided from his comfortable chair at home that the straits in reality separated Asia and North America, and because the land to the southeast was called Ania by Marco Polo, the name Straits of Anian was given to this body of water. This was all right with the mythical Admiral de Fonte, who picked up the name and used it in his tongue-in-cheek tale of the Northwest Passage. A little later the fanciful tale of Juan de Fuca was added to the overall picture, and in *Chart 2*, it will be noted that the beginning of the passage was called the Straits of Juan de Fuca.

The myth of the Northwest Passage was so generally accepted that the Hudson's Bay Company sent explorers to find the Atlantic opening. When they failed to find the entrance to the passage, the company was accused of withholding information on the strait for the monetary benefits of the Great Company of Gentlemen Adventurers of the Hudson's Bay. In the Pacific, the English sent the experienced Cook and Vancouver to search for the strait. The French sent La Perouse. The Spanish had Perez and others in the field and the Russians were there also, although it is not known whether the Northwest passage was their primary goal.

Chart No. 3. This chart was originally printed in St. Petersburg, Russia and this is an official copy made by the British in 1780 in London, giving full credit to the original explorers and cartographers. It is one of the first reasonably accurate charts of the Pacific Northwest and was made following the voyage in 1771 of those tough navigators, Vitus Bering (a Dane) and Alexei Tschirikov (Russian) on what is generally believed to be the first authentic voyage by Europeans to the northwest coast of America. They discovered Alaska for the Russians at Mount St. Elias, and the furs that they found when they landed instigated the Russian fur-trade and led to the establishment of Russian trading posts along the coast as far south as Fort Ross, in what is now California — just north of Bodega Bay.

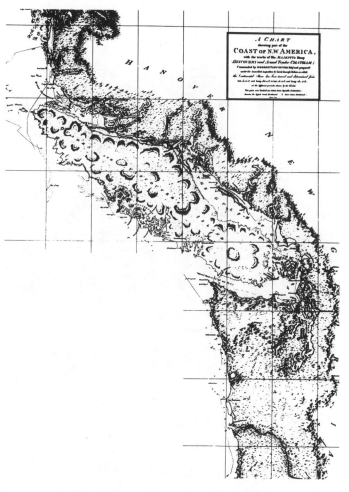

CHART NO. 5 — Vancouver's chart of Vancouver Island area. Reproduced from the original atlas printed in 1798.

174

This chart is also of interest as it shows another version of the Northwest Passage — that of the River of the West (said to have been discovered by Martin d'Aguilor in 1603) leading from the Pacific through Lake Winnipegon and connecting with Kris Krik flowing into the Hudson Bay. It was reported by one navigator of this passage, that his ship could not pass the shallows between the two systems but that he visited aboard an American trader which had come in from the Atlantic and was lying at anchor in the River.

The tracks of the two ships, *St. Peter,* under Bering and *St. Paul,* under Tschirikov, are marked by dotted lines on the chart. Of all the individual voyages of exploration to our country, this one ranks as the most difficult and exhausting by far. Few members of the expedition survived the years of hard labor, privation, cold and suffering. Bering, himself, died on the expedition after losing the *St. Peter.* The history of this rugged journey would make a story in itself.

Chart No. 4. This is a section of a larger chart that included the whole of the Pacific Northwest area and also the Asiatic coastline. It is a result of Captain Cook's voyages, and the outline of his tracks can be seen on the chart. Lieutenant Roberts was his cartographer; the original chart was printed in 1786 and this revised copy in 1794. It was the first authentic chart of this general area and the chart I have has been used for navigational purposes.

However, there are some major errors. The first is that Vancouver Island is not defined. The Straits of Juan de Fuca are mentioned; but Captain Cook did not know that Nootka was on a large island. The Queen Charlotte Islands had been discovered, charted and named by Captain Dixon, who named the islands after his ship the *Queen Charlotte.*

His ship in turn, was named in honor of Queen Charlotte, George III's pretty wife.

Some of the notations printed there are of interest, particularly the areas called *Northwest Georgia of Captain Colnet of 1793.* I cannot understand this reference, because as far as I can find out Captain Colnet was whaling in the southern hemisphere about that time. He is of historical interest as the British captain who was arrested and his ship seized by the Spanish at Nootka in 1789, thus becoming the *cause celebre* that triggered the Nootka controversy. That controversy over who had jurisdiction over Nootka almost precipitated war between England and Spain. It eventually ended peacefully with Captain Vancouver coming out to meet Captain Bodega y Quadra at Nootka to settle the matter and at the same time explore the Pacific Northwest for any remote possibility of a northwest passage.

Underneath the name of Captain Colnet, one can make out *The land of Foo Sang, the Chinese navigator about the year of 458 A.D.* The Sea of the West, the North Sea and the Great Sea are all indicated in general areas and these were part of the legends of the Northwest Passage.

Chart No. 5. This again is an excerpt from a larger chart which is primarily directed at the Vancouver Island area. It is the chart which resulted from Captain Vancouver's explorations and indicates the tracks of his Majesty's sloop *Discovery* and armed tender *Chatham.* The ships were commanded by George Vancouver, Esquire.

It will be noted that new names have been added to the mainland, namely, Hanover and also New Georgia. Vancouver Island is known as Quadra's and Vancouver's Island. The Gulf of Georgia is labeled here for all to see, particularly those new sailors who insist on calling it the "Straits."

47

The Northwest Explorations of Captains Cook and Vancouver

by R.E. McKechnie M.D.

From time to time in the history of the world there are great men who would have been great in any century. Captain James Cook was such a man. His influence on the Pacific Northwest was great, not only because of his ability to conduct important voyages of exploration, but also because he was able to inspire his junior officers to such an extent that they later returned to our coast as captains and conducted exploratory voyages of their own. Vancouver was a midshipman on the *Resolution*. Portlock (Portlock Canal) was master's mate and Dixon (Dixon's Entrance), the armourer for Cook. Colnet was another midshipman who came back as captain. His ship was the *Argonaut*, the cause of the Nootka controversy when it was seized by the Spanish in Nootka Sound.

Cook was born in October, 1728, the son of a poor farm laborer in England. He received a very minor degree of education and then started to learn his father's trade. At the age of 18 he joined the Merchant Marine and eventually moved into the Royal Navy. Once in the navy, his ability to get things done was recognized and his promotions were inevitable.

When it was decided to send a scientific expedition to the South Seas to observe the transit of the planet Venus, Cook was selected to take charge of the expedition and promoted to lieutenant. On this expedition, 1768 to 1771, he charted the whole of the east coast of New Zealand and the eastern coast of Australia.

The second exploratory expedition to the South Seas was 1772 to 1775. The third expedition was the one which eventually came to the Pacific Northwest. Cook left England in July, 1776, sailing on his ship *Resolution* with the *Discovery* as his consort. During this voyage he discovered the Sandwich Islands (Hawaiian Islands) and made a general survey of the western coast of North America from 44 degrees north latitude to the Arctic regions, including a plan of Nootka Sound. Cook was killed in the winter of 1778 in a savage encounter with natives in Hawaii. The

CAPTAIN COOK

London, Published as the Act directs Sep 1 1784 by No...

expedition was carried on by Captain Clerke, and the two vessels arrived in England in 1789.

In these days of exploration of the moon, it is easy to forget that past generations were also scientifically minded. It is interesting to note that in spite of hostilities between France, Spain, England and other countries, these countries recognized the worth of Captain Cook's scientific explorations and gave him letters of safe conduct in case he was stopped by any of the warring factions. In fact, France was so intrigued by the value of these explorations that a French expedition under Compte de la Perouse was sent to explore the Pacific northwest.

Captain Cook was not only regarded as a great geographer of the globe, but was also noted for his ability to preserve the health of his crew at sea. This was a most important consideration, inasmuch as scurvy usually took its toll on these long sea voyages. However, Cook developed a regime and diet of his own, strictly enforced by the cat-o'-nine-tails when necessary, which cut the scurvy to a minimum.

Cook was a strong man and a clear and logical thinker. It was my privilege to examine the original manuscripts of his third voyage to the Northwest in the British Museum. I was most impressed by his clear and distinct handwriting done in black India ink with excellent narration of the events of the voyage and few errors in his writing. This is in contra-distinction to some of the logs of the more junior officers, whose writing was at times almost illegible and whose narration of inconsequential events often took precedence over more important happenings.

Captain Cook had an artist aboard, by the name of Webber, whose task it was to sketch and record the various interesting scenes that he saw along the way. Again I was very fortunate to have the opportunity to examine in the British Museum the original drawings made by Webber on this third voyage with Captain Cook. They

Captain Vancouver's ship Discovery on the rocks in Queen Charlotte Sound with the Chatham standing by to give aid.

were magnificent drawings, some beautifully colored, and all tremendously detailed. They gave excellent impressions of the things the explorers saw on the way. These pictures were much copied when they were engraved and printed on the return to England.

One of Webber's drawings shows the *Resolution* and the *Discovery* lying at anchor in Friendly Cove in Nootka Sound. This is a beautiful picture and if one examines it closely, one can note the detail. Another picture is that of a sea hunt for the walrus which they called sea horses and used for fresh meat. Note the exaggerated size of these animals, in keeping with the tendency of explorers to exaggerate.

Captain Vancouver also had an artist aboard, Zachary

Mudge, after whom Cape Mudge is named. He has left us a number of excellent sketches of Captain Vancouver's explorations. An outstanding one is that showing Captain Vancouver's new ship *Discovery* hard and fast aground in the group of small islands and rocks, now known as the Walker Group and in the southeast portion of Queen Charlotte Sound. It had been raining that day and a fog was present. A light wind came up and the *Discovery* and *Chatham* began to move, but unfortunately the *Discovery* went aground on a rocky ledge with a falling tide. The forefoot was fixed and the stern began to drop. Captain Vancouver, like all good sailors, started to lighten the ship. Note that the top masts are down and that the long-boats are loaded with equipment. All the water, ballast and fire-

Captain Cook's Resolution and Discovery lying at anchor in Friendly Cove, Nootka Sound, on Vancouver Island.

Captain Vancouver's ship Discovery ending her days as a convict ship on the beach at Deptford, England.

wood were thrown overboard and shores or braces were used to prevent her from capsizing altogether. The stern was in deep water, floating relatively free, and sank downwards as the tide lowered. This meant, of course, that at any given moment the ship could slip off into deep water and might either capsize or sink.

About an hour before low water, the crew was suddenly terrified by a lurch of the ship as the water receded but the shores held. At low tide, the main deck was within two inches of the water, but fortunately there were no waves or turbulence and when the tide turned, the ship floated free without any apparent damage. This is the first recorded grounding of a ship in Queen Charlotte Sound.

The *Chatham* shortly afterwards touched bottom for a brief period and then was taken off.

It is said that old ships never die and this would seem to be true as far as Captain Vancouver's ship is concerned. A picture of Captain Vancouver's *Discovery*, done in 1828 by A. W. Cook and published in 1829, mistakenly describes the ship as Captain Cook's *Discovery*. But George Godwin in *Vancouver: A Life* states unequivocally that this is Captain Vancouver's ship. The super-structure shown in the picture was added when she was beached at Deptford and was used as a convict ship. A sad and ignominious ending for such a great ship.

Captain Cook's crew members hunting "Sea Horses" (walrus) for fresh meat.

48
In Honor of Kings and Commodores
by R.E. McKechnie M.D.

King George III — Georgia Straits

In 1792 Captain Vancouver gave the name *Gulf of Georgia* to this inland sea in honor of His Majesty, King George III of England. The previous year Lieutenant Eliza, A Spanish explorer, had named it *Gran Canal de Nuestral Senora del Rosario la Marinera*. The use of the name "Gulf" was changed to the more correct "Strait" by Captain Richards in 1865, after he had been appointed Canadian Government hydrographer.

Not withstanding this official alteration, old-timers and wet-backs in conversation today nostalgically refer to their old adversary as an entity, almost a personality, *The Gulf*, knowing it was the same "Gulf" that had challenged Captain Vancouver and practically every local sailor since then.

A picture of George III, drawn by Edridge in January 1803, shows Windsor Castle in the background. King George (whose wife Queen Charlotte loaned her name to Queen Charlotte Sound) became a most important man among the Indians of our coast in the days of the fur-traders. During his long reign he was so frequently mentioned by British subjects and others, that in the native mind, his name became synonymous with power and authority. Such so that all Britishers were called *King George men* and their ships, *King George ships* in contradistinction to those of other nationalities with whom the natives came in contact. Other traders were styled *Boston men* because they nearly all belonged to American vessels which were fitted out and hailed from Boston, New England. In the Chinook jargon, which is generally understood by the Indians on this coast, these meanings are still preserved.

Admiral Rainier — Mount Rainier

Captain Vancouver named the snow-capped mountain after his friend, Rear-Admiral Rainier, shortly after Captain Vancouver's return to England. This picture, drawn at a later date, shows Rainier as Admiral of the Blue and wearing some unusual, broad-rimmed spectacles which give him a most extraordinary appearance.

England's King George III

In spite of this appearance he was a very popular and efficient man. He was sent to the East Indies in 1794 as commander of the British naval forces protecting the great English trading group known as the Honorable East India Company. He remained there for eleven and a half years, during which time he saw considerable action and founded his personal fortune, as was the custom of the time, with his share of the booty that was captured. When he returned to England he was in command of a convoy of thirty merchantmen that were estimated to have an overall value of £15,000,000 sterling ($75,000,000). Needless to say, the privateers and warships of every country attempted to capture this convoy, but Rainier brought it home to England untouched.

As evidence of his popularity in India he was given a farewell party by the civil servants of the Honorable East India Company in Madras. The party was so successful that it was fully written up in the Madras Gazette on the second of March, 1805. Apparently the toasts were frequent and, reading between the lines, copious. Many tunes were played, but the tune reported as being considered most suitable to the all powerful Honorable East India Company was *Money in Both Pockets* and the tune most suitable to Admiral Rainier was *Hearts of Oak*.

At his death he left one-tenth of his fortune of £250,000 to be applied to the British National Debt. This action was criticized severely as perhaps it would be even today by those who said that the amount he gave was more or less a drop in the bucket, whereas widows and orphans of brother naval officers and sailors needed this more than the government.

Admiral Rainier

"Lord Thurlow — Thurlow Islands"

On the 16th of July, 1792, Vancouver noted in his journal (as his ship *Discovery* was working up Johnstone Strait), "after we had proceeded about ten miles from Point Chatham, the tide made so powerful against us as obliged us about breakfast time to become again stationary in a bay (Knox Bay) on the northern shore in 32 fathoms water. The land under which we anchored was a narrow island which I distinguished by the name of Thurlow Island."

Lord Thurlow

The island has since been discovered to be divided into two islands and is now known as Thurlow Islands. Edward, Lord Thurlow, the son of a clergyman, started life in a solicitor's office and was eventually appointed Lord Chancellor and raised to the peerage on the 3rd of June, 1778. Shortly after this, he was publicly reproached in the House of Lords by a reference to his plebeian origin and his recent admission to the peerage. Lord Thurlow's reply is a gem of English oratory: "My Lords, I am amazed, yes, my Lords, I am amazed at His Grace's speech. The noble duke cannot look before him, behind him, or on either side of him without seeing some noble peer who owes his seat in this House to his successful exertions in the profession to which I belong. Does he not feel it as honorable to owe it to these, as being the accident of an accident? To all those noble lords, the language of the noble duke is as applicable and insulting as to myself. But I do not fear to meet it single and alone. No one venerates the peerage more than I do. But my Lords, I must say that the Peerage solicited me, not I the Peerage........!"

Lord Thurlow was tall, well built and singularly majestic in appearance. It was said, "No man ever was so wise as Thurlow looks."

"A Man of Nootka — Nootka Sound"

On Cook's arrival in the Pacific Northwest in 1778, he first named the inlet on the west coast of Vancouver Island, now known as Nootka Sound, *King George's Sound*. Later he changed the name to *Nootka*, under the impression it was the Indians' name for the area. There has been considerable controversy as to how the name was mistakenly applied, but the general opinion is that Cook, having made a tour around the sound in his boats starting from the small bay now known as Friendly Cove, may have asked the Indians, with a comprehensive sweep of his arm and other motions, what was the name of the place. The Indians, misunderstanding him, but knowing that he had been around in his boat, had replied with the word *Nootka*, that in their language meant to go around or make a circuit. Cook, believing this was the natives' name for the sound, labeled it as such on his charts.

The Nootka Indians were not only an intelligent group led by a very outstanding chief by the name of Maquinna,

Man of Nootka Sound

but they were also very fierce and ruthless. They behaved well most of the time but the story of the massacre of the crew of the American ship *Boston* in 1803 is blood-thirsty enough for any modern TV show. Chief Maquinna, angered by a fancied insult by Captain Salter of the *Boston*, craftily attacked the ship when most of the crew were out fishing for salmon. The armourer, by the name of Jewett, was working below decks and when the attack took place he ran up the ladder, but a savage clutched him by the hair from above and he received a deep gash in his forehead from an axe, the wound penetrating to the skull. He fell into the steerage stunned and bleeding and was discovered later on by Maquinna, who, after Jewett had recovered, ordered the savages to spare his life because of his usefulness in making weapons. The severed heads of the captain and crew, arranged in a row on deck, were shown to him and he was told to name them. That of Thompson, the sailmaker, however, was not among them. Thompson was afterwards captured in the hold and his life was spared through Jewett's pleading with Maquinna for Thompson (an elderly man) as his father, saying that if they killed the father the useful son would die. After two years of captivity, a rescue was effected by Captain Samuel Hill of the brig *Lydia* out of Boston. Their experiences as captives and their method of escape is another tale that would bear telling.

Sir Harry Burrard Neale – Burrard Inlet

Burrard Inlet, the lovely waterway leading to and forming the harbor of the city of Vancouver, was examined by Captain Vancouver in June, 1792, and named by him after his friend, Captain Harry Burrard, Bart. R.N., who was an acting lieutenant with Vancouver in the ship *Europa* in the West Indies in 1785. Sir Harry married Grace Elizabeth in 1795, the heiress of the House of Neale, and assumed — for reasons that no one ever suggested to be other than monetary, but blessed by a Royal License — the additional surname and arms of Neale. He became groom of the bedchamber of both George III and William IV and one of

the Lords of the Admiralty. From then on, he played a great part in the navy and was a member of Parliament for forty years.

The Spanish officers Galiano and Valdez examined Burrard Inlet about the same time as Vancouver and named it *Canal de Sasamat*, which was understood to be the Indian name and it is thus given on their charts of 1792. Eliza, another Spanish officer, on his exploring voyage in 1791 had named the inlet *Boca de Florida Blanco* after a Spanish notable, and this name Galiano adopted on the large copy of his chart dated 1795.

Vancouver explored and charted Burrard Inlet himself, leaving his ship *Discovery* and the armed tender *Chatham* at Birch Bay near what is now the town of Bellingham. His boats were propelled by oars or sail and they traveled great distances. Part of his task was to set aside naval reserves for defense purposes and as a potential source of masts and spars for His Majesty's ships of war. One of these areas he allocated is still a naval reserve and is known as Stanley Park in Vancouver. It still has many fine straight trees, although the need for spars is gone.

On the 13th of June, 1792, Captain Vancouver wrote in his log about his tired crew, "the shores of this situation were formed by steep, rocky cliffs that afforded no convenient space for pitching our tent, which compelled us to sleep in the boats. Some of the young gentlemen, however, preferring the stony beach for their couch, without duly considering the time of highwater mark, found themselves incommoded by the flood-tide of which they were not

Sir Harry Burrard Neale

appraised until nearly afloat; and one of them slept so sound that I believe he might have been conveyed to some distance had he not been awakened by his companions." What a breed of men!

181

49

Vancouver:
The West Side Story

by Edwin Monk

Here are some observations of our cruise along the West Coast of the gigantic, "Unspoiled Island to our East." We refer to rugged, harbor-slotted Vancouver Island, this continent's greatest and most varied island cruising-coastline, one of the most distinctive in the world.

But most yachtsmen think of Vancouver Island and its gorgeous, unequalled passages that create a great inland sea off the main coast of British Columbia. It is vastly less-attainable for many boaters out there on the western side. When we say "Island to the East" we are also saying, "and a tremendous, exposed Pacific Ocean to our west."

There is certainly nothing wrong with the inner side of Vancouver Island and the intrigue of its many satellite islands and passages. We have cruised there for years and enjoyed every minute of it. But, the spirit of adventure does still survive in most of us. While it is fun to touch at familiar spots and rewarding to develop friendships that are renewed on our summer cruises, eventually an urge to see new places, touch into strange harbors and anchor in new coves prompts us to look around to see where we might turn, where there are no "Private Property" signs and where anchorages are not filled with boats and water skiers.

Such a cruising ground can be found on the west coast of Vancouver Island provided we are willing to pay the price in perhaps some uncomfortable hours spent in getting there and in the several ocean hops between inlets and a real gamble weather-wise. The lower part is fast becoming a cruising ground for the Portland yachtsman and this year a sailboat race and cruise was made to Barkley Sound by a large number of Puget Sound boats.

The writer in 1950 made it up as far as Refuge Cove, now Hot Springs Cove, and hoped to some day circumnavigate the Island, a rewarding cruise recently completed.

To one contemplating such a venture many questions come to mind. The foremost might be the adequacy of his cruiser. Bill Thompson made it in an outboard, Bill Garden and John Adams in their 24-foot sailboats, Bert Cruise in a fast 34-foot twin-screw V-bottom cruiser and Rex Bartlett no less than three times in a 36-foot double-ender. No doubt if one had the time it could be done in almost any seaworthy boat. The catch, however, is that after several days waiting out the weather in some snug harbor boredom overcomes prudence and we venture forth rather than wait it out a little longer. There are two fairly long jumps, one from Bull Harbour to Quatsino Inlet, the other around Cape Cook. The first hop, however, can be broken at Sea Otter Cove now easily entered thanks to several beacons erected by the Canadian government. It is listed in most publications as "Not recommended" but this would no longer seem applicable.

Weather-wise the west coast has a reputation for fog and rain. Last year it was rain with a vengeance and fog on the last lap. The former was general throughout the Pacific Northwest though worse on the west side of Vancouver Island's mountain ranges. There seems slightly better weather near the ocean with the rain increasing as one ventures farther into the inlets. In spite of the weather, however, it can be a very enjoyable cruise.

Will Dawson, in his book, *Coastal Cruising*, tells us that fresh NW and W winds for fair weather rise about mid-morning and reach full strength about mid-afternoon and calm by evening. Experiences of others verify this though 1964 was an exception with almost constant southeasters. The Canadian weather reports are excellent and are broadcast for the fisherman and seafarer over their weather station at 1630 kc.

This is one cruise where the company of another boat or boats is both prudent and most welcome. There are outside stretches where prompt help is not available. We were three, Bob Taylor with his 83-foot *Elfin*, Bill Paine and his 58-foot *Una Mae* and our 44-foot *Tatoosh*. One could not but observe the easier motion of the larger boats and following in the wake of one of them was often a decided advantage.

What of the navigational hazards and what equipment should one have? There are a great plenty of the former, a multitude of surf-pounded reefs and rocks. The Canadians have turned out some splendid large scale charts, most apparently quite new, and to make the cruise no less than 20 fine charts are available to the navigator; the B.C. Coast Pilot is a great help although one should keep in mind that it is written for deep-draft ships and not for pleasure cruisers. And, of course, a Canadian current table is a necessity.

A radar would be wonderful but most of us have to be satisfied with more modest equipment. A good depth-sounder is a real help and a 100-fathom instrument is ideal, although a good look at the general chart of the entire

Island (No. 3593) will show that one can get along very well with a shallower instrument. Needless to say a good compass (adjusted) is a necessity and we would certainly have a direction finder on another trip. It is difficult to hold an exact course in a small boat in high steep seas in the fog with only a compass for directional guidance. The tidal currents in Juan de Fuca Strait run up to three knots and further complicate dead reckoning on that stretch.

It is a rewarding experience with every day an adventure. Alert Bay with its totem poles and local color is very interesting. Bull Harbour on Hope Island is the first ocean stop and one can walk across the end of the island, only about 100 yards, where there is a wonderful ocean beach with all its driftwood and interesting flotsam.

We barely saw Cape Scott through the rain and murk and could not see the Scott Islands at all. Cape Scott is the Cape Horn of Vancouver Island and the books mention heavy rips and overfalls dangerous to small vessels so we reached there shortly after slack water, the reference point being Prince Rupert. The wind velocity was 25-30 miles which can whip up a nasty sea.

We were very glad to follow the *Elfin* into Sea Otter Cove where four trollers were waiting out the weather, one with a deer hanging in the rigging. The Canadians have placed two rows of mooring buoys here as they say the holding ground is not good and several trollers have come to grief. The weather held us there the next day but it was interesting exploring the beach between rain squalls.

Quatsino Inlet comes close to cutting the Island in two.

The next jump was to Quatsino Inlet with the weather somewhat moderated. The fishing village of Winter Harbour with its boat shop, hotel, store and fish camp provides an opportunity to stock up. From here on fish-ice only is available; placed in a canvas bag it is quite satisfactory. The stores in these out-of-the-way places are always interesting and turn the clock back to our frontier days.

Quatsino Inlet comes close to cutting the Island in two and Coal Harbour is only 14 miles from the east coast. Here is located a whaling station and when we were there they had, during the season, brought in 418 whales with about eight more that day. It is a very interesting operation, the whales being pulled out on a ramp, the blubber removed in large strips by steam winches and the meat cut up and frozen for shipment to Japan. We were given a large piece and it seemed quite similar to beef. The bad odor attached to the whaling station has been all but eliminated and we were told that 98 percent of the animal was used. Five killer

From Barkley Sound it's a short and scenic cruise to the Strait of Juan de Fuca.

Tatoosh, Elfin and Una Mae

boats range out to sea as far as 150 miles and drag in the whales with their tails lashed to the bulwarks.

Varney Bay only a few miles away is an excellent anchorage, and here lives Miss Varney, a very remarkable woman for whose father the bay was named. She lives alone on the old homestead, is a licensed guide, has 19 cougars to her credit and is an excellent gardener.

Klaskish Inlet is typical of the many inlets: here we tied to an unoccupied fish camp float. It is a pretty spot and like many of the inlets without human habitation although there are occasional abandoned shacks. Eagles are seen in most of the inlets. We explored the Klaskish River in one of the small boats.

Brooks Peninsula jutting out like a huge domino seems transplanted from another region with its rolling hills and its Cape Cook next only to Scott in reputation. The south shore of this peninsula is a beachcomber's paradise as it catches much of the drift along this coast, including glass balls from Japan and acres of driftwood.

The fishing village of Kyuquot is located in an almost perfect round harbor and can be reached only by plane or boat. It is the home-port of seemingly hundreds of trollers and very well worth a visit. When we were there they had been weather bound for two weeks.

Our next stop, Notchatlitz Bay, is a good spot to set the crab pot. Crabs seem to abound all along the coast and are of the large delicious Dungeness variety. A good-sized river flows in with a fairly high falls and at high tide one can outboard right up to the waterfall.

Friendly Cove on Nootka Sound is of great historical interest. Here was located the first Spanish settlement on the Northwest coast and here Vancouver took over possession of practically the entire Pacific Northwest from Spain. There is a monument to the event, as well as one to Captains Cook and Vancouver.

Hot Springs was our next stop where genial host Ivan Clarke made us welcome. There are ample floats and Clarke's general store. The hot springs are about 1½ miles over a good trail. There is a natural hot water falls, a natural shower albeit a little too hot, and below it several pools for soaking up the medicated waters and a much needed bath.

Tofino just down the coast is interesting and here is a crab cannery where the most delicious canned crab may be purchased by the case. It is a short hop to Barkley Sound and then it's a short and scenic cruise to the Strait of Juan de Fuca and we are back in U.S. waters.

For those with a sea-going feel of adventure, a desire for different and relatively untouched cruising waters and sufficient time, circumnavigating Vancouver Island or cruising its west coast can be most rewarding providing proper plans are made and with suitable equipment aboard.

Billy Paine smiles proudly as he boats a good-sized cod

Giant Dungeness crab abound in Klashkino Inlet

50
Cruise of the Calcite

by J.A. McCormick

This story, written nearly half a century ago, covers waters, names, people and points of interest known to many Northwest skippers. It was discovered in the "archives" at Roche Harbor as part of an extensive photograph album. Feeling that families who cruise in these same waters today would enjoy this narrative, we present it through the courtesy of the late Mr. Reuben Tarte of Roche Harbor.

During the late summer of the year 1908, one of the unrecorded miracles of the Puget Sound country took place, and it is left to me, a witness of said miracle, to set down the facts. What was it? Why, John S. McMillin took a vacation! Yes, it could be stated that he took several vacations in one, since I heard him say that he had been promising himself a summer cruise for many years. On this occasion he made up for all of those promises by having a trip of a lifetime.

Did he vacate by his lonesome? Well, hardly! J.S. is not the exclusive kind. He wants cheerful company if he can get it, but company he must have. So that is why I am writing of the cruise: I was a participant in the "Joy Ride."

Our party consisted of the following: John S. McMillin, our host, Commodore of the Roche Harbor Yacht Club and President and General Manager of the Tacoma & Roche Harbor Lime Co., San Juan Islands; Fred H. McMillin, our genial captain, his father's chief assistant in the management of the lime works; Mr. R. P. Butchart of Victoria, B.C., Manager of the Vancouver Portland Cement Company of Tod Inlet, Vancouver Island; J. A. McCormick, official photographer of Seattle, who stands ready to take any measure of credit or criticism due for the way in which this record is handled.

The crew consisted of Harry Horst, First Officer, a deep-sea sailor and a man that kept our good ship, the *Calcite,* clean and trim; Guy Wheeler, Chief Engineer, who knew his engines and ran them for 17 days without missing a stroke; and last, but most important, our chief steward, Jim Nagioka, a man with a yellow skin but a white understanding when it came to tickling the palate of the hungry horde aboard our good ship. He was never at a loss for something new in pastry or pudding, and was continually giving us the last word in delicious compounds from his three-by-five-foot galley.

The *Calcite* is 50-feet-10 overall, 12 feet moulded beam; 50 even horsepower, speed clear, nine knots. She is 14.91 gross tons, and nine tons net. She swings a 45° propeller, and makes 300 revolutions a minute. She is equipped with a compressed-air pilot-house control, and is handled by the man at the wheel with perfect ease and absolute safety. She is also equipped with a Brush direct-connected direct-current 110-V, 4-KW generating set which operates the lights, one-and-one-half-mile searchlight, heats the boat with electricity.

Calcite has an up-to-date electric galley in addition to a gasoline stove galley. She swings one life boat, and has sleeping and living accommodations for ten persons besides the crew, which consists of engineer, captain and cook. She has the inverted Kewanee water system, which enables her to have running water under pressure throughout the boat. Her engine is a San Francisco Standard.

All of her dead space is taken up by lockers and drawers, which, with the space beneath the after deck, allows of the stowing of all baggage and equipment of the party, making for perfect comfort. Her pilot house is furnished with all required equipment for deep-sea navigation. And she carries a full supply of flags and bunting for all occasions.

PRELIMINARY: Upon the morning of Wednesday, Sept. 9, 1908, at 10:50, with all flags flying, the club flag at the masthead, the weather ideal, the *Calcite* slipped her halters, and with her exhaust drowned by the parting salute from the factory whistles of Roche Harbor, she started upon a cruise that will forever stand as one of the ideal outings upon the land locked waters of Puget Sound and of British Columbia.

The run was made through Mosquito Pass, just south of Roche Harbor, without incident, but while crossing the Straits de Haro in a choppy sea, the master's helmet was carried away and a half hour was lost in rescuing it, owing to the elusive tide currents.

Upon arrival at Oak Bay at 12:50 p.m. the Commodore landed from the Captain's gig and secured a season's permit to cruise in British Columbia waters. As Mr. Butchart and I joined the party at this point, and as that is really a separate story, I will beg the indulgence of the readers while I tell of it in the first person.

About the middle of August I had received a letter from J. S. McMillin asking me to join his party for a cruise and instructing me to meet him at the Empress Hotel in Victoria. I quote one paragraph of that letter: "Now Mac., be sure to come and bring a gun, a rod and a stock of good stories." Well, I was there with the gun and the rod, but modesty forbids that I say more about the stories than this: In twelve days and nights one can think of many stories if properly encouraged, and the audience was in the receptive mood.

Dinner aboard the Calcite... (from left) R. P. Butchart, whose home is now the famous Butchart Gardens; John S. McMillin of Roche Harbor; J. A. McCormick and Fred H. McMillin.

On the morning of the 9th of September, 1908, I took the steamer *Princess Victoria* for Victoria. When the customs inspector asked me if I had any dutiable goods, I told him that I had a box of ammunition, a portion of which I might leave across the line, and a few boxes of dry plates which I hoped to bring home with me after they had each received an impression of some portion of the magnificent scenery of Vancouver Island and the Mainland of British Columbia. He gruffly ordered me to move on, and then called to me to have a good time. Poor man! I know he must have been homesick to join me.

After a most delightful trip up the Straits, I arrived at Victoria, went at once to the desk of the Empress Hotel and inquired for J. S. McMillin. I was informed that he was not there. At that moment a gentleman at my elbow volunteered the information that he had just received a phone message from Oak Harbor that the *Calcite* was about to come to anchor. This was my first meeting with Mr. Butchart. We had a pleasant visit while awaiting the McMillins'. Upon their arrival we proceeded at once to that splendid edifice, the Parliament Building, then to the Customs Office, secured our permit, and after a few purchases of supplies we took the car for Oak Harbor and the *Calcite*.

THE CRUISE: At 4:45 p.m. we had all of the party with their baggage aboard, the order to heave anchor was given, and the expedition was immediately under way with the Union Jack floating at the masthead. After passing the reefs of Oak Harbor and getting well into the stream, we very reluctantly went below to get our luggage stowed in lockers and drawers while we still had the daylight to assist us. Many trips were made to the deck to admire the splendid coloring of the sunset and the island scenery through which we were passing. Space forbids an adequate description of the islands and channels of this most wonderful land-locked body of salt water, with its varying tides and currents. Suffice it to say that there are hundreds of islands in the British Columbia and Puget Sound waters and that the islands are of a rocky formation, gray predominating, with a growth of dark green forest and wide grassy slopes and open areas that turn yellow by midsummer. The sunsets are brilliantly colored and the influence of the sun's evening rays upon the shores, the foliage and the grassy fields is truly iridescent in its effect, causing the most indifferent visitor to enthuse over this unusual splendor. You approach one of the islands, you pass a rocky point that ends in a broken reef. Just beyond you see a beautiful stretch of sand and gravel beach in the depths of a deep bay, backed up by an open valley with here and there a farm house, a lone tree, a stretch of fence. You pass another point with a low rocky nose, grass grown; you see beyond, in another bay, a beach of rock and coarse gravel backed by a heavy timber growth. You pass a high perpendicular wall where the main body of the island ends in many fathoms of water; just beyond you see a long crescent of beach, first backed by a portion of this wall, then by a body of timber as the country drops away; then a long neck of land finally terminating in a decided peninsula. You know that just over this low neck of land you will find another fine beach sweeping on to perhaps other forms of shore, until the shoreline meets with your starting point. All is beauty without the monotony of most island groups. The channels between the islands will in some cases be open, winding and charming; in others they will be narrow, with swift currents, and delightfully exciting.

You pass from an island group into the Straits of Juan de Fuca, or the Gulf of Georgia, and for hours you have really and truly an ocean trip. Just as you are tiring of the heavy swell of the open gulf, you plunge into another group of islands with its glassy waters and picturesque shores.

At 10:45 p.m. of this, our first day, we dropped anchor in the Bay of Chemanis, in seven fathoms of water. It rained during the night, clearing the atmosphere perfectly.

Thursday, September 10th. Upon awaking we found that we had been under way since 5:30. While we were dressing, Fred called to us to hurry as we were nearing Dodds Narrows. This was worth seeing as it is one of the narrow channels mentioned. We had to negotiate it against a heavy head tide. This took some time as we could make little headway against such a strong current. We made the pass at 7:15, entered Northumberland Channel for a day's run to Campbell River. During the day we passed the steamers *Transit, Yucatan and Thorbus.* and arrived at the mouth of Campbell River at 5:00 p.m. While the officers were sounding the river channel, Mr. Butchart and I tried salmon trolling, which resulted in Mr. Butchart landing a fine silver salmon with his tuna gear. For the benefit of those who do not know him, I will say that Mr. Butchart in everyday life is a very quiet, dignified gentleman, devoted to the successful management of a very large business, and is the last man one would choose as an enthusiastic fisherman. But I am here to say that when he got that strike there was not a word of criticism to offer for the way in which he conducted himself. He played that salmon for 15 minutes, giving it all the chance that a true sportsman could be expected to give; at the same time he handled his "gear" like an expert, bringing the fish to "gaff" without a sign of the usual awkwardness of the "once-a year" fisherman. The catching of this Silver was all that was required to put Mr. Butchart at his ease and he was wholly human on the balance of the trip, recovering his wonted dignity only upon our arrival at his beautiful home on the shore of Tod Inlet and the end of our outing.

Returning to the launch with the gleam of first honors in our "sporting eye," we found that we could not enter the mouth of the river until high tide on the morrow, near noon. We spent this, the second night, at the mouth of Campbell river, with Seymour Narrows to the north, Cape Mudge in sight to the southeast, the log booms to the south, all forming a picture of promise for the coming day.

Friday, September 11th, we weighed anchor on the scales of Butchart's Silver salmon at 8:20 a.m. and crossed the channel to visit Gowlland Harbor and some mining friends of the McMillins'. After a short stop at the camp we cruised for a time along the broken west shore of Valdes Island while awaiting the incoming tide. We then returned to Campbell River and worked our way up the river with the rising tide until we reached a large pool near the south shore, that made an ideal place to moor the *Calcite*. Reached this pool at 3:07 p.m. and at once prepared for a trip up the river, trout fishing. Returned in the evening with a mess of fish and spent the fore part of the evening in playing the phonograph for the people ashore. Soon after dark the Northern Lights began to illuminate the Heavens and we spent two hours or more watching the changing form of the Aurora. It was a splendid exhibition and at times took on considerable color. We became thoroughly chilled and as the lights were dying we retired about midnight.

Saturday, September 12th, after breakfast we got into our waders and spent the forenoon whipping the stream for trout and later made a trip up one of the side streams. Had a delightful day, but without canoes we were unable to go up the river far enough to get the best of the fishing, so we returned to the launch. At 4:15 p.m. we dropped down the river and after getting clear of the river mouth, we set our course for Powell River on the mainland, where we arrived at 11:55 p.m. in a light fog, and tied up to the Company float.

Sunday, September 13th, with the *Calcite* trimmed in bunting, we spent a good portion of the day fishing,

The small boats take off for another day of exploration.

while the chief steward was preparing the commissary for our trip to Powell Lake. We caught some fine trout in the mouth of the Powell River, below the falls. J.S. landed a fine silver salmon while trolling on our return to the launch for lunch. During the day we also visited the logging camp and made a trip up the river above the falls, where we did some fishing with rather poor success, owing perhaps to the bright sunlight. We spent the evening in preparing our personal outfits for the lake trip, and played the phonograph until midnight, entertaining the logging population ashore. We were not far from shore and the weather was very calm, so with the horn turned shoreward, the people were given a rare treat, as we had dozens of the finest of records, including a number of the Sacred Hymns. During the day, while on our trip to the lake, we met a moccasined, leather skinned individual who volunteered considerable information that sounded reliable, and upon inquiring, we found that this was Tom Ogburn, a guide. He was invited to dinner aboard, and during the evening J.S. made a bargain with him to guide us on our lake trip.

POWELL LAKE

Monday, September 14th, we were up early getting our camp equipment ashore, and at 9:20 we had all aboard the flat car, including our boats, and began our climb to the lake end of the railroad, about one and one quarter miles away. While the engine is climbing the grade I will say a word about the lake. Powell Lake is 45 miles long, with one large island lying in the eastern or mountain end of the lake, which divides it into two channels of about equal width. There are a few smaller islands, one of which lies near the lower end in sight of the long landing, and this is known as Little Island. At the head of the lake there are several quite large streams that are fed by the perpetual snow and ice of the main ranges to the east and north. Along the shores on both sides of the lake there are numerous smaller streams flowing down from the foothills, carrying plenty of fish food for the innumerable trout to be found both in these streams and in the lake. At the mouth of some of these streams, one will find low flat country, here a marsh, there a delta, being an ideal home for the wild duck and kindred fowl. The immediate shores of the lake are overrun with deer, bear, mountain goats and grouse, making this an ideal lake for a stay of from ten to 60 days, while we had but six days to enjoy its blessings. The steep and rugged shores of the entire lake have been scourged by fire within recent years, marring the beauty to a great extent. Nature is slowly repairing the damage done on the lower reaches.

We arrived at the log landing in short order, and with the assistance of the logging crew we soon had our boats in the water, loaded for the trip and free from the log booms. With a parting cheer, we headed for the right arm of the lake, with the intention of taking plenty of time to the up-trip. The south shore for several miles is backed with low rolling hills and wide, flat country covered with a good growth of timber that escaped the ravages of the recent conflagration. After an hour's rowing we landed in a sheltered bay, and after a leisurely lunch we made a trip over a moss-grown trail to a small lake that lay about two miles to the south, buried in the heavy forest. We did not spend much time on the shores of this splendid little lake, but we all agreed that one would find the trout fishing ideal during a day's stay.

Returning to our boats we moved on to the flats at the mouth of a small stream where we secured a mess of ducks and then we crossed over to Little Island and put up our tents for the night. We camped in a small bay at the lower end of the island, where we could have a large beach fire, sheltered under a high bank from the crisp night breeze that was blowing up the lake. After our camp dinner we spent hours talking of the few happy days that had passed and planning for the days to come. We had just comfortably settled in our freshly-cut bough beds when we were called from our slumbers by the breakfast yell. Sound sleep makes short nights.

J. S. McMillan and his guests prepare to leave the Calcite for a six-day trip around Powell Lake in the small boats

Tuesday, September 15th, soon after leaving camp we came to a stream that fell directly into the lake, and at the foot of this falls was some of the best fishing that we had encountered. We stopped here until we had trout enough for our immediate wants and then proceeded to the head of the lake with an occasional stop to shoot a duck or cast a fly. At one place I found Mr. Butchart sitting in his boat shaving while he was waiting for the stragglers to come up. We camped at the mouth of one of the larger streams at the head of the right arm of the lake, and enjoyed a good night's rest after our strenuous trip of the day.

Wednesday, September 16th, we were up early and on our way through the narrow channel back of the island, headed for the left arm of the lake, which lies between foothills of great height and picturesque form. During the forenoon, while skirting a low point, John S. had a shot at a black bear. As he was in a canoe and used his shotgun, it is not likely that he did Bruin much damage, but this left us in a sufficiently excited state to cause us to spend the next hour looking for his lordship. I pushed my boat ahead past the point, and had the satisfaction of seeing either the same bear or another, leisurely walking a log across a gulch. Upon landing I was unable to trace him as the trail was worn smooth with much travel. In half an hour we were in camp and spent the balance of the morning getting our camp in shape for our stay. It would take pages to properly describe the beauties of our surroundings, so will only attempt to give a brief outline to assist the imagination.

Our camp was just on the edge of a partially cleared bench, or flat, perhaps 20 feet above the water and 75 feet back from it. We faced directly down the lake, with a shallow beach to our front and left, with good but rather cold bathing. Still farther away to our left was the bear point. On that account we named this "Camp Teddy." Just to our right a small stream entered the lake, at the mouth of which the trout fishing was good. At a distance to our right we could hear the deep murmur of a waterfall. To the right and

down the lake there was a group of high peaks with scattered snow fields, and our guide said that mountain goats were numerous up there. Just back of us was a broad face of high rocky range, almost devoid of timber, that was undoubtedly the home of the Grizzly. Altogether an ideal outing place, and three days were all too short a stay. It would take weeks to become sufficiently intimate with the many beautiful peaks that were in sight of camp, and no doubt a climb to any one of them would bring us in range of dozens even more attractive.

After lunch, Fred, Butchart and I started for a hunt among the breaks to the south of camp, incidentally looking over our bear pasture of the morning, but as the beasts were apparently housed for the day, we moved to the higher benches where Fred left us to climb to the peaks beyond. I killed a grouse and while cooning down a log to get it, I had a fall into a patch of undergrowth from which a bunch of deer escaped while I was buried in much bark, brush and profanity. Such is the hunter's luck.

Thursday, September 17th, we spent the fore-part of the day visiting points of interest near camp, until we heard Fred on the slope beyond. We crossed the bay with a boat to get him and spent the lunch hour listening to his description of the beauties above. After lunch we made a short trip to the mouth of the river and up to the falls. This looked so promising that we planned a day's outing for the morrow to this delightful spot, and returned early to camp.

This falls is not high, but a good-sized body of water slips over a slope of polished granite and brings up against a hollow wall, giving off such a deep roar that John S. christened it "Thunder Falls," which is truly a name that applies. The pool just at the foot of the falls was named by Mr. Butchart "Trout Eddy," and this also applies, so we hereby give notice to all the world that these names are to be used in this connection. While at the falls we saw a badly-used canoe pulled up among the rocks, and soon after our return to camp a trapper from up the river arrived on his way to the outer world for supplies. He had been buried among the hills all summer preparing his winter camp. He certainly looked the worse for his long absence. Our party had commenced to look rather weather beaten, but we were still delightfully civilized in dress by comparison with this individual. He looked as though the vermin of ages had lived and died upon him.

He insisted on starting down the lake at once, although it was nearly dark. Soon after we saw his campfire just across the bay within a mile of us. After a sumptuous dinner and a comfortable smoke, we retired, well pleased with the world and all that was in it, even the trapper.

Friday, September 18th, after a hearty breakfast we prepared our fishing gear while Jim got together one of his irresistible lunches, and we took boat for the River and "Thunder Falls." We went up the river above the falls for a mile or more until we found it so tangled that we could scarcely believe that the trapper had come this way. We returned to the Falls where we fished and photographed for a while, after which Jim served on the rock table above the falls. After lunch we beat the flats at the mouth of the river for a deer, but finding none, we returned to camp, arriving about 2:30 p.m. Jim had returned ahead of us and you can imagine our surprise when he said, "You go down lake? This Friday! Log train no run Sunday." Here we were 45 miles from the landing, with one day intervening. Not one of the party except Jim had noted the flight of time. After some discussion we decided to get up so as to start at daylight, but Jim knew us well and he said: "You no get up. Log train stop six o'clock. We no can ketch it. You go tonight!" All of which was true.

So we prepared a lunch to eat upon the way, packed up and rowed all night, reaching Little Island at 4:00 a.m. Jim and Mr. Butchart had pushed ahead, built a fire, and had a hot lunch waiting for us.

Saturday, September 19, after a late breakfast, we loaded up for the remaining six miles, which we made with ease. Upon arrival at the log landing we found that the engine was out of commission and the camp shut down for repairs. Anticipating our return on that day, the logging crews were soon on hand·with a push car. With ropes and pole breaks, our outfit was safely lowered down the steep grade.

During our absence the launch had been in charge of Harry Horst, First Officer, and Guy Wheeler, Engineer, and they had been compelled during the week to run for shelter from a storm a couple of times. But when we arrived we found them lying quietly at anchor, the weather having improved. We soon had everything safely aboard and lashed fast and were under way for Jervis Inlet. Thus ended as fine a week's outing as could well be arranged for a party of poor-conditioned men who not only desired but required a touch of the strenuous. But I dare say that the night's work at the oars will live in our memories as one of the most severe tests of human endurance and good nature that could well be devised.

We left Powell River at 2:40 p.m., and after an uneventful trip we arrived at the Brandon logging camp at 7:15 p.m. Mr. Brandon was in Vancouver, but his foreman and crew helped us to tie up safely to the log boom, and then our versatile musician, Mr. Fred McMillin, entertained all parties for a couple of hours with both vocal and instrumental selections. If anything, Fred's "tenor" is better than his "soprano;" his baritone is splendid; he plays exceedingly well on both the banjo and the xylophone, but his marches in full brass can only be equalled by the March King himself. His last selection was a military instrumental in which the bugles sounded taps, so we will say good night.

Sunday, September 20, after a late breakfast, we trimmed the ship with the Sunday bunting, and while the crew was filling the water tanks, the foreman of the logging camp took us over the foothills and showed us the work that had been done in the timber. The country stands on edge throughout this region, making the work of logging both difficult and dangerous. Returning to the launch we started for Sechelt Arm to pick up a guide — Joe Sylva, a native — but found that he was out on the mountain. We ran over to where he was supposed to have left his boat, and the boys landed and killed a few grouse. Later, while drifting off shore, we saw what we supposed to be the guide's two dogs, but they proved to be timber wolves. Before we recovered from our surprise they had disappeared. We soon picked up Sylva and ran over to Egmont logging camp, where we tied up to the log boom at 6:00 p.m. We laid there until 10:20 p.m. while our guide prepared for his trip with us. When all was ready we cast loose and made the run to Hotham Sound, arriving at 11:50 p.m.

Monday, September 21, we were out at 5:20 a.m. for a deer hunt in the mouth of a neighboring river. Returned at noon with two deer. We landed on the beach where a large fire was built and John S. proceeded to "plank" a leg of venison.

We left at 1:20 for Briton River, arriving at 7:20 p.m. where we anchored in 16 fathoms with doubtful bottom. At 12 midnight the wind from up the river caused the launch to drag her anchor so the boys proceeded to run for the head of the inlet where we arrived at 4:20 a.m. and found good bottom at eight fathoms.

Calcite, with her shore boats on booms, waits at Egmont at the entrance to Sechelt Inlet, for their guide

Tuesday, September 22, we left the head of the Inlet at 8:20 a.m. for a day's cruise. We located Mt. Lord Wellington too late to secure the best picture of it, but the face on top of the mountain is very striking indeed when viewed from the proper position.

A little later we stopped at a waterfall that dropped directly into salt water. Here we secured some fresh drinking water. If our tanks had needed filling we could easily have run the nose of the launch up to shore and taken water direct from the Falls, and it is well to state here that there are numerous places in the British Columbia waters where this can be done. Miles of the shore line are so steep that a large vessel could be tied up with only the guard rail touching. At 9 a.m. we reached "Calcite Narrows" at the entrance to Princess Louisa Inlet, which was negotiated without mishap at about half tide. This would undoubtedly be dangerous when the tide was running full strength, for the channel is narrow and winding. After passing the Narrows one would think that one had entered a wind sheltered lake, as the reflections were perfect.

While Jervis Inlet throughout is so beautiful that it seems more like a dream than a reality, Princess Louisa is the most charming of the many arms and reaches. It is only a few miles long, extending in a narrow winding channel between foothills from 3000 to 5000 feet in height, and so steep that one is often compelled to lean out from beneath the canopy of the afterdeck to be able to see the tops of the hills. As we passed openings between these foothills, we saw just beyond snow capped peaks of unbelievable height. From the top of the immediate hills numerous snow fed streams plunged over cliffs so high that the plume of falling water broke into mist before reaching the cliffs below, there to gather form once more and rush to the crest of another cliff where it repeated the performance, then rushed through the timber of the near slopes, visible for a moment, then all hidden except its loud murmur, it finally plunged noisily into the salt water at our feet.

As we reached the head of Princess Louisa there were seven of these streams visible at one time. At the extreme head of the Inlet a larger stream could be seen leaving the nose of an immense glacier, plunging over the rocks and cliffs through the timber, now visible, again hidden, and finally reaching the Inlet in the most perfect water representation of a bride's veil; therefore, the name of "Bridesveil Falls." To the left of these falls there is a perpendicular cliff of terrific height, where it is said that the Indians secure their year's supply of goat meat by driving the animals over the sheer precipice.

We reluctantly drifted under slow bell to the narrows, with a promise of sometime returning for a week's stay and a goat hunt. After passing the narrows we ran direct to Marble Mountain, where we visited the slate quarry; and here there seems to be slate enough to roof the buildings of the world, and furnish every pupil with a desk top of solid slate. At 12:33 we reached Deserted Bay, where we anchored for the afternoon alongside a beautiful yacht, the *Bonita*, if I remember correctly. We exchanged calls, and found that Corporation Council, Scott Calhoun of Seattle and a jovial party were aboard, having been out some weeks. At 3 p.m. we poled up the river and took our stands for a bear hunt. We returned at 7 p.m., chilled through. Fred was the lucky man, having secured a fine black half-grown bear. At 7:15 we left for the Brandon logging camp, hoping to find that Mr. Brandon had returned, and reached there at 11:30, when we tied up for the night.

Wednesday, September 23, not finding Mr. Brandon at his camp, we left at 8 a.m. for Narrows Arm, reaching the head waters at 2 p.m., proceeding at once up the river for a bear hunt. We went by boat as far up the river as possible then struck off across the heavily timbered flats, our guide dropping us one at a time at the various bends of the stream to await the approach of evening, when the bear would begin fishing for salmon. We returned at 6:10 with two black bear of goodly proportions. After hoisting our bear to the bow of the launch, using the anchor tackle for the purpose, we cast loose from the raft and started for Vancouver, this being our last day in Jervis Inlet.

After passing the entrance of Narrows Arm, leaving Fred at the wheel, J. S. Butchart and myself answered the dinner call. While comfortably partaking of one of Jim's best efforts, our launch suddenly turned upon her side, spilling our dinner upon the floor. Rushing to the deck we found that we were in the heart of Sechelt Rapids, breasting a terrific incoming tide which was boiling and seething in its effort to pass this narrow channel. After many minutes, gaining inches only, we succeeded in getting through. Returning to the dining room and our badly wrecked dinner, Jim opened the door to the galley and with a rather sickly effort at humor said — "Look! My dinner!" Everything that was loose in the galley had been precipitated to the floor.

An early September morning mist hovers over the still waters of Princess Louisa Inlet as one of Calcite's guests sets out for a bit of fishing

In a triumphant return to home port at Roche Harbor, hunting prizes are displayed on the bow while one final picture is taken . . . from left, Jim Nagioka, chief steward; R. P. Butchart; J. S. McMillin; Guy Wheeler, chief engineer; Fred H. McMillin; Harry Horst, first officer. J. A. McCormick, writer of this narrative, took the picture.

We soon reached Sechelt camp, where we left our guide, Joe Sylva, and then at 10:20, with a parting salute, we started for the open gulf. After negotiating the long and treacherous Agamemnon Channel south of Nelson Island, and gazing our last gaze upon these mountain beauties, we headed direct for Vancouver, where we tied up at 5:50 a.m.

Thursday, September 24, J. S. had some business to attend to. While he was engaged, we were taken in tow by Mr. Butchart. We were entertained at lunch and at the clubs, visited the public buildings and points of interest, and altogether had a fine day in this beautiful city.

Our good ship *Calcite* had been under the focus of many jealous eyes during our stay, with the two big bear lying on the forward deck. All pleasant days have an end, as this one did, for at 6:00 p.m. we cast loose and ran down the bay, headed for home. After a smooth passage across the Gulf of Georgia we reached Active Pass at 10:40 p.m. in a heavy fog, so at 11:02 we dropped anchor in Maine Harbor for the night.

Friday, September 25, while the entire crew was interested in the skinning of the bear, we lost our *bear*ings in the fog so that when the fog lifted we were seemingly in strange waters. While looking for a familiar landmark, Mr. Butchart recognized the island in front of his home, so instead of landing him at Sydney as contemplated, we took him to Tod Inlet, his home and the location of the cement plant of which he is managing director. After showing us through the plant he proceeded to circle the beautiful grounds surrounding his home, approaching his house by the tennis courts and croquet grounds, when his wife and two daughters came down the steps to greet him. After a fine luncheon and a pleasant hour's visit with his charming family, we walked down to Mr. Butcharts' private dock, where the *Calcite* lay. With every assurance from Mr. Butchart that he had had a delightful outing, we boarded our launch.

After a pleasant trip over a choppy sea that interfered somewhat with the skinning of the bear, we arrived at the private dock of Fred H. McMillin at 4:25 p.m. We here took to swing our bear and pelts into sight, making a photograph, and trim ship for our triumphant entrance into the home port. At 5:30 we ran up to the home dock at Roche Harbor, with the whistles blowing a din of welcome.

Thus ended one of the most delightful outings ever experienced upon the waters of Puget Sound and British Columbia. We were out just 17 days, and now that it was over, it seemed more like seven.

51
A Huck Finn Cruise in the Pacific Northwest

by Eric Wahleen

The whistle of a river craft echoes thinly above the levee. The shrill cry of a high-wheeling bird mingles lonesomely with the muted gurgle of a backwater current. A lone calf bawls for its mother and scrambles through the brush toward a weatherbeaten barn.

One almost expects to see Huck Finn and "ol' Tom" lazily fishing from a raft in the slough, or glimpse a youthful Sam Clemens at the wheel of a steamboat 'round the bend as the cry "Mark Twain!" reenacts a long-gone version of life on the Mississippi.

Surprisingly enough, the scene isn't the deep South. This transplanted replica of the Mississippi levee country lies at the opposite end of the United States between Puget Sound and the Cascade mountains in Washington state.

The Northwest has always been noted for beautiful lakes and mountains. Not so well known are the many river deltas sandwiched between the mountains and the one and only Puget Sound.

Seven swift streams cascading from the high peaks flatten out at sea level to meander slowly into the east side of the Sound. Five of them, the Nooksak river at Bellingham, the Skagit at Mt. Vernon, the Stillaguamish at Stanwood, the Duwamish at Seattle and the Puyallup river at Tacoma offer smooth waters for small boats.

Sixth and largest of the navigable rivers on the east side of Puget Sound is the Snohomish river and adjacent sloughs. Sometimes known as "the world's shortest river," the 17 miles from Snohomish to Everett is a year-around waterways attraction.

A sloop with auxiliary motor uses its foresail to glide upriver at a leisurely pace. Homeowner sitting on porch in background, like other river dwellers, waves to passing boats.

A man, a dog and a boat make up ingredients for a Huck Finn cruise of the Snohomish River delta, starting at the Puget Sound docks of the city of Everett.

Six sloughs, three large islands and over 50 miles of navigable water are contained in the 27-square-mile lowland area stretching nine miles south from Marysville and five miles east of Everett.

Tugs, barges, mills, log dumps, farms and waterways, criss-crossed by many bridges, offer an unending panorama of river activities totally different from the well-known wide sweep of Puget Sound so close at hand.

The Snohomish river and sloughs were an integral part of early Washington history. Indian canoes cruised the

191

sloughs for centuries. When the white men came to Puget Sound over a hundred years ago they chose the riverbanks to settle on. The river was their highway that contacted the rest of the world.

Today the river banks mix relics of early Washington history and a hustle and bustle of maritime activity that is an extension of the busy docking area of the city of Everett on Puget Sound.

The quiet waters, protected from gales by the surrounding hills and kept from flooding by miles of dikes, offer year-around use by watercraft of all descriptions.

The backwaters that bear such a surprising resemblance to the bayous of the deep south seem almost unreal between the high peaks on one side and the vast waters of Puget Sound to the west.

Though the delta area lies at the backdoor of a busy city of nearly 60,000, a turn into the nearest slough brings utter peace and quiet, stirring a Huck Finn instinct to turn back to the days of Mark Twain and life on the Mississippi.

Snohomish's river was a miniature Mississippi when big canoes carried as much as 3,000 pounds of goods in the 19th century. The railroad trestle was abandoned in 1940.

A tug with several sections of log-raft in tow heads down-river to a mill.

"Hangman's Island" reflects picturesque names that river landmarks retain from the past. Channel at left is "Devil's Hole."

52
How to Follow the Rock Painting Trail of Jervis Inlet

by Lester R. Peterson

E VER SINCE the rather romantic discovery of prehistoric art on walls and ceilings of the Altmira Caves, the world has been intrigued by this type of relic from an otherwise unrecorded past.

During the twentieth century, examples of these pictographs, more commonly known as rock paintings, have been discovered, scattered here and there throughout most of the world.

Rock paintings from Europe, Africa and Australia have been studied, photographed and reproduced again and again. Relics from the New World have been traditionally considered less significant and North American rock paintings have received comparatively little attention.

True, some, particularly those located near highways, are well enough known to the traveling public. But, while these comparatively few examples of aboriginal art are visited by an unending cavalcade of automobile tourists, hundreds of fascinating and significant sites along the Pacific coastline remain literally unseen.

To the representative traveler, sea- or land-borne, the shores of British Columbia are hardly associated with aboriginal rock paintings. Neither native Indians or fishermen ever said much of what each knew of this unique art form, and passers-by seldom noted the unobtrusive protected galleries.

Summer after summer a steadily increasing number of argonauts have found their way to Jervis Inlet to view its breathtaking mountain scenery, to fish, to pick oysters or to rally beneath Chatterbox or Freti Falls. Many of these travelers have undoubtedly brought with them burning curiosities, yet fortunate indeed have been those few who have managed to find one reminder that a once numerous people, the Sechelts, used to roam these shores and waters.

I saw my first rock painting, (No. 9 on the accompanying map), during a visit to the head of Jervis Inlet in the company of Jack Gooldrup, fisherman-boatbuilder of Gibson's Landing, and Basil and Clarence Joe, of the Sechelt Indian Band. Basil, 80-year-old patriarch, and his son Clarence, had volunteered to make a journey to the innermost reaches of their people's ancient domain to point out features named by their ancestors and to tell legends and stories from bygone days.

Discovery of this painting added a new dimension to our search. On succeeding expeditions, we looked for further sites as well as for other storied spots. The even dozen numbered on the map indicate results to date.

All Jervis and Sechelt Inlet paintings are red in color. According to Basil Joe, they are the work of medicine-men, who used a natural cinnabar, most commonly known as vermilion, to depict mythical and legendary events from their people's history. Exactly when and by whom they were done cannot now be known; Basil Joe's grandmother told him that they were already very old when she was young.

Durability of the color used by prehistoric peoples was illustrated recently, when stalactites blasted off the roof of a cave in Sicily disclosed paintings thousands of years old, their colors still discernible. Walls of ancient Aztec buildings, excavated from beneath 25 feet of debris, have retained colored designs. The cinnabar seems to have penetrated the granite, becoming as durable as the ageless rock itself.

Suk-Wah-Main, on the map, is Garden Bay, Pender Harbor, popular stop for yachtsmen headed into Jervis Inlet.

Rock painting No. 1 is located on the shore of Sakinaw Lake, on a bluff a few hundred yards above its outlet. The bay, prominently marked by a huge sloping spar-tree, affords good anchorage, and a light dinghy can be readily carried the few hundred feet to the lake, along a road over which logs have been dragged from it to salt water. The base of the paintings appears at little more than eye-level of a rower. The characters extend, in disconnected sections, for 30 or 40 feet. According to tradition, Sechelt boys were once obliged to swim the lake at this spot, under water, as part of their initiation into manhood. The fact that the lake was an accustomed haunt of Tchain'-Ko, the evil serpent of the deeps, would have added psychological fear to physical challenge.

No. 2, is located on the curved face of the bay's upper entrance, at about 30 feet elevation. It consists of markings of no distinguishable design. It marks the spot from which, so Sechelt legend has it, a young brave once threw into the sea a creature which his spirit-man father had endowed with magical powers to kill.

The site of No. 3 is indicated by a small cave, about 15

feet above sea-level, in a tiny bay three nautical miles up Agamemnon Channel, Leal-Ko-Min on the map. This spot, so the oldtime Sechelts said, was a bad place. Lightning would strike here as a storm gathered. Any ordinary person entering the cave would die from poisonous fumes. But a medicine-man once upon a time entered it, and painted a doubleringed circle, his insignia, and symbol for the sun, from which he drew his power. Clearly he meant to show that his sun-derived power could overcome the cave's evil. Geologists say that the locality contains zinc sulphide. An investigator must scramble to the cave's entrance to see the circle and other symbols painted within.

No. 4 is to be found at the lower entrance to the small bay immediately below Earl's Cove, the ferry landing, on a flat rock rising above a wide ledge, near gunwale-high at most tides. Although quite dim, it will still photograph, and is a most significant painting. The concentric circle in the mural here represents the rainbow, symbol of a promise made by the Sechelt people's god that he would never flood their world again. Basil Joe, living "memory" for the Sechelts, says that the medicine-man who painted it, ages ago, first journeyed to a spot in Princess Louisa Inlet — No. 8 on the map. There, with the aid of a certain leaf he knew of, he induced a vision, and what he saw in his vision he painted on the site many miles to the south.

No. 5 depicts men in a canoe. It appears on a "gallery" directly across from the beginning of Moorsam Bluff, where mountain goats were hunted in times past. Nothing is known now of the painting's meaning, but the style of the canoe, quite different from those in use anywhere on this coast when Europeans arrived would tend to suggest great antiquity.

No. 6 lies about midway between Seshal and Osgood Creeks. Twelve to 15 feet above sea-level, it is a miniature of a round-eyed man, or god, with what appears to be a skipping rope held over his head. This painting, one of several which seem to have been lost track of since aboriginal times, requires quite diligent searching. It appears in a small triangular niche above a sloping black rock, and is not more than a foot and a half in height.

No. 7, like No. 1, marks a spot associated with initiation ritual. It is marked by a sheer cliff, 40 feet or so in height, with a pronounced overhang at its top. From this abbreviated spring-board, boys wishing to attain manhood status were obliged to leap into the sea below. The paintings show a mass of fish, thinly outlined and interwoven. An oxide stain which now is interposed over a part of the painting was not likely in existence at the time it was put there.

No. 8, already mentioned, is located about a mile up Princess Louisa Inlet, on the right hand shore. Water trickling down the sheer rock helps indicate the spot, marked by a concentric circle, similar to that in No. 4.

No. 9 is located in a beautiful setting, amidst the inlet's highest waterfalls, between two and three miles above Malibu Rapids. Outlined on the dry wall of a niche, ten feet or so up an accessible rock slope, it is the largest and clearest of the Sechelt pictographs. In bold outline appear, prominent among other symbols, the circle, the killer whale and the serpent. It depicts the very crux of Sechelt mythology — the sun, symbol of all good; the killer whale, symbol of perceptive evil, guiding the serpent, blind evil.

Sechelt Inlet has few paintings, and can be entered only at slack water through the rapids below Egmont. One painting, however, No. 10 on the map, located on a point about a mile below the head of Salmon Arm, is quite interesting, and different from any other. It depicts, on a vertical rock face, accessible by means of a ledge, an open "U", beside which stand a pair of deer, most accurately drawn. Strangely enough, it is the very symbol found years ago by James Churchward throughout the Pacific's islands and periphery, used, so he found, to depict the immersion of the legendary continent Mu. Near this painting, another shows the double-headed serpent encircling a tiny deer, and, near that again, a sort of herringbone pattern, which could well represent the primordial Tree of Life.

No. 11, located on a concave cliff midway between Nine Mile Point and Gray Creek, depicts a face, full view. At this spot, so legend has it, a hunter was pulled overboard from his canoe by a porpoise he had speared, and was drowned. His spirit, seen sitting in a niche near the site of the painting, refused to come back to his people, but told them that he wished to return to the kingdom beneath the sea. There are overtones to the legend of the Greeks' boy on the green dolphin.

No. 12, on Four Mile Point, consists today only of a few vertical stripes. Any story that may have been once connected with it is now lost.

Jervis and Sechelt Inlets are becoming known to more and more Pacific Coast voyagers. To those interested in aboriginal American culture, time spent in seeking out some of the unusual, ageless relics would certainly prove rewarding.

Painting #10, just below the head of Salmon Arm, shows an open "U" and a pair of deer...(right) double-headed serpent encircles a tiny deer

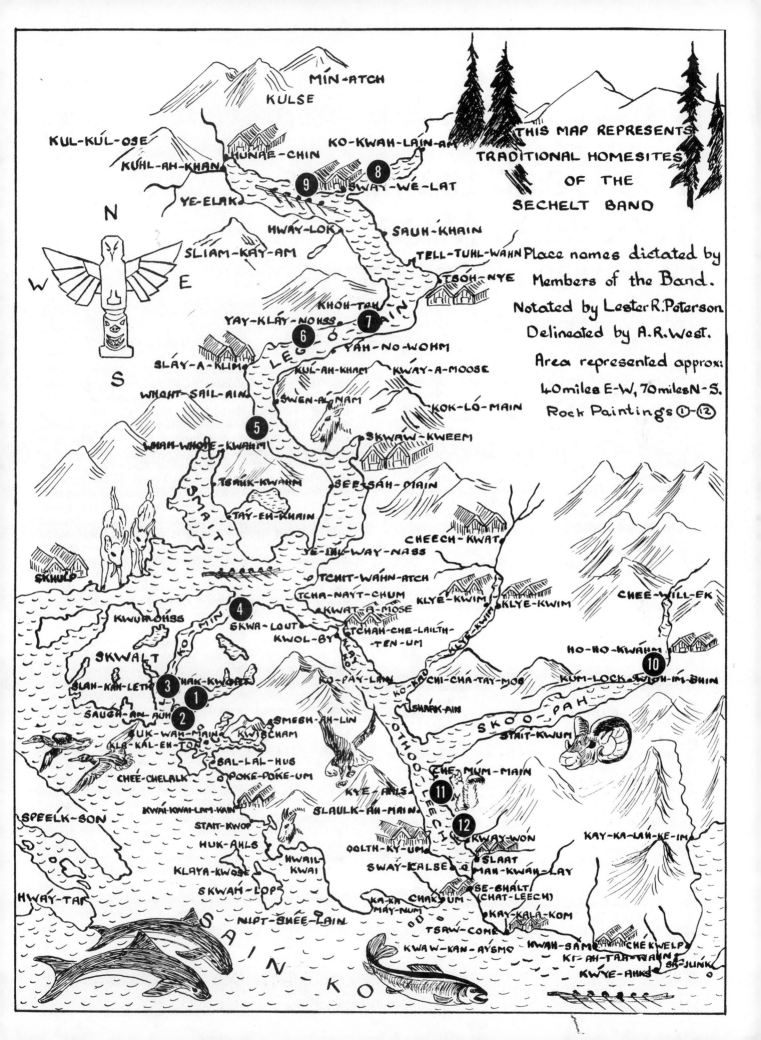

53

The Columbia River's Thousand Miles of River Ramblings

by Yvonne Montchalin

Not knowing from whence trailering cruiser enthusiasts may come, you will have to make your own decision as to whether you wish to enter the Columbia River from launching ramps in the Portland and Vancouver areas . . . or halfway down from the Longview area . . . or clear at the river's mouth at Astoria for a cruise up the river. Or in reverse, you might wish to launch farther up the Columbia and cruise down. This is the log of a journey made by Yvonne Montchalin and her skipper in both directions. They cruised and trailed Ca Va *from Camas, Washington up to the Arrow Lakes in British Columbia. Then, as a postscript, trailed back to Camas, re-launched and cruised down to the Pacific.*

The Columbia River, which forms the boundary between Oregon and Washington from its mouth in the Pacific Ocean for a distance of more than 300 miles, is no ordinary river. True, it carries less water than the Mississippi, but because of its rapid fall, it is the greatest power river in the world with the possible exception of some of Africa's rivers. One third of the potential water power on the North American continent runs between its banks.

My skipper and I had lived all our lives upon the banks of this great western river, loved her many moods and were. haunted by her invitation to exploration. When we took delivery of our 23-foot Uniflite with Interceptor-165 inboard-outdrive power, we could think of no better way to prove her performance than to navigate as much of the Columbia River as possible. We brought her home from the factory in Bellingham, Washington, in March, christened her *Ca Va* and set forth to explore the further reaches of the river which we had never before visited.

We left our home port of Camas, Washington, with the river running at flood stage and full of drift. Chart #6156 covers the course of the Columbia from Vancouver, Washington, to Bonneville Dam. Leaving Camas and cruising up-river, one begins to anticipate the drama v hich will be unfolded.

We proceeded easterly on a river so broad as to resemble a lake. The beautiful, angular, snow-clad peak of Mt. Hood seemed to bar the way. As we left the low hills on either bank and moved up the river, the terrain and the character of the Columbia itself changed. We proceeded past Rooster Rock Park on the Oregon side and a little further, past Cape Horn on the Washington side, and we realized that we were entering the world famous Columbia River Gorge that cuts deep through the Cascade Range to the north of Mt. Hood.

Surely no land is more beautiful than when seen from the surface of a river. As we looked up at the beautiful rock cliffs we were filled with awe. There are many waterfalls in the Gorge, among which are dainty Mist Falls, second highest water fall in the United States, and Multnomah Falls, full and white, tumbling from a great height out of the rugged rock and quickly spilling into the river. A little further east and on the Oregon shore, St. Peters Dome stands like a cathedral away from the mountains behind it and Beacon Rock rises on the Washington shore. At the base of Beacon Rock there is a snug harbor well protected from both the east and the west winds, which in the Gorge are the only winds. The dock is a part of Beacon Rock State Park; there is good water and a picnic area on shore, but no other facilities are provided and no gasoline or supplies are available.

The river narrows and the current swiftens a little at Bonneville Dam, but no power boat will experience any difficulty. There is a good dock to which the boater may tie while waiting to enter the lock at Bonneville. In the locks in the upper dams, the mooring facilities are for barges. While we waited for a barge to be let out of the lock, we took out chart number 6157 which covers the river from Bonneville to The Dalles. A barge leaves the lock at so slow a speed that no suction or wake is created which might endanger the safety of a small boat in this restricted area. Bonneville lock is 500 feet long, 76 feet wide and has a maximum lift of 66 feet. It is equipped with floating bits, as are all of the locks on the Columbia; no fee is charged for the use of any of the locks.

We proceeded up-river past Bonneville and North Bonneville, over that part of the river into which the legendary Bridge of the Gods fell, past Cascade Locks in Oregon and Stevenson in Washington. Here, on the lake formed back of Bonneville Dam, there is often rough, sometimes

Nakusp on the Upper Arrow Lake

breaking water in the afternoons. We followed the Oregon shore as closely as we could for easier passage. The area above Stevenson from Wind River to above Cook is as rough a section of the river as one will find, except at the mouth and possibly on the lakes behind McNary and Grand Coulee Dams under the certain wind conditions. The river is wide and the combination of wind and current can cause a heavy sea. The *Ca Va* has a deep V-hull design and we were pleased to find that she cut through the chop and waves rather than pounding down on them. She has not yet taken a drop of water over the bow.

If you travel this river, be alert as you approach Underwood, for here the White Salmon River comes rollicking out of a canyon in the Washington Cascades. For a fleeting moment Mt. Adams, snow covered at 12,307 feet, may be seen framed by the canyon walls. On the Oregon shore Mt. Hood, which we last saw as we left Camas, stands free and alone at 11,245 feet. The elevation of the river here is 100

Minimum Time Table	
Mouth of the river to Vancouver, Wash.	1 day
Vancouver to Pasco	3 days
Pasco to Grand Coulee, trailering	1 day
Grand Coulee to Northport	1 day
Northport to Syringa Creek	1 day
Syringa Creek to Arrowhead	1 day

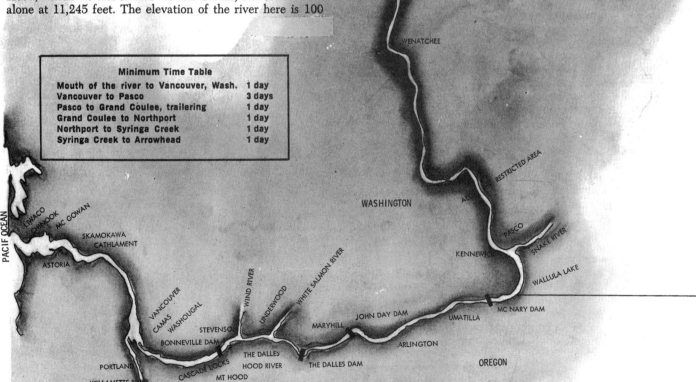

feet. So far as we could determine this is the only spot on the river where both mountains may be seen at the same time.

There is a small boat harbor and yacht club at Hood River, but we chose to go on to The Dalles before nightfall. As we left Hood River behind, we detected another change in the appearance of the rock formation of the shores. We left the deep cut of the Gorge with its jagged cliffs formed against a background of forests and entered the east of the mountainous area where the lava flows are clearly visible, one over another, some horizontal and others tilted at rakish angles, all quite bare of forest cover.

At The Dalles we found a very welcome sheltered small boat harbor in which The Dalles Yacht Club makes its headquarters, complete with guest dock and gasoline pumps. It gives a tired traveler a warm feeling to see a guest dock posted and at The Dalles the hospitality of our hosts was felt as soon as we nosed *Ca Va* around the breakwater. The harbor is within a few minutes' walking distance of the business center of this bustling little city.

In the morning we broke out our up-river charts. Chart 6158 would take us from The Dalles Dam through Lake Celilo to Preachers Eddy below John Day Dam.

For pleasure-boaters without radios, there may be some uncertainty before entering the three upper locks on the Columbia. The confusion does not lie in giving the required signal: we do as the sign directs and pull the slender cable which is suspended for that purpose. The problem occurs when there is no response from the control tower. The boater does not hear the signal and has no way of knowing if the system is functioning or not. Moreover, there is no place to tie in while one waits for the gates to open. In this instance, we waited an hour before receiving the order to enter the lock, which is 675 feet long, 86 feet wide and has a maximum lift of 90 feet.

Once through this lock we passed Big Eddy into Fivemile Rapids, then Memaloose Island, now almost covered by the waters of Lake Celilo which is formed back of The Dalles Dam. To those of us who knew Celilo Falls as it was before the dam was completed, the very name brings a tingle — and here we were riding over it in a small boat. Until the advent of locks, difficult portage for those traveling by river was always required at Celilo Falls and the Cascades near the Bridge of the Gods.

As we approached Miller Island the skipper decided that rather than follow the South Channel we would go through Hells Gate. We were mindful of the unfriendly reputation which Hells Gate has earned through a century of navigation. However, because of the accurate chart and fine range markers, we enjoyed a good passage through the narrow cut.

We tied in for lunch at an abandoned ferry slip at the pretty little village of Maryhill, then on to Preachers Eddy, John Day Dam and chart 6159. We entered the approach to the lock, pulled the signal cord, and waited for two and one-half hours for orders to enter the lock. This is quite a while to hold a boat to a slender wire in the absence of a ring or bollard to which we could secure the boat. This is a lift gate and apparently there was some mechanical difficulty. Finally at 1600 the lockmaster called us in through the partly-lifted gate. This lift was only a few feet, as the dam is not completed. When the lock is finished it will be 675 feet long and have a maximum lift of 113 feet. °

°*The John Day Dam locks were opened in mid-1968, thus forming another 62 mile long lake of quiet water. There are 16 major recreational areas including a large boat basin planned on this lake.*

Chart 6159 is a marvel and so are the ranges. It seemed as if there were as many range markers here as there are quills on a porcupine. The river was high and swift and all we had to do was to pilot the boat precisely as directed by the chart and the ranges. This is not the place to second guess the men who have been there before you!

We did Indian Rapids, John Day Rapids, Squally Hook Rapids, Rock Creek Rapids, Four O'Clock Rapids, Blalock Rapids (change to chart 6160) and Owyhee Rapids before we put in at Arlington for the night. It was a run that kept the skipper too busy to give orders, and the first mate on her toes with the chart clutched tightly in one hand, the other arm embracing the depth sounder and her eyes hunting the next set of ranges. And we loved every second of it!

The buoys which are used in this part of the river are unlike those in the lower river; for instance the red buoys look like 25-gallon oil drums painted white, with a red stripe around the center — and maybe they are. Most of them were pulled either all or nearly all of the way under the surface of the water by the swift-moving current.

The next day it was an easy six-hour run to cover the 90 miles from Arlington to McNary Dam, using charts 6161 and 6162. The chart brought us up the south shore of the river. Below the bridge at Umatilla, with the spillway of McNary Dam in full view, we began to look for the range which would take us across to the north-shore and into the lock entrance.

We went under the bridge before we found the range, and unlikely as it seemed, it took us at about a 45-degree angle across the tailrace of the dam, and to compound our discomfort, as we turned to go behind the wingwall of the lock entrance, we were hit with a vicious sidewash from the spillway. Crossing this bit of fast water, we were glad that *Ca Va* was adequately powered with an Interceptor 165. She performed like a perfect lady.

Here we re-enacted our signal operation with a pull cord, but with one welcome change; we were advised by loudspeaker that there would be a delay of 15 minutes before we could go through the lock. The only hazard here, after gaining the protection of the wingwall, was the great amount of very heavy drift which had accumulated. This lock is 675 feet long, 86 feet wide, has a maximum lift of 92 feet and fills rapidly. In each of these locks we had been alone — a 23-foot boat in a huge lock. After the gates close behind you, you trust that the attendants do not forget that you are down in that cavern.

Charts 6163 and 6164 cover the course from McNary Dam to Pasco. We had been warned that Wallula Lake back of McNary Dam would probably have a heavy chop and that we could find refuge at the Hat Rock parksite. Instead of chop we found a mirror-like lake with no sign of motion on the water except that caused by our boat.

As we rounded the bend above the dam and looked toward Port Kelly, the ancient rock walls of the canyon looked almost fluid as they unfolded to our view. Much of the surface is covered with lichens in reds, bronzes and greens and there are many strange and contrasting formations. Here the river turns sharply northward and no longer marks the boundary between the states of Oregon and Washington.

We soon passed the mouth of the Walla Walla River and then the mouth of the Snake River. At the confluence of the Snake and Columbia Rivers is located Sacajawea State Park with overnight moorage and water available.

We went on in to Pasco and had no difficulty in finding an excellent sheltered moorage, with gasoline at the docks, a loading ramp, marine supplies and a lunch counter. Again we found the residents could not do enough for the stranger. The marine facilities are within easy walking distance of the center of Pasco.

With such marvelous boating water and so much of it, we were and are at a loss to understand why we had encountered no other pleasure boats on the river between Camas and Pasco, except one outboard boat under way and except, of course, the boats at the dock in The Dalles and now at Pasco. Wonderful water for cruising, sailing, skiing and all water sports.

For the boater the way is restricted between Pasco and Grand Coulee Dam by Priest Rapids, Wanapum, Rock Island, Rocky Reach, Wells and Chief Joseph Dams, in no one of which is there a lock. We are advised, however, that a study is underway by the Corps of Army Engineers on the feasibility of extending barge navigation from the pool behind McNary Dam upstream to Wenatchee. This would require the installation of locks in Priest Rapids, Wanapum and Rock Island Dams. The 57-mile open river channel between the head of McNary pool and Priest Rapids Dam would then be improved either by dredging or by the construction of an additional dam and lock. Because there is no lockage provided in these dams, we trailed *Ca Va* from Pasco to Grand Coulee Dam.

If any of you are planning to navigate the Columbia River and are unfamiliar with the phenomena which has taken place along its course through thousands of centuries, you may wish to do some advance reading. Many books concerning the Columbia River are available in libraries, or you may send to the Superintendent of Documents, U.S. Government Printing Office, Washington, D.C. (15c) for the brochure "Coulee Dam National Recreation Area, Washington." If you trail from Pasco to Grand Coulee Dam you will be traveling through beautiful and exciting country and a part of the way you will actually drive in the ancient channel of this great Columbia River.

There is some confusion in the names of the communities near the dam, one being Grand Coulee Dam itself. We were unprepared for the great display of raw, naked power of this dam. We know that it is disciplined, but it does not give this appearance as it roars and spills over the top of the dam, each snowy white, highly agitated drop of water seeming to be vitally alive and in a tremendous hurry. The plate glass windows in the shopping center on the northwesterly side of the river are in constant vibration due to this great free force.

Our first need here was to find a launching ramp above the dam. A Washington State Patrolman gave us the necessary directions and then followed in a few minutes to see that we had found a ramp; he also contacted the National Park Ranger for us. There are two ramps above the dam, but one is quite steep. We chose the one in closet proximity to the dam — concrete, wide and with a gentle slope. The first mate admits to having had a queasy feeling as *Ca Va* floated off the trailer as a thin chain of boom sticks formed the only barrier between the boat and the spillway of the dam. Boom sticks, which are peeled poles chained end to end and ordinarily used to encircle rafts of logs, had never looked fragile.

The campsite and harbor are in the Coulee Dam National Recreation Area and are operated by the National Park Service. There are mooring buoys inside the barrier which forms the boat basin, and there is a dock which is

for the use of the Park Rangers. The Rangers were kind enough to permit us to tie to the dock. There is also a swimming area, a concession, a gasoline pump at the water's edge and ample space for storing boat trailers and vehicles. The Ranger directed us to a place where our equipment would be under his surveillance as he made his rounds of the campsite. The State Patrolmen, Park Rangers and the Security Guards for the dam were all very helpful. We found that this part of the river is subject to sudden, short-lived and very violent wind and thunder storms. We were told of a protected moorage across the lake, but it was unnecessary for us to take advantage of it.

There were just two pleasure boats moored there, and the owner of each was friendly and generous with advice. Before we left for the north they carefully marked our charts with two danger spots within a short distance of the dam. What neither so much as breathed a word about was a short, narrow, deep cut through a mountain of marble which lies just beyond China Bend and is designated as The Little Dalles. We were in this maelstrom before we knew what had happened! Here is a boiling, vicious stretch of water filled with boulders, where a chart is clutter.

We came through this quick experience with two thoughts: we were happy that we had an inboard engine with an outboard drive, and we are convinced that we could navigate the Rhone River in France from Lyon to the Mediterranean Sea without a professional pilot! We did not put so much as a nick on our propeller. When we returned to Grand Coulee sometime later, one of the men who had so carefully marked our chart asked what we did at The Little Dalles, and then told us that he had once taken his 28-foot cruiser up that far, that a whirlpool turned him around and that he just kept on going back to Grand Coulee.

Roosevelt Lake extends from Grand Coulee Dam a distance of 150 wonderful boating miles, almost to the Canadian border. We experienced no difficulty in finding safe harbors. Gasoline is available at the mouth of the Spokane River, at Hunters Landing, Gifford, Daisy and Kettle Falls.

Our first day's run after putting in at Grand Coulee brought us to the mouth of the Spokane River. This took four hours, which included almost an hour for lunch tied at the national parksite at Welch Creek Cove near Lincoln. This run was made through spectacularly beautiful country.

Just beyond the gasoline dock at the mouth of the Spokane River is the Old Fort Spokane National Parksite. There is a launching ramp and there are excellent finger

Wallula Lake

docks, with drinking water on shore. The park boasts a swimming area with a life guard on duty, picnic and camping areas, clean rest rooms, and for those who need to be entertained, a slide show in the evenings. We found the slide shows, which are held in open air amphitheatres under the beautiful and fragrant Ponderosa Pines, to be very worthwhile. The government brochure mentioned above gives data on the many national recreation area campsites bordering Lake Roosevelt.

Our moorage was utterly peaceful, with the sound of doves in the trees and the movement of jumping fish in the water. We did not fish, but noted that others were doing so. Fishing is excellent in Lake Roosevelt and good catches of Rainbow, Kamloops and Dolly Vardens are to be made. We observed increased boating activity at this point. Boaters from Yakima to Spokane and Walla Walla come here to launch small craft.

The Colville Indian Reservation lies on the west shore of Lake Roosevelt and the Spokane Indian Reservation on the east side, north of the Spokane River. We were told that there are no rattlesnakes on the east shore, but that there are on the west bank.

As we proceeded on our northerly route under perfect conditions of weather and water, we noted small farms tucked picturesquely into the hills to our right. We used our charts (6168 and 6169) mostly to test our powers of orientation. We find a fascination in locating a contour, a draw or the southwest gable of a barn as shown on the charts and thus establishing our position. You know from the names on the charts as well as from past reading, that this area is rich in the history of the northwest.

At Kettle Falls there is a well protected moorage in conjunction with a national recreation area campsite. We found ample moorage with a gasoline dock and a small launching ramp. We often have our evening meal ashore if there is a restaurant available. At Kettle Falls we found a very good restaurant across the river at the west end of the highway bridge. It is within walking distance, but we took the boat across and found a small float with a stairway leading to the highway level.

From Kettle Falls it is only a short distance to Northport, but the water is lively in spots. As we approached China Bend above Kettle Falls and Marcus, we could see the lake narrowing consistently and the water moving a little faster.

At Northport we expected to find a dock readily accessible, but we experienced difficulty in locating it. You must keep to the west side of the river until you pass under the bridge, then cut across into what appears to be a quiet pool to a slender, floating dock. The dock is secured to shore by a single cable. What we did not know when we tied to the dock was that we were in an eddy and that the dock moves around at the whim of the current. We found a little city park on the bank above our moorage and beyond that the stack of a now unused smelter, a lumber mill and then the town. Gasoline and water? To fuel up, the gasoline must be carried about a half mile from one of the service stations in the town and then it is a little awkward to lower the gasoline down over the steep bank to the dock; water would present the same problems. However, we found that the friendliness of the people in this village more than compensated for any inconveniences.

It is obvious that the river above Northport is turbulent and here again we were given advice on how best to proceed. Each advisor said that there was really only one

bad spot above Northport, and then described it. The only trouble was that no two persons had the same spot in mind, and none could mark our chart. There are no lights or other aids above China Bend, not even a warning concerning The Little Dalles. We made a decision about which neither of us was very happy, but after all, we still wanted to cover the Arrow Lakes and we still wished to return to Camas and to travel from there to the Pacific Ocean via the Columbia River with an undamaged boat. Our decision was to trail to Castlegar in British Columbia.

McNary Dam

At Castlegar we found the best launching ramp to be at the Arrow Boat Club at Syringa Creek above Robson. At the Arrow Boat Club we found a good concrete ramp, excellent moorage, gasoline, marine supplies and rental boats. Our hosts were Alf and Ella Waldron; they are warm, friendly and hospitable people with whom we spent many happy hours. They opened the clubhouse to us so that we might enjoy the luxury of hot showers and they furnished much information about the Arrow Lakes and the excellent hunting and fishing in this rugged area of British Columbia. The recent construction of the high dam at Castlegar has raised the water behind the dam and the Arrow Boat Club and the marina have been re-located in the same general area.

The Lower Arrow Lake and the Upper Arrow Lake, which are connected by a narrows, total 130 miles in length and are a part of the Columbia River. The color of these lakes is a deep emerald green; the water clear and cold and beautiful. The lakes extend generally north from Castlegar and Robson and are set between the Slocan Range and Selkirk Mountains on the east and the Monashee Range on the west. As can be expected, there are sudden, very sharp wind and thunder storms on the lakes, but one soon learns to be conscious of any change in the feel of the air and in its movement, and to seek shelter or check lines. The beauty of the Arrows and of the mountains rising high above them is breathtaking.

We were visiting in the home of the Waldrons one evening before we made the trip up the lakes when a young boating friend dropped in. We asked about securing charts for these waters and he told us that there is no need for charts because everyone in the area knows the waters. There you have it — they know the water, so we do not need charts! There seem to be charts, but where they can be found we do not know. We left for Arrowhead at the upper tip of the Upper Arrow Lake with no worries about the water, however.

The narrows are about 18 miles long and are a little sticky in places. However, there are a few range markers along the way; they are white triangles which, when lined up, gave us confidence. Our only cause for concern was when we met the tugs with log rafts in tow. We had been spoiled by having had the river pretty much to ourselves, and here where it is narrow and quite shallow we met these not very maneuverable vessels. Our depth finder was put to good use.

Through the Narrows and into the Upper Arrow. We tied up at a dock at Nakusp, weathered a thunder storm and then walked to the village. There is a hotel with a nice dining room, and stores and shops for provisioning. However, when we moved to the government dock the next morning in search of a gasoline truck, we were advised to go to St. Leon, about 20 miles further up the lake, where we could get gas at the dock. So far as we know, the only dockside gasoline pumps on these lakes are at the Arrow Boat Club and at St. Leon.

We found this interesting spot, beyond another Cape Horn, with the little dock and gas pump located in a beautiful, well-protected bay. The lodge was built in 1902, close to a hot spring. There are few roads along the Arrows even now; residents and travelers on the lakes were formerly served by stern wheelers, the last of which was the S.S. *Minto* which operated from 1898 until 1954. The lodge is now owned and operated by Mr. Gates as "The Gates of St. Leon." °

To complete our trip in the upper reaches of the Columbia River we loafed along past Halcyon, an abandoned hot spring resort, and past all that is left of mines long abandoned, to Galena Bay and the town of Arrowhead which is at the upper tip of the Upper Arrow Lake. We were sorry that we were unable to travel the remaining 300 miles to Columbia Lake at an elevation of 2650 feet, and which is the actual headwater of the Columbia River. The elevation of Arrowhead is about 1400 feet above sea level. Compare this with the 380 foot elevation at Pasco and an elevation of 8 feet at the lower side of Bonneville Dam and we realize how the mighty Columbia gets her power.

°*The St. Leon Lodge burned to the ground late in 1968.*

There are countless streams entering the Arrow Lakes, and there is no problem in getting to shore almost any place to permit exploring on foot. The shores of the Arrows abound with birch trees.

We poked along back down the lakes to the Arrow Boat Club and the hospitable Waldrons. Here we loaded *Ca Va* out for the return trip to Camas. We trailed her all the way down-river, put her in the water again and were off to complete our journey down the Columbia to the sea. We had a date with some salmon in the cool waters of the Pacific.

The Little Dalles

54

Lower Columbia River

by Charles K. Sparks

The lower Columbia River country had long attracted us as a vacation-cruise project. We wanted to poke around in all the little bays, inlets, sloughs, towns and villages that exist along the perimeters of the river. And so, one July afternoon, my wife, Bettye, and our dachsund, Heidi, boarded our 28-foot Chris-Craft *Pu-Kii* and set off downriver from the Portland Yacht Club.

We proceeded down North Portland Harbor, past Hayden Island. Idling along at 1800 rpm we cruised under the Interstate Railway Bridge and felt we were really on our way to a pleasurable week of cruising.

It was a beautiful day. The water was silky smooth as it reflected the clouds and trees, then passed into our stern wake. Unbelieveable that one of the world's great rivers could be so strikingly serene in contrast to other of our experiences when it was so violent that we felt we were riding the high seas.

Shortly after entering the main stream we approached the Corps of Engineers busily dredging. Apparently the winter snow run-offs had built up some shoaling. This, of course, must be kept under continuing surveillance to maintain a deep clear channel for the large sea-going vessels.

Continuing, we saw many fishermen at Reeder and Willow Points and Warrior Rock on the Oregon side, all ambitiously trying their luck catching summer steelheads. Several boats were also gathered at Hewlett Point, Bachelor Point and at the mouth of the Lewis River.

About 1630 hours we approached St. Helens and decided it would be interesting to explore Scappoose Bay. We turned the *Pu-Kii* to the port and entered the lower end of Multnomah Channel, motoring into Scappoose. The entry is interesting because of its many contrasts. On our left were little fjords of blue-green water with grass and trees growing right to the water's edge. On the other shore were huge barges taking on tons of wood chips for delivery to the nearby paper mills. Very shortly, we entered the bay and sighted the Bayport Marina. Checking our depth finder we found the channel to be a very satisfying 12 feet right up to the floats.

Upon coming alongside we were greeted by John Ewen, who had recently taken over as owner and was busily en-gaged in plans for modernizing. There are covered slips, fueling facilities with a complete marine way, boat repair and engine service available.

Scappoose is a beautiful bay offering many excellent and amply protected anchorages. Fishing comes with challenge and variety. You can apply your wily touch at bass, catfish, steelhead and crappie. Just above the marina is the beautiful grass-covered park with large shade trees, picnic tables, outdoor fireplaces and plenty of fresh water which is the gathering site for the famous annual St. Helens Salmon Barbecue. Scappoose Bay should be marked as a *must* on a Columbia River cruise.

Leaving Scappoose, we eased into the Columbia with the idea of selecting a moorage for the evening. Our choice was Martin Island, about halfway between St. Helens and Kalama on the Washington side. Either entrance to Martin Slough is acceptable, though more caution in picking the channel is recommended from the upper entrance. Since the evening tidal waves were rather gusty we entered from below and worked our way back to a secluded moorage. With many log booms lining the shore, we selected one and tied down the *Pu-Kii*.

A nice spot, we thought, until with our engines silenced we realized that we were moored directly under a freeway. Heavy trucks, trailers, automobiles and a freight train were whizzing overhead. However, as nightfall came, so did stillness. We enjoyed a delicious first-night-out dinner of fried chicken from our barbecue, a green salad, corn on the cob and fresh raspberries for dessert.

Early the next morning Heidi roused us with her barking. Peering out of the cabin, we saw a tug had pulled in and was busily attaching cables to our moorage. John Erickson of the Smith Tug and Barge Company greeted me, "I'm sorry to wake you, but work's work. We're going to have to take this boom out. Weyerhaeuser needs it down at their mill in Longview."

I freed *Pu-Kii's* lines and in a matter of minutes we were out of the way. We had breakfast, gave Heidi a run on the beach, and were soon underway again.

As we passed the granaries above Kalama, we saw many fishermen steelheading from the beach. And we noticed a

Skamokawa with its enticing sloughs and finger bays provides a winding foliage-cruise

The broad, placid waters of the Columbia with forested shores stretched before us as we left Prairie Channel

good trick worth remembering: one fisherman, after beaching his fish, buried it in the sand right at the water's edge, to keep it cool and moist.

Stopping at the Port of Kalama docks for water, we met Victor Gamble, the marina manager. Vic was most accommodating with the deck lines and in providing information. Gas is now available dockside after an absence of any service for over two years. Floating moorage is very convenient to this Indian-named town of Kalama. Just a short walk via the underpass leads you safely to the other side of the freeway and in the center of excellent shopping. This is an old community with a colorful history built around the early-day activities of Indian tribes who gathered to fish, hunt and trade. There are some of the finest hand-carved totem poles to be seen anywhere. In town you'll also find some interesting antique shops. Kalama is another *must* on the cruising itinerary.*

Leaving Kalama we moved slowly downstream to Longview, Washington. Noticing the Cowlitz River on our charts we decided to explore the lower reaches. We found the river to be softly flowing in a clear, beautiful blue green. The depth ran between seven and twelve feet. We cruised about one mile above the highway bridge, noticing a very good launching ramp and several boats skiing. This would be an excellent evening's layover with ample protection.

We returned to the main river and continued downstream to Longview. Minutes later we came to massive docks where ships were loading cargoes. We saw vessels from Manila, Monrovia, Stockholm, Japan and Germany. Shortly after, we entered Fisher Slough and visited the Longview Yacht Club. We noticed gas and water were available. Since the sun was still fairly high over the yardarm we continued on to our original distination of Coal Creek Slough an extensive waterway winding far into the interior.

Entering the slough you pass Stella, a colorful old community perched high on rocky ledges supported by piling. Stella has floating moorage, a restaurant and groceries. The meandering slough is enchanting and suggestive of new things to see around every bend. Many log booms, commercial fishing villages and summer cottages line the shoreline. Securing *Pu-Kii* in a snug cove we were ready to relax. The sun streamed across our stern and the water provided an almost diamond-like effect, slowly changing to a golden red as the sun set. With a warm beautiful sunset, swallows sweeping over the water's edge, catching their evening's meal, carp breaking the water's surface in large circular ripples and soon a delightful meal to be enjoyed, we were truly at peace with the world.

The next morning shortly after 0830 we were greeted by a large tug lumbering up the slough. As the *Cougar* came alongside, we introduced ourselves and became acquainted with John Hafenbrack and Harry Swift. John skippers one of the Smith tugs out of Longview. He has been on the river for over 25 years and has many interesting experiences to relate. Harry Swift assists John and had just recently been released from the U.S. Marine Corps Air Force.

As the *Cougar* moved away John hollered, "Remember, Charlie, if you ever have any trouble on the river, give the tug boys a signal. They're always ready and willing to help."

We proceeded on our way to Cathlamet. When passing out of Coal Creek and into the Columbia *keep to the star-board* and follow the channel markers carefully. There's a spit and shoaling to your port side which can cause some grounding problems.

Cruising at a moderate speed in the down-river current we passed Bunker Hill, Abernathy Point, Eagle Cliff, Waterford and finally Cape Horn. Coming up on the Cape I spotted a boat that looked familiar. It was *Miss Charlie*, George and Charlie Smith's beautiful Uniflite, fishing and just waiting for us. After a little persuasion we talked them into joining us on our cruise, and together we headed on to Cathlamet Channel.

Coming into port we stopped at Allen Johnson's Standard Marine Dock, right under the bridge that connects the mainland with Puget Island. We took on fuel and water and then moved a short distance to the public docks.†

Fishing gear came out as soon as Pu-Kii and Miss Charlie moored to a log raft in Deep River

Just a few steps from the dock you'll locate the Wahkiakum Cold Storage Company. They have good hard ice and are very accommodating in cutting it to size. Uptown we shopped and explored the business center. There is a fine old church overlooking Cathlamet that was built over 80 years ago. An historic carved plaque stands in front of the County Courthouse at the far end of the business center to commemorate the colorful Cathlamet history and its founders. A fine museum is nearby. Cathlamet is an old river settlement — bustling with activity. The town looked scrubbed and polished; the people were friendly and made us feel welcome.

From Cathlamet we went around the bend and entered Elockoman Slough. Here again the shoreline is lined with massive log booms. We asked one of the boom men if it was safe to cruise the length of the slough. "No", was the answer. "It gets pretty shallow." With that we turned around and proceeded to Price Island and Steamboat Slough.

Turning into the slough, we were careful to stay offshore at least 150 yards, noting the big farm home and barns as our guide. This stretch is very shallow and can cause some grounding and bent wheels. For the sturgeon fisherman, I've been reliably told, it's well worth while to stop here. Anchor on the shelf and fish the deep water. Using herring, anchovies or raw meat as bait, you might be lucky in catching one of these delicacies of the Columbia.

With *Miss Charlie* close astern, large heron taking flight

*The Port of Kalama opened a new marina in 1977 with complete facilities including slips, fuel dock and pumpout station.
†The fuel dock is closed.

from the shore, we moved in to an acceptable anchorage, tying the two boats together in raft form. This is a marvelous anchorage; quiet, well protected from the river tide winds, with plenty of deep water for even the largest cruisers. Steamboat Slough was so named because of the many early day ships that came in from the ocean and up the Columbia to discharge their cargoes and take on supplies. Though small, it is one of the few natural bays that could, and even today receives the larger draft ships. Trees grow to the water's edge and it's very beautiful. You might even find time to trap for crawdads, dangle a worm for a catfish or flip a streamer fly for the sea run cutthroat.

At the lower tip, around the spit of this inlet, is the colorful historic community of Skamokawa. Here at the confluence of two fairly navigable creeks you find a secluded, but fairly large harbor with many of the old homes, boardwalks and stores that came into being in the late 1800's. It's the site of one of the first cooperative creameries, established in 1898.

Close by you can visit the old Town House where Archibald Silverman and a man named Morgan built a fine mercantile store and hotel. Though the hotel has since been dismantled, the store still stands proudly as a symbol of another era where pioneers came and settled at the river's edge. Skamokawa has harbored many peoples: fishermen, farming folk, Indians, Chinese laborers and seafarers. Even today many Indian and Chinese artifacts, coins and buttons are found as new homes and highways are being constructed.

We were lucky to have Dan Silverman, descendant of the original family, tell us first hand of the early-day activity, and were so fortunate as to collect some old newspapers, receipts and memorabilia of the early 1900's. Dan had some fine pictures of ships and early scenes which I copied to add to our growing pictorial history of the Pacific Northwest.

Motoring into the inner harbor we spotted some old weathered structures with nets drying on the high dock and a float below. Here we found ourselves in the heart of the old Skamokawa. A rickety ramp leads up to the side of Silverman's store. Walking between two buildings you are led to the store's more interesting front.

We met young Mike Thacker, whose dad runs the store. When we told him of our pictorial history project, he offered to show us his fine collection of old papers and pictures taken when the town was in its heyday. Mike took us into the store to show us a massive old safe that was truly a collector's dream. It was a thing of beauty with ornate lettering and fine cartouches in a range of rich colors.

Shortly, Hoby Thacker and his wife Clara greeted us in the store. More friendly people you'll never find. Very graciously they offered us moorage and water for as long as we wished to stay. Wandering through their colorfully old but spotlessly clean store we noticed they had everything in hardware, groceries, fishing tackle, etc.

With their suggestions of what to see, we set out for more picture taking and exploring. Directly across the highway, perched high on the hillside, stands the old Redmen Hall and church, where we saw old Indian mementos and

Bettye and Charlie hold two juicy wild blackberry pies ready for the oven

Photographer's still life, river style

No one is going to board this dinghy when Heidi is standing watch

items collected from the historic past. Walking up the hillside you enjoy a view looking over the town and harbor, across the Columbia, west to Astoria and the Pacific Ocean. It's spectacular in the late afternoon.

During our hike, George located some tremendous patches of wild blackberries, and suggested we get busy and gather enough for a pie. In a matter of minutes we had gathered a big rusty gallon can full of berries. Upon returning to the boats, Bettye and Charlie pitched in on the pie making, and produced two big golden brown, fresh wild blackberry pies.

Our next destination was Deep River. We cruised directly down the Columbia River with our check point being Harrington Point. Arriving there we had to decide whether to go to Astoria and follow the Ferry channel or go across Grays Bay. The latter is considerably more tricky since the area has a tendency to shoal and the channels shift. With the weather being in our favor, a good flood tide, information provided by our tug friend John Hafenbrack regarding the buoy locations and a very reliable Sonar depth finder we chose to take the short route. It was a successful crossing and we reached our goal, Portuguese Point.

From there we headed for Rocky Point. Keeping a close watch with our binoculars, we were searching for the ghost town of Frankfurt. This town was settled many years

A section of the Astoria hillside. Probably more history and more fishing, logging and shipping industry have been woven into this famed city's life since the days of fur-trading John Jacob Astor than any other city of 10,000-plus citizens

ago by farming and fishing families. For some unknown reason, epidemic, economic strife or whatever, these people left their homes. It has been said that this river village was established as a quarantine station where personnel and livestock would be cleared for communicable disease and sickness before being permitted to dock at towns such as Astoria, Ilwaco or other up-river communities.

This part of our trip was like walking back into history. Plunging into the heavy underbrush and coming upon the old town, we could imagine the people and activities that took place possibly a hundred years ago. Many of these homes had beds, tables, stoves, chairs, pianos and even dishware on the shelves. In the old weathered sheds and buildings adjacent to the homes we found firewood left cut and neatly stacked, the chopping block still in position ready to be used. Drying racks for nets were still in good repair. Old bales of hay were piled high in the barns and some implements for farming and livestock care were hanging or standing nearby.

In the gardens and orchards surrounding the homes we found blackberries, raspberries, squash, cucumbers, cherry, apple and pear trees. Interesting small items such as old labels from canneries, freight receipts of old steamship lines, grocery receipts with low, low prices of foodstuffs made us all somewhat nostalgic. If you are interested in the history

Westport Slough, with its houseboats and busy sawmills is an interesting anchorage . . . cat-fishing and crawdadding made for fun during idle moments

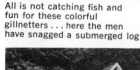

All is not catching fish and fun for these colorful gillnetters . . . here the men have snagged a submerged log

"Just an old shack," some would say . . . but this old home perched on weathered pilings is a part of the gay, romantic, robust history of the Columbia River country

Scappoose is a picturesque bay with excellent moorage and a waterside park which is home of the famed annual St. Helens salmon barbecue

Pu-Kii and Miss Charlie lie quietly at Hoby's store floats where fishermen repair nets and prepare their gear

Skamokawa Harbor, deep and well protected, provides excellent moorage and colorful exploring

of the Columbia River, this is worth your time and effort to make as a port o' call.

Reluctantly, we returned to our boats and headed up the bay to the entrance of Deep River. This is truly a deep river, for we followed the buoys carefully and recorded depths of 10 to 50 feet. Many small fishing boats and villages are along the lower reaches. Further up the stream are farm homes and lumber mills. The area is clean and offers many scenic spots where you may anchor or tie for a quiet overnight moorage.

We were wakened by the rural sound of a rooster's proud crowing. We were anxious to get underway, as George wanted to cross the Columbia Bar early in the day for some salmon fishing. After breakfast, *Miss Charlie* took off like a scared rabbit while we meandered downstream, finally arriving in the vicinity of Megler about noon.

Before us, stretching across the great Columbia, was the newly-constructed bridge that connects Astoria with Megler and the entrance to the Olympic Peninsula. Arriving at Astoria, which was established in 1811 as a fur-trading post, we turned downstream. We passed under the new bridge and soon approached Skipanon Slough, the entry to Warrenton Yacht Basin. The basin is a colorful harbor with lumber mills, fish boats, canneries and many excellent marinas. It is the base of the annual sportfishing and charter fleets that cross the bar for the well known silver and chinook salmon. Warrenton is also the home of Oregon's only whaling station. The town is closeby and offers a complete source for food, clothing, ice, restaurants and banks. Summer cottages and golfing are relatively close as is Seaside, a favorite ocean resort community.

Hendricksons is probably the most complete marina in the harbor, with marine goods, repair shops, boatways and fuel. Several other waterside fuel stations are available, all offering excellent facilities and service.*

Just down river is Hammond. Located below the Coast Guard station, they now have excellent launching facilities. A protected moorage with floats is being added by the men of the business community. It will provide a much needed marina facility for the growing fleet of sportfishermen.

We then pointed east for Astoria. I had promised Bettye we would have dinner at least one night ashore at a place of her choice. Having listened to some tempting radio advertising promoting the Seafare Restaurant, she decided this was the place for her night out. The Seafare is located on the dock directly above the Astoria public boat slips and is very beautiful. The food, cocktails and service are excellent. The Seafare features many fine water color and oil paintings of this colorful area.

About 0730 the next morning, we left Astoria and headed upstream planning to go around Tongue Point and cruise the inland waterway via Prairie Channel. Upon an ebb tide, we passed the pilot boat exchanging pilots on a seagoing vessel and entered John Day Channel. Before us lay row upon row of ships anchored bow to stern. Their dark gray hulls, silhouetted against the sun and haze, gave us the impression of a floating city with their towering structures and masts. These are combat ships of World War II

carefully "mothballed" and ready for any world emergency.

Moving on we checked channel markers and periodically referred to our depth finder. In spite of the low tide, we found the depth to be very acceptable while cruising both Prairie and Clifton Channels. In one or two locations where the situation may have been marginal, high tide would have resolved the problem very simply.

For the individuals who enjoy solitude this entire area offers complete seclusion. There is a great abundance of wildlife, interesting flora and excellent opportunities for photography, fishing and even the recording of bird calls.

Upon clearing Tenasillahe Island we proceeded up the main stream passing Puget Island on our port side and Wauna on our starboard. Wauna is the site of the new Crown Zellerbach paper mill which will make a very welcome contribution to the economic development of the area.

Above Pancake Point on Puget Island the ferry was seen carrying passengers and cars to Westport. We chose Westport Slough as our moorage for the evening. The waters were placid and the scenic outlook breathtaking. The coastal range with its fleecy evening fog banks, is covered with large stands of fir timber extending almost to the water's edge. The evening was delightful as large clouds shaped themselves into castles, faces and other formations. The warm reddish tones of the setting sun brought to a close another pleasant day.

Tuesday morning we arose to a sun-filled cabin. Leaving Westport Slough regretfully, we slowly poked *Pu-Kii's* bow towards the Portland Yacht Club. We noted a fuel dock at the Puget Island ferry dock in passing. Our trip was uneventful as we moved along against the river current. We stopped at Rainier for a short shopping stint. Gas is available on the public floats. With enough gas on board we moved towards St. Helens.

Upon arriving at St. Helens we refueled and filling our water tanks, we moved into high gear for the first time since leaving nearly a week previously. Passing many of the familiar landmarks we hugged Sauvies Island enjoying the colorful umbrellas protecting the fishermen and their families from the sun and evening breezes.

Home was almost in sight as we passed the mouth of the Willamette River. Minutes later we again glided under the Interstate bridge and shortly after entered our boat house at the Portland Yacht Club.

We had cruised about 250 miles during our week's expedition. We used approximately 70 gallons of water and slightly less than 200 gallons of gasoline. We experienced no mechanical malfunctions of equipment at any time.

We enjoyed the pleasures and privacy of many fine anchorages. Weather throughout was excellent. The scenery and sunsets were spectacular. And we had the great pleasure of making many new friends. The people we talked to and questioned about their communities were informative and congenial. Many went out of their way to be of help.

We are already planning new cruises and explorations of the Columbia River. The Columbia country and its waterways offers some of the finest cruising to be found anywhere.

This is now the Skipanon Marina.

55

Bridge of the Gods

by Gary Pfingsten

In keeping with the old thought that the most cherished things often come in small packages, it frequently seems that the smaller cruises often provide more enjoyment and closer friendships...giving many hours of enjoyable post-cruise conversation and recollection.

A Columbia River Cruise is a great source of enjoyment, good river cruising, whether one goes forth in a super safari, attracting 80 boats from one yacht club (I've seen it myself!), or in a small pocket-party.

One such small cruise was plotted through the Bonneville Locks with myself as cruise director. My boat *L'Argo* was still in drydock as cruise time neared, having her chine replaced. At the going rate of work there was no hope of having her ready in time for the cruise...and fellow members of the Northwest Outboard Trailer Sailors seemed somewhat less than amused at the idea of a cruise director with no boat.

So, *April 27,* we set out to borrow a boat for the weekend cruise. Norm Jones of Jantzen Beach Marina was sympathetic to our plight and offered the loan of a 26-foot stern-drive Tollycraft. The cruise director was reinstated and ready for the adventure.

April 29 — We made preparations for an early start Saturday morning, moving the Tolly from Jantzen Beach up to Tyee Yacht Club to eliminate that slow, slow run through the Oregon Slough. The cruise we were leading was to begin at 1000 hours from the launching ramp at Corbett Landing, just below Rooster Rock and Crown Point. The disadvantage of a larger cruiser in a mobile club is sometimes keenly felt — although we had more room aboard, we had to pay for it with an early start for the 17-mile run to Corbett.

(Our original intention was an afternoon departure on Friday, a lazy evening run to Gary Island and a restful night spent at Peanut Point; we go on the river to relax, and not to fight with crowded schedules. When the First Mate became indisposed, however, a change of plans was indicated and an old friend, Mac McElroy, agreed to join us.)

April 30 — In the words of the popular song, "What a day this has been!" The bunk felt good tonight.

We took our departure from TYC late, as always — our friends generally introduce the Skipper as "The Late Mr. Pfingsten" — since we had more gear to stow than we had planned. However, we had left a generous time allowance in our plans since the Tolly was not yet broken in and could not be run at full throttle; we found that even a conservative setting gave us a better speed than we had hoped for, and arrived at Corbett five minutes early, at 0955.

This was one of the smallest club cruises either Mac or the Skipper had been on; only two other boats met us at Corbett, and we saw no one else all day. Our cruise companions were Ray and Julia Bowcutt and family aboard the 20-foot *Whatacrew,* and our newest members Earl and Jan Ruby aboard the 17-foot *Ruby I.* This was the *Ruby I's* first cruise with us, and she solved one problem that had us worried. A borrowed 26-foot cruiser is not the ideal craft for gunkholing; since *Ruby I* carried both radio and depth sounder, she would enter the unfamiliar coves first to check for depth, sandbars, etc.

We left Corbett promptly at 1000 hours, heading up through the scenic Columbia River Gorge. To port, the sheer rock wall of Cape Horn drops straight into the river — giant gray lava formations shaped by wind and water into a fantastic colonnade. This is a good place to follow the channel closely; we did so, passing between the colonnade and Phoca Rock, then following the ranges past Multnomah Island to clear Fashion Reef.

To starboard, along the Oregon shore, we could see where inconsequential streams, reaching the edge of the Gorge, suddenly leap into space in a bid for recognition, creating the picturesque falls for which the area is famous — Latourelle, Bridal Veil, Multnomah, Horsetail.

From here we could already see the imposing mass of Beacon Rock, the world's second largest monolith, exceeded only by Gibraltar; on earlier cruises we carried the Trailer Sailor burgee to the top of its 840-foot height, but today our convoy stopped only long enough for lunch.

From Beacon Rock to Bonneville Dam is only a short step, but an interestnig and scenic one. Along the bank are scattered the remains of ancient fish wheels, now illegal, and the stretch is a favorite with fishermen. Indian relics are to be found on Pierce and Ives islands, and farther upstream one can see Tanner Creek and the entrance to the fish ladder at Bonneville.

Since the *Ruby I* had called the locks on the radio before we left Beacon Rock, we arrived to find the gates open and waiting for us. We ran a line from the Tolly's midships cleat to a floating bitt, put out fenders bow and stern for protection against the concrete wall, and took the *Ruby I* alongside. Meanwhile *Whatacrew* had chosen the bitt across from us; having no midships cleat available, the skipper moored the stern to the bitt while the mate took a boathook onto the foredeck and snagged the rung of a ladder.

Then the fun began. As soon as the lift started, the *Whatacrew's* position revealed two disadvantages. One, the bitt her skipper had chosen was directly over the water inlet; two, the ladder which the first mate was holding was fixed, requiring her to change rungs as the water rose. When she missed one hold, the force of the water from the inlet swung the bow out. As the rest of us watched helplessly from the opposite side of the lock, shouting conflicting advice, Ray and Julia battled to keep their motor from being crushed against the concrete wall.

Reaching any sort of hold from the bow was impossible; a line hurriedly run from the bow to the floating bitt proved equally unhelpful, while holding the boat off by main strength was out of the question. Ray found the answer — quickly ordering Julia off the foredeck, he put the engine in gear and opened the throttle; since the stern was still secured, the bow swung in nicely, striking the rubrail against the wall. As the bow struck, Ray cut the engine, seized the boathook and sprang to the foredeck to recover their hold on the ladder; he missed by inches as the bow swung out again.

Once again the same remedy was tried; this time, with the engine left in gear to hold the bow in place, the lift was completed without further incident.

Leaving the lock, we once more gave our attention to the scenery, which is magnificent here. For about two miles above the dam the river is narrow and deep; the charts show more than 100 feet in places. This is the site of the Bridge of the Gods, the natural rock arch spanning the Columbia, which plays so large a part in Indian legend. Today, instead of a legendary arch, the yachtsman passes under a Bridge of the Gods created by architects, a graceful, silver-lattice-work structure just below Cascade Locks.

After passing the bridge, we explored the old lock which was used by steamboats to bypass the Cascade Rapids before the days of Bonneville Dam. The lock is now a favorite fishing spot, and we cruised with impunity over the rapids, for the rocks and the steep drop are hidden under a thick blanket of water tacked up behind Bonneville Dam.

We had chosen two possible overnight moorages on our charts, and proceeded to explore them. Sending the *Ruby I* ahead, we entered Rock Cove on the Washington side, seeking a protected spot with space on shore for a bonfire. A couple of pleasant spots presented themselves, but none with the protection we wanted from the west wind which was now kicking up. Government Cove, on the Oregon side, showed even less promise of getting ashore, and after a hasty conference we set our course downriver again to Eagle Creek, just half a mile above Bonneville.

Here in the throat of the Columbia Gorge we found the west wind strong enough to make our boat drift up-current as we waited for the *Ruby I* to investigate the creek entrance. To the east of the creek, the water is shallow for some distance from shore; we noticed the *Whatacrew* drifting into the shallows, and turned on the loud-hailer to warn her skipper of the danger. Before we could shout, however,

Ruby I (foreground) and Whatacrew pass the Bridge of the Gods on their way back to Eagle Creek

we saw him rapidly tilting up the motor, which had stalled and would not start. He fended the drifting boat off several rocks until it reached shore, then tied to a tree and set to work repairing the motor while we conferred with the Rubys on a rescue procedure.

The Tolly couldn't move in close enough to heave a line, so we dropped our hook, then passed the spare anchor rode to the *Ruby I*. She worked in close enough to heave the line to the *Whatacrew*, then backed out of the way. Ray took the line, belayed it to his boat cleat and went back to work on the motor; Mac and the Skipper heaved in on the line, pulling the *Whatacrew* out to us.

At least, that was the plan! After a moment it was clear that as the line was heaved in, the Tolly was moving steadily toward shore, dragging her anchor. A few minutes of fast work brought the anchor up and got the engine started; we pulled out a safe distance, anchored again, and this time succeeded in bringing *Whatacrew* almost alongside. Ray had meanwhile been working on his motor, and now it started. Calling out his thanks, he promptly cast off our line; just as promptly, the motor died again and the *Whatacrew*, already out of reach of a heaving line from our anchored Tolly, drifted back toward shore again.

Rescue duty once more fell on our new member. Catching the casualty just short of the shallows, *Ruby I* brought her back to lie alongside the Tolly until the motor was repaired. Then, having proved themselves valuable cruising companions, the Rubys led the way into Eagle Creek where we found a pleasant spot to moor and room for a bonfire.

The water here is clear and quiet, without a ripple, and we were protected against wind from any direction. The bank is steep and overgrown with trees and bushes, but enough clear space remains for a picnic, and the youngsters in the party received permission to spend the night ashore in their sleeping bags.

As the Skipper was writing the log, a tug boiled past in the river channel, throwing a high wake straight into the

Cape Horn's colonnade provides an imposing backdrop for two small boats bound up the Columbia River

creek mouth. The bow of the Tolly had been moored against a large rock, for use as a boarding platform, and all hands rushed to fend off. As the wake passed under the highway and railroad bridges which cross the creek mouth, however, it collapsed with a roar like ocean breakers, and scarcely a ripple reached the boats. There is protection!

May 1 — Some of the crew members had to be home by afternoon, so we left Eagle Creek early. The clearness of the water there is amazing; even more so is the sharp line of demarcation between creek and river, as definite as if it were drawn with a knife. The water of the Columbia is cloudy at best, yet in the creek mouth we could see every pebble on the bottom. As we left, passing under the bridges, we were suddenly in murky water as though some unseen hand had drawn a shade across a window.

Yesterday the *Whatacrew's* motor seemed fiendishly inspired; today it was merely stubborn. As we circled, waiting for the lock to open, the motor quit for the day, but the rescue operation seems hardly worth mentioning after yesterday's circus. *Ruby I* was closer, so she towed *Whatacrew* into the lock where we took both boats alongside the Tolly.

After a brief discussion, it was agreed that *Ruby I* would tow *Whatacrew* downstream to the nearest launching ramp, at Dodson, while the Tolly took Julia and some of the crew back to Corbett to pick up the truck and trailer.

We made arrangements for a rendezvous, and after dropping our passengers off at Corbett, we anchored at Reed Island to await the *Ruby I*. When she arrived, we celebrated her successful towing job by cleaning out our respective larders for lunch; then the two boats separated again, each heading for home port.

A challenge to hikers and lazy skippers, Beacon Rock looms up over the bow rail.

210

56

Where Rolls the Mighty Columbia

by Ed Goetzl

With pleasure boating—as with anything else— what is familiar is easy, fun and safe. What is unfamiliar is difficult, questionable and perhaps dangerous.

An old-time boater in Seattle or Vancouver, for example, wouldn't hesitate much to take off for almost any of the San Juan islands. Likewise, a veteran Portland boater would give hardly a second thought to heading his craft up or down the Columbia River to one of the beautiful white sand beaches lining the river's banks and islands — or even heading a hundred miles down the mighty river to Astoria just for a cruise or to pursue the big salmon on either side of the Columbia entrance.

Fortunately, more and more adventuresome pleasure boaters — buoyed up with Power Squadron and Coast Guard Auxiliary training and barricaded behind some first-class, workable navigation equipment — are getting out of their backyard ponds and exploring the excitement of strange waters.

This shifting attitude of skippers is truly fortunate for several reasons. Today, pleasure boaters seek newer ways to use their relatively expensive and cruisable toys. They are gradually becoming attuned along with the old salts to finding new adventures—adding more track, tunnels, signals and switches to this sea-going electric train system.

Familiarization is the thing. Familiarization with new boating waters.

One of the least publicized major pleasure boating waterways in the nation is the Columbia River. In this, the river is part of that thing called a last frontier.

Most persons probably know that the Columbia is the largest river in the western United States, one of the largest, actually, in the world. But "largest" is a relative term. The river's size and function don't readily come into focus. Its position clears somewhat viewed through the statistic that more waterborne dry cargo moves through the Port of Portland than through any other port on the Pacific Coast. The Columbia is a wide and long navigable river with several navigable tributaries. And all these streams are beautiful, safe pleasure boating waters.

Heart of Portland, center of Columbia River navigation, is 88 miles up the river from the Pacific and 9 miles up the Willamette River, largest tributary of the Columbia.

The city has commercial and pleasure boating facilities on both the Columbia and Willamette, with about 30 miles of cruising waters through the center and along one boundary of the city. Weekend cruises in the city are common—complete with fishing, camping, swimming, beach parties and the like.

There probably are 30,000 to 40,000 pleasure boats in the Greater Portland area, but the waters are not crowded. And, taking the full navigable (without portage) length of the Columbia and its tributaries, waters handling boats up to 65 feet, the expanse is downright lonesome.*

Portland generally is considered to be near the head of the lower navigable Columbia. From Portland to The Dalles Dam, about 80 miles, might be called the middle navigable Columbia. And from The Dalles Dam to Richland, Wash., another 125 miles, is the upper navigable river.

In addition, it now is possible for large pleasure boats to go up the Snake River 34 miles to the site of the Lower Monumental Dam.° Such boats also can go up the Willamette 74 miles to Salem, capital city of Oregon. At high water they also can run up the Cowlitz River about 5 miles to Kelso, Wash.; up the Lewis River about 6 miles to Woodland, Wash.; at flood, up the Sandy about 5 miles; and up Wind River a few miles. Smaller pleasure boats can push these limits considerably farther.†

Moreover, the Columbia has Prairie Channel; Cathlamet Channel; North Portland Harbor; and a dozen or so other interesting alternate navigable channels and sloughs. And the Willamette has its 19-mile-long Multnomah Channel and some shorter alternate channels.

All-in-all, the Columbia and its tributaries offer more than 500 miles of safe, fun-type cruising. That means more than 1,000 miles of shoreline. And each side of these rivers is highly individual and interesting. The rivers meander or rush through thickly forested, barren, populated and isolated areas and have both precipitous and sloping shores.

So when we talk about the Columbia River as a cruising

°Lower Monumental Dam will be completed sometime in 1969.

*These figures are only a fraction of today's boating population in the area.
†With the completion of the Lower Granite Lock and Dam in 1975, there is navigation to Lewiston, Idaho, 120 miles above the mouth of the Snake River.

waterway, we are talking about pleasure boating waters with tremendous expanse and variety — a waterway, really, which in passing through three states brushes most of the geology, geography and social culture of the Western United States.

Much western history still lies relatively unspoiled along the route, but also there is considerable evidence of the greatest forces the contemporary world has unleashed in the name of progress.

Here is the heart of world atomic power development. Here is the early center of hydro-electric power, with several of the world's largest dams. Here are huge and beautiful bridges and tremendous highway, town and railroad relocation projects, both completed and abuilding. Here is the center of the world's greatest commercial forest area. Here are the remains of the once fabulous, but not dead salmon industry. Here is the cradle of western democracy.

History the region's got — history and a natural geographic beauty that would keep an eager and inquisitive boating family hopping with pleasure for a long time. And a lot of all this richness can best be enjoyed by boat.

Astoria waterfront, rich in atmosphere, covers a wide area. Center background shows Tongue Point, with protected Prairie Channel running off to right. Public boat basin is at lower left.

Here the mighty Columbia flows through portion of famous Columbia Gorge a few miles above Portland. Beach at lower left is Rooster Rock State Park, which on sunny weekends becomes the Coney Island of Oregon.

Here are a few seeds of thought for those who want to get the most from cruising in the region and who this year might plan to open the locks to new adventures in pleasure boating.

Much of the Columbia offers year-around cruising, but best months along any of its stretches are from June through October. The fall is particularly good.

Accommodations of every sort are available within comfortable running distances — service, launching, repairs, housing, club facilities, night life, land transportation, fishing and skiing spots, the works.

The region has both highly civilized and very remote and isolated areas within less than a day's run of each other. Camping or sleeping aboard is no problem in the center of towns or along sandy beaches or in the sage brush and desert isolation of the upper Columbia and Snake.

The full 335 mile run from the Pacific up the Columbia

and Willamette to Portland and thence on up the Columbia and Snake to Lower Monumental Dam site and return can be made in a two-week vacation period with comparative ease.

The entire route is charted, well marked and relatively safe for any skipper who can read charts and run ranges and follow buoys.

The Columbia, like any large body of water — it's five miles wide in some sections — can and does get rough, real rough during a blow. But by following directions and by getting local information and using good boating sense, few skippers with seaworthy boats would run into serious problems anywhere along the waterway.

To every skipper comes the desire one day to try his craft in the Big Water.

"Big Water" doesn't necessarily refer to the ocean. In the thinking of a boater the term usually is associated with the most challenging, the most dramatic and generally, to him, the least-known piece of water in which he can wet his hull.

Usually, a skipper doesn't prefer the water too rough; but if it offers a challenge, that's all to the good. The water must be somewhat unfamiliar so that a skipper can do some big dreaming and thus double his fun. The water must have strong natural attractions — scenery, beaches and the like — to capture the skipper's eye. It must have many man-made "dives" and service facilities to answer a skipper's desire for association with other persons who have portholes in their heads.

To western boaters the Big Water should be the Pacific. No skipper who has run a pleasure boat off the coast of California, Oregon or Washington can fathom how Magellan ever pulled the name *Pacific* out of the mists to describe the 70 million square miles of water between the American continents and Asia and Australia. There was a man with real big portholes in his head! But the bodies of water emptying into the Pacific or funneling off the up and down movements of that great ocean do provide excellent fun waters for family cruising.

As a major, there is the Columbia River, one of the great boating rivers of the world. Here is a waterway with 1000 miles of shoreline whose natural allure and variety are hard to beat. The mates, too, can take to the Columbia without many reservations.

This is the story of the lower Columbia from the river

bar to Portland. Size-wise, here is the big part of the river — eight miles wide in one spot and having a 38-foot channel to the sea. This is the stretch of river with numerous islands that nestle clean white sand beaches onto which even big pleasure boats can have their bows pushed up and on for safe, overnight stops. This is the stretch of river plowed by thousands of boaters during the spring and fall salmon runs each year in pursuit of the stream-lined Silvers and chunky Chinooks. This is the heavy traffic section of the river. But it still is uncrowded.

What should a pleasure boater, new to the region, expect to find?

There are three ways to get to this stretch of the Columbia: run down through the locks at dams on the upper and mid-river areas; come into the river over the Columbia Bar from the ocean; trailer (or ship) a boat to Portland or one of the many other spots in which the craft can be put into the water. Such facilities are everywhere.

Let's begin our cruise of the lower Columbia at Portland, 97 miles up the rivers from the Columbia Bar.

The Willamette River is navigable for big ships from where it joins the Columbia for nine miles into Portland. And for some pleasure craft it is usable for about 74 miles to Salem, state capital of Oregon.

There are half a dozen public moorages within 3½ miles of the city's center, two of them with fine restaurants. Up the river 14 miles is Oregon City with its falls, navigation locks and rich historic background. Much of the city perches on high cliffs which rise precipitously in steps from the water. On one cliff is the big white house which once was the home of John McLoughlin, famed Hudson's Bay factor. It is a rewarding experience to leave the boat at one of the Oregon City moorages and walk the streets of the historic town.

The Willamette wanders on its way from Oregon City to Portland through some fine residential areas. Lawns and rock gardens slope down to the water's edge. There are gravel beds in this stretch of river, so charts should be carefully followed.

Portland's harbor area generally is lined with freighters from many countries. The view of the city from the water has pulling power.

A good spot to tie up overnight in Portland is at the

Fishermen's Dock in Astoria, near mouth of Columbia — a snug place to tie up.

Harbor Patrol dock. This public dock is free for use by anyone for a 24-hour period, or longer in special cases. The walks are wide and clean, electricity and water are available. A ramp leads to the heart of the city — only a ten-minute walk to the town's shops and night life.

If the lower Columbia cruise is to begin and end in the Portland area, the first day's run from the city probably should be upriver as far as Multnomah Falls, about 28 miles above the mouth of the Willamette. Or, if later Columbia cruising is not to include the midsection of the river, run all the way to Bonneville Dam, 38 miles above the confluence of the Columbia and Willamette.

A run to Bonneville and return is a good day's cruise for any boat. There are, however, several good islands in this stretch to duck behind for the night. Beacon Rock, about 3½ miles downriver from Bonneville, is a cozy harbor. Arthur Lake, about seven miles downriver is another possibility, but don't go far inside. The northwestern portion of Reed Island is a favorite overnight spot. At Reed, come in from downriver side slowly and watch the chart and depth sounder.

There is a fine marina at Parker Landing between Camas and Washougal, Wash., which offers various services. Fuel and other services also are available at Corbett Station on the Oregon shore just off the eastern end of Reed Island.

It is assumed that no skipper would run these waters without up-to-date charts. C&GS chart No. 6156-57 (one chart printed on both sides) covers the Columbia from Vancouver to The Dalles, Ore.

Main navigation aids on the Columbia are ranges and the traditional red and black buoys. Columbia ranges are two square white boards, one behind the other and at different heights, with each one having a single vertical red stripe through the center. These stripes are lined up, one over the other, when the center channel is held. Some ranges are read forward and others aft. They are a little tricky to follow until mastered, but then they are excellent to keep a skipper out of trouble.

Anyone who can read a chart and follow it would have little difficulty staying out of navigation troubles along any stretch of the Columbia. The river is well marked and aids regularly maintained.

The Columbia between Vancouver and Bonneville seldom gets extremely rough. A west wind in late afternoon can kick up some white stuff, but no one usually is going very far.

For skippers who like to duck into marinas and yacht clubs, eat and drink at waterside restaurants and bars or turn the kids loose in parks, the Portland-Vancouver area is a natural. There are more than 50 miles of accessible shoreline in the Portland area, dotted with all types of service facilities. And visiting boaters will find the natives very friendly and helpful.

Heading downriver from the Portland area, first stop should be St. Helens, Ore., 13 miles below the mouth of the Willamette. The city has a good public dock in front of its picturesque courthouse. A stroll up into town is well worth the few minutes it takes.

About 12 miles below St. Helens is Kalama, Wash., another interesting stopping place. Fuel, supplies and services of all types are available at both communities.

About six miles below Kalama is Rainier, Ore., which also has a good public dock and facilities. On the Washington side are Longview and Kelso, but the cities can be reached by boat only by running five miles up the Cowlitz River, a passable but somewhat tricky stream to navigate during low water.

If the skipper wants to spend a night behind an island in this area, an excellent spot is along the Oregon shore behind Walker and Lord Islands, a half-dozen miles below Rainier. Come in behind the islands from the downriver side, around red buoy ten, for easy access.

The lower Columbia has tidal action all the way to Vancouver and Portland — about a two-foot tide at Vancouver and gradually getting larger all the way down the river. So in tying up along a beach, allow for tidal rise and fall. Best program is to drop a stern anchor as you move slowly onto the beach, bow first. The bow line then can be played out or pulled in from the shore to compensate for tidal movement.

Another factor to watch is the wake or surge caused by ships passing in the main channel. A stern anchor with adequate scope usually will handle this problem.

There are numerous islands between Rainier and Cathlamet, Wash., about 25 miles downriver; and most of them provide good protection for a short or long stop. Most of the various sloughs running off the main channel behind the islands are navigable with careful checking of charts.

In addition to large public moorages along most stretches of the lower Columbia, there are also many small private docks — such as this one below St. Helens, Oregon — which are interesting to visit and which could be a haven in case of necessity.

The Columbia in this area can kick up, not seriously in most cases, but in a strong wind choppy enough to necessitate taking the glasses off the drainboard. Best chances of smooth water are in the early morning hours. In summer, a wind generally springs up in mid-afternoon.

Cathlamet is the last easy spot to pick up fuel or supplies until reaching Astoria, about 14 miles farther downriver. However, if necessary or if a skipper has time and enjoys historic riverfront atmosphere, he can run into Skamokawa, about six miles below Cathlamet.

Don't worry about leaving the main channel to run into Cathlamet Channel. There is plenty of water, but a skipper needs to watch the chart. There are some shallow spots just below Cathlamet on which careless operators have run aground.

The nine-mile stretch of water between Harrington Point and Astoria gives many skippers the willies. Here the river and contiguous bays provide more or less open water eight miles wide and over 20 miles long. A strong wind from almost any direction will cause chop, and when the wind is blowing against the tide, it can get real

sloppy. On the other hand, the nine-mile run into Astoria can be very gentle.

Thing to do is prepare for rough stuff and relax when it doesn't show. Big consolation is that the run is short.

The range and marker system from Harrington Point into Astoria is somewhat confusing. Sand spits are all around. So skippers are advised to go slowly until they know, through reference to the chart and markers, exactly where they are. The channel is well marked, but the range and buoy system must be followed closely.

In case of a real blow when a skipper doesn't want to lay to behind a protecting island, one good out is to duck into Prairie Channel by crossing the main Columbia channel after leaving Cathlamet and running in behind Tenasillahe Island and Welch Sands (on island) and continuing on down the Oregon shore into John Day Channel around Tongue Point into Astoria.

This Prairie Channel route is favored by tugs moving log rafts and such and wanting protection from the wind. The route also is picturesque — rather tricky but not rough to run provided adequate attention is given the chart. It is especially recommended for an upriver run on a very windy day.

Astoria is a delightful waterfront town. Great to explore. It has two protected public docks — one, Fishermen's Dock, near the downtown area, has about as much salty atmosphere as any skipper could desire, also a good restaurant and bar.

Entrance to the dock is a little difficult to find. It is at the lower end of town; so move along the waterfront until the big buildings of the port terminal and fish cannery are spotted and then look for the "go slow" sign on the breakwater projecting out from the entrance. If there are a lot of boats inside, that's the spot. Select any unfilled mooring space and check with office on the dock for place to tie during your stay.

Astoria has a fine Maritime Museum of artifacts from the entire Columbia basin historic years. The Museum is at 16th and Exchange Streets, still growing, and features extremely fine models of early-day riverboats, boating and bits and pieces from maritime lore. The exhibit is well presented, and, the Lightship *Relief* is in juxtaposition to the museum for boarding and viewing.

Warrenton, Ore., about three miles nearer the ocean than Astoria, also has fine mooring and service facilities. And across the river behind Cape Disappointment is Ilwaco, Wash., with facilities to handle around 700 boats.

This section of the Columbia, near its mouth, is the big river area — two to eight miles wide, but dotted with sand spits. So, again, careful attention to the chart and the buoy and marker system is a *must*.

In this region almost full ocean tidal forces prevail, so one doesn't give way to a temptation to put a boat's bow on the beach.

Tidal currents, although noticeable in the area inside the Columbia Bar, give no particular worry except near jetties and the bar itself. It is considered extremely hazardous for pleasure boats to attempt crossing the bar during the last hour or two of an ebb tide. Runoff in area of the two jetties protecting the river entrance reaches seven knots or more at times. Wind working against the runoff causes a very nasty situation.

If a skipper wants to cross the bar just for kicks, recommended time is slack time — particularly slack following an ebb. Incoming tide then will give a lift on the run back in.

The Columbia Bar is not always as tough as generally assumed. But it can be, and even fatal. *Know* what you are doing. Thousands of fishermen in small boats cross it every day during the good August and September salmon runs. But these waters are not to play with. And except for the thrill of having done it and value as a talk piece, crossing the Columbia Bar isn't the sort of thing to suggest for general family fun.

But cruising around from Warrenton to Ilwaco to Astoria can be great fun, and it provides the feel of big water without the smash-bang force of the ocean to combat. This is truly a salty area and worthy of much more cruising traffic than it gets — particularly in the late summer and early fall.

Pleasure boats coming into the Columbia from other ports should try to make the crossing as near slack tide as possible. Again, a flooding is better than ebbing tide. Fighting the river runoff is no sport. If water is breaking over the bar, no boat should try to run in until things simmer down.

The run upriver? If a skipper is in no great hurry, there are enough navigable channels and sloughs to provide a different route from that used going downriver for a considerable portion of the run back to Portland. Running these alternate channels is a fine way to come to know the mighty lower Columbia.

The section of the Columbia River with the greatest potential for pleasure boating is the 205-mile stretch between Portland, Oregon, and Richland, Washington. And that is a sentence so loaded with understatement that it hardly makes sense.

The Columbia River and its major tributaries, the Willamette and Snake Rivers — about 1000 miles of shoreline from the mouth of the Columbia to Lower Monumental damsite on the Snake — unquestionably is one of the great pleasure boating regions of the world. But, as everywhere else, the people who live in the region hardly recognize what they have in their front harbor.

The Mediterranean, the Aegean, the Caribbean all have charms which drive a cruise-happy pleasure boater right out the portholes in his head. Puget Sound, the San Juans

and Canadian Gulf Islands, likewise, stir a skipper's heart into a fast beat. But any man who has cruised all these waters will come back to the Columbia River and its tributaries with appreciation and respect. These are pleasure boating waters with less immediate dramatic appeal than the Caribbean and without the delectable oysters and clams of the Canadian Gulf Islands. But for the Sunday boater who has at best a 48-hour cruise in which he would like to relax by pulling the bow of the old tub onto a clean sand beach and pushing the kids overboard, you just can't beat the Columbia and its tributaries.

The 97-mile stretch of the Columbia from Portland to the Pacific Ocean is loaded with fine white-sand-beached islands, as is the 38-mile section from Portland to Bonneville Dam. The mid- and upper-Columbia from Bonneville to Richland, Wash., has few comfortable islands or sloughs into which a large pleasure boat can safely pull for the night. But there are sufficient night tieup spots; and the attractions which this 205-mile stretch of the Columbia offer are great enough to entice any boater who likes adventure.

For a new or old boater on the Columbia, the run from Portland to Hood River is 60 miles of pure joy — provided it is made at the right time of day. The Columbia Gorge is one of the scenic wonders of the world; and until you've seen the Gorge from the river, you really haven't seen it.

Portland area boaters are a bit reluctant to make the run up the Columbia behind Bonneville Dam because they know the waters above the dam can become very rough. During the summer months, a west wind usually springs up between 10 and 11 a.m. By 4 p.m. the wind can whip the pool behind Bonneville into a whitecapped hell for boats under 30 feet. The chop is short and steep and relentless. Running up the river, you have the wind and wave movement with you, so things are not so bad. Coming down the Bonneville pool in late afternoon is wet. On our last run down in the 52-foot *The Living End*, we took spray over the 15-foot-high pilothouse windshield hour after hour.

Obviously the answer to this inconvenience is to run in the early morning hours and pull in for a full afternoon and evening of relaxed exploration and fun. This practice is recommended for every stretch of the Columbia from its mouth up.

There is no guarantee that the west wind will not blow in the morning. Roughest ride we ever had in the Bonneville pool was a few years ago on a three-day run from Lewiston, Idaho, down the Snake and Columbia to Ilwaco, Wash., near the Big River's mouth. This was in a 21-foot twin-powered outboard rig. We left Hood River shortly after daybreak with ominous black-grey clouds choking the Columbia Gorge. As soon as we cleared the breakwater protecting Hood River's fine relatively-new boat basin, the west wind hit us in the face; and that 21-footer was pounded and pushed for the full 22 miles to Bonneville Dam.

Generally, however, the westerly summer winds do not reach great intensity until mid-afternoon, so run in the mornings. The Columbia, like most waters, is most beautiful at sunrise and sunset anyway.

Of considerable concern for many boaters are the navigation locks along the Columbia and Snake. Today there are five locks in operation, four on the Columbia and one on the Snake. In the next 10 or 15 years there should be three more locks operating on the Snake, making it possible for pleasure boats to run all the way from the Pacific

Most persons do not realize the size of Willamette River in downtown Portland. Here heavy cruiser USS St. Paul is moving in to tie to seawall near heart of city during Portland Rose Festival activities early in June.

Ocean to Lewiston-Clarkston, about 120 miles from where the Snake joins the Columbia and 402 miles from the Pacific. When all eight Columbia and Snake dam locks are in operation, this 402-mile run from the sea will provide a pleasure boating paradise.

In full operation now on the Columbia are Bonneville, The Dalles and McNary locks and John Day locks are now completed. On the Snake, only Ice Harbor Dam- 10 miles from the river's mouth—is completed. However, Lower Monumental Dam, 34 miles up the Snake, is well along; so soon there should be smooth sailing in deep clear water for about 50 miles or so up the river.

The Columbia and Snake dam locks are some of the finest and highest in the world, all expertly operated for the convenience of pleasure boaters and all easy to navigate provided common sense and directions are followed.

No boater, old timer or newcomer to the Columbia, should try to run the river without purchasing and carefully reading *United States Coast Pilot 7*. This excellent book put out by the U.S. Coast and Geodetic Survey, in fact, should be the No. 1 purchase of any skipper using Pacific Coast waters. It sells for only $2.50 at any agent handling CG&S charts and is, among other things, a detailed supplement for such charts.*

It is assumed, of course, that no skipper will try to run the Columbia without new charts — and by "new" we mean charts for the current year. A year ago when *The Living End* apparently became the first large pleasure boat to run the upper Columbia and lower Snake without an experienced river pilot aboard, we had only "working charts" of the Snake; but today the Coast and Geodetic Survey has a fine Snake River chart available.

Getting back to *United States Coast Pilot 7,* what the book adds to chart information is detailed advice on proper signals to use in approaching or leaving locks, how to get through bridges over the river, what to look for in identifying land formations and what to expect in the way of navigation hazards and aids. As we said, no boater should try to run the mid- and upper-Columbia without having studied this book. You might, for example, never get through a bridge if your boat's mast is high above the water.

The book has detailed instructions on how to use the five locks on the Columbia and Snake; so we needn't labor that point. However, what boaters probably want is assurance that the locks will give them little embarrassment or trouble.

All five locks are single-rise. Only one tieup is necessary in each, but that tieup is important. Every skipper has his own way of doing things, but most find the easiest way to get through the locks is to have one end of a line secured to both bow and stern cleats. Bollards through all locks are the floating type. So, with bow and stern lines secured at one end, all that is required is to bring bollard amidships and toss each line over it, running bow line and stern line back as spring lines and securing at cleat suggested by size of boat. Adjustments may be made as needed. We have taken small boats through with single line running from bow to stern. Have plenty of fenders out and be prepared to hold boat off concrete sides of lock. Most common mistake made by skippers is to forget that water coming into the lock may exert considerable pressure as it hits the rear lock and moves against the boat's stern. The stern generally will give the most trouble.

Lock tenders will give instructions as to which side to tie; so come into locks slowly and watch for attendant along wall or listen for instructions over loudspeaker system. Don't get in a hurry. The locks are not going off without you.

In other words, none of the Columbia Basin system locks are anything to worry about. We have found that calling the locks on 2182 kc about half an hour before approaching and letting the lockmaster know our desires helps considerably. General conversation, of course, is not supposed to be carried in 2182 kc; but after raising the dam, you give and get instructions in about four sentences. †

So drop dam lockages from your mind as a cruising problem.

There are, however, a couple of major problems in running the mid- and upper-Columbia: rough water in the pools behind the dams when the wind is whistling and lack of comfortable tie-up spots for the night.

But neither of these problems are of the type to keep a boater home. Again, it's mainly a matter of applying common sense and seamanship

Problem No. 1 — Rough water in pools behind dams: run, as we said, at early morning. If conditions look really rough, stay in port. Force of the Columbia is not as relentless as that of the ocean, but it is powerful. Currents are the hazard, but it doesn't take an awake boater long to determine which way the water is running and react accordingly.

Problem No. 2 — Lack of comfortable tieup spots for the night: this really is no problem except for those throttle-happy persons who insist on asking their craft to do more in a day than is realistically possible.

First day's run from Portland should end at the boat basin in Hood River, regardless of size and speed of boat, if the skipper and crew are to relax and savor scenic attractions of the trip. Hood River is about the point where weather breaks away from the too-frequently grey overcast of the lower Columbia and gives the boater the heart-speeding force of warm sunshine.

It is worth the possible tribulations of a Columbia River run just to sit aboard in the Hood River boat basin and watch the late afternoon sun slant across the hills. Underwood Mountain off to the right, with its dry farms making a patchwork pattern on the eastern slope, is balm to a boater's soul. ‡

And don't fail to take a tour of the *USS Banning*, Hood River's war memorial ship. When we were there last, basin manager Ralph McDaniel and Mrs. McDaniel and their daughter Jean gave us the friendly royal tour, and we enjoyed every second of it.

Our recommended second night's stop is Miller Island, 10.5 miles above The Dalles Dam.

A look at the chart will show this island to be navigable on both sides. Take the left-hand channel going upriver and pull into the small cove on the upriver side. Stay in close to the cliff and anchor at the north edge of the small sand beach for best protection. Water shallows quickly south and east of the beach.

*The U.S. Coast Pilot sells for $6.00 and is updated annually.
†VHF Channel 16 has replaced 2182 kc.
‡The Port of Hood River has a new facility east of the old basin.
 The USS Banning is no longer there.

Good spot for a third night's tieup is the boat basin at Umatilla, 74 miles above Miller Island. Opening to the basin is rather small and located about 500 yards west of the highway bridge on the Oregon shore. Fuel and water are available, and operator Frank Garred probably will be happy to provide transportation into town if desired.*

There is a yacht club on the Oregon shore a short distance above McNary Dam at Umatilla, but Pasco and Kennewick are only about 35 miles above the dam and Richland 40; so the club probably would be left to a leisurely exploration of Lake Wallula, the pool behind McNary Dam.

The three cities of Kennewick, Pasco and Richland all are conscious of what the river means to them in way of recreational returns and are eager to make a pleasure boater' stay pleasant. Beacon Marina in Pasco Yacht Basin and Metz Marina back of Clover Island at Kennewick are two of the finest marinas along the Columbia. Sacajawea Boat Club and Tri-Cities Power Boat Association both call Desert Marina home, and members are happy to make visiting boaters comfortable. All types of services are available at marinas in the area.†

The 40-mile stretch of the Snake River from its mouth to the site of Lower Monumental Dam provides several comfortable and interesting spots to tie up. There are eight public marine park areas, five of them at Sacajawea State Park at the mouth of the Snake and three of them in Lake Sacajawea behind Ice Harbor Dam. The three are Levey, Fish Hook and Windust. C&GS Chart No. 682-SC is a must for every skipper running up the Snake, and it clearly indicates these recreation areas.

There are dozens of other coves and beaches in Lake Sacajawea that provide comfortable tieup for any size boat. Important thing to watch is the wind.

The day we chose to run up the Snake was hardly typical. We left the Beacon Marina at Pasco in a fairly sharp breeze. But by the time we reached the narrows at Burr Canyon, about 20 miles above Ice Harbor Dam, we could see a dust storm blowing in behind us.

The Snake really came alive. White caps cut deep furrows from shore to shore. And when we turned downstream after shooting colored pictures of Lower Monumental Dam construction, spray was flying over the pilot house as fast as it did when we hit rough water off the Columbia Bar.

The Snake, like the Columbia, the ocean or any body of navigable water, can be vicious. The weather changes quickly here. In a two-hour period, water can change from a beast to beauty. One does not soon forget the mad whitecaps nor the midnight solitude of a moon illuminating the hills, the rocks and the sand holding the Snake River in bounds.

It is rather startling to be awakened by a seagull screaming outside the cabin in the middle of a desert. It is equally startling to have come up through the desert by boat during a sand storm. But the 40-odd-mile stretch of the Snake from Pasco to the Lower Monumental damsite today is mostly an area of sagebrush, straw colored cheat grass, moving sands, rock and trains with far-away sounding whistles.

When we made the run last year, The Living End tied up two nights in an isolated spot we called Driftwood Cove, where we could have shot sagehens from the bow of the boat. In the relatively clear water of the Snake we could see two-foot fish swimming lazily alongside.

Like something out of Egypt — the lower gate of John Day Dam locks

It is not necessary, of course, for small boaters to make the run up the Columbia and Snake to use the waters. There are launching ramps of sorts at about every spot a road runs down to the river. At the Tri-Cities, at Sacajawea State Park, Levey, Fish Hook and Windust public ramps are maintained. Likewise, about every community on the Columbia from Portland to Pasco has a usable ramp. So a cruise of the mid- and upper-Columbia and lower Snake can start and end just about anywhere a skipper desires.

So, getting back to problem No. 2 — lack of comfortable tie-up spots for the night — the problem seems almost to have taken care of itself. But the point we want to make is that planning is necessary. There are places to tie up, but runs should be made to reach them at the right time of day. The upper Columbia most times of year runs too fast to permit a boater, even in a powerful, fast small boat, to pull in anywhere he chooses.

Charts show dozens of islands and coves and several communities between Bonneville Dam and the mouth of the Snake. Islands and communities along the shores or in the pools behind the dams have relatively quiet water; but those along open stretches of water are brushed hard by powerfully running river and generally do not provide a comfortable tie-up spot for boaters who lack local knowledge.

Formerly the 62-mile rapids area between John Day Dam and Umatilla was a problem that rightfully scared most skippers.

Ever have a nightmare involving climbing the Alps in a 52-foot boat? Well, taking The Living End from John Day Dam to Umatilla made such a nightmare become reality for us. Relatively few pleasure boats have made the run all the way from Portland up the Columbia and Snake; so far as is known The Living End is the only large pleasure boat to make the run without employing an experienced river pilot. Aboard were only the author and his first mate. But there never was any hint of real danger. The nightmare was the grueling slowness.

A skipper soon learns not to panic when he rides beside a buoy or rock for minutes without making progress. It took The Living End 11 hours, 45 minutes to cover 38 miles. For boaters familiar with the San Juan and Canadian Gulf Island area, running this stretch of the Columbia was like running Deception Pass, Dodd Narrows, Gabriola or Agete Pass for a 12-hour stint.

217

*Umatilla Marina at the south end of the Toll Bridge was completed in 1970 and offers complete facilities.
†Beacon Marina is no longer in existence.

The pull by water over the Cascade Range into Eastern Oregon is a long rough haul. There were eight tricky rapids in the 62 miles from John Day Dam to Umatilla. We still get a thrill at sound of names of Indian Rapids, Squally Hook Rapids, Rock Creek Rapids, Four O'Clock Rapids, Blalock Rapids, Owyhee Rapids, Canoe Encampment Rapids and Devils Bend Rapids. These names were real personalities for us and for any skipper who tried his skill in mastering them.

Ranges through the rapids generally were well defined, but they were tricky. They did not necessarily follow a clockwise progression. Range No. 3 through a rapid may be on a starboard tack, Range No. 4 on a port tack, and Range No. 5 on a starboard tack but with markers more to port than those used for Range No. 3. In other words, a skipper and his observer must have studied the range progression system for every rapid before entering. It took two people to run a boat every foot of the way through those 62 miles of rapids-filled waters. But with necessary preparation and with application of seamanship, running these rapids was a challenge exceedingly gratifying to meet—not relaxing, but gratifying.

It took *The Living End* more than 19 hours to make this 62-mile run into Umatilla from John Day Dam. That means the boat made good just over 3 knots; so the current was running faster than 4 knots average for the 62 miles. And that's moving! Running back downriver was easier than going up.

Actually, the water wasn't moving much faster in the rapids than in the open stretches. In one six-mile stretch of the Columbia between Rock Creek Rapids and Blalock Rapids, the river climbed ten feet. That is more than it climbs in the 88-mile stretch between the Pacific Ocean and Portland.

Completion of John Day Dam has now covered these eight rapids, and the nightmare of long hours of running in fast water has vanished. The 282-mile run from the mouth of the Columbia to the mouth of the Snake can hardly be called a breeze, but it is much more relaxing—as we think all cruising should be.

The question that most often has been asked us since we completed our 18-day run up and down the Columbia and lower Snake last year is, "Would you go back?"

Answer to that is, "At the first opportunity." It took considerable soul searching to determine that this year's extended cruise for *The Living End* would be north from the Columbia up into San Juan and Canadian waters rather than a return trip to the upper Columbia. And those who know the attractions of the San Juan and Canadian Gulf Islands readily can understand what power Columbia River cruising might possess.

One big question with all boaters in strange waters is, "How about facilities?"

The mid- and upper-Columbia, like the lower river, has everything any boater will need. Any boat can carry enough fuel and ice cubes to get from Portland or Washougal, Wash., to Hood River, from Hood River to The Dalles, from The Dalles to Umatilla and from Umatilla to Pasco or Kennewick. Precautions should be taken, however, to have ample fuel for that 62-mile slow run through the rapids from John Day Dam to Umatilla. *The Living End* almost doubled its hourly diesel fuel consumption on that run. It was like running a car in low gear for 19 hours.

Gasoline can be secured at Boardman, Ore., 84 miles above The Dalles Dam and at Biggs Junction, about 17 miles above the dam by running into the old Maryhill ferry landing and packing the fuel from a service station on the highway. Larger boats should have no trouble by fueling at the regular spots listed above. At The Dalles, fuel up at The Dalles Yacht Club, which has some fine facilities in behind a good breakwater.

Final word for those boaters who this year or in the future plan to make the very rewarding Columbia River cruise — completely or in part — get the area charts, a copy of *United States Coast Pilot 7* and all other printed information on the region, talk to people everywhere you pull in to get local information on where to go and what to see. The Columbia cruise then will be a standout in your pleasure boating life.

Navigating the Columbia, Willamette and Snake Rivers in spots is not easy, but neither is it dangerous. One great advantage over waters where tidal forces exert more pressure is that if the old tub conks out, you never are a great distance from a shore where an anchor can be tossed out to hold you until your panic subsides. Highways line the river banks, towns are seldom far away; so, despite the isolation the waters seem to give, you are never a pioneer in a wide world of Douglas fir, cliffs or sagebrush. If you have to, you always can walk home.

57
Alaska in a 17-footer

by Don de Forest

Cruising into Southeastern Alaskan waters on a small boat is adventure for which not everyone is suited. It is for those who love motor boating, who admire magnificent scenery, who have daring tempered by good sense and judgment. It is for those who willingly endure hardships. Most of all it is for people who take time enough to prepare conscientiously for their cruise.

Two of us went in a 17-foot Glasspar Sunliner (no cabin, no galley, no head, no bunks), launching at Campbell River and cruising 1750 miles, living aboard night and day.

We chose July and August because these are the months with least rainfall and calmest seas.

Tramp steamers, Canadian and Alaskan ferries, mailboats, innumerable commercial fishing vessels, ocean-going tugs with huge barges and many large pleasure boats navigate the Inside Passage. Most vessels which cross Queen Charlotte Sound, Dixon Entrance and other large bodies of water of the Inside Passage are 30 feet or more in length. The small boat operator may look upon a cruise in these waters as being formidable; but it is not impossible. The rewards are tremendous.

You *should* have some experience in salt water navigation. No amount of reading can prepare the fresh water sailor for the rise and fall of the tide or the currents produced by tidal flow in estuaries of the Inside Passage. To meet the challenge of the Inside Passage as captain of a small boat, you must have physical endurance. Salt air, wind, spray, wave motion and hours and hours of engine noise produce physical fatigue and mental strain.

The expanses of the Inside Passage require that you cover over a hundred miles each day if you are to complete a long cruise within the limits of a vacation of only a few weeks. This means you must be prepared for 12 to 15-hour days. Begin your voyage with six or eight-hour days and work up to the big ones. Expect to be exhausted at the end of each day. Don't attempt this trip unless you are cleared for such exertion by your physician. You will sleep magnificently, lulled to rest by the motion of your vessel as you lie at anchor or moored to a float.

The *Marine Atlas* (two volumes) by Morris, Heath and Berg is used by pleasure and commercial craft plying the Inside Passage. It provides information on interesting sights, government and private facilities, resorts, service stations and possible courses between harbors. You must spend hours and hours poring over these charts long before you set sail on your cruise.

The Hydrographic Office of the United States Navy publishes *Sailing Directions for British Columbia* (two volumes). This is available at marinas and navigation equipment dealers.

The United States Department of Commerce Coast and Geodetic Survey publishes *United States Coast Pilot 8* which covers from Dixon Entrance (where volume II of *Sailing Directions* leaves off) to Cape Spencer (all of southeastern Alaska). This is also available at navigation equipment dealers.

The prevailing summer westerlies sometimes blow all night but usually calm descends shortly after sunset on the Inside Passage and continues until midmorning. Brisk wave action becomes reestablished by noon or midafternoon on waters which have a western exposure. Johnstone Strait is one of many examples of such waters. Small craft should elect to cross such waters in the early morning when the weather forecast indicates fair weather with only light wind. For the small boat operator on the Inside Passage, the best hours for cruising are from daybreak until noon.

However, one rainy day will sometimes follow another during part of the summer. Because westerlies are fair weather winds, and rainfall is accompanied by southerly winds, timetables must be altered with the change of weather.

For safety and comfort you will wish to avoid rough water. It is well to study your charts so as to plan your movement over various bodies of water at times of day which are appropriate. Johnstone Strait and similarly oriented waters must be crossed early in the morning when the weather is fair because the westerlies make such waters rough in the afternoon.

Small boats should stay in port when the going is rough. If it is necessary to put to sea, do so only in the company of a vessel of 30 or 40 feet or larger. Do so with the approval and understanding of the master of that vessel and with the agreement that you will remain astern, taking advantage of the relatively smooth wake behind the larger

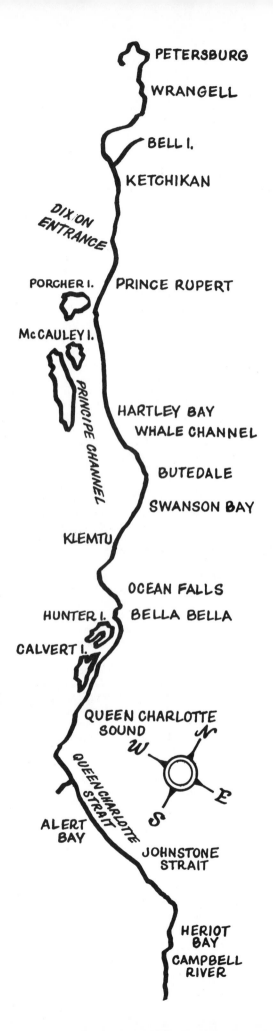

PETERSBURG

WRANGELL

BELL I.

KETCHIKAN

DIXON ENTRANCE

PORCHER I.   PRINCE RUPERT

McCAULEY I.

PRINCIPE CHANNEL

HARTLEY BAY
WHALE CHANNEL

BUTEDALE

SWANSON BAY

KLEMTU

OCEAN FALLS

HUNTER I.   BELLA BELLA

CALVERT I.

QUEEN CHARLOTTE
SOUND

QUEEN CHARLOTTE STRAIT

ALERT
BAY

JOHNSTONE
STRAIT

HERIOT
BAY
CAMPBELL
RIVER

craft. The higher bow and broader beam of the vessel you follow can make a temporary path of relative calm for you through the rough seas. Remain in his protection in this manner and he will be available to you for succor in case of mishap.

Engine failure can occur any time. It is more likely to occur in rough seas than in calm seas. Travel in the wake of a large vessel, when the sea is rough, can add to your comfort and your safety.

Study of your charts will help you select alternative routes when such are available. Every vessel going from Campbell River to Alert Bay must enter Johnstone Strait for part of its voyage but for other parts of that trip there are several alternative routes. Although these are longer, they do not expose you to the summer westerlies for long

Floating docks at Bell Island Hot Springs Resort, 50 miles from Ketchikan. Our small boat is docked on the far side behind the bending figure. Off to the right is a seaplane landing. Up the path above the ramp are numerous cabins and an Olympic-size swimming pool with piped-in water from the hot springs.

distances and therefore travel over the alternatives may be accomplished in a shorter period of time.

Similar alternatives are available in many parts of the Inside Passage. Another example is between Meyers Chuck and Wrangell, Alaska. A small boat can usually move more rapidly over the Eastern Passage route than over Clarence and Stikine Straits because the narrower channels give less exposure to westerlies.

Another point to study on your charts is current flow. Official Pacific Coast current books will give proper directions, high water and low water slacks and velocity of current.

This is important to you, if you are anxious to travel economically and speedily. You will want to be moving in the same direction as the tide as much of the time as possible because the tidal currents in these passages are often five knots per hour or more.

Remember the prevailing wind in fair weather is from the west. Because the wind is usually not strong before 1000 hours, movement of your vessel in the early morning will not be greatly affected by wind action. After 1000 hours, a westerly wind can produce very rough seas for small vessels when the westerly is blowing against the direction of the tide. An outgoing tide carrying water to the west, will be churned into a rough sea by wind blowing from the west. This is particularly true when funnel action is evident.

A west wind of 15 miles per hour, observed out over the ocean, may become a much stronger wind in a narrow strait with high canyon walls and a funnel mouth opening to the west.

Some bodies of water lead into the Inside Passage from the Pacific Ocean through canyon-like straits with cliffs 500 to 3000 feet high. Many miles inland, the narrow strait may open into a broad sound. When tide rises or falls, a tremendous amount of water (on incoming tide) sweeps through the strait into the sound. You can imagine the effect this has in producing strong currents. On outgoing tide the tremendous volume of water (representing a tidal fall of 15 feet) from the sound will rush through the narrow canyon back into the ocean. In a few places such currents reach six to 20 knots in velocity.

Refueling is not a problem if you study your *Marine Atlas* carefully. The maximum distance between service stations is approximately a hundred miles — meaning that you must have fuel capacity for at least that distance (additional, if you encounter strong opposing tides and wind).

Our 17-footer docked at the government float at Naha Bay. Up the trail from the ramp we enjoyed fly-fishing for Alaska salmon.

Marine service stations have not learned to provide the personal services of automobile filling stations. Many of them have no toilet. In a few places, you will find recognition of the peculiar needs of sailors. Twice on our cruise we visited stations with clean, flush toilets and clean sinks with a supply of hot water, soap and paper towels. After several days on a 17-foot boat, a flush toilet and sink with hot water are welcome. Once we were treated to the luxury of a hot shower, supplied as a personal service available to all customers. This is really living!

Fresh fruit, vegetables, milk and eggs are not readily available. Plan your menus without these luxuries.

Ice for perishables can be obtained from fishing boats and canneries. Canned goods, candy, tobacco and postal services can be found at most of the same ports where motor fuel is sold.

A cruise in Alaskan waters could be initiated by loading your small boat and trailer on a cruise ship, ferry or freighter sailing from Seattle to Alaska. You could return home the same way, after enjoying local cruising in Alaskan waters. This is probably a good answer for some people who would enjoy cruising in Southeastern Alaska.

We did not do this. After landing at Campbell River, we cruised up Johnstone Strait and connecting waters to Queen Charlotte Sound. We visited Bella Bella, Klemtu, Butedale and Prince Rupert. Beyond Dixon Entrance we crossed the international boundary into Alaska where we visited Ketchikan, Wrangell and Petersburg. Porpoises, whales, salmon and icebergs were all encountered on this memorable small boat cruise.

Sailing to Alaska in a small boat from below Queen Charlotte Sound is not for everyone. Neither is it out of the question for those with adequate experience and a sense of adventure. The cruise of the Inside Passage can be safely, sensibly and enjoyably undertaken even in boats under 20 feet in length. The degree of comfort experienced depends upon the particular vessel available. Even more, it depends upon the study and planning which you are willing to make prior to the time your vacation rolls around.

58

Alaska...
not just a Place to Reach

by Betty Nunn

Alaska is not just a place one has reached,– it is an achievement, an experience, a feeling. Here is all man could wish of primitive untouched wildness. The handful of settlements throughout Alaska and man's industry and man's entertainment pursuits are scattered with distance enough between that one is forgotten before the next crops up around a headland. Steeped in history when really its history has hardly begun, Alaska seems to be marking time while the rest of the world is busy whizzing complicated spacecraft to the moon. Our new state is standing by to preserve what is beautiful, simple and magnificent right on our own planet.

After months of planning, our *Bee Jay III* was ready to set forth on her maiden voyage to Alaska. On the preliminary part of the trip from Santa Barbara to Seattle she proved herself in the rough waters off Point Conception, the gales north of San Francisco, the log-infested turbulence at the mouth of the Columbia River and angry weather in the Straits of Juan de Fuca.

In Seattle she passed her check-up of engines, hull and equipment with flying colors and was ready for the great Alaskan adventure. A last-minute addition to *Bee Jay's* equipment was a selection of crab balls. These brilliant inflatable round floats were to serve as bumpers when we drew up to the rough pilings of the northland area fueling docks and moorings.

As *Bee Jay* passed through the Ballard Locks, wheeling sea gulls and a stiff breeze welcomed us into the sparkling waters of Puget Sound. Our route took us to the right, or inside, of Whidbey Island as we proceeded north. Houses nestled in tiny clearings in the dark evergreens on top of the bluffs as we cruised smoothly past one softly rounded headland after another. Evening cast her enchanting shadows across the mirror-calm water of a surprise bay as we rounded a spit, naked except for a single cluster of trees etched on the sunset sky. Our wake made smooth rounded humps that hardly disturbed the perfect reflection of the cloud and blue-patch pattern of the sky.

Rounding a woodland bend, a strong current running toward us warned that we were at Deception Pass at flood tide and we glimpsed the graceful bridge spanning the deep, narrow chasm between Whidbey and Fidalgo Islands.

We veered to pŏrt and spent the night in serene Cornet Bay at the State Park landing. Fuel was available at a private dock nearby, as well as a store, a small cafe and telephone.

Lulled to sleep by the sound of rain tap-tapping on the flying bridge, we were awakened by an early morning stillness broken only by lilting birdsong from shore. Suddenly one roar followed another as nearby outboards moved out to catch slack water in Deception Pass. We crossed Rosario Strait and spent the balance of the day touring the San Juan Islands, wishing we had time to linger at Lopez Island, and at Friday Harbor on San Juan Island, and visit Orcas Island. But our ultimate goal, Alaska, was too strong a lure and we opened the throttles for Sidney, Vancouver Island, where we went through Canadian customs.

We spent the night in cozy Canoe Cove just north of Sidney, sitting top-side in the warm evening, broiling steaks.

Up and away early the next morning we headed through the Canadian San Juans. The sky was mostly overcast, but whenever the sun did break through, the trees on the rock-footed bluffs came alive with the unreal opulent green of the northwest. The white-breasted gulls would glide alongside our mast which was most festive with our red and white British Columbia courtesy flag. We cruised past Panther Point into Whaleboat Passage, by Thetis Island and into Georgia Strait.

The Straits were kicking up a fuss that afternoon and most of the crew surreptitiously swallowed Dramamine tablets. Across the frisky water on the mainland side were the Powell River Paper Mills with the snow-topped Coast Range looming darkly above. To our port were the tall snowy peaks of Strathcona National Park on Vancouver Island. With all that snow the air was brisk.

Campbell River, Vancouver Island, was the stop for the night. At the fuel dock the attendant drily asked our destination and then motioned toward a yacht moored at the dock opposite. "They were going to Alaska, too, but hit a log near Phillips Arm and broke a shaft. Now they're waiting to be towed home to Vancouver." The crew of the *Bee Jay III* soberly vowed to double the log-watch from then on.

Campbell River is a salmon fisherman's paradise. There

are good docking facilities and the town is fair-sized with excellent accommodations, stores and a theater. For those heading north, it is a last touch with the bright lights.

Waking in a drizzle, we set the course for the day for Seymour Narrows at slack tide. It is a neat trick to navigate these waters and one must be on the charts constantly to identify each of the myriad islands and reefs — and they all look alike. Even on the well-marked channels it is easy to make a wrong turn into a bay. Especially is this true when it is raining, as it so often is. In the rain the landscape becomes eerie and ghostly with the tops of islands lost in wraithlike cloud, the beaches narrow and cold and covered with dark water-soaked drift logs and somber gray boulders.

Large freighters emerged from the gloom and as they passed there would be an exchange of horn blasts and a hand-wave from bridge to bridge. Also, in both directions, many little fishing boats passed, their outriggers clasped above in prayer or dropped aside like butterfly wings.

In Johnstone Strait, past Ripple Point to port, a waterfall tumbled in steps down the rock-ribbed island wall — and another and another. In Queen Charlotte Strait it was a little rough, but the weather report indicated that all gale warnings were down and that the wind would be less across the Queen Charlotte Sound that day than it would be the next. We crossed it most comfortably and were soon in the lee of some craggy weatherbeaten rocks — islands of a sort. The trees were noticeably spindlier and twisted and flattened by the elements.

It is not wise to cross the Sound too soon on the heels of gale warnings because even though the wind might be down the sea is still whipped into an angry roughness that hasn't had time to lie down. Also, it is advisable not to travel at night because of hard-to-spot logs and debris. Other hazards to be avoided are the prop-fouling snarls of ocean hemp, the seaweed which extends in stringers a quarter of a mile or more across the seaways, like long, thick, brown snakes.

Once across Queen Charlotte Sound and in the comparative protection of Fitzhugh Sound, the ladies started dinner. What a passing panorama out the galley picture window! Darkly forested headlands and islands seemed pinned on a soft blue backdrop of high mountains with here and there a filmy veil of falling snow on the higher peaks. What scenery to peel potatoes to! It was hard to keep the mind on the fresh salmon steaks on the Teflon electric griddle — the salmon given us freshly caught by fishermen in Campbell River, British Columbia.

Namu, British Columbia was reached just as daylight faded. We settled for the night at the fishing dock having thrown our bow line to a most obliging Indian youngster who soon had us expertly fast fore and aft. We all were amused by this same youngster's capabilities as the chronicler of the town, for we hardly had the engines off before we had learned all the recent events of Namu, happy or otherwise.

We strolled the high wooden sidewalk typical of all of the towns of the northland as they are located where the variance of tides is so extreme — often up to 30 feet in these northern waters. All docks and habitation must be on high pilings. When the tide is out the old weatherbeaten clapboard houses look like old ladies caught in wading, their skirts tucked up and their skinny legs showing. Trash and odd bits of discarded machinery and household items strew the tide shore of the towns in the area and they are consequently more attractive when the tide is in covering the family "skeletons."

Namu is a quaint little company town of the British Columbia Packers. All night the tiny fish boats riding low in the water sputtered up to the big cannery dock. The *Bee Jay III* was moored on the opposite side of the small harbor near the net-drying racks and in the morning several fishermen were straightening out and mending their nets and re-reeling them aboard their small, sturdy fishing craft. Most of the fishermen and the personnel in the packing house are Indian. They are friendly folk, but would be a very bad advertisement for a toothpaste commercial as there is such a scarcity of teeth in the young and old alike.

Leaving Namu we were cruising under cumulus clouds lazing in an unbelievably blue sky. All day our route followed one narrow passage after another of tree-girded rocky shores, desolate, yet beautiful. And then at the end of a long inlet nestled the colorful miniature town of Bella Bella. Fueling and limited shopping was done at New Bella Bella, a settlement across the inlet from the main village, which is Indian. The water here was not too good, but we took some aboard since we have a purifying filter system throughout the boat.

Between Bella Bella and Butedale, British Columbia, lies Klemtu Passage, a narrow waterway paralleling the main channel. Although narrow, it offers no navigational difficulty and there is a quiet beauty here. The Indian village of Klemtu clinging to the abrupt shore is worth visiting. As we traveled through the passage, several bald-headed eagles soared and screamed overhead as our wake rolled fast and broke in a glory of white spray on the close-enough-to-touch rock-girt shores.

Back in the main channel again many small whales were sighted, their vapor plumes erupting suddenly, and their dark backs and flukes humped over. Long-necked cranes rising regally from the lonely shores and dark little clusters

Bee Jay III cruises past totem poles in Revillagigedo Channel near Ketchikan

of chubby mudhens spattering clumsily across the water were the commonest specimens of wildlife along these waterways.

Butedale, British Columbia, with its cascading waterfall an integral part of the town, was a pretty place to dock for the night. We had added excitement watching the natives help a tugboat save its tow. Coming up the strait to Butedale, the tug was towing three small fishing boats like little chicks, one-two-three — boats destined for Alaskan waters. Churning along the channel like a mother hen, the tugboat hit a partially submerged log, and although it did not harm the heavy tug, the impact pushed the log far under the water and it bounded back up and hit the hull of the more vulnerable fishing boat, number two of its brood. It took the entire crew and help from shore to save the stricken craft.

The day's travel between Butedale and Prince Rupert through the beautiful Grenville Channel was outstanding in magnificence. The channel is a fairly straight chute for 20 miles, lined with heavily forested mountains, mostly snow-topped. Through each little draw or canyon can be glimpsed a cirque valley left by glacial action — a rim of noble yet grim-faced peaks, their steep escarpments etched with veins of snow, like wrinkles on old men's faces. These granite peaks formed a protective circle around a sapphire lake or inlet, their sternness softened by a graceful waterfall spilling into the main channel. The lower, rounder mountains were densely forested.

Prince Rupert is not just another settlement on the inland waterways of British Columbia. It is a fair-sized city with some paved streets, signals, and drag-racing teen-agers. Yet its modernness is tempered by the uniqueness of its position in the wilderness. It is not only the jumping-off place or last stop before the Dixon Entrance crossing into Alaska, but it is also the terminus of one of the few roads in British Columbia that link the inland area with the sea.

The docking facilities at the long established Prince Rupert Rowing and Yacht Club were more than adequate. The town is large enough to have good stores and some good restaurants in the better hotels.

The Dixon Entrance is much discussed and cussed by all who have wet their hulls in this stretch of water open to the not so pacific Pacific. Weather predictions originate in this area close to the Aleutians; therefore it is difficult to say what is going to start up when one is so close to where it all starts. The Coast Guard does a superb job trying to outguess the wind and sea conditions with its well-equipped stations. This particular stretch of water is more apt to be rough than smooth, so if the gods are smiling when you tentatively poke your bow past Dundas Island and all looks well — go!

It is comforting to see the impressive mountain range of Prince of Wales Island, even though far distant oceanward, shouldering its way between the Pacific and the route to Ketchikan up Revillagigedo Channel. We passed Cape Fox, Tree Point and Foggy Bay on the mainland of Alaska and then Duke Island and Annette Island and their sheltering buffer.

Ketchikan doesn't have the Indian Rain Bird for its mascot for any idle reason. We arrived at our first Alaskan town in a heavy downpour and were glad to find docking facilities good and handy to town.

Ketchikan is located on Revillagigedo Island, separated from the Alaska mainland by the Behm Canal. It is one of the largest and is the most southerly of the southeastern Alaskan towns. The long, often rough, route up the Pacific coast to reach this town is just a preamble to the great beauty of this area.

Ketchikan clings for dear life to the steep mountainsides, spreading out lengthwise along the rugged shore, barely grasping a toe-hold, and ever crowded from behind by the dark forest. It rains in Ketchikan as though the clouds are determined to dissolve the town and melt it away into the swirling waters of Revillagigedo Channel, which waters, in turn, often cooperate by clawing and raging as if to tear out the docks, canneries and lumber mills.

Defiantly man uses for his success here the very items challenging him — the inland arm of the sea for the fish for the canneries, the encroaching forests for the large pulp mills.

We were glad to come out of the wild seas of Dixon Entrance into the calmer water of the Channel with the difficult to pronounce name, Revillagigedo.

A new unity has been brought about between the towns of southeastern Alaska by the great new blue Alaska Ferries. Suddenly the great inland passages become unifying water highways. Where before only a few tourist steamers each summer could penetrate the area, now this ferry system, the "Greyhound Bus" of Alaska, plies these waters all year long on regular schedule, carrying freight, cars and people.

This entire area of southeastern Alaska constitutes the largest national forest in the 50 states — Tongass National Forest. Most of this forest area is on islands, but also includes the mountain-peaked mainland strip with its fjords, bays and inlets. It has the distinction of being the only national forest where timber crop must be transported by marine waterways. The symbol of the national forest is the totem pole, for the entire northwest coast region of British Columbia and Alaska is known as the home of the Totemic Indian culture. All the towns have their totem pole collections and displays.

It is impossible to say just how long it takes to see an Alaskan city. This depends upon who is doing the seeing and the amount of time available. The course of the Bee Jay III was to cover as much of southeastern Alaska as possible, so individual stops were far too short.

We found that eating aboard the Bee Jay beat most anything ashore except in Juneau and in the new Glacier Bay National Monument. The curio stores in Alaska are still fascinating as the labels "Made in Japan" or "Made in West Germany" have not yet corrupted the Alaskan Indian and Eskimo art.

Heading north from Ketchikan, Wrangell is the next town. The friendly wood smoke from the lumber mill reached us before the town came in sight. All the Alaskan towns are picturesque and all have certain peculiarities of their own, too. The docking facilities, usually right in with the fishing fleet, were always adequate though not deluxe. Good bumpers are vital as the docks are not buffered in any way.

Wrangell is the second oldest settlement in southeastern Alaska. It was settled by the Russians in an effort to keep the British Hudson Bay Company from hunting on the Stikine River. Today a four-day riverboat trip up the Stikine is a spectacular side-trip from Wrangell.

The economy of Wrangell is based on the Alaska Wrangell Mills which export lumber, and on the shrimp business. The shrimp boats bring their catches to the cannery to be canned and frozen for export. Every evening while in Wrangell the crew of the Bee Jay III received as a gift delicious cleaned and steamed delicate Alaskan shrimp from the cannery.

Between Wrangell and Petersburg are the exciting and challenging Wrangell Narrows. In the 20 miles of these Narrows there are no less than 80 channel markers. Alaska does not set unnecessary markers as they are difficult and expensive to install and maintain, so it behooves the navigator to follow them carefully.

Petersburg, at the end of Wrangell Narrows, is a picture-postcard town. It scatters over a couple of rounded hills, each house clean-cut, and the tall-spired church adds a European flavor. With the towering snowy peaks behind, it is like a sea-level Alpine village.

The first icebergs were sighted from the *Bee Jay III* just north of Petersburg. They had originated at the La Conte Glacier, the most southerly of the tidewater glaciers. We were impressed by the blue shades in the bergs, which from a distance looked like white or blue boats lined up along the channel like a flotilla on parade.

From Petersburg we cruised the smooth waters of Frederick Sound past some of the most impressive and rugged mountain ranges yet seen. The "Devil's Thumb" rises nearly 2000 feet above the surrounding peaks which are all at least 9000 feet of almost perpendicular cliffs topped with snow fields and ice packs.

Around Cape Fanshaw and north up Stephens Passage we came upon the Five Finger Islands around the well-dressed snow-garbed peaks of Admiralty Island.

Thirty miles south of Juneau the *Bee Jay III* veered out of the channel into the Tracy-Endicott Arm area. Here in an iceberg-filled fjord we were surrounded by beautiful free-forms of nature, protected from wind and tide by the steep canyon walls and topped by jagged pinnacles.

Still spellbound by the beauty of the scene, we re-entered Stephens Passage. Hurrying northward we almost missed tiny Taku Harbor. Turning sharply starboard we entered this round emerald inlet. Taku Harbor is where Father Hubbard, the glacier priest, maintained his headquarters. Reluctantly we eased out of the refuge into the main channel again, which had become a little choppy in the brisk afternoon breeze.

Juneau at last, and the *Bee Jay III* cruised under the steel bridge spanning the Gastineau Channel. Here in the capital city of Alaska are the first reminders of the old gold rush days. Today the economy of the town is tied to governmental administration and tourist trade.

A few miles out of Juneau an overall understanding of the forceful role that glaciers have played in shaping the landscapes of southeastern Alaska can be obtained at the Mendenhall Glacier. Here in the beautiful new Visitor's Center the geologic history is graphically given and explained by rangers. A restaurant and observation room allow travelers to view the massive ice chasms of the glacier face in comfort.

In Juneau, the Baranof Hotel dining room gave the ladies a well-deserved rest from the galley and the whole crew enjoyed the entertainment in the Red Dog Saloon. The curio and gift shops received their share of attention and the first mate went to a beauty shop.

Via Wien Airlines we flew inland from Juneau to Whitehorse in the Yukon Territory, great supply center of gold rush days for prospectors heading for the Klondike. The air route carried us over the Alaskan Coastal Range and Juneau ice fields. We looked down on this great remnant of the ice-age, blinding white ages-old snow packs and powerful rivers

of moving ice. Abruptly the sheer mountains were gone, and sparsely forested gentle slopes gave way to the flat valley floor of the Yukon. And there the river snaked its way into Whitehorse and beyond.

Whitehorse has adequate but not deluxe accommodations. We rented a car and drove out the Alaskan Highway 40 miles to Marsh Lake and stayed overnight at a hunting lodge, rustically simple but modern enough for comfort, and excellent frontier food.

The next day we caught the narrow-gauge Yukon and White Pass Railroad for the all-day scenic trip from Whitehorse down the old 1898 Trail to Skagway. The train cuts back through the mountains to the sea down a tortuous grade. It carries flat cars for autos and freight cars and two or three cars for passengers. The engines are now modern diesels, but the lounge cars are still heated by pot-bellied coal stoves.

Skagway is strictly for tourists, but has done a superb job in keeping a true flavor of old Alaskan days in the original buildings, dirt roads, museums and entertainment offered.

We sampled the ocean-liner type service of the big blue Alaska ferry by cruising aboard it down the Lynn Canal, stopping briefly at Haines and arriving in Juneau in the early morning. We readied the *Bee Jay III* for her trip to Glacier Bay National Monument located west and north of Juneau. Here are found more live and grinding glaciers than in any other similar area in the world. The massive Coast Range, topped by Mt. Fairweather rising 15,300 feet straight up from the edge of the sea, spawns these ice mon-

(Left) Bee Jay III leaves a smooth wake in Sergius Narrows. (Right) A mooring in Namu, B.C. Note typical wooden sidewalk on pilings

sters. Many of the glaciers reach tidal water and so the many inlets of this region are choked with icebergs. The only access to this far-north National Monument is by private boat or chartered float plane. The government has just completed a beautiful lodge at Bartlett Cove in Glacier Bay with dining room, lounge and excellent accommodations.

The days were now close to 22 hours long and we used the time to cover the waterways. Leaving Glacier Bay we traveled down Icy Strait to Chatham Strait and into Peril Strait which separates Chicagof Island from Baranof Island. We turned into Poison Cove which led into Sergius Narrows, crossed Salisbury Sound, whizzed through Whitestone Narrows, crossed Krestof Sound, passed Halleck Island, and crossing Sitka Sound, found ourselves in Sitka.

Sitka is the oldest settlement in Alaska and the center of Russian activities until 1867. It was founded in 1799 by Alexander Baranof and many relics of Russian life are found here. Sitka's main geographical highlight is Mt. Edgecumbe, an extinct volcano. There are many places of historical sig-

nificance in Sitka and one of the finest collections of native arts and crafts is found at the Sheldon Jackson Museum. The influence of the Japanese current is more evident in Sitka than in the other areas of Alaska. Here the few rocky beaches had flocks of swimmers in the gentle waters.

We left the grand new boat anchorage at Sitka, and threaded our way back up to Peril Straits and thence back into Chatham Strait, heading southward for the first time. We made a stop at Baranof Warm Springs, just across Baranof Island from Sitka. A spectacular waterfall crashes out of Baranof Lake into secluded Warm Springs Bay. Ashore, high on the pilings, are quaint old wooden houses. One is a bathhouse with running warm mineral water filling wooden tubs. These baths were built by the Russians and the tubs looked old enough to be the originals.

The crew of the *Bee Jay III* had scarcely finished its trip to this stupendous country before we were planning the next, pointing out inlets to cruise, bays to fish, and Indian villages to explore. We'll be back!

Bee-Jay III is a 46-foot Cedros Island Express, custom-designed and built by Santa Barbara Yachts, Inc., Santa Barbara, Calif. The 18-ton cruiser is the wooden prototype for the firm's new line of fiberglass-hulled craft.

She has two staterooms, one amidships, the other to port, comfortably sleeping six. The dinette in the main salon has a couch that can double as additional sleeping accommodation for two. The completely-equipped head has shower and large hanging locker.

She is powered by Cummins V8-300M diesels, 300 hp each, with Capitol 2-to-1 gears, using 1¾" Armco 17-4 PH shafting and swinging Federal Equi-quad 4-bladed wheels of 24" diameter and 22" pitch. Top speed is 20 knots; continuous cruising speed is 17. Her 840-gallon fuel capacity allows a 1000-mile maximum range at reduced speed.

All electronics are by Bendix: MR-4 waterproof radar; two depth sounders, DI-8 600-ft. and DI-6 100-ft.; radiotelephones are a Skipper 673, Captain 250 and MM8 Citizens Band; the Autopilot is a Model 14.

Electric power is supplied by a Kohler 7.5 KW diesel 115-v a.c. generator, La Marche Invert-A-Volt 600-w 12-v

d.c. to 115-v a.c.; and 60-amp. 115-v a.c. to 12-v d.c. La Marche Constavolt.

Other equipment includes a Marvel refrigerator and freezer, both 12 volts; King Refrigerator Co. deepfreeze in the equipment room, 117v a.c.; two 8-gal. Raritan hot water heaters; Ling-Tempco apartment style dishwasher; G.E. washer-dryer combination; G.E. disposal; Princess 4-burner stove with oven; built-in Arvin electric heaters; Lear Jet 8-track stereo; Nu-Tone intercom. Additional galley equipment: Teflon electric griddle and Farberware spatterless electric grill.

Compressed air is supplied by a Cummins compressor which powers the horn and windshield wipers. Fresh water is supplied from a 240-gal. stainless steel tank by a PAR pump, through a Crowell Hydro-Cell pressure accumulator. There is a 75-gal. fiberglass holding tank for toilet wastes, and an engine-driven centrifugal pump to discharge the tank when the vessel is in open water.

The ship's dinghy is a Boston Whaler with 18-hp outboard, carried on the flying bridge. There is an electric hoist on the dinghy, handling mast and boom.

59

Ford's Terror

by Frank Morris

Frank Morris, the contributor of Fords Terror, is a long-time compadre of SEA & *Pacific Motor Boat staff members in marine publishing. His name has appeared in our columns for the news that he has made in the Pacific Northwest and it has appeared as a contributing author many times across more than 25 years beginning with Pacific Motor Boat. A Commander in the Coast Guard Reserve, Frank Morris has accomplished more for pleasure boating than can be listed in this introductory. Washington, British Columbia and Alaska waters are his specialty. We have frequently reviewed and recommended his two fine chart books, Marine Atlas 1 and 2, volumes covering from Olympia to Skagway with charts, distances, courses and air photos of harbors. He is a leading predicted log racer and navigator and has won the International Cruiser Race, the Northwest prize of powerboating prizes.**

About sixty miles southwest of Juneau, Alaska, off Endicott Arm, nestles a seldom-cruised but renowned little inlet named "Fords Terror." The name implies something frightful, to the extent that many pleasure boats avoid making the 40-mile round trip voyage off the main traveled route in Stephens Passage from Petersburg to Juneau. Research on place-name originations for Alaska fails to divulge any information on why the name "Fords Terror."

Implications are that something horrendous is involved; however, like so many narrows and rapids in the Northwest, all that is needed is 'local knowledge' to make this bit of wonderland one of the most spectacular scenic beauties of the world. There are times and conditions when the narrow passage leading into the five-mile inlet is strictly *verboten*. Whoever named it must have been there at one of these precarious moments.

Conjecture is that the name "Fords Terror" was meant to apply to the narrow passage which leads into the inlet. This is where the "Terror" lies. The name "Fords" or "Ford" does not seem to have any related historical meaning, so again conjecture indicates that the inlet was originally referred to as a "fjord", or, "fiord", which Webster defines as "a narrow inlet of the sea, between high banks or rocks, as on the coasts of Norway and Alaska". Hence, the "terror"

of the "fjord" turned out to be "Fords Terror" on the hydrographic charts.

In navigating to the inlet, one would take the main channel route up Frederick Sound from Petersburg, round Cape Fanshaw into Stephens Passage and proceed into Holkam Bay, an approximate distance of 60 miles north of Petersburg, and to the east of Stephens Passage. Entering Holkam Bay between Harbor Island and Wood Spit, there generally are several icebergs which originate from the twin Sawyer glaciers at the head of Tracy Arm to the north, or from the twin Dawes glaciers at the extreme southern end of Endicott Arm. The current near Wood Spit can reach a velocity of about five knots at times, producing noticeable swirls and making it quite important to study the actions of the numerous bergs, large and small, the purpose of course to avoid collision with the ice. The bulk of the ice being submerged, it is mandatory to keep the hull away from this hazard.

Much of the ice collects on the shoals inside of Wood Spit Light, or across the bay where the Sumdum Glacier spills its waterfall. From Sumdum Island on into Endicott Arm, the ice flows can sometimes clog up the entire channel. At other times, fairly clear navigation can be made all the 15 miles into Fords Terror inlet. When the channel is clogged with ice, the next flood or ebb tide probably will clear the route some, although generally a boat is required to do a bit of backing and filling along the journey to avoid collision with icebergs.

Fords Terror is deep and steep for five miles to the upper reaches, which break into two branches, the south arm shoaling up fast about half way to the end. At the entrance of Fords Terror, however, in the narrow channel, there are only two fathoms of water at a minus tide. With an approximate 25-foot tide range here, the currents can reach a velocity of over 16 knots on the bull ebb. During this time, the white foaming water literally boils out of the narrow cut, making a considerable roar which at times will echo from the surrounding granite-like walls on each side.

If this weren't enough to discourage one from entering, a look at the rocks and shoals at low tide in the bay outside of the rapids would be sufficiently ominous. Near the entrance is a rounded rocky shoal about 60 yards long and

*Frank Morris is deceased but the two volume MARINE ATLAS is available completely updated in book or marine stores or direct from the publisher: Bayless Enterprises, Inc., 427-9th Avenue N., Seattle 98109.

20 yards wide which covers at zero tide, and on which no kelp seems to grow — to warn navigators. Other smaller (but just as solid) rocky shoals exist in the center on the eastern half, or starboard side, on entering the narrowest part of the channel. Much of the time the glacier-like water is milky-white, not clear enough for the shallows to be detected. Needless to repeat, 'local knowledge' is recommended in negotiating this spot.

In reference to the "terror" part of "Fords Terror", at times flows of icebergs coming out Endicott Arm from the Dawes glaciers can float with the currents into Fords Terror. Some of these bergs are several hundred feet in measurement, with the bulk being submerged and of unknown shape below the surface. When they come tumbling and rumbling out of the canyon into the shallow and narrow entrance, they hit the bottom with great force, roll over and break up, spilling tons of ice in various directions with a thunderous roar and creating a virtual holocaust for any small boat in the vicinity.

Recommendations are that navigating into Fords Terror should be done at slack tide, preferably high slack, as at low slack the kelp floats to the surface in the summer months and chokes up the entrance. When the current is running a knot or so, the kelp lies almost horizontal along the bottom and is of no particular annoyance. Slack current, on the faster spring tides, will last nearly half an hour, and longer on the slower neap tides. High slack, neap tides, would logically be the best time for going through, but that would spoil the opportunity to lie in the bay to watch and hear the bull ebb rushing out. The most spectacular time to safely negotiate the entrance is about ten minutes before low slack, going in against a slight ebb current when the kelp is low, then coming back out about an hour later against a slight flood, with the same conditions in reverse. Or, lying inside the inlet viewing the upper reaches until the next tide change.

On the inside of the passage, the scenery is almost indescribable. Rock cliffs several thousands of feet high drop straight down into the salt chuck. If the sun is shining, it is difficult to get an entire scene into focus with your camera. Waterfalls drop off the top ledges, spilling their way over the ragged cliffs, sometimes disappearing in a deeply wooded area, then coming into view again closer to the water's edge. Gorge-like ravines extend between granite rock cliffs, for some four to five thousand feet in height, on the north side of the inlet. In the spring and early summer there is no shortage of spectacular waterfalls, some of which are thin trails of water disappearing into a mist after dropping a few thousand feet; others quite large, with some splitting into double falls on the long drop down from the tremendous heights.

The clue to entering Fords Terror is to locate the very conspicuous high thin waterfall, southeast of the narrow entrance about 1000 yards distant. The water is deep where these falls spill into the bay, over 20 fathoms. Then, with this waterfall dead astern, proceed to the left center of the opening, past the sand spit on the port side. This course will avoid the shoals and rocks in the middle of the little bay. After passing the sand spit, a mid-channel course, with no steering error to the right, will lead to safe deep water inside. The same course is taken on the exit: after passing the sand spit on the west side to your right, head for the conspicuous high thin waterfall on the opposite shore, making no steering error to the left.

Chances are, it could be like a mill pond on a Sunday afternoon when you go there. But don't count on it!

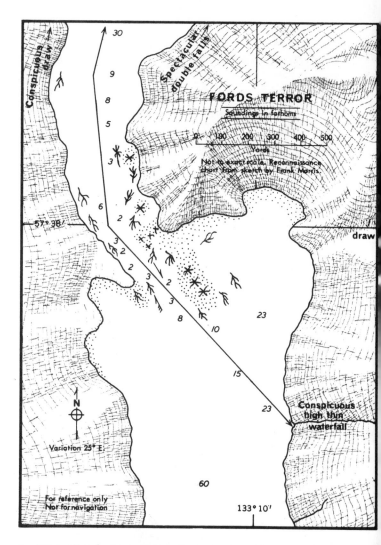

Dr. Mitch Bilafer's Doressa, St. Francis YC, takes her turn on the high, thin waterfall and heads for the entrance of Fords Terror

60

Folly Explores the Remote Reaches of Rivers Inlet

by Trevor Roote

If you have ever been to Rivers Inlet you will know that it has a reputation for huge salmon, 50 pounds and up And although our family has a reputation for not catching any, we still enjoy exploring this rugged, exciting cruising country.

For the past two years we had come up to the area of Queen Charlotte Sound, only to be beaten back by weather and time. This year, however, we were determined to reach our goal.

In July we left Vancouver, made the long run through Georgia and Johnstone Straits toward Bull Harbor, headed for Queen Charlotte Sound and that vast, little-cruised area around Calvert Island and up Rivers Inlet.

Our cruiser *Folly*, a 37-foot Chris-Craft tri-cabin model with hardtop, slid steadily by Port Hardy and swung on to the last leg for the day through Goletas Channel. Our twin engines pushed us along at steady 13½ knots and we slowly overtook waves being driven by a moderate S.E. wind. The red ensign flag hung limp and wet on the stern staff as steamy exhaust curled up around the transom then whished away as it rose out of the shelter of the deck railings. Nigei Island was now on our starboard side and we hugged the shoreline using the small sheltering effect from the south-eastern it afforded. Vancouver Island lay opposite us across two miles of dark rain swept water.

We took out our binoculars and scanned Shusharties Bay on the Vancouver Island side. A lonely house and a large storage or work shed appeared to be the only things left of an early settlement. In earlier days a trail ran from Shusharties Bay through the rugged forests to Cape Scott and served a group of Scandinavian settlers who had tried in vain to establish farms in the area.

We noted on our chart that Loquililla Cove on Nigei Island was where James Strange took possession of this part of the world for Great Britain in 1786.

On the starboard side, we moved out past the end of Nigei Island and opened the view north-eastward through Bate Passage; Hope Island now lay dead ahead. We picked up the small white light beacon perched on Gallows Point near the entrance to Bull Harbor. As we neared the entrance of the harbor, which is really a cleft in the walls of hundred-foot rock cliffs, skies to the west showed patches of blue. We slowed down to four knots and scanned the northern end of Vancouver Island. There, far out past the tip of Cape Scott, we could see the Scott Islands sparkling in bright sunshine.

Folly slipped through the narrow slotted entrance into the confines of Bull Harbor. Three floating fish camps were moored in to channel with a fleet of trollers clustered around each. Fishermen were sitting around in groups waiting for the winds off Cape Scott to abate and the seas to settle down so they could start salmon fishing.

We nosed into an open space alongside an Imperial fuel barge and tied up. The time was mid-afternoon and we watched salmon being taken out of a cold storage locker and loaded on board the large fish packer *M.V. Fort Ross*.

After wandering through the various parts of the floating camp and visiting the store, we turned our attention to the surrounding harbor. Out towards the entrance, another scow camp was moored around the edge of a bluff. Two Standard Oil tanks sat on top of the bluff, all the surrounding trees were burned and the rocks blackened. We learned that the year before lightning had struck and burned out a store built on a log float and had ignited the fuel tanks. The charred remains of the log float were pulled up on a nearby beach.

Looking to the north, we could see the end of the harbor on a shelving beach. There in a fringe of trees stood the white and red trimmed houses of the government radio station. Several large radio masts rose above the wind-twisted trees.

Our charts showed us that the narrow strip of land holding the radio station sheltered us from Queen Charlotte Strait. The bay on the other side was aptly called Roller Bay.

It was still several hours to dinner so we decided to launch the dinghy and row to the head of the harbor. Susie gathered up our children and along with Sandy, our Sheltie, we headed out. A walk of less than a hundred yards put us through the trees and out on Roller Bay beach. A crashing surf surged up and down the strand, rolling thousands of small round rocks over the beach. The exposed beach was piled high with these fist-sized rocks and rose very steeply just before going into the trees.

That night we had our usual conference on next day's

plans. If weather permitted, we would cross Queen Charlotte Strait, round Cape Caution and visit Rivers Inlet. We turned in early with our fingers crossed. Our alarm clock woke us at 4:30 a.m. to a dull red glow of dawn and clear skies. We headed out, hoping to cross the Strait before the wind came up.

As we eased out of the harbor, fishing vessels were also slipping from their moorings. We turned east and swung northward into Bate Passage between Hope Island and Nigei Island. We rounded a headland, expecting to look out into the open strait, but were confronted instead with a solid fog bank in the channel. We took a few bearings, established a compass reading to put us through to open water and proceeded under reduced speed. Soon we had broken into the clear open waters of Queen Charlotte Strait.

On the beach at Roller Bay near Bull Harbor

the surface of the ground swells. Within minutes, we were back in sheltered waters and headed for Goose Bay.

We pulled into the float at Goose Bay Cannery and started to relax. We had crossed the strait; it was a "piece of cake." We were to eat these thoughts a week later on our return trip.

The water supply was running low, as we had not been able to obtain good water since Shoal Bay on Thurlow Island. It is odd that in this area, where over 100 inches of rain falls every year, good water is hard to obtain. The heavy rains fall into low swampy land along the coast which becomes stained to the color of tea. It is referred to locally as "cedar water" or "iron stain." When we opened the tap at Goose Bay, brown cedar water gushed out and we decided to hold out longer. After stretching our legs and wandering through the old cannery buildings, we pulled out and headed up the inlet.

No sooner had we moved back into the main channel of Rivers Inlet than we realized that the sockeye salmon run was on. There were hundreds of gillnets stretched out along the inlet, each tied to the end of a 1200-foot net. A small colored ball or a flag indicated the far end of the net. The further up the inlet we ran, the thicker the nets became. We learned later from a fisheries patrol that some 1600 boats were fishing the inlet that day. The night before they had averaged 200 fish per boat, one of the biggest nights on record. Small packers were busily shuttling among the drifting gillnetters, collecting the catch and moving it to various fish-buying camps.

We slid by Duncanby Landing, Wadhams, Good Hope Cannery and on to Kibella Bay near the head of the inlet. The fisheries patrol vessel was tied alongside a float below the abandoned cannery.

We trolled up and down without so much as a nibble. Sockeye salmon were jumping all over the bay, but they rarely took a hook. So thick were the sockeye running that next day as we idled up to the very head of the inlet, I leaned over the side of the boat with a dip net and just slipped over the back of a five pounder. Later on, I scooped one out of the water as it swam by the float at Rivers Inlet Cannery.

The cannery at the head of Rivers Inlet

We took a compass reading which would pass us well off Cape Caution and on towards the Egg Island lighthouse, some 21 nautical miles to the north and out of sight over the horizon. The water was glassy smooth with a slight heaving swell. Within the first half hour, I spotted what I thought was the top of Egg Island. It was some five or six degrees further west than I had anticipated; correcting course, I steered by site bearing. The sun had now come up over the pinnacled snow capped peaks on the mainland, far to the east. We looked around and there was not a boat of any description in sight, only a few pairs of sea ducks diving after the plentiful schools of herring.

A morning breeze was putting a little chop onto the ever increasing swells. As we passed Egg Island, we could see these swells crashing over the inshore rocks. A few gillnet fish boats appeared off False Egg Island. The mouth of Smith Inlet, inshore of us, had a heavy mist covering the confines of the inlet. Calvert Island lay eight miles or so off our port bow to the west with billowing white clouds hiding the top of its peaks.

We now turned our attention to entering Rivers Inlet. We passed south of Dugout and Paddle Rocks and gave a wide berth to a rocky area which was just breaking under

Floating fish camps at Finn Bay

None of the canneries along the shores of Rivers Inlet are operating. Fast modern fish packers move the fish catch down the coast to the Vancouver area or up to Namu where a new cannery has just been built to replace the old plant that burned to the ground. Some of the old cannery buildings, such as Goose Bay, Wadhams and Good Hope are now used as net storage lofts and many of the bunkhouses and resident cottages have been taken over by Indian families.

At Rivers Inlet Cannery we found the old buildings were slowly rotting away. A young boy and his grandfather were caretaking and trying to repair the cottages for use as a future sport fishing and hunting camp. The grandfather had just that morning successfully pieced together the old wood water line which ran some mile and a half back up the side of a mountain to a waterfall. Great geysers of water were spurting out of leaks in the pipe. We watched as he turned on the valve controlling a water turbine. As the pressure built up, the belt drive to the generator started a steady click, click sound as the old leather lacings sped around the pulleys. The needle on a voltage meter on the wall slowly crept up to 110 volts and lights hung on wires around the plant started to glow. With minor adjustments to the valve, the 50-year-old turbine settled down to a steady speed.

We decided to walk through a trail to an Indian village about a mile up the river which joins Owikeno Lake to River's Inlet. The caretaker warned us to keep an eye out for grizzly bear as one had been prowling around camp the previous night. This changed our mind and we decided to head back down the inlet. We filled our water tank and headed into the mass of gillnets stretched across the inlet. As we headed into the afternoon sun, a fresh westerly breeze made the water dance and it became extremely difficult to see the low float lines supporting the nets. Suddenly a long low line of black net floats appeared dead ahead. I slammed back on the throttle and into reverse. The pressure on the props stalled the engines. The net slid underneath and caught.

Rather than start up again and entangle the net still more, we went down on our transom platform and secured both ends of the net where it came out from under the chine. While we attempted to free the net, the net's owner, a jovial middle-aged Indian, dropped his end of the net and came over to help. A small packer, whose crew noticed our plight, also ran alongside and took our bow line to hold *Folly* up wind. This left the net streaming out the stern and still clinging to the props. Susie volunteered to duck-dive down to inspect the problem. The net was not around the shafts, just caught on one blade of each prop.

Folly moves up through Queen Charlotte Straits

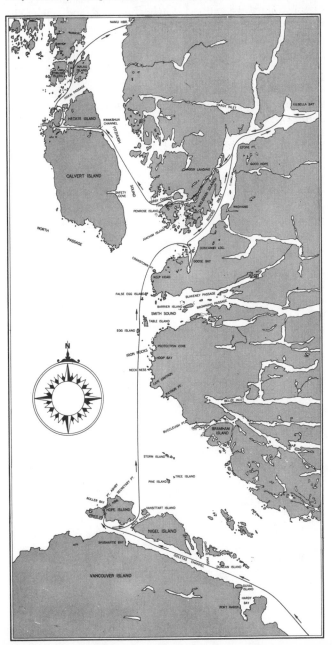

Mile-long West Beach at Calvert Island

In three quick dives we were clear. I quickly moved off, and we once again got under way at a more cautious speed.

We had left the main course of Rivers Inlet at Dawson's Landing to refuel and visit the most interesting store we have seen on the coast. Grizzly bear traps hung from the walls of Dawson's Landing store and much of the other merchandise hung from hooks in the ceiling. It reminded us of a real old-fashioned country general store or trading post.

A short stop at a nearby fish camp allowed us all to take showers and purchase fresh vegetables. The fish company utilized the hull of the retired B.C. auto ferry *Quillyuit* for a net loft and dormitory. The retired stern wheeler *Samson* served as a mess hall and fish-buying scow. Still another barge served as a store. The whole camp moved off to follow the various salmon runs. The snow capped peaks and glaciers were all behind us now as we ambled down Darby Channel to Finn Bay. Our afternoon ended at Finn Bay, nestled into a float with dozens of fish boats.

Kwakshua Channel on Calvert Island was our next destination. A friend had told us of a beautiful ocean beach with a sheltered anchorage within walking distance. Early next morning, we crossed Fitzhugh Sound and anchored at the head of Kwakshua. It was a day of brilliant sunshine. Within minutes, we rowed ashore.

A small cabin stood at the edge of the forest; behind the cabin a well worn trail led off into the deep green shadows cast by towering cedars and hemlocks. The numerous entries in the cabin's log-book signed by yachtsmen indicated the popularity of this "off the beaten path" anchorage. We noted with particular interest the remarks referring to wolves roaming the beach at night.

The walk took about 15 minutes and we emerged on one of the most beautiful beaches we have ever seen. The sand was so fine that it creaked as we walked along the shore. The bay was open to the Pacific with minor headlands and small islands at either end of its one-mile length. Small waves rolled in and out over a gently sloping beach. The day was calm and our children swam all afternoon as the tide crept in over the warming sands. We cooked our supper over a bonfire and swapped boating stories with two other couples who were cruising out of Ocean Falls. Back on board the *Folly*, I jigged for halibut, which were reported to run up to 80 pounds.

Next day we visited the beach again, but a brisk westerly wind was blowing and it was too cool to stay. We once again upped anchor and started out. On our way into Kwakshua, we had noticed a micro-wave station to the south of the channel, built high on a wind-swept bluff. We spotted a wharf in one of the many small bays below so we stopped to investigate. Mr. Carson and his wife were the sole inhabitants of Calvert Island, some 18 miles long and seven wide. Mr. Carson supervised the micro-wave station and had to run his speed boat into Namu, some 20 miles away, for supplies.

A rough jeep track was blasted out of the rock up to the micro-wave towers. We hiked to the top and ambled through the scrub pine and heather, all wind-swept and gnarled. At the top we had a wonderful panorama of open ocean to the west. Heavy seas were breaking over off-shore rocks. The still waters of Kwakshua Channel lay below us and to the north, Hakai Pass swept in from the open Pacific between Hecate Island and Hunter Island to join with Fitzhugh Sound.

We only had a day or so left, so we turned *Folly* up through Hakai Pass and stopped at Namu for supplies before turning south and home.

61
Cold-Water Cruising in Alaska

by Mary Lind Morrison

For those who like beautiful clear water, towering mountains, an abundance of water life, and an "it's all mine" feeling, I recommend Resurrection Bay out of Seward Harbor. It is all these and more.

Since last September, Johnny and I have counted the days until March, the earliest time we could take *L'il Lindy,* our 19-foot cabin cruiser, over the 128-mile trek to one of our favorite boating spots. Seward Harbor is open year round, but Alaskan winters offer no welcome to boaters in a small craft which has not been outfitted for winter.

March finally dragged its feet onto the calendar this year, and we were off for a weekend of boating. We pulled our reluctant trailer down Turnagain Arm, coaxed it over icy Johnson and Summit Passes, and finally into Seward Harbor, only to find the wind blowing like sixty. We found a sheltered place on the wharf to leave the boat, and spent the night with fingers, eyes, and toes crossed in hopes the errant wind would find a new playground.

White caps were dancing all over the bay the next morning. We had no desire for an enforced swim and gave up the idea of boating for that weekend. Survival time in these waters is limited to between seven and eleven minutes.

The following weekend, March 21, we tried our luck weather-wise again. We couldn't have asked for a more perfect Saturday. There was some wind, but not enough to prevent our going out. The snow-covered mountains smiled down at us from all sides under the bluest of blue skies.

Just past the rock jetties we saw a sea otter lying on his back, his round eyes staring at us from his whiskered face. He bobbed along until we approached within 25 feet, then submerged. Otters have been protected since 1911; before then they were almost made extinct by fur hunters. Now anyone killing one does so at the risk of a $10,000-dollar fine.

We passed Thumbs Cove with its old barges washed ashore and stopped in Humpy Cove to debate the pros and cons of going on to Rugged Island. It was a pointless debate. We always go.

I scrunched down in a corner of the cockpit while we roared across the ten miles. Even with insulated underwear beneath wool clothes and a surplus army parka, an Alaskan north wind has a way of getting through to you.

Johnny yelled with excitement as we neared the island. There on the rocks dead ahead were 30 or 40 harbor seals. We inched our way forward. They were as interested in us as we were in them. They felt safer in the water, however, and when we got within 30 feet of them they began diving in, reappearing nearer the boat and swimming around us with their mouths wide open as they gazed at their human circus.

As we approached the entrance to Mary's Bay we found three more groups of about 40 seals each and at least as many in the water.

After entering Mary's Bay, we ate our snack of sandwiches and milk near the old military dock sheltered from the wind. The whole island is dotted with military installations left from World War II.

Dusk brought on an evening calm and we were able to plane across the 15-mile stretch to Seward, passing a few scattered seals, three leaping porpoises and a couple more sea otters. Startled sea parrots ran out of our way.

Sunday morning was dark and dreary. Although there was no wind, with workday Monday staring us in the face, we couldn't risk having to sit out the weather in some cove. We had had the whole bay to ourselves the previous day so there was little chance of a larger boat getting us back in time. For me that thought was enticing!

It began snowing as we pulled the boat out. But — wait till next weekend! We're out of hibernation now. If you have a venturesome spirit, a love for beauty, and a yen for nature in its primitive state, come on up and join us. We've not yet scratched the surface.

Seals off Rugged Island. (Inset) Li'l Lindy

62

Cruising Temperamental Cook Inlet

by Mary Lind Morrison

So few pleasure boats cruise temperamental Cook Inlet that our trip in our 20-footer will be of interest to those who wish to try it someday. We only suggest that the pleasure boater know what he is doing, use good equipment and choose the right season to make sure that it is a pleasure cruise and not one that tests Cook's uncertainties.

After a long Alaskan winter, while the *Lindy* beckoned us provokingly, it was that time of year again — the earliest time we could launch our little cabin cruiser in calm water.

Saturday morning found us busily stowing last-minute gear, gassing the boat and trundling down to the Anchorage small-boat harbor. I use this term loosely. Before the 'quake in March 1965, Seward had fine docking facilities. So did Valdez. Homer still does. But Anchorage, the largest town in the state, had only mud-filled, undredged, unberthed, unramped Ship Creek. And apparently there is no relief in sight for this situation. High tides at Anchorage, second only to those in the Bay of Fundy, apparently makes the authorities chary of taking action.*

This day's launching proved no worse than usual. The Scout only had to be buried slightly above floor level to set *Li'l Lindy* afloat. Johnny, my husband, was in no mood for the "Up, periscope" someone hurled at him as the water gushed Niagara-like from the Scout.

We threaded our way around the bar, past the fishing canneries and into Cook Inlet. We missed a picture of Joey Reddington, one of our famous dog-team racers, who had just been casting off when we arrived at Ship Creek. In his long, narrow river skiff he was accompanied by his entire team of Huskies. Apparently some of them were reluctant to return to their summer home because they kept hopping overboard. Joey seemed quite unperturbed as he headed for the big Susitna River across the Inlet with his canine cargo.

We passed the bar, our cares fading as we headed for Kenai, 75 miles away. The Inlet was akin to a large, placid lake. At a distance it looked blue. But when we looked directly down, it was boiling, swirling liquid mud. The combination of extremely swift currents, high tides and silt-saturated glacier-fed rivers emptying into it is not conducive to clear water.

Five miles down the Inlet on our left we passed Fire Island at the mouth of Turnagain Arm. This is one of the passages explored by Captain Cook in his search for the Northwest Passage. After some 30 or 40 miles he turned back to the Inlet, and named the arm for his disappointment. In the early days of Alaskan history it was used by boats for passage up to Portage and the gold towns, Girdwood and Hope, a route now made impassable by silt raising the bottom.

Continuing on we crossed the Inlet to see one of the oil wells being drilled. A number of boats were working on the project, one of them exploding charges which sent up 50-foot spouts of water.

We then recrossed the Inlet and passed through the Forelands, the narrowest part of the Inlet, an area often too rough for a 20-footer. However, like the rest of the Inlet, conditions were glassy smooth. Rounding the Forelands we soon reached the town of Kenai. The harbor at the mouth of the Kenai River has a shallow entrance strewn with enormous boulders, some of them submerged. There is an unmarked opening through the boulders on the south side,

Oil drillers send up 50-foot water spouts in Cook Inlet

*In 1978 the small boat situation is no better. The single concrete ramp is silted in and no dredging is planned. Furthermore, the basin is dry at low tide. There are no berths, only a floating dock open from April 1st to about Oct. 1st.

but we had gone in too near shore. When the propeller of our inboard/outboard ticked a rock and mud boiled in our wake, we were forced to anchor to await higher tide. After a couple of hours we had sufficient water.

We proceeded into and through the harbor and tied up at the end of the road to visit our friends, the Gene Morans. Since so few pleasure boats cruise so far up Cook Inlet, our friends refused to believe we had come by boat. Fearful that the receding tide would leave us high and dry, we soon returned to our floating cabin. During our visit, Gene and Johnny had driven to a gas station with jerry cans to replenish our gas supply.

We cruised down the river and tied up near shore to eat our sandwiches. When the mosquitoes grew bold, we decided to anchor for the night further out in the river. The day's disasters involved Legs, our canine shipmate, who fell in the river; and our anchor which dropped on one of the cabin windows.

We left Kenai early to catch high tide in Anchorage, and were half-way home when I awakened at dawn the next day and went out to relieve the captain at the wheel. The late May days had been warm, and the trees were tinged with spring green. But the early-morning breezes were reminiscent of winter.

After an hour at the wheel I had to summon the captain from his nap to cope with a debris-filled rip tide. He took over, and in another hour we were back in the Anchorage harbor.

Now we'll be watching the weather and waiting for the next inviting weekend.

Li'l Lindy is launched the hard way at Ship Creek

The author in heavy-weather garb

63

Alaska Reflections

by Betty Nunn

Vancouver Island to Bella Bella

On the eve of her second adventure in the Pacific Northwest, *Bee Jay III* rested easily in her slip in Canoe Cove in water reflecting the orange tint of the summer sunset. Summer also spoke in the scales of birdsong echoing from the dark forest . . . in the raucous honk of a lone goose . . . in the shrill scream of a fishing seagull. The sudden sound of the ferry horn ricocheted off the rocky shore, startling a beaver into the water. A long-necked loon swam by. Nearby boats rocked gently as the light faded and the marker lights gleamed in the entrance to the cove.

It was the first week in June 1967. We had had *Bee Jay* skippered to Canoe Cove, near Sidney, Vancouver Island from her home port, Newport Beach, California, so that we could spend all the time possible in continuing our exploration of these fabulous northwest waters. After months of planning we were ready to get underway, crew assembled and last-minute supplies stowed. The crew was comprised of three couples — a perfect number for *Bee Jay*. Each couple had a private stateroom and the division of watches and stores would leave much time for individual freedom.

At noon *Bee Jay* churned through Moresby Pass, past Beaver Point on Saltspring Island, into Trincomali Channel. We approached the tiny opening of Dodd Narrows with a 4.5-knot current going our way, and popped through like a cork out of a wine bottle. Passing Horswell Bluff north of Nanaimo, we entered the open channel.

The Strait of Georgia was kindly that day and after a pleasant afternoon of cruising along Vancouver Island, we dropped anchor in Union Bay just below Comox. Since we were following the Vancouver shoreline we watched our depthmeter closely, for there are many oyster beds near the surface in this area.

In the morning we slipped out over the sand bar at high tide and headed for Campbell River. The skies were gorgeous and the water sparkling. Summer clouds drifted above the snow-topped peaks of Vancouver Island, across the Strait of Georgia and on to the magnificent Canadian Rockies.

It is a blue, blue world in the northland. Sky, moun-

tains, forests, even the clouds and snow reflect the color. This day the waters of the Strait were smooth, and we seemed afloat in an immense bowl of sapphire-blue water.

Nearing Campbell River we passed through a tide rip opposite Cape Mudge on Quadra Island. This innocent-looking current can be rough in certain tide changes and wind conditions, but the boat handled beautifully. At Campbell River we bought a freshly-caught salmon and grilled it. The delicate-flavored fish caught in these cold waters and cooked immediately is delicious.

The route we traveled this second summer duplicated much of the first, but the flavor was always new. We had a feeling of confidence on this second passage through Seymour Narrows and Johnstone Strait. We enjoyed pulling into fuel docks and anchorages in out-of-the-way places and being greeted as old friends.

The days were fantastically beautiful until one grim day when we left Alert Bay to cross a strange, brown-colored Queen Charlotte Sound under a misting overcast. Our radar scope whirled comfortingly, proving for the tricky check points across this unprotected opening to the sea. Gradually visibility improved and the eerie sea-worn islands of the Sound appeared in their appointed places. Heavy swells lifted and lowered us into Fitzhugh Sound and the sun greeted us as we neared Namu.

Bella Bella to Ketchikan

At Bella Bella we fueled and spent a serene night before tackling turbulent Milbanke Sound the next morning. We started out at sunrise in a sea choppy with brilliant blue and pink waves. As we passed Jorkins Point on Swindle Island we were grateful to relax in the unexpected calm of Finlayson Channel.

When hat-shaped Cone Island loomed into view, *Bee Jay* darted to the left out of the main channel to follow the narrow, deep passage between the Indian Village and the cannery town of Klemtu. Moving carefully through the fog, we headed north up the Tolmie Channel, past Waterfall Point and Cougar Bay. As we turned out of Graham Reach with its myriad waterfalls the sun burned off the mists and we anchored in Khutze Inlet to lunch and explore. Dancing apple-green waters, luxuriously verdant shores and a plumy fall of water from the snow-covered peaks seemed exclusively our own.

Underway again we passed Butedale and pressed through Fraser Reach and McKay Reach, entering Wright Sound beside a pod of whales blowing their spume in rhythmic cadence with their movement through the water. We spent the night at Prince Rupert where the newcomers to the crew prowled this fascinating port. In the morning we awoke to a dense white mist drifting through the island-dotted Ven Passage and Metlakatla Bay. Radar helped a little, but we were grateful to the tiny fishing boat which blazed a trail for us on this unfamiliar route.

We emerged from the fog abruptly onto a stage-set of unbelievable clarity. The water rippled with flecks of sunshine and the seaward islands from Melville to Dundas seemed sewn like dark felt on a blue flannel sky. This was Chatham Sound.

Passing stark Green Island with its quaint red-roofed marine station we found Dixon Entrance flat as a pane of blue glass, and so it was across the Alaskan border. The crew sunbathed on *Bee Jay's* spacious sun-deck and by the time we reached Ketchikan it was actually hot.

Alaska's Totem-Land

Each Alaskan town has a unique, individual charm. Superficially they are alike, but each has a different flavor. The towering mountains and dense forests of the Panhandle Islands act as a barrier to protect the towns along the inner estuaries. The people are bound together by geographic isolation and by their common industries — fish, lumber, tourist, and those complementary industries which serve all three. But the fishing fleet of Ketchikan does not resemble the fishing fleets of Petersburg, Juneau or Sitka. And the same atmosphere of differences appears in other fields. Travel in Alaska is a study in human nature.

No matter how many times one may cruise to Ketchikan, the thrill of approaching this city after the miles of ocean wilderness is not lessened. Known as Alaska's "Totemland," Ketchikan was already on the scene when explorers, gold-seekers and homesteaders took up the challenge of Alaska. Indian villages of the Tlingits, Haidas and Tsimshians were established here because of the abundant salmon, shellfish, berries and game. Totem poles were important to the culture of both the Tlingit and Haida tribes, serving as the decorative record of the events in the life of a family or clan. Many of these are still standing. A unique collection of Tlingit carvings is found in Saxman Totem Park, three miles south of Ketchikan. Nine miles to the north is the replica of an Indian community house and a park where many types of Tongass poles are displayed. In Ketchikan itself is the Chief Skowl totem, famed as the Haida Memorial.

Ketchikan still has the atmosphere of a vigorous frontier fishing and lumber town. The growing city stretches out along Revillagigedo Channel with 20-foot tides snapping at its waterfront and 3000-foot mountains crowding it from behind. This "Salmon Capital of the World" boasts Southeastern Alaska's largest fishing fleet. North of the town is the famous Ketchikan Pulp Company which is the first large manufacturing plant in Alaska and has been responsible for developing Alaska's great timber industry.

Exploring the Behm Canal

Ketchikan is situated on Revillagigedo Island, and to circle the island on the Behm Canal is a rare experience. On this trip the weather was lovely, the water happy; and we fairly flew out of Tongass Narrows past the old Guard Island Light and into the canal. Our wake washed ashore on Betton Island and over the partially submerged Tatoosh Rocks; we peered into darkly-shadowed Smuggler's Cove on Cleveland Peninsula; binoculars came out as we passed Naha Bay to spot lurking bears. Next came Escape Point and Traitor's Cove then Bushy Point and Cove.

Around us porpoises paced our cruise, surfing in our wake in pairs and darting across the bow in a precise criss-cross pattern. We passed Snail Point, Bug Island, Chin Point, Nose Point and Brow Point as we made our way past Gedney Passage and turned left at Bluff Point to enter Yes Bay with its yellow seaweed-covered islets. Here we moored at an old hunting lodge where the caretaker and his gracious wife gave us coffee and entertained us with interesting side-lights on living year-round in this wild country.

Our next stop was Bell Island with its hot springs and naturally heated pool. The pleasant dining room and lounge and excellent accommodations make this a mecca for those who fly in by sea-plane. But on this Fourth of July we were the only visitors. *Bee Jay* idled at the dock while her crew experimented with firecrackers and Roman candles from the flybridge.

The crew went salmon-fishing in earnest and stocked the freezer with pink filets. In a cove across the Arm we dropped the crab pot and soon had the skipper boiling some big ones on our little butane stove. Later, exploring the interior of Bell Island we found a lake flipping with darting trout.

We resumed our circle tour with *Bee Jay's* windshield wipers ticking briskly. Alaska wears well in the rain, even with the islands and spectacular peaks reduced to dim silhouettes. Through Behm Narrows on the back side of

Giant icebergs spill out of Tracey and Endicott Arm into Stephens Passage.

(Above) Fishing is excellent at Bell Island—and crabbing, too. (Above, right) 20-foot tides beset the anchorage at Ketchikan. (Right) Sawyer Glacier deposits icebergs in Holkham Bay.

the island the water seemed heavy and thick. We visited lovely coves where white, splashing water tumbled into the sea.

Where the Unuk River spills into the Canal through Burroughs Bay the skyline changes abruptly from low, timbered slopes to massive snow-covered pinnacles. On the down side the Behm Canal developed a short chop that slapped the bow and showered arctic water clear up to the flybridge.

In Walker Cove we marveled at the plummeting waterfalls, the ancient ice sculpting great valleys and the still waters in which the raindrops rippled.

The night was spent anchored in the Punchbowl of Rudyard Bay — the Valley of a Thousand Waterfalls. In this isolated haven no navigation markers marred the shore. Fishermen, commercial or sport, never frequent these waters as the entire area of the Canal and its bays are closed to fishing. Waterfalls drifted across the austere cliff faces; the vivid beach grass vibrated in the rain; broad snowfields lay among the mist-covered peaks. The few trees in this bay of imprisoning walls clung to the smooth slabs of the cliff face, with the only semblance of forest rising where the waterfall tumbles out of Punchbowl Lake high above.

The sun reappeared as we passed New Eddystone Rock, a tree-covered rock shaft jutting 230 feet from a

tiny sand shoal in mid-channel. We rounded Point Alava into Revillagigedo Channel, heading for Ketchikan. At the confluence of Ernest Sound and Clarence Strait, 40 miles north of Ketchikan, is Meyers Chuck where we planned to anchor for the night. The only navigable entrance to this unique cove is an intricate slalom run of rocks projecting from the water to deck height. We maneuvered *Bee Jay* into this beautiful hideaway and spent a happy evening watching the changing colors of the brilliant sunset.

From Ketchikan to Wrangell

There are several routes to cover the 88 miles from Ketchikan to Wrangell, and *Bee Jay III* has tried them all. The route we chose this time was the one around Wrangell Island, through Blake Channel and Eastern Passage. We passed near Humpback Bay and Anan Creek on the Bradfield Canal, where we decided to stop over. We spotted a bear as we entered the bay, and hoped this meant the salmon were running in the creek. We lowered the dinghy and headed for the golden sandy beach. A large brown otter supervised our mooring as we tied the Boston Whaler high on shore to allow for the 20-foot tide. No salmon were working their way upstream that day, but we found enough Loch Leven Trout to feed us all. A U.S. Forest Service trail along the creek provided spotting places to watch the bear catching salmon during the runs. This trail

238

(Left) Bee Jay III anchors by a lumber camp log pond at Thomas Bay. (Lower left) Lodge at Glacier Bay's Bartlett Cove is set in lush forest. (Below) The fishing fleets at Ketchikan and Meyers Chuck.

penetrates the primeval forest where ancient moss-covered trees and massive boulders are highlighted by reflections from the stream.

Leaving Eastern Passage, we passed Simoniof Island at the north end of Wrangell. Simoniof is also known as Dead Man Island, since in winter it becomes a temporary graveyard. Chinese laborers brought in to work in the Wrangell canneries request that if they die, they are to be buried in their homeland. In the frigid months the bodies are stored in barrels on the bleak little island to be shipped home in the spring.

Wrangell, the town with the sweet wood-smoke smell, was established by Russians in 1834, and has since lived under both English and American flags. Wrangell is the largest lumber-exporting point in Alaska, with much of the tonnage going to Japan. There are also enormous exports of salmon, crab and shrimp.

We moored for several nights near Shake's Island in Wrangell Harbor. This is the tribal home of the Bear and contains totems which are several centuries old together with many ancient carvings. Petroglyphs may be found along the beach at Wrangell, and are said to pre-date the totem poles.

Wrangell to Petersburg

Her freezer loaded with shrimp (called Alaskan Pop-corn by the natives), *Bee Jay III* left for Wrangell Narrows, one of the trickiest passages in the world. This 22-mile waterway lies between Mitkof Island and the Lindenberg Peninsula of Kupreanof Island.

Petersburg, or "Little Norway" lies at the entrance to Frederick Sound from Wrangell Narrows. Primarily a fishing town, Petersburg's population is mainly of Scandinavian descent. Moose and bear are prevalent, and Petersburg is frequented by hunters as well as sportfishermen.

Some 12 miles out of Petersburg and off Frederick Sound lies Thomas Bay. Dodging tiny slivers of blue icebergs floating across the entrance, we passed Spurt Point and, rounding a headland, found ourselves bow-to-face with massive Baird glacier. We slipped through a slot in the towering cliffs to the right into Scenery Cove, a narrow, deep canyon harboring a shoreless pool.

Thomas Bay has a glacier hanging at either end, and we chose to spend the night under Patterson Glacier, moored to a solid log-boom at Reid Lumber Company. Warm and comfortable aboard, the crew listened to the cold wind whistling in the rigging and ruffling the shallow water beside the blueberry bogs ashore.

Petersburg to Juneau

The raucous cry of a bald-headed eagle fishing for his breakfast awoke us. These birds fish the inland passage

239

and their appetite for salmon rivals that of the bears. As we cruised past the junction of Frederick Sound and Stephens Passage, we were entertained by a pod of immense black whales which balanced erect on their tails, then crashed back into the sea with enormous upheavals of water.

Stephens Passage, one of the widest channels of these inland waters and one of the most beautiful, runs between the mountainous mainland to the east and the peaks of Admiralty Island to the west. Hobart Bay is a pleasant hideaway along this marine thoroughfare between Petersburg and Juneau. At dusk we maneuvered *Bee Jay* past Entrance Island, which conceals the opening to this bay, and drew into a haven of serene beauty.

We anchored near a ramshackle dock, as abandoned as the sagging gray trapper's cottage nestled nearby in tall grass and wild roses. We were greeted noisily by the croaking of a pair of Great Blue Herons nesting on a platform of sticks high in a tree. Never have we found such a varied abundance of sea-life as in Hobart Bay. We found it strange to collect tidal water sea specimens in this alpine setting.

En route north to Juneau, huge icebergs spill out of Tracy and Endicott Arms through Holkham Bay into the main channel, their source two great tidewater glaciers, Sawyer and Dawes.

Then, Juneau, its narrow, uneven streets haunted by echoes of Alaskan frontier days, the derelict remains of its large gold mine hanging over the Gastineau Channel. Juneau's historical museum covers all phases of Alaskan life from the days of the earliest aborigines through the Russian interval to the present.

Juneau to Sitka

Glacier Bay National Monument north and west of Juneau is worthy of an expedition to Alaska for itself alone. This 3600-square-mile remnant of the Ice Age is an unforgettable lesson in geology. Bartlett Cove, near the entrance to the Bay, is the setting for a lodge and pier where sea and aircraft may moor.

For a warmer climate, we headed for Sitka-by-the-sea. We dropped out of Icy Strait, down Chatham Strait and along high-mountained Chichagof Island. We spent the night in the unique floating town of Tenakee Springs in Tenakee Inlet where large seiners were making ready for the early-morning race to the fishing grounds opened by the Fish and Game Service.

Through Peril Strait, past Hoonah Sound and Sergius Narrows we fairly flew. In Salisbury Sound *Bee Jay* left a zig-zag wake as she picked her way between fishing boats. After the final run through Neva and Olga Straits, we arrived in Sitka, nestled against the rugged mountain slopes of Baranof Island. The Japanese current sweeps close here, giving Sitka a mild climate. In summer, beaches swarm with clam diggers, abalone divers, and happy children.

Sitka's recorded history originated in the late 1700's when the fur trade attracted vessels from Spain, Britain, Russia and the States. In 1804 it became the capital of Russian America. In 1867 it served as a capital city for the United States until Alaska became a territory and Juneau its capital. We visited the Sitka National Monument with its displays of native crafts, as well as several of its excellent schools.

The route home led back through Wrangell Narrows, past Ketchikan, across the Dixon Entrance. Our last night in the wilderness was spent in a tranquil inlet called Kumealon or West Inlet, just off the Grenville Channel in British Columbia. *Bee Jay III* rode at anchor silently, as if in a world suspended in time.